Charles Eugene Banks

The Artistic Guide to Chicago and the World´s Columbian

Exposition

Charles Eugene Banks

The Artistic Guide to Chicago and the World's Columbian Exposition

ISBN/EAN: 9783741118395

Manufactured in Europe, USA, Canada, Australia, Japa

Cover: Foto ©Lupo / pixelio.de

Manufactured and distributed by brebook publishing software
(www.brebook.com)

Charles Eugene Banks

The Artistic Guide to Chicago and the World's Columbian Exposition

GUIDE TO CHICAGO

AND THE

WORLD'S COLUMBIAN EXPOSITION.

ILLUSTRATED.

From ice-bound lands where weary stars
　　Look down on nights a half-year long ;
From lands by old historic wars
　　Made rich in legend and in song
From every country, every clime
　　Will come the peoples of the earth
To join the pageantry sublime
　　In honor of thy birth,
　　　　COLUMBIA !

✣　✣　✣　✣

1892
MONARCH BOOK COMPANY,
CHICAGO, PHILADELPHIA, STOCKTON, CAL.

THE
Artistic Guide
TO
CHICAGO
AND THE
COLUMBIAN
WORLD'S
EXPOSITION

Illustrated

Preface.

THE wonderful growth of Chicago, from a moorland traversed only by Indian trails in 1831, to a splendid metropolis with a million and a quarter of inhabitants in 1891, furnishes food for a story far beyond the possibilities of this small volume.

No more has been attempted here than to acquaint the reader with the principal events in the history of the city; to point out such places and things as would be most likely to awaken a lively interest in the mind of the visitor, and to give the general public at least a faint impression of what the World's Fair is to be.

Our information has been gathered from the most reliable sources. We have endeavored to present it in a clear, concise and interesting manner. Our aim is to furnish the public with a guide to the pleasant, the instructive and the amusing, and not to compile an encyclopedia of dry facts.

THE PUBLISHERS.

BIRD'S-EYE VIEW OF CHICAGO.

INDEX TO GUIDE TO CHICAGO.

4

INDEX.

Fresh-Air Fund, 133; Hospital for Women and Children, 134;
Orphan Asylum, 134; Nursery and Half-Orphan Asylum, 134;
Erring Woman's Refuge, 134; Foundling's Home, 134; Good
Samaritan Society, 135; Holy Family Orphan Asylum, 135;
Home for Incurables, 135; Home for Self-Supporting Women,
135; Home for Unemployed Girls, 136; Home for Working
Women, 136; Home for the Friendless, 136; Home for the Aged—
Little Sisters of the Poor, 136; House of the Good Shepherd,
136; Home for Incurables, Number 2, 136; Newsboys' and Boot-
blacks' Home, 136; Old People's Home, 137; School for Deaf
and Dumb, 137; Servite Sister's Industrial Home, 137; Soldiers'
Home Fund, 137; Waif's Mission, 138; Young Men's Christian
Association, 138.

Rose Hill Cemetery, 144; Calvary, 145; Graceland, 145; Oak-
wood, 146; Aushemaariv, 146; Austro-Hungarian, 147; B'Nai
Shilom, 147; Chebra Gemilath Chasadim Ubikar Cholim, 147;
Chebra Kadisha Ubikar Cholim, 147; Concordia, 147; Ger-
man Lutheran, 147; Mount Greenwood, 147; Mount Olive, 148;
Ohavey Scholom, 148; Waldheim, 148.

Public Library, 149; Newberry Library, 149; John Crerar
Library, 150; Armour Mission Library, 151; Chicago Athe-
naeum, 151; Historical Society Library, 151; Union Catholic
Library, 151.

Auditorium Hotel, 152, Grand Pacific, 153; Wellington, The,
153; Richelieu, The, 157; Leland, The, 158; Palmer House,
158; Sherman House, 159; Tremont House, 159; Chicago (or
Northern), 159; Saratoga, 160; Atlantic, 160; Briggs House,
160; Burke's European, 160; Clifton House, 161; Commercial,
161; Continental, 161; Gault House, 161; Gore's Hotel, 161;
Hotel Brevoort, 161; Hotel Drexel, 162; Hotel Grace, 162;
Hotel Woodruff, 162; Hyde Park Hotel, 162; Southern Hotel,
162; Virginia Hotel, 162.

Alexian Bros.' Hospital, 168; Dr. Chas. W. Earl's Private Asy-
lum, 169; Mercy Hospital, 169; St. Joseph's Hospital, 169;
Martha Washington Home, 169; Washingtonian Home, 170;
Leslie E. Keeley's Institute, 170.

Argo Club, 173; Calumet Club, 173; Chicago Club, 174; Iroquois Club, 173; Union League Club, 175; Union Club, 175;
Chicago Woman's Club, 175; Chicago Electric Club, 176;
Illinois Club, 176; Fortnightly Club, 177; Harvard University Club, 178; Hyde Park Suburban Club, 178; Irish-Ameri-
can Club, 178; Lakeside Club, 179; Kenwood Club, 179; Evanston Country Club, 179; La Salle Club, 180; Newsboys' Club,
180; Standard Club, 180; Sunset Club, 181; Wa Na Ton Club,
181; Press Club of Chicago, 182; Phœnix Club, 183; Park
Club of Hyde Park, 183; University Club, 183; Washington
Park Club, 184; Whitechapel Club, 184.

INDEX TO GUIDE TO WORLD'S COLUMBIAN EXPOSITION.

OLD FORT DEARBORN.

CHICAGO, ✣ ✣ ✣
1779 TO 1812.

Early Settlers—Building and Destruction of
Fort Dearborn—Massacre of the Garrison.

EARLY in the spring of 1779, a fugitive San Domingoan slave named Baptiste Point de Sable found his way from the French settlements of Louisiana to the south-western shores of Lake Michigan, built a rude cabin on the north bank of the Chicago River near its mouth and began in a small way to trade in furs with the French and Indians. For many years previous to his coming the French mission-aries had made this point a camping ground on their travels back and forth in their explorations of the Mississippi country. Marquette, Joliet and other early missionaries, in their letters and records, often speak of the "Checagau River" and the "Portage of Chicago;" but there is no mention made anywhere of a permanent dwelling or fort in this vicinity. The treaty of General Anthony Wayne, signed at Greenville, Ohio, August, 1795, in which the Indians ceded to the United States "six miles square at the mouth of the Chicago River," further describes the locality as "the place where an old fort stood;" but the oldest Indians of that time had no recollection of such a building. If such a structure ever occupied this ground, it could have been nothing more than a temporary affair for the storing of provisions, and was never permanently occupied. It is therefore safe to say that Point de Sable's rude log hut was the first dwelling erected on the present site of Chicago, and that the refugee slave was its first permanent resident and land-holder.

9

He is described by one writer of that time as "a large, handsome, well-educated negro,' and by another as "a negro trader, pretty wealthy, who drank freely and was much in the French interest." Previous to his settlement on the lake he had spent some time among the Peorias with a friendly countryman named Glamorgan, and was familiar with Indian traditions and customs. During his long residence at Chicago he was intimately associated with the Pottawatomies, and, it is said, aspired to become the head of the nation. This was no mean ambition; for the Pottawatomies were at that time a numerous and warlike people, rich in territory, great in council, and among the most intellectual and humane of all the savage tribes. It is more probable, however, that he was well content in the possession of untrameled freedom, and the prominence which came with the growth of his business. At least he lived quietly on in his narrow cabin until 1796, or for seventeen years, when, broken in health, he sold out his business and holdings to a Frenchman named Le Mai, and returned to Peoria, where he soon after died in the home of his friend Glamorgan.

Le Mai, his successor, was a shrewd, industrious Frenchman, with a keen desire for gold and an accommodating conscience. He considerably enlarged the business of De Sable and grew rapidly toward affluence. Other traders came to share his prosperity, other cabins sprung up about the mouth of the harbor; and when Le Mai, in 1803, disposed of his business and returned to the pleasures of civilization, there was quite a little settlement at "Checagau Portage," and the trading post at the mouth of the Chicago (or Onion) River was known all along the lakes.

The Revolutionary war, while it resulted in victory for the colonists, left them with many new and serious responsibilities, which they, in their reduced and enfeebled condition, were illy prepared to assume One of the most difficult and important of these was the "Indian question"—which, like Banquo's ghost, occasionally rises to trouble and perplex their descendants to this day. The English still hoped to gain possession of the vast territory which the colonists had wrested from them, and as a means to this end kept among the savages many well-paid and skillful emissaries, whose business it was to destroy the confidence which the Americans sought to awaken in the bosoms of their dusky neighbors. This was not a difficult task. The savages, ignorant and suspicious, were easily persuaded that the Americans meant to rob them of their lands and drive them out of the country. The rascally spirit of many of the government's trusted agents materially assisted the English to spread this belief among the more restless tribes that roamed along the borders of the great lakes. The purchase of Louisiana from the French, which was about to be consummated, would open a vast territory for settlement. But unless something was done to keep the hostile tribes in check, the hardiest pioneer would hesitate long before trusting the fate of his family or of himself to the mercies of so treacherous and pitiless a foe. And so the Government, in order to establish a wholesome respect for its power among the more savage tribes and at the same time cultivate more intimate relations with those disposed to be friendly, decided to build and garrison a fort somewhere on the southern shore of Lake Michigan. St. Joseph was first selected; but this, not meeting with the approval of some of the friendly tribes, Chicago Portage, which was situated in the six-miles square of territory lately ceded to the Government, was selected, and work on the fort began. The building was finished sometime in the fall of 1803, and called Fort Dearborn, after General Harry Dearborn, then Secretary of State, and garrisoned as follows:

One captain, one second lieutenant, one ensign, four sergeants, three corporals, four musicians, fifty-four privates and one surgeon's mate.

"The fort," says A. T. Andrews, in his "History of Early Chicago," "stood on the south side of the Chicago River, where the stream turned to enter the lake. It had two block-houses, one on the southwest corner, the other on the northwest. On the north side a subterranean passage led from the parade ground to the river, designed as a way of escape in case of emergency or for supplying the garrison with water in time of siege. The whole was inclosed by a strong palisade of wooden pickets. At the west of the fort and fronting north on the river was a two-story log building, covered with split oak siding. This was the United States

agency house. On the shores of the river, between the fort and
the agency, were the root-houses, or cellars, of the garrison. The
ground on the south side was inclosed and cultivated as a garden.
Three pieces of light artillery comprised the commandment of
the fort."

Captain John Whistler, the builder of Fort Dearborn, was its
first commander, and during his stay of seven years the garrison
enjoyed a season of unbroken peace. American settlers, with
their families, took the place of the French traders with Indian
wives, and Fort Dearborn began to assume the manners and
adopt the customs of civilization. While the fort was in process
of construction in 1803, John H. Kinzie brought his family from
St. Joseph, across the lake, and took up his residence in the
trader's house of Le Mai, which he had bought from the Frenchman some months before. This was the first family to settle in
Chicago, and the first home in the settlement. It consisted of
John Kinzie, his wife Eleanor, their infant son, John Harris
Kinzie, and Margaret McKillup, daughter of Mrs. Kinzie by a
former husband.

John Kinzie, justly styled the father of Chicago, was a silversmith by trade, but for years previous to his advent at Chicago
he had followed the business of Indian trader with marked success. The dialects of the different tribes were as familiar to him
as the language of his fathers, and he enjoyed the fullest confidence of the Indians throughout all the lake region. He was
strictly honest in all his dealings with them, and during the most
stormy times and under the most trying circumstances they never
refused him their protection. He was a hospitable man ; and his
humble home on the north bank of the Chicago River, fronting
the lake, was the favorite resort of every hunter that strayed into
the post. As time went by other American families came to
settle about the fort. New cabins, larger and with more preten-
tions to comfort were built; and the French trader, with his
Indian wife and half-breed children, gave place to the American
pioneer, whose ideas of life, if crude, were of a much higher character. The frontier post now began to assume some of the airs
of older civilization. The social line, which had at first been
drawn at the palisades, was extended to take in the whole village.

The wife of the veteran soldier sipped tea with the farmer's daughter in the rude home of the trader; the village maiden, listening to the pleadings of the corporal, was led to pity his lonely lot, and there were weddings and births and gossip. Thus the inhabitants of Fort Dearborn, far in the wilderness, went on making history, and the great world beyond the woods and lakes and prairies gave them seldom a thought, if it gave them a thought at all.

In 1810 Captain Whistler was relieved by Captain Nathan Heald, a native of New Hampshire, where he was born in 1775. When quite a young man he entered the army, where he received rapid promotion; was lieutenant in 1799 and captain in 1807. His wife Rebekah was a daughter of Captain Samuel Wells, a noted Indian fighter of Kentucky.

The Indians of the country about Fort Dearborn were Pottawatomies, and generally inclined to be friendly. But at the beginning of the war of 1812 they began to show signs of restlessness, and the garrison was frequently startled by the report of some isolated settler being murdered, his butchered offspring given to the flames and the broken-hearted mother dragged into cruel captivity. On the 18th of June the United States declared war on the British. On the 15th of July the American fort at Mackinac surrendered. When this news reached them, many tribes that had hitherto been neutral went over to the English. In the south and west that wily old warrior, Tecumseh, was hastening from council to council, stirring up the Indians to join forces and make general war on the white settlers. Fort Dearborn was far removed from civilization and completely at the mercy of the hostiles. On the 5th of August General Hull, then in command at Detroit, dispatched an Indian messenger to Captain Heald with orders to evacuate the post at once and proceed with his forces by land to Detroit. Captain Heald was a brave. soldier. To abandon his post before a blow had been struck or a hand raised against it savored of timidity at least. Besides, the Pottawatomies still professed to be friendly, and promised him safe escort through their country whenever he should decide to go. The fort was strong and well stored with ammunition and supplies. The route from Chicago to Detroit was a long and tedious one, and should his Indian escort prove treacherous he would be with his small force entirely at their mercy. Debating thus he delayed his departure six days. On the evening of the 13th Captain Wells, the uncle of Mrs. Heald and Indian agent at Fort Wayne, arrived with thirty friendly Miamas. Captain Wells was well-acquainted with the nature of the Indian and his tactics. Stolen by the Miamas when a boy of twelve he passed his youth and early manhood as a member of that tribe, the adopted son of its most powerful chief, Little Turtle. At the outbreak of 1790 he fought with the Indians. After the battle in which St. Clair was defeated he realized that he was warring against his own kinsmen, and in a noble speech informed his adopted father that he could serve with him no more ; then making his way to the camp of General Wayne, he joined the American forces and was made captain of a company of scouts. When peace was again restored he settled at Fort Wayne, where he was joined by his wife, the daughter of Little Turtle.

Upon his arrival at Fort Dearborn Captain Wells advised the destruction of all extra arms, ammunition and liquor, and the immediate abandonment of the fort. His advice was followed. The muskets were broken and destroyed and the whiskey thrown into the river. Some prowling Indians learned of this, and immediately hurried with the news to their camp, which was not far distant. The young bucks were furious, and a council of war was held, at which it was decided to destroy the fort and garrison.

Black Partridge, who carried a medal presented to him by General Wayne at the signing of the Greenville treaty, and who had always maintained a friendly feeling for the whites, came into the fort and returned the medal to Captain Heald. " My young men," said he, " say they have been betrayed. You have destroyed the arms and provisions which you promised to leave here for us. My braves are resolved upon taking your lives. I cannot restrain them. I return you the token of peace, for I will not wear it while I am compelled to act as an enemy."

The only hope for the garrison now lay in speedy departure. The officers went quietly about their final arrangements, cheering the soldiers by word and example. At nine o'clock of the following morning, August 15th, the little band passed out of the fort, and its gates closed upon them for the last time. The evacuating company consisted of the garrison, about seventy-five men, including officers, Captain Wells and his band of thirty Miami braves, the women and children of the officers, soldiers and settlers, and brave John Kinzie, who, although warned by several chiefs who held him in high esteem, resolved to use all influence to avert the massacre of his white friends. The women and children were in wagons or on horseback. Captain Wells, according to the Indian custom, had blackened his face in premonition of his fate. With fifteen of his Miamis he led the advance. The band played the dead march. The waves of the swelling lake broke sobbingly upon the shore, and the beleaguered garrison moved slowly southward along the beach. At the same time a band of five hundred Indians left their camp and trailed along behind a ridge of sand-hills that stretched between the path that ran along the beach and the prairie beyond. A mile and a half from the fort the troops were attacked. At the very first volley the Miamis ran away, accompanied by their chief. The battle was short and sanguinary. The soldiers felt that escape was impossible. To surrender meant death. Already they felt the winds of eternity in their hair, and fought like men resolved to enter its borders full-handed with revenge. While the battle was in progress a young Indian savage crept unseen into a wagon and tomahawked twelve of the children. The troops, without shelter of any kind, were soon cut to pieces. Captain Heald, himself badly wounded, fought his way through the lines, and with the surviving remnant of his band, escaped to a little knoll out of range of the Indians' guns. From here a half-breed boy was dispatched to Chief Black Bird, offering to surrender on condition that their lives would be spared. This was agreed to, and the battle which totally annihilated the embryo Chicago was over.

Of the original number that left the fort, less than one-third escaped with their lives. Captain Wells, who fought like a demon through it all, was at last overpowered and killed. His head was cut off and his heart taken out and eaten by the savages, who hoped by this means to become possessed of the courage and prowess of the heroic scout. Ensign Ronan and Surgeon De

Isaac Van Voorhis also lost their lives in the engagement. All the wounded, with the exception of Captain and Mrs. Heald and Lieutenant Helm and his wife, were dispatched on the field.

The women fought with the same fierceness and bravery which distinguished the men. Mrs. Helm, daughter of Mrs. Kinzie, was snatched from the clutches of a young savage who was trying to tomahawk her, by a friendly chief, Black Partridge, who bore her to the lake, and, plunging her in up to the chin, cautioned her to remain there, which she did. After the battle he returned and conducted her to a place of safety. Mrs. Heald, mounted on a fine thoroughbred Kentucky horse, fought her way to the prairie, and refused to surrender until she was wounded six times. The savages spared her life in admiration of her bravery.

The prisoners were distributed among the different tribes, to be all finally ransomed or returned to their friends. John Kinzie, and his family, were allowed to depart in peace. The fort and surrounding cabins were burned, and the savages hurried away to join in depredations elsewhere. For a few days the winds tossed the remnants of the settlement about the sand-hills and then the last vestige of early Chicago disappeared. The mink and beaver came back to sport under the quiet banks of the river, and the elk fearlessly sniffed the air and pawed the turf where the gardens of man had been.

STATE STREET, LOOKING NORTH FROM MADISON STREET.

OF CHICAGO.

1816 to 1891.

FOR four years after its destruction by the Pottawatomies, Fort Dearborn lay a scattered ruin in a wilderness of weeds, and the bones of the murdered garrison
bleached whiter than the white sea-sands on which they
rested. But when the war, which, during this time raged all
along the Canadian border, was ended and the English flag
driven from the lakes, the Government turned its attention
once more to the settlement of its frontiers, and Fort Dearborn was ordered to be rebuilt. In July, 1816, Captain
Hezekiah Bradley, who had been commissioned for that service, arrived at Chicago with two companies of infantry, and
the reconstruction of the fort was begun on the site of the old
one—but larger and on a somewhat different plan. A high stockade inclosed the barracks, officers' quarters, magazine and provision store. Two bastions, one on the northwest and one on the
southeast corners, rose above the palisades, commanding a wide
view of the surrounding country. The officers' quarters were on
the west side of the stockade, the soldiers' barracks on the east;
a block-house stood at the southwest corner.

The site of the old fort is now occupied by a massive five-story
business block, within the angle formed by the junction of River
Street and Michigan Avenue. On its north front is a marble
tablet, with the following inscription:

19

THIS BUILDING OCCUPIES THE SITE OF OLD FORT DEAR-
BORN, WHICH EXTENDED A LITTLE ACROSS MICH-
IGAN AVENUE AND SOMEWHAT INTO
THE RIVER AS IT NOW IS.

THE FORT WAS BUILT IN 1803-4, FORMING OUR OUTMOST
DEFENSE.

BY ORDER OF GENERAL HULL, IT WAS EVACUATED AUG.
15, 1812, AFTER ITS STORES AND PROVISIONS
HAD BEEN DISTRIBUTED AMONG
THE INDIANS.

Very soon after, the Indians attacked and massacred about
fifty of the troops and a number of citizens, including women
and children, and next day burned the fort. In 1816 it was
rebuilt, but after the Black Hawk war it went into gradual
disuse, and in May, 1837, was abandoned by the army, but was
occupied by various Government officers till 1857, when it was
torn down, excepting a single building, which stood upon the
site till the great fire of Oct. 9, 1871.

At the suggestion of the Chicago Historical Society this
tablet was erected, November, 1880, by   W. M. HOYT.

Fort Dearborn was kept constantly garrisoned from this time
until 1823, when, the frontier line having moved westward to the
Mississippi, a garrison at Chicago was considered no longer necessary, and the troops were withdrawn.

It was garrisoned again from 1828 to 1831, Major John Fowle
commanding. Again, in 1832, when Black Hawk and his warriors
became hostile, Major William Whestler, with a small body of
troops, was stationed here to protect the settlers, who had sought
refuge in the fort. He was relieved in July of the following year
by Major John Fowle, and he, a month later, by Major De Lafayette Wilcox, who commanded until Dec. 18, 1833, and again
from Sept. 16, 1835, to Aug. 1, 1836. Major John Bendee, Major
John Greene and Captain and Brevet-Major Joseph Plympton
held command during the interval for varying periods. On Dec.
29, 1836, the troops were permanently withdrawn; the last salute
sounded, the last bugle was blown, and Fort Dearborn, the scene
of many stirring dramas and of one of the saddest tragedies which
the history of American frontier life records, was, as a military
post, forever abandoned.

John Kinzie, who, after the massacre of the garrison and destruction of old Fort Dearborn, removed with his family to Detroit, returned to Chicago in the autumn of 1816, and moved into his old log house on the north bank of the river. During all those troubled years, while the Indians, made furious by their many losses, had butchered and burned on every hand, that one lone cabin stood unmolested in the heart of the wildnerness. What better proof could be had of the esteem in which these untutored savages held the silversmith, Shaw-nee-aw-kee, who, in all his dealings with them, never used deceit and never broke his word? They gave additional evidence of their affection for him when, in the treaty of Sept. 20, 1828, the year of his death, the Pottawatomies inserted a provision which gave "to Eleanor Kin. zie and her four children, by the late John Kinzie, $3,500, in con sideration of the attachment of the Indians to her deceased husband." Other settlers followed Kinzie. The Indian Agency was resumed, and once more Chicago became the scene of social and business life. Friendly chiefs came once more to the fort, and around the firesides of former acquaintances recounted tales of the tragic war which had proved quite as disastrous to the Indian as to the pale-faced conqueror. Many a powerful tribe had been annihilated, many an Indian village swept away. The chief of a once numerous people, Black Partridge, came to sit in the cabin of his old friend, John Kinzie. He was now a lonely, broken-hearted man, whose tribe and kindred were either dead or scattered, whose village was in ashes and whose voice, once powerful in council, was listened to no more.

From the time of the rebuilding of Fort Dearborn Chicago's advance was steady if not rapid. There was peace and quiet in all the region round about the harbor. The soil of the rich prairie lands was broken up by settlers, who came in numbers from the Eastern States, and well-tilled farms supplied the traders with the necessaries of life. Fish were plenty in the streams, and game in abundance stalked through the woods, or roamed over the undulating prairies. Vessels came to the harbor for furs, and brought such luxuries as the simple tastes of the hardy pioneers demanded. These at the same time kept them in communication with the outer world. Thus by slow degrees the little frontier

2

post grew to the dignity of a thriving village, with a population of several hundred souls. Communication was established with towns farther to the south. The Homestead act increased the tide of emigration to the West. In 1818 Illinois was admitted to the Union, and the settlement of her rich domains increased. Chicago became the commercial center of a rich and rapidly developing country. Commodious dwellings took the place of cabins, and well-filled stores the place of traders' huts. The goddess of commerce touched the marshes with her wand of gold, and there sprang up a splendid city.

The first territorial legislature of Illinois met in 1812, and the territory became a State six years later. In 1829 the Illinois and Michigan Canal received Congressional sanction. The county of Cook was organized in 1831, and Chicago made its county-seat. In 1833 the town of Chicago was incorporated with twenty-eight voters. Its first trustees were: T. J. V. Owen, George W. Dole, Madore B. Beaubien, John Miller and E. S. Kimberly. Its first public buildings were a log jail and an estray pen. The prominent families living in the city in 1832 were those of James Kinzie (son of the silversmith, John Kinzie), Elijah Wentworth, a tavern-keeper, Robert A. Kinzie, Alexander Robinson, William and Samuel Lee, John Miller and Mark Beaubien, who kept a tavern on the east side of the South Branch just above its junction with the North Branch. These, with a few French traders, went to make up the town of Chicago in the first year of its existence. At this time there were no post-roads in this section, and Chicago was without a post-office. The mail was brought once in two weeks by a half-breed Indian from Niles, Michigan.

The first newspaper of Chicago was established in October, 1833, by John Calhoun, and was called the *Chicago Democrat*. It was published at the corner of La Salle and South Water Streets, and between its editorials urging the necessity of work on the Illinois and Michigan Canal and its reports of the arrival of an occasional lake schooner, it chronicled the bear and wolf hunts that took place in the corporate limits of the town. During the summer of 1834 a lake schooner came regularly once a week from Lake Erie, unloading its cargo with lighters outside the bar. But during the year a freshet swept away the bar that had heretofore obstructed the mouth of the river, and the schooner *Illinois* sailed up the narrow stream into the town—the first vessel to navigate that channel, which is to-day, for nine months in the year, a moving forest of masts.

The embryo city already boasted several taverns, a newspaper, a packing establishment, two ferries, several supply stores and a marine list. Neither were these early pioneers neglectful of their spiritual welfare—four religious denominations, viz: the Catholic, Methodist, Presbyterian and Baptist, being represented.

During the year 1836 a ship was built and launched here; work was begun on the Illinois and Michigan Canal, and the necessary steps taken to incorporate Chicago as a city. The latter did not take place, however, until March 4, 1837. At the first city election William B. Ogden (Democrat) was elected over his opponent, John H. Kinzie (Whig), by a majority of 237. The total vote cast was 706.

Chicago was at that time confined within the limits of North Avenue on the north, Wood Street on the west, Twenty-second Street on the south, and on the east by the lake. For some years the municipal authorities met to transact the business of the city in a building at the corner of Lake and Clark Streets, known as the "Saloon Building." When the city market was built, on the ground where State Street is now intersected by Randolph, the upper floor of that building was arranged for municipal uses. A building of liberal proportions and beautiful architecture was, in 1851, built jointly by the city and county on Court-house Square, the site of the present county building. Here the business of both city and county was transacted, much as it is to-day, until the building was destroyed by fire in 1871.

The speculative fever caught Chicago in '35 and '36; and the city experienced, even in those early days, a "boom" which deserves to rank with the wildest and haziest of this class of commercial baubles. Real estate changed hands with a rapidity which hardly allowed time for signing the papers, and at such rapid advance in prices as made anybody rich who was able to float his paper for a day. The panic of 1837 placed things once more on a stable basis; and, while it caused a momentary hesitation in the growth of Chicago, it never really checked it, and when the flurry was over and real values once more established things moved forward more rapidly than ever. The astonishing increase in the value of Chicago realty in those early years is shown by the following figures: In 1832 lots 3 and 4 in block 1 were worth $102. In 1853 they sold for $108,000. A small tract held by the Kinzies in 1832 at $346 sold twenty-one years later for $540,000. These are fair examples of the general rise in Chicago property during those years.

While the city enjoyed a season of unparalleled prosperity during these years, it was not without serious troubles. In 1836 the Black Hawk war sent the settlers for miles around flying into Fort Dearborn, and at the same time the cholera, more terrible and more deadly than the savage redskins, came to scourge the city. Then the panic of 1837–38 left many of the citizens without means to supply the necessaries of the plainest living. The most serious set-back, however, was the flood of 1849. In March of that year the Desplaines River overflowed and came pouring into the South Branch of the Chicago, breaking up the ice and gorging the stream. This, sweeping onward toward the lake, caught the vessels which had wintered there, and, crushing them into a common mass, moved with an irresistible force upon the city. More than forty vessels were destroyed, and the only bridge in the city swept away. The damage to the shipping, wharves and city generally was more than $130,000. This does not seem large to the Chicagoan of to-day, who saw the flood of flame that swept over the city in 1871; but, to the struggling city of that time, it was a great calamity. But with the same perseverance, energy and pluck which has since made Chicago the wonder of the world, the citizens set about repairing their losses, and Chicago from that time went steadily forward, with no reverses worth recording until the great fire of 1871.

At that time Chicago was a city of wood. Not that there was a dearth of fine buildings of stone and brick. Even before the fire the "Queen City by the Inland Sea" boasted many structures that would have done honor to the greatest metropolis in the world. But its growth had been so rapid that it had had no time to harden, and wood was the predominating material. The towering stone business blocks six stories high in the business

center of the city were flanked on either side by rambling wooden
shells. Outside the heart of the city it was all wood. Even the
showy brick structures were lined and beamed and raftered and
shingled with wood. The lumber yards were great piles of sea-
soned wood; the ships at the docks were loaded with it, and even
the docks themselves groaned under great loads of wood, lately
arrived and ready to take part in the coming carnival of flame.
For weeks previous to that fatal night, the wind had been blowing
dry and hot over those acres and acres of warped boards, sucking
out the last bit of moisture, till their black knots ran hot pitch as
they turned their cracked and splintered edges to the sky, as
if pleading to heaven for relief. The night of Oct. 8, 1871,
found Chicago a city of tinder; the night that followed left it a
bed of blistering ashes. A cow on DeKoven Street put her
cloven hoof to a lighted lamp and 20,000 buildings lay in ruins;
100,000 people were homeless; $200,000,000 of money was con-
verted into smoke, and the lives of 200 citizens had been sacrificed
to the god of flame. The fire, which started in a little frame barn
in the vicinity of DeKoven and Jefferson Streets, west of the
river and south of Van Buren Street, was never under control
from its discovery until it had burned over an area of nearly three
and a third square miles and destroyed 17,450 buildings. It first
crossed the river at Van Buren Street, and the gas-works, which
then stood at the corner of Adams and Franklin Streets, were
soon wrapped in flames. The wind blew a gale, and the conflagration swelled every moment to greater heat and fury. A
granite block was no more in its path than a house-fly in the path
of a swallow. At one o'clock in the morning the Chamber of
Commerce fell. The Court House across the street was the next
to go. Crosby's Opera House, Hooley's Theater, the *Times*
building; the whole length of Randolph Street went in a breath.
The Tremont and Sherman houses were already burning; and by
morning all this part of the city, from the West Branch of the
Chicago River to the lake and north of Congress Street, at that
time the very best portion of the city, composed of splendid
blocks of commercial houses, magnificent public buildings, handsome hotels and places of amusement, lay in ruins. About three
o'clock in the morning it crossed the river to the North Side, and

by daylight that part of the city was a blackened ruin. From the river to the city limits, three and a half miles north and east as far as the lake, everything was swept clean. Only one building in all that district was left standing. This was the "Ogden House," on the north side of Washington Square, between Clark Street and Dearborn Avenue. It was a square frame structure of comfortable dimensions. The trees which grew rather plentifully about it are credited with saving it from destruction. This building, which has been an interesting landmark for residents and visitors, has lately been torn down to make way for the Newberry Library building, which is being erected on the grounds. It was the one link remaining between the Chicago of to-day and rude log huts of the trader and trapper settlers of a century ago. There is a "Relic House," a quaint structure built of molten relics picked up after the great fire, standing at the junction of Clark Street and North Park Avenue; but this is more of a curiosity than a souvenir of the early days of Chicago. There is also a large collection of relics in the rooms of the Chicago Historical Society, mostly donations from Maria G. Carr, Mrs. E. E. Atwater and business firms, which were gathered from the ruins of the city's merchandise.

The condition of the inhabitants of Chicago directly after the conflagration was pitiful in the extreme. The millionaire and pauper were alike houseless, homeless and without food. Families were separated, and roamed from place to place searching for each other in vain. Trampled turf took the place of downy beds, and the sky roofed in the couches of those who had been wont to sleep under curtains of silk. The pangs of hunger added to the misery of loss of fortune, and tears and lamentations were everywhere. When the news that Chicago lay in ruins flashed over the wires, the heart of the world melted with compassion, and the magnitude of calamity was surpassed by the universal charity that it awakened. From every quarter of the globe came not only expressions of the deepest sympathy, but substantial offerings of relief. The capacity of every railroad leading into Chicago was tested by the continuous flow of supplies pouring in from everywhere. The contributions in food, clothing and money amounted to over $7,000,000. It was the grandest illustration of that great wealth of sympathy underlying the seeming indifference to the sorrows of others in the every-day affairs of mankind that the world has ever seen.

Encouraged by this generous expression of sympathy and assistance, the citizens of the stricken city set bravely to work to retrieve their broken fortunes. Private dwellings were turned into manufactories, and temporary shanties were put up on the ruins of stores and dwellings before the stones in the cellars were cold. The city was rapidly rebuilt. Forty millions of dollars were expended,in improvements during the first year after the fire. The new buildings were of grander proportions and were constructed with regard to ornament as well as use.

In the reconstruction of the city the erection of buildings of wood was restricted to certain limits, and fire-proof structures six and seven stories in height and of imposing appearance arose on every hand. It was not many years before every vestige of the fire had disappeared, and out of its ashes arose a new Chicago, incomparably superior to the one that had met with such sudden and fearful destruction.

On July 14, 1874, the city suffered from another disastrous fire. That portion of the city east of State Street and south of Twelfth Street, which had escaped the conflagration of '71, was completely burned over, $4,000,000 worth of property going up in the flames. This fire consumed the greater part of the wooden buildings still remaining within the fire limits of the city. These were at once replaced by those of a more substantial character; and what would otherwise have been a serious calamity was after all of great advantage, and hastened forward the time when Chicago might justly claim, as she does to-day, to be the most solidly built and fire-proof city in America.

The wonderful recuperative powers displayed by Chicago in so rapidly recovering from the effects of two such disasters, following one another in quick succession, aroused such a feeling of confidence in her ultimate greatness that everybody became imbued with a desire to become a landholder, and speculation in real estate for a time ran riot. Previous to the fall of 1873 unimproved property was held at prices almost equal to those of to-day. But the panic of that year proved disastrous to speculation, and prices of Chicago realty settled back to their normal condition. Wild speculation was succeeded by rational improvement, and lands which had long been kept vacant by fictitious values became sites for splendid business structures or beautiful residences.

When, in 1837, Chicago was first incorporated as a city, with a population of 4,170, and an area of 10.70 square miles, it comprised "the district of country in the county of Cook, etc., known as the east half of the southwest quarter of section 33, township 40 north, range 14 east; also the east quarter of sections 6, 7, 18 and 19, all of fractional section 3, and of sections 4, 5, 8, 9 and fractional section 10 (except the southwest fractional quarter thereof, occupied as a military post, until the same shall become private property), fractional section 15, sections 16, 17, 20, 21 and fractional section 22, township 39 north, range 14 east." The city limits have since that time been twelve times extended, and its present area covers 181.70 square miles. The population, according to the census of 1890, was 1,098,576. The school census gave it 1,208,669. Since that time several new districts have been added, and an estimate of 1,300,000 for the present population of the city of Chicago would not be far from correct. Chicago, which is only one-quarter as old as New York, ranks second in the United States and sixth in the cities of the world.

The rapid growth of Chicago, while it may puzzle the casual observer, is after all but the natural effect of an easily discerned cause. Situated at the extreme head of a great chain of lakes that open a direct waterway to the sea, surrounded by a country that two decades ago was in great part a wilderness, and which to-day supports 10,000,000 of people, who, in the occupancy and development of 500,000 square miles of forest and prairie, have invested no less than $2,000,000,000, what wonder that Chicago should become a great city? A great mass of men and a great mass of capital came together on this land to develop it, and Chicago has but kept pace with the result. It is an inland city! London is an inland city, and yet it is the world's metropolis. In the course of events New York must take the place of Liverpool, and Chicago of London in the New World. Man will not bring this about: man could not

CLARK STREET, FACING COURT HOUSE—GRAND OPERA HOUSE.

bring it about. The geography has done it already, and nothing short of a general upheaval of Nature can change the result.

Chicago is situated on the southwest shore of Lake Michigan, in 41° 52′ north latitude and 78° 52′ west longitude. Its mean elevation is 75 feet above Lake Michigan, or 591 feet above mean sea level.

Baltimore, its nearest port on the Atlantic, is a distance of 854 miles, while 2,417 miles lie between it and the Pacific Ocean. It lies directly on the high way from the Lakes to the Gulf, and from the Atlantic to the Western States. Besides being a great inland feeder, it has all the advantages of a sea-port city. It is because of these things that from a small hamlet a little over half a century ago, Chicago has grown into a metropolitan center, whose arteries of trade extend to every portion of the world.

The climate of Chicago is generally delightful. Cool breezes from the lake blow almost constantly during the summer months, and the winters, which in this latitude are generally long and severe, by this same agency are tempered to moderation. There is an exhilaration in the atmosphere of Chicago which stimulates and arouses the latent energies of the human system, and in no other city can such an amount of mental and physical labor be performed with so little fatigue. Statistics prove Chicago to be the healthiest city in the world. The highest death rate it has known 'for many years was in 1875, which was 20.29; the lowest in 1878, when it fell to 15.70 per 1,000 population. The death rate of New York averages over 29 per thousand, of Boston 23 per thousand, Philadelphia about 24 per thousand, while the great European cities give up every year from 25 to 45 of every one thousand of their inhabitants to the fell destroyer. During the year just passed, notwithstanding the ravages of *la grippe*, there died in Chicago but 21,856 persons, or about 18 per cent. of the population.

Almost the whole of "down town" Chicago rests on an artificial foundation. All the ground lying east of Wabash Avenue from Sixteenth Street north to the river has been reclaimed from the lake, while the grade of the entire business portion of the city has been raised from eight to fifteen feet above its original level.

The entire absence of any rise or fall of the country on which Chicago is located made the question of adequate sewerage a serious one. Skillful engineering has, to a great extent, overcome the difficulty; and there is no city in the country to-day that can boast of a purer atmosphere or more cleanly surroundings.

The Chicago River, which was at one time the sneer and scoff of her own citizens, has become the city's most useful, if its most humble servant. With its two branches, stretching out like the extended claws of a crab to the extreme northeast and southwest quarters of the city, the arm or main channel meeting the lake on the east, it formed a natural arterial system. It was, however, too sluggish by nature to do the work required of it, and artificial means had to be employed. A system of pumping was introduced, with works at Bridgeport and Fullerton Avenue. The former, in the extreme southwestern part of the city, throws the water out of the river into the Illinois and Michigan Canal at the rate of 40,000 cubic feet per minute; the latter, in the extreme northeastern part of the city, throws in fresh water from the lake in quantities something less, but enough to dilute its contents and form a head sufficient to set its current from the lake. While the system has thus far proved measurably successful, the rapid growth of the city and the approaching Columbian Exposition suggested the need of improvement, and steps have already been taken to that end. The gravity channel that is to connect the Chicago with the Illinois River, when finished, will be of sufficient compass to relieve Chicago of any fear of the pollution of her water supply for all time to come. It is believed, also, that this canal will receive aid from the government sufficient to make it a navigable waterway from the Mississippi to Lake Michigan.

Chicago, considering the heterogeneous character of its population, has been remarkably free from riotous disturbances. When, in 1877, the whole eastern country was on the eve of convulsion, and labor riots, which had their origin in Pittsburgh, were threatening the peace of every American city, Chicago was but slightly agitated. The militia were called out, but their services were never required, except for the protection of private property and the guarding of public buildings. The local police were sufficient to quell the disturbance. Less than a score of people lost their lives during the three or four days which the riot lasted, and peace was easily restored. The Haymarket massacre, on the night of May 4, 1886, was much more serious and far-reaching in its consequences. A crowd of Anarchists had gathered near the Haymarket, at the entrance to an alley that opens on Desplaines Street, and their speakers were making incendiary speeches from the bed of a wagon which stood partly in the street and partly in the alley. Six companies of policemen were sent to disperse the mob and arrest the speakers. As they wheeled from the Haymarket and advanced into Desplaines Street, a bomb was thrown from the mouth of the alley and exploded in their midst. Seven policemen were killed outright or so badly wounded that they died shortly afterwards. Many more were crippled for life. Instantly all was confusion. The policemen opened fire, and the mob fled in every quarter. Just how many of these were killed and wounded will never be known. The excitement in the city was intense; and their friends anxious to conceal the fact of their being at the meeting, concealed the bodies of their dead and gave them quiet burial, and in secret nursed the wounded. Those known to be leaders in the Anarchistic movement, Fielden, Lingg, Spies, Engel, Schwab, Neebe and Fischer, were arrested. The office of the *Arbeiter Zeitung,* with which several of these men were known to be connected, was searched, and quite a supply of dynamite arms, bombs and infernal machines discovered. Parsons, one of the principal Anarchistic leaders, and who escaped on the night of riot, a few days later surrendered himself to the authorities. A long and sensational trial followed, which resulted in a sentence of death for the prisoners. The sentence of Fielden and Schwab was commuted to imprisonment for life. Lingg, the "Tiger Anarchist," committed suicide in jail by means of a bomb stolen in to him by his sweetheart; and the others, Parsons,

Spies, Engel and Fischer, on the 11th day of November, 1887, went to the gallows.

When the fatal drop fell on that still autumnal morning, Anarchy was dead, and nothing approaching a riot has been since seen in Chicago.

In railroad facilities Chicago is much superior to any other American city. This, together with its cool lake breezes, its splendid hotel accommodations and its many fine assembly halls, make it the ideal place for holding conventions of all kinds. The great Exposition building, in which Lincoln was nominated in 1860, as was McClellan in 1864, Garfield in 1880, Blaine in 1884 and Cleveland again in the same year, affords seating capacity for 20,000 persons. The new Auditorium, the largest theater building in the world, is now the favorite assembly hall for the great conventions; and the candidates for President will no doubt continue to be named at Chicago.

The bonded indebtedness of Chicago is about $17,000,000. The $500,000 of the $1,000,000 invested in the World's Columbian Exposition is included in this estimate. The number of buildings erected has grown from 4,086 in 1883 to 11,608 in 1890. In the former year there was expended for this purpose $22,-162,610; in the latter year, $47,322,100. The building industry of 1891 will be far in advance of this.

Chicago, during the year 1890, slaughtered 5,733,082 hogs and 2,219,312 cattle; and the total value of live-stock handled during that time reached the enormous sum of $231,344,879. The commerce of the city has increased from $20,000,000 in 1850 to $1,380,000,000 in 1890. The wholesale business is now more than $500,000,000, and the value of manufactured products over $100,-200,000. The total receipts of grain amounted to 177,353,461 bushels, and of flour 4,358,058 barrels; 2,050,000,000 feet of lumber were shipped or consumed in the city, and it took 515,000,000 shingles to supply the trade. These figures show that Chicago leads the world in the business of stock and lumber. The banking business of Chicago ranks next in volume to that of New York, although second place is given to that of Boston in the published reports of the clearing houses. The total clearings of the twenty-one associated banks in Chicago for 1890 were $4,093,-

THE AUDITORIUM, STUDEBAKER BUILDING AND ART INSTITUTE.

145,904; and the Comptroller of Currency at Washington, in his report for the last quarter of 1890, said: "The general showing is a good one for the country at large, but the Chicago banks seem to be in especially good shape, and the reserve of 31.42 per cent. indicates a healthy condition of that city. Philadelphia's reserve is 28.38 per cent., while New York's is 28.11 per cent.; so you can judge of the relàtive standing of Chicago." The custom duties collected at Chicago for 1890 were $13,518,896.33, and the general commerce of the city reached in 1890 the magnificent sum of $1,380,000,000. The commercial and manufacturing interests of Chicago increase at such a rapid rate that the figures of a preceding year are necessarily far below those which would be required to give an idea of the current business of the city. The preparations now going forward for the World's Columbian Exposition have greatly increased the volume of trade in all lines, and the statistics for 1891 will show an advance of at least 30 per cent. over the figures quoted above.

GUIDE TO
CHICAGO.

Giving the Principal Points of Interest, Parks, Boulevards, Railroads, Street Railways, Suburban Towns, Public Buildings, Etc., Etc.

COUNTY ORGANIZATION. — The government of Cook County, Illinois, is vested in a Board of Commissioners, consisting of fourteen members, elected for four years, half of whom retire biennially. Their salaries for 1891 amounted to $33,551. The board elects its president, selecting one of its own number. This board has the direction and control of all county officers; collects the revenues of the county through the County Treasurer; appropriates money for the maintenance of the courts, jail, insane asylum, poor-house, county hospital, court-house building, sheriff's office, county clerk's office, coroner's office, etc., and has general supervision of county highways, bridges, etc. The County Board is entirely independent of the City Council, although the jurisdiction of the latter extends over a large portion of the county included within the corporate limits.

Cook County Court-House—Occupies the entire east half of the block bounded by Washington, Randolph, La Salle and Clark Streets, in the center of the business district of the South Side, the west half being occupied by the City Hall. This magnificent pile was erected in 1876–77 at a cost of about $3,000,000, and is one of the handsomest public buildings in the country. In this building are located the County, Probate and various Circuit and Superior Courts, the Law Library, and all the County offices, except that of the State's (or Prosecuting) Attorney, which is located in the Criminal Court building, North Side.

County Insane Asylum.—Take train at Union Depot, Canal and Adams Streets. This institution is located at Dunning, a suburb of Chicago. It is a costly structure of imposing dimensions, surrounded by spacious grounds, far enough removed from the city to make the location a quiet and healthful one. Numerous cottage wards relieve the overcrowded condition of the main building. The current expenses of 1890 were: Salaries, $44,-111.68; supplies, repairs, etc., $112,006.87. The total number admitted for treatment in 1890 was 1,483; of these 717 were men and 766 were women; 30 per cent. were native-born and 70 per cent. were of foreign birth. The number remaining under treatment at the close of 1890 was 1,083, of which 509 were men and 574 were women. In his annual report the Superintendent makes this important statement: "I would here call attention to a fact, and that is, where those that are insane are placed under proper treatment in well-arranged hospitals within the first three months of the inception of the disease the chances for recovery are about as good as from any serious bodily ailment. The average of cures when this class of disease is thus treated will range as high as 60, 65 and even 70 in 100."

County Jail—Situated in the rear of the Criminal Court building, Michigan Street, between Clark Street and Dearborn Avenue, North Side. Entrance from Michigan Street. Visitors admitted by permission of the sheriff. Both the jail and the Criminal Court building long since ceased to meet the demands made upon it by the extraordinary growth of the city, and the consequent and natural increase in the number of criminals. It lacks almost every modern improvement, and will, doubtless, soon be replaced by a larger and more convenient structure. The Criminal Court building is connected with the jail by a "bridge of sighs," over which the culprits pass for trial and after conviction. This entrance is never used except by deputy sheriffs and jailers in discharge of their duties. The only other entrance is up a narrow flight of steps leading from the open court between the two buildings. At the head of these steps is a double iron gate, where stands the outer turnkey. On one side of the prison entrance is the head-jailer's room; on the other, the office of the jail clerk. No one is allowed to go beyond this corridor without a permit. Beyond this is the "Cage," an iron-bound arrangement covered with several thicknesses of wire netting, from which the prisoner may hold communication with his friends. It was here that the "Tiger Anarchist" Lingg received from his sweetheart the dynamite cartridge which he exploded in his mouth, killing himself the day before that set for his execution. There are a number of cells on this floor. Just above, on the next balcony, is "Murderers' Row," from which many unfortunates have gone forth to the gallows during the last twenty years. The cell balconies run all around this interior building. At the northeast corner of the cell-building the gallows is always erected. There are four departments: Men's, Women's, Boys' and Debtors'.

County Poor-House.—Located at Dunning, a suburb of Chicago. Take train at Union Depot, Canal and Adams Streets. This institution is not remarkable in any sense, save as the home of the most wretched class of paupers of the county. The cost of conducting it for 1890 was $105,666.91. This included salaries, supplies, repairs, and the expense of operating the county poor-farm, which returns some revenue.

The Judiciary of the county consists of one probate and eighteen judges of the Superior and Circuit Courts. The salaries of the judges of the courts of Cook County amounted in 1890 to $69,415.40; for clerks of the Superior and Circuit Courts and their assistants, $59,582. The repairs on court rooms amounted to about $2,000.

CITY GOVERNMENT.—The City Government is well organized in both its legislative and executive branches. There are departments of police, fire, health, law, finance and a department of public works, which is supposed to look after everything which does not come under the supervision of any of the other branches of the administration. The legislative power is vested in the Mayor and a Board of Aldermen, more familiarly known as the City Council. The Mayor's term of office is two years. The board has thirty-six members—two from each of the eighteen wards, elected in alternate years for a term of two years each. The Mayor presides over the deliberations of the body, or, if he be absent, a member from the quorum present is called to the chair. The following is a complete list of the Mayors and the dates of their election:

William B. Ogden,	May 2, 1837
Buckner S. Morris,	March 6, 1838
B. W. Raymond,	March 5, 1839
Alexander Lloyd,	March 3, 1840
Francis C. Sherman,	March 5, 1841
Benjamin W. Raymond,	March 7, 1842
Augustus Garrett,	March 7, 1843
A. S. Sherman,	March 7, 1844
Augustus Garrett,	March 5, 1845
John P. Chapin,	March 3, 1846
James Curtiss,	March 2, 1847
James H. Woodworth,	March 7, 1848
James H. Woodworth,	March 6, 1849
James Curtiss,	March 5, 1850
Walter S. Gurnee,	March 4, 1851
Walter S. Gurnee,	March 2, 1852
Charles M. Gray,	March 14, 1853
Isaac L. Milliken,	March 13, 1854
Levi D. Boone,	March 8, 1855
Thomas Dyer,	March 10, 1856
John Wentworth,	March 3, 1857
John C. Haines,	March 2, 1858
John C. Haines,	March 1, 1859
John Wentworth	March 6, 1860
Julian S. Rumsey,	April 16, 1861
Francis C. Sherman,	April 15, 1862
Francis C. Sherman,	April 21, 1863
John B. Rice,	April 18, 1865
John B. Rice,	April 16, 1867
Roswell B. Mason,	November 2, 1869
Joseph Medill,	November 7, 1871
Harvey D. Colvin,	November 4, 1873

3

Monroe Heath, ...	July 12, 1876
Monroe Heath, ...	April 3, 1877
Carter H. Harrison, ...	April 1, 1879
Carter H. Harrison, ...	April 5, 1881
Carter H. Harrison, ...	April 3, 1883
Carter H. Harrison, ...	April 7, 1885
John A: Roche, ...	April 5, 1887
Dewitt C. Cregier, . . .	April 2, 1889
Hempstead Washburne, . .	April 7, 1891

In 1863 the term of office of Mayor was extended from one to two years. In 1869 the time of holding the city election was changed from April to November. and the persons then in office were continued until the first Monday in December. The city was reorganized under the general incorporation act in April, 1875, and consequently no election was held in November of that year, but the persons in office held over until July, 1876. In that year the City Council provided for an election for city officers under the new incorporation, but omitted all reference to the office of Mayor. Nevertheless, a popular vote was taken for Mayor at the election, and Thomas Hoyne received 33,064. The canvass of the returns being made, the Council disregarded the vote for Mayor, but the new Council canvassed the returns and declared Mr. Hoyne elected. Mr. Colvin, the incumbent, declined to yield possession, and the matter was taken to the courts, where the case was decided against both contestants. A special election was then ordered by Council, and held July 12, 1876, resulting in the election of Mr. Heath to serve till after the next regular election. Measures can be passed over the Mayor's veto only by an affirmative vote of two-thirds of the council. The regular meetings are on Monday evening of each week.

The Law Department consists of a Corporation Council, City Attorney and Prosecuting Attorney.

The Department of Finance is under the City Comptroller, City Treasurer and City.Collector.

The ·Building Department.—A Commissioner of Building, assisted by a secretary and a corps of inspectors, has charge of

1is department. No building can be erected in the city without permit from this body. Fire escapes and elevators are also nder its supervision.

The Health Department.—This is in charge of a Commissioner ppointed by the Mayor. It has supervision over the cleanliness f streets, alleys, factories, workshops, vaccination, etc. The ffices of these several departments are in the City Hall.

The Department of Public Works.—This department has en- re charge of the machinery connected with the public works of hicago, and is too ponderous in its operations to be described ere. All the streets, sewers, bridges, viaducts, etc., are in charge f these commissioners. It formulates all plans and executes all nprovements of a public character in the city. It supervises the perations of corporations, and is powerful in every quarter of 1e city.

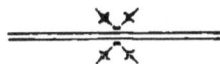

Parks and Boulevards.

As the glory of woman is in her hair—so is the glory of Chi- 1go in her parks and boulevards. Here are gleams and glints of eauty; shifting light and shade; the profusion of prodigal wealth ombined with unassuming gentleness and unobtrusive modesty. Iiles of meadow, mead and dale have been converted into acres f emerald lawn, smooth shaven as a priest. Undulating plats f rare and beautiful flowers on every hand charm the eye with 1eir infinite variety of colors, harmoniously blended; here deep- ning into carnation, there flashing into scarlet, and fading away onder into a bank of pale blues, crystals and whites. There are 1iniature lakes, upon whose surface move vast flotillas of deli- 1tely tinted lilies, and sailing slowly among them the stately van. There are shady banks spread thick with emerald grasses, hereon to lie and watch the white clouds drift across the smiling 1y, the lake droning on in dreamful music at your feet. The 1lendid public building is something in which the citizen takes just pride, but it is for a special purpose and entrance to it is necessarily restricted. The city's parks are the citizen's property, and as much to be enjoyed by the humble toiler at the counter, in the factory or upon the high ascending wall, as by the rich man, whose proud steeds spurn the gravel of the smooth boulevards themselves. Thus it is that the plutocrat and the plebeian alike join in praise of these grateful breathing places in the endless struggle for supremacy. The Chicago parks and boulevards have not only kept pace with the marvelous growth of the city, but they have outstripped every other improvement—public or private. No other city can boast such an extensive system of pleasure grounds. The chain of boulevards, which, with the improvements now under way, will encircle the city, make the longest continuous pleasure drive in the world. The recent transference of Diversey Avenue to the control of the West Park Board by the City Council removes the last obstacle to the completion of the system of parks and parkways encircling Chicago. When this gap of two and a half miles of common street shall have been transformed into a boulevard, it will be possible to start on Michigan Avenue at Madison Street, drive south to Jackson Park, thence by way of the west parks and boulevards to Diversey Avenue down to Lincoln Park and along the Lake Shore Drive to the starting point, a distance of about thirty-five miles. All this length of road will be a pleasure drive, not surpassed by anything of a similar kind in the world. By the time the Columbian Exposition opens, and Chicago begins to bid welcome to all the nations of the earth, this superb succession of parks and pleasure roads will be completed and ready to be offered for the use and admiration of the visitors. They will be as pleased with it as Chicago will be proud of the beauteous adornment.

Another notable addition to the boulevard system will be the Sheridan Road, now in course of construction. This driveway, beginning at Byron and Sheffield Avenues, where it connects with the Lake Shore Drive, will wind its way along the lake shore over a stretch of picturesque country, through tastefully laid out villages, through shadowy ravines lying between broken and ragged cliffs, to Waukegan, a distance of thirty-six miles.

For diversified scenery, both artificial and natural, the great

SEA LION POND LINCOLN PARK.

sweep of roadway stretching from Madison Street on Michigan Avenue by way of Jackson Park to Waukegan is not excelled by any urban drive. The view, the incidents, the quality of the surroundings, change with each furlong. From the lines of stately palaces on Michigan Avenue the eye is feasted with successive varying sights until it comes to the restful green of the maple, beech, birch and pine along the upper reaches of the north shore. When improved and beautified in accordance with the plans already accepted by its projectors, the great boulevard will surpass in extent and attractiveness either Euclid Avenue, Cleveland's boast, New Orleans' famous "Shell Road," Riverside Drive, Gotham's pride, or the Bois-de-Boulogne, of Paris. Even "Unter den Linden," where Kaiser Wilhelm and the German imperial family take their outings, and "Der Ringstrasse" of Vienna. over which the royal scions of the house of Hapsburg spin, will have to retire from the front rank of world-famous drives.

But one short gap remains to make the chain about the city complete. That is the connection by a proper pleasure driveway of the Lake Shore Drive with Michigan Avenue. This is near its solution. It is probable that a light yet strong viaduct, of ornamental design, will be built from Michigan Avenue at Randolph Street to the Lake Shore Drive at Ohio Street, passing over the river at the present Rush Street bridge. The great boulevard is spoken of as the Sheridan Road, Sheridan Drive, Lake Shore Road and Lake Shore Drive indiscriminately. Properly speaking, the Sheridan Road begins at Byron and Sheffield Avenues, while it is the Lake Shore Drive south of that point.

The original idea of our magnificent park and boulevard system was at the time of its conception so far ahead of the city's needs and so far beyond her power to construct, much less keep in order, that its projectors certainly deserve the title of prophets. More than a score of years ago the land which is now used for park purposes was purchased, and a plan laid out for a system or chain of parks and boulevards, which differed but little from that which is now so nearly perfected, and of which the city is so proud. Chicago then had little more than 300,000 inhabitants, and the wildest enthusiast would not at that time have ventured to predict a population of one and a quarter millions in 1891. Yet they were wise enough to secure these broad stretches of country, then lying on the confines or just without the borders of the corporate limits of the city. They are all inside the city limits now, and their entire compass will soon be in a state of the highest cultivation. The area covered by the different parks and public squares of Chicago embraces 1,974.61 acres. This is exclusive of the ground covered by park boulevards. The park system is divided into three divisions, and each division is under the control of a separate board of park commissioners, elected by the courts. These are known as the South Park Commissioners, the West Park Commissioners and the North Park Commissioners. The public parks of each division are maintained by a direct tax upon that portion of the city in which they lie. There are a number of smaller parks, squares and "places" throughout the city, under the control of the City Government.

NORTH SIDE.

LINCOLN PARK.

Take North Clark or Wells Street Cable Lines for Main Entrance;
or North State Street Cars to Lake Shore
Drive Entrance.

This is at present the most attractive park in the city. It is 250 acres in extent, beautifully laid out with sinuous driveways, quiet walks, extensive flower plats and miniature lakes. It has many heroic statues, a zoölogical garden, avaries, green-houses, a magnificent palm-house, just being completed, and almost every innocent and restful attraction that the ingenuity of man, combined with the munificence of Nature, can establish. Twenty years ago the old Chicago cemetery occupied the southern portion of the land, but as it was encroached upon by the city the ground was condemned for park purposes, and the bodies removed to different burial places. The tomb of the Erich family only remains. The park at first contained about 60 acres, but it has since been gradually extended until its area has grown to 250 acres. Its connection with the boulevard system dates from 1869, when the legislature provided for its maintenance and improvement, and appointed its first board of commissioners. The park has eight miles of drives, nine miles of walks, seven bridges, two tunnels and twenty acres of lake surface. From the magnificent Lake Shore Drive, which extends from Oak Street to the northernmost limit of the park, the panorama on either side is one of unrivaled beauty. On the west is the park with its succession of landscapes, each different from the others, yet perfect in itself; and on the east is the lake flashing its ever-changing hues upon the vision, its rippled surface dotted with sails and steamers, and at night the red gleam of the light-houses in the distance, and the lights of the vessels that move fitfully about, and the weird moonlight that, falling upon its dimpled face, is shivered into millions of radiant beams. There is a long artificial lake of some twelve acres in the southern half of the park, and a smaller one of eight acres in the northwest section. The zoölogical department contains an interesting collection of animals and birds. The list embraces sea-lions, prairie dogs, several varieties of bears, antelopes, buffaloes, deer, foxes, raccoons, wolves, etc. The floral department is a striking and attractive feature. About 100,000 plants of different colors are displayed in beds artistically shaped and arranged, and the conservatories contain a large array of the most beautiful and curious tropical plants and flowers. A striking Indian group in bronze, life-size and standing upon a massive granite pedestal, is the gift of Mr. Martin Ryerson. The Lincoln monument, provided for by the munificent legacy of $50,000 left by the late Eli Bates, of this city, faces the south entrance. It was designed by St.-Gaudieur, is a splendid likeness of the Great President, and is said to be among the finest pieces of sculpture in the world. Farther up the Lake Shore Drive and facing south is a magnificent equestrian statue of General Grant. This is of beaten bronze, heroic in size, and its attitude strongly suggestive of the character of the "Man of Will." The "Indian Group" marks a spot farther inland. There are also the La Salle monument, presented by Lambert Tree; the Schiller monument, presented by the German residents of the city, and the monument of Herr Linnæus, that eminent German who was to flowers what Audubon was to birds or Agassiz to minerals. Here, too, is a beautiful electric fountain, presented by C. T. Yerkes, which delights the eye with a thousand prismatic hues as the waters rise and fall in musical chorus. Pretty well toward the north end of the park, beyond the zoölogical gardens, and facing the flower garden, is the new grand conservatory, the finest building of its kind to be found anywhere. The palm house area is 156x90 feet, the fernery 90x56 feet, conservatory 90x31 feet, while the orchid and cape houses are 41x31 feet each. There is also a potting shed 12x90 feet. The style of the building is not unlike that of the grand palm house at Kew Gardens. The building covers a total area of 23,800 feet. The conservatories in other parks of this city are as follows: In Humboldt Park are the exotic house, 48x64, and 65 feet high; two houses, 25x60 feet each, and four propagating or plant houses, each 12x100 feet, costing $22,594.08. The Garfield Park conservatories are almost an exact counterpart of these, costing about $20,000 to build. These were constructed in or prior to 1887. Douglas Park has what they call a winter garden of quite pretentious appearance, covering an area of 178x62 feet, and the cost was about $40,000.

WEST SIDE.

HUMBOLDT PARK.

Take Madison Street Cable Cars marked "Milwaukee Avenue."

This is the most northern park in the city. It has an area of 200.62 acres, and is situated four miles from the Court House, in a northwesterly direction. It is bounded on the north by West North Avenue, on the south by Augusta Street, on the east by North California Avenue, and on the west by North Kinzie Street. It is handsomely laid out, and one of the most beautiful parks in the system. It has several large lakes, clear as crystal, which afford excellent opportunities for rowing. There is a refreshment pavilion and a band-stand near by, from which, during the summer evenings, music floats out over the waters; a delightful addition to the pastoral surroundings. An artesian well, 1,155 feet deep, yields water of high medicinal qualities.

A FLOWERY DELL, IN LINCOLN PARK.

Thousands of shade trees, a forest of pines, winding driveways, a pavilion, a band-stand, a lake, a play-ground, two lily ponds, a monument and a parade ground are to be added at once to the features of Humboldt Park. The portion to be improved is the western section, running three-quarters of a mile long and one-quarter of a mile wide from North Avenue to Augusta Street. Humboldt Boulevard runs north from the park to Logan Square, and thence east to Western Avenue, and when completed will connect Lincoln and Humboldt Parks. A driveway, very nearly straight, will connect Humboldt Boulevard and Central Boulevard, and pass along the eastern border of the newly improved portion or through the center of the park. Another driveway will make the same connections by branching off at the entrance on North Avenue and winding around to and along the extreme eastern border of the park, and back again to the entrance on Central Boulevard. In the very pathway of the central driveway the monument to Von Humboldt will stand. The monument will be the donation of Frances J. Dewes. The present lake at Humboldt Park is to be continued in a northwesterly direction, 400 feet wide, a distance of 1,200 feet. Not far from the bridge where the central driveway will cross the lake, will be a new casino of generous dimensions. A band pavilion will be by its side, around which a grove of shade trees will fling wide branches over seats for 1,000 people. Around a graceful curve of the lake and stretching a sweep of green sod for several acres to surrounding woods, a play-ground will be created for children. A branch from this drive follows the shore, crosses a little neck of water that flows to make the lily pond, and joins the central drive at the monument. But the main western driveway continues past where the flat white flowers float, past a great, open stretch of sod, where ball grounds will be made, and where brave soldiers will parade, and finally meets the central driveway at the entrance on Central Boulevard. Here they will pass out together in an asphalt boulevard by stone and marble mansions to Garfield Park, and from there to the grounds of the World's Columbian Exposition. The unimproved lands of this park cost $241,157, at a time when Chicago property was very much cheaper than it is to-day.

GARFIELD PARK.

Take Madison Street Cable Cars, marked "Garfield Park."

This park lies four miles directly west of the City Hall. It was formerly called Central Park, but its name was changed to the present one in honor of President Garfield, soon after his death. It lies between Madison and Lake Streets, and runs west a mile and a half from the head of Washington Boulevard. It contains 186 acres. A lake in its center covers seventeen acres. There, as in the other parks, are many beautiful walks and drives, a wilderness of flowers, shady retreats, sylvan glades, pretty boat-houses, and a great conservatory filled with tropical trees and plants. In the lake are two miniature islands. The boat-landing is 300 feet long. Breezy balconies run along three sides of the refreshment pavilion, and from its pleasant piazzas there is afforded a fine view of the lake. Over 40,000 plants are propagated in the conservatory every year. There is an artesian well here 2,200 feet deep, whose waters are wonderfully effective for the cure of some diseases—such as anæmia, indigestion, rheumatism, and kindred complaints. Hundreds go daily to drink of these waters, and many carry away jugs full of the health-giving beverage. A handsome drinking fountain for horses was presented to the park by the Humane Society, the cost of its construction being contributed by Mrs. Mancel Talcot. The analysis of the water is as follows:

	GRAINS.
Chloride of Magnesium,	8.352
Chloride of Sodium,	87,491
Bromide of Magnesium,	0.301
Sulphate of Lime,	1.114
Carbonate of Lime,	14.802
Carbonate of Iron,	0.712
Sulphate of Soda.	13.645
Silicate of Soda,	0.508
Alumina,	traces.
Organic Substances,	none.
Sulphureted Hydrogen,	none.
Total,	146.925
Free Carbonic Acid,	13.44 cubic inches.
Temperature at the Well,	71.4° Fahrenheit.

Water flows from the well at the rate of 150 gallons per minute. A small cataract, known as " Miniature Niagara," falls from a basin on the top of the rocky grotto at the mouth of the well. Here, as in the other parks, are shady retreats, sylvan glades, pretty boat-houses, wooden, stone and iron bridges, and different shaped lawns, with walks and drives, all of which are bordered with trees and beds of flowers. There is a great conservatory filled with tropical plants, giant palms, cork trees, ferns and hundreds of varieties of rare and beautiful trees and flowers, all heightened and made charming by the ingenuity of the landscape gardener's art here displayed. There are three miles of foot-paths and a driveway of about two miles.

DOUGLAS PARK.

Take Madison Street and Ogden Avenue Cable Cars.

To the south and east of Garfield Park, and directly south of Humboldt Park, lies Douglas Park, somewhat smaller than the two previously mentioned, but still of goodly proportions. There are 180 acres in Douglas Park. It is bounded by Twelfth Street on the north, Nineteenth Street on the south, California Avenue on the east, and Alabama Avenue on the west. Ogden Avenue runs diagonally through the park from east to west. It lies on the chain of boulevards, and is connected with Garfield Park by Douglas and Central Boulevards, and with Jackson Park by West Boulevard and others. It has two beautiful lakes, fed by an artesian well, also highly charged with medicinal properties.

There is a spacious conservatory with propagating houses, from which over 70,000 plants are transplanted every year. Base-ball, lawn-tennis and croquet are played on the shady lawns. From the balconies of the unique refectory is had a fine view of the lake, eleven acres in extent, and the most striking vistas of the grounds. In the month of August, in Douglas Park, the Chinese congregate to perform one of their religious ceremonies, which is celebrated by the flying of curious and queer-shaped kites, representing impossible animals, outrageous in design—fitting offsprings of their poppy-fed imaginations! The original cost of the lands of Douglas Park was $241,157.

SOUTH SIDE.

SOUTH PARKS

Is the name by which Washington and Jackson Parks, connected by Midway Plaisance, are collectively known. There are in all about 800 acres. These grounds now form part of the site for the Columbian Exposition, and will contain many of its finest buildings and most attractive displays.

WASHINGTON PARK.

*Take State Street and Wabash Avenue Cable Cars, over Indiana
and Cottage Grove Avenues; Michigan Avenue, Drexel and
Grand Boulevards, and the Phaetons and Dummy
Line from Oakwood Boulevard.*

This park lies between six and seven miles south of the City Hall, and extends from Fifty-first to Sixtieth Streets, between Cottage Grove and Kankakee Avenues. It is more than a mile from the lake shore, and contains 371 acres.

In many respects Washington Park may be considered the finest in this system of beautiful surprises. Drexel and Grand Boulevards contribute greatly to its natural beauties. Their entrances to the park are gorgeous panoramas of tempered light, shifting shade and artistic blending of form and color. There are long drives under wide-spreading elms and ancient oaks, whose roots were in the soil before the English tongue had been heard this side the Atlantic. There is the "Meadow," with its hundred acres of velvet sward inviting you to come and bury your flushed face in its fragrant coolness, and a glinting lake covering more than thirteen acres, dimpling and sparkling and showing silvery white through careless openings in the green foliage. If Washington Park cannot boast of a long stretch of pebbled shore whereon Lake Michigan dashes in stormy weather and dances in the quiet days, it can boast of one of the most picturesque little lakes in the world; and it is all its own. This park has also a great conservatory, and in flower plats and foliage painting is far ahead of any of its sisters.

A pavilion known as the "Retreat," where weary ramblers may be served with refreshments to their liking, stands invitingly near its center. As permits for sports are readily obtained, baseball, archery, lawn-tennis and croquet parties select Washington Park oftener than any other for a day's outing. Both Grand and Drexel Boulevards are traversed by park phaetons, making regular trips to Oakwood Boulevard for passengers. These obliging conveyances are said to carry not less than 100,000 passengers during the year. The stable in which the park phaetons are kept is one of the attractions of the park. It is 325x200 feet, and accommodates 100 horses. The portion allotted to the horses is unique and interesting. It is circular in form, and the stalls are ranged in two consecutive rings with an alley between. The horses used to draw the phaetons are all grays, and resemble each other very much in form and deportment. If you take a park phaeton, you may be driven through these stables.

JACKSON PARK.

Take Cottage Grove Avenue Cable Cars or Illinois Central Suburban Trains.

Eight miles to the southeast of the City Hall, along the shore of Lake Michigan, lies Jackson Park, memorable now from having been selected as the site of the World's Columbian Exposition. It contains altogether 593 acres, only eighty-four of which were improved before work was begun on the World's Fair grounds. Its northern boundary is Fifty-sixth Street, its southern boundary Sixty-seventh Street. Stony Island Avenue runs along its western border, and its eastern line is washed by the blue waves of the. great lake. It is easily reached by the Illinois Central suburban trains, which run almost constantly, or by Wabash Avenue and Cottage Grove cable cars. Many other lines, both surface and elevated, are projected, and will, no doubt, be completed in time for the great Columbian Exposition. Cercle Français and the Federation of Franco-Belge, two French societies, have undertaken the erection of a bronze statue of Victor Hugo,

to be placed in Jackson Park. The work will be designed b,
Architect Albert Blitz.

There is much beautiful scenery in Jackson Park of the wild
and picturesque kind. The woods are of native trees; and the
lakes, which form a sinuous chain throughout the park, were,
many of them, the result of the broken and undulating nature of
the ground before it came under the cultivating hand of man.
The shore along the lake at this point is high and the ground
solid. The work which is to be done on these grounds during the
next two years will entirely change the topography of the place ;
but the opportunity will present itself to make Jackson Park, at
the close of the Exposition, the grandest park in the city, if not in
the world.

MIDWAY PLAISANCE.

This is a woodland drive connecting Jackson with Washington
Park. It contains eighty acres, not hitherto improved to any
extent. This, too, forms a portion of the site of the World's
Columbian Exposition, and will undergo so marked a change that
a present description of it would be a waste of words. (See
Columbian Exposition.)

GAGE PARK,

A small but neat park of twenty acres, four miles west of
Washington Park, at the junction of Garfield and Western
Avenue Boulevards. It is covered thickly with trees, and will
eventually become a pleasant resting place on the drive around
the city.

UNION PARK,

Situated on Washington Boulevard, one and three-quarter
miles from the Court-House. It contains 14.3 acres of land, and
is one of the most delightful as well as useful parks in the city.
It lies between Ashland Avenue, Lake Street, Ogden Avenue
and Ashland Avenue; is in a thickly settled portion of the city
and is a blessed breathing spot for hundreds of children who, but
for it, would have to pass the hot summer days under a burning

roof. This is one of the oldest parks in the city. Some years ago the citizens whose property abutted on the park petitioned to have this pleasure-ground turned over to their care, and their prayer was granted. As a consequence, Union Park was soon in the condition of other parks in charge of the city government. It became a dry and trampled waste. The park commissioners were again given charge of it; and once more it blooms, the lakes sparkle, its fountains dance in the sunlight, beds of flowers perfume the air; there is music of birds and the laughter of children, and all within fifteen minutes walk of the roaring center of the city. The headquarters of the West Park Board are here.

PARKS NOT IN THE SYSTEM.

All the other Chicago parks are in charge of the city government. They are laid out with no particular regard to order, and seem to have become parks through the wise beneficence of Providence rather than through any design of man. As health restorers, they are of incalculable benefit; and, were there half a hundred more of these breathing places in the city, where the children might stretch their limbs and broaden their chests, it would be a glorious thing.

In the west division are Jefferson, Wicker, Vernon, Congress and Campbell Parks. The largest of these is Jefferson Park, a beautiful, shady retreat on West Adams Street, between Troop and Monroe Streets. It has a lake, a fountain, and a grotto. Its walks are well kept, and its trees are wide-spreading, and make friendly shade for the citizens of that vicinity.

Vernon Park is a four-acre strip two miles southwest of the Court-House on West Polk Street, between Center Avenue and Loomis Street. Wicker Park is three miles from the Court-House northwest (take Milwaukee Avenue cars). It lies within an angle formed by the junction of Park, North, Robey and Fowler Streets. It is well kept and attractive. Congress Park contains seven-tenths and Campbell Park five-tenths of an acre.

In the north division are Washington Park and Union Square. Washington Park is on North Clark Street, between Dearborn Avenue and Lafayette and Washington Places. In the northwest quarter of the block bounded by Goethe, Scott, Aster and Stone Streets, lies a half-acre park, called Union Square. In the south division of Chicago is Lake Park, or "The Lake Front," as it is more familiarly called. It lies between Michigan Avenue and the Lake, and stretches from Randolph Street to Twelfth Street along the blue waters. It has never been cultivated to any extent, and is little used except by the lower class of idlers. There has been so much controversy about the rights of the Illinois Central Railroad in this quarter that nothing has as yet been done towards beautifying this valuable property. With a bridge across the river, such as is now contemplated, connecting the Lake Shore Drive and Michigan Avenue, and with this ground turned over to the Park Commissioners, it could be made a delightful as well as a most convenient resort for those living near the business center of the city. Dearborn Park is nothing more than an uncultivated open half-square on the west line of Michigan Avenue between Washington and Randolph Streets. Groveland and Woodland Parks lie farther south, near Thirty-fifth Street, between Cottage Grove Avenue and the Lake. Each four and a half acres in extent. Groveland is covered by a deep wood of wide-branching elms, through which run serpentine walks, vine-embowered and quietly restful. The Chicago University, which is directly opposite these parks, was, together with the grounds forming them, donated to the city by that gifted son of Illinois, Senator Stephen A. Douglas. For many years prior to his death he lived near this spot, and the mausoleum containing his remains is located on the border of Woodland Park, near the eastern terminus of Douglas Avenue, overlooking the Lake. A noble monument towers above the mausoleum to the height of 104 feet, on the top of this stands a life-like statue of Douglas in bronze, executed by Leonard Volk, a Chicago artist. The monument is a fitting tribute to the distinguished orator, patriot, statesman and public-spirited citizen. The mausoleum and shaft are of granite. At the corners are four bronze female figures, seated on granite pedestals, each inscribed with the character · respectively represented, viz: "Illinois," "History," "Justice," "Eloquence." The marble sarcophagus in the cript bears on its side the following inscription:

THE BEACH, JACKSON PARK.

STEPHEN A. DOUGLAS,

BORN

APRIL 23, 1813,

DIED

JUNE 3, 1861.

"TELL MY CHILDREN
TO OBEY THE LAWS AND UPHOLD THE
CONSTITUTION."

The cost of the monument was about $100,000. Lying four miles south of the Court-house, between Cottage Grove and Vincennes Avenues, at the Thirty-seventh Street crossing, is Ellis Park, a pleasant little place of three and three-eighths acres. At Thirty-seventh Street and Vincennes Avenue is Aldine Square, an inclosed park of one and a half acres, handsomely arranged, and, like Groveland and Woodlawn Parks, surrounded by elegant and costly mansions. All three, too, are maintained in the same manner, viz: by special tax levied for the purpose on abutting property.

PARK CONSERVATORIES.

Among the most attractive features of the Chicago parks are the conservatories, where, when winter has despoiled the landscape of its foliage and flowers, bloom and fragrance, dainty fern and spreading palm still whisper of the summer gone and prophesy of the summer to come. Visitors at Lincoln Park during this season may wander for hours through its large conservatory, and with each changing glance be delighted by the strange or beautiful in Nature. Here is a sago palm from Mexico, a century old; a tree fern over fifteen feet in height; a carludonico palmata, which, if the visitor is fortunate, he may find in bloom; a date palm of great size; and many other rare plants and trees from the tropics. Here are propagated the many varieties of lilies which beautify the park lakes during the summer months. Among them are groups of Victoria tuberose lilies, a North American variety, Hymphotea Alba of England, the Oderete rosea from Cape Cod, and several species of the nelumbeum of Japan. All through the summer these, together with water pop-

4

pies and water hyacinths, spread their variegated blossoms to the
sun, and trail their dainty edges in the limpid waters of the lakes;
and, when winter comes again, they find safe refuge in the conservatory. There are others from the warm waters of the Nile
and Amazon, such as the African lily (a night bloomer), the
Victoria regia from South America, and the India Sanzibar Afri-
canus, with many other varieties of hybrids which only thrive in
waters tempered to 90 degrees Fahrenheit. These have a lake to
themselves. Mr. Stromback, chief gardener, informed me that
the managers of Lincoln Park were the first to bring these wonderful lilies to Chicago. This conservatory has also a fine
collection of chrysanthemums, ferns and orchids. The green-
houses at Lincoln Park have a great number of admirers, and
visitors are numerous all the year round.

The Washington Park conservatory is another "joy forever."
One of its chief attractions is a large aquarium, made picturesque
by hundreds of fern fronds, delicately traced, which spring up
along its borders and nod gracefully to their reflections in the
water below. Giant palms suggest the splendors of the tropics,
and the shadowy pathways winding about beneath their inter-
lacing branches bring to mind the pastoral scenes in the lives of
Paul and Virginia. In the green-room are large stocks of diminu-
tive plants with tiny leaves of variegated hues. These are for
the lawn decorations of the coming summer, but even in their
propagation they are so arranged as to make a pretty and artistic
display. There is a large assortment of the homely, but for some
undefined reason, attractive cacti. In the palm-room is a plant
from the West Indies, bearing an edible fruit which is said to
resemble honey in taste, and quite a favorite with the natives of
the islands. It somewhat resembles the American pawpaw ; but
the rind is more delicate—so much so as to prevent its being
handled for shipment.

Next to the new conservatory at Lincoln Park the one at
Douglas Park, erected one year ago, is by far the handsomest
and costliest of any of the public green-houses. Its roomy
dimensions are filled with the rarest and most delicate flowers
obtainable. A large circular basin of water in the east wing is filled
with aquatic productions, among which the Victoria regia lily

shines supreme. Unique exotics trail or peep from baskets suspended around the margin of the miniature lake, showing an endless variety of blossoms, no two of which are alike. It is an ideal place for the flower lover.

Humboldt Park has also a splendid conservatory. The greenhouses here have the most attractions. A eucalyptus tree, growing indoors in free ground, has reached the hight of forty-eight feet. There are rows upon rows of dainty and fragrant flowers growing in banks of emerald verdure, and the air is heavy with mingled perfumes. Graceful ferns climb up rocky ledges, overrun by trailing vines. From a plateau in the center a tropical forest waves its feather-edged leaves or stretches out its broad palms in welcome invitation. The fernery is one of the most artistic and pleasing rooms in the building. There are, beside tuberoses and lilies, hyacinths and orange blossoms, with a host of minor flowers nestling everywhere.

LAKE SHORE DRIVE.

That part of the Boulevard system which is known as the Lake Shore Drive is the grandest portion of that broad belt of yellow roadway, smooth as marble and level as a floor, which encircles the city. Beginning at the northern extremity of Lincoln Park (where it makes connection with the Sheridan Road), it follows the gentle curves of the lake shore through the park to the southwestern extremity of North Chicago, where it is soon to be carried across the river by a steel bridge of light and graceful proportions, with the northern terminus of Michigan Avenue Boulevard at Randolph Street. Through the park the drive is pleasing beyond expression. Rows of large, graceful elms cast their shadows over it from either side. On one hand stretches the Lake, dotted with white sails; its dancing waves bright with sunbeams, or showing green and cool under drifting clouds; on the other, the well-cultivated park, with its tiny lakes and gorgeous flower plats peeping through vistas of trees. Between the park and Oak Street, and fronting on the drive are some of the most magnificent mansions in the city. The State legislature three years ago authorized the Lincoln Park Commissioners to expend $300,000 on a shore-line defense against the encroachments of Lake Michigan. This sum, while far from sufficient for the completion of the work necessary, nevertheless enabled the commissioners to commence operations, and several thousand feet of beautiful sea-wall has been erected, and many acres of valuable land reclaimed. The work is altogether so valuable and adds so much to the beauty and utility of the drive that there is no question now of its speedy completion. The breakwater rests on piles driven thirty-five feet into the sand. On this foundation granite blocks are laid and securely cemented. A paved beach forty feet wide slopes on a gentle incline to meet the granilithic promenade, and along its inland border runs the boulevard. A more charming promenade could not be imagined. On one side Lake Michigan, beating against the curving sea-wall and dashing its spray high in the air; on the other, a swiftly changing array of carriages, with a background of stately stone dwellings of many shades and numerous styles of architecture, and then the park with all its variegated beauties. The promenade will be three miles long, and is destined to become one of Chicago's most famous resorts. The long, sweeping curves which the constant movement of the waters against the shifting sands of the beach have formed have been religiously followed by the commissioners in the selection of the sea-wall line, thus avoiding the usually tiresome stolidity of such improvements, and giving to the grandeur of a great continuous stone-wall the pleasing sinuosity of a natural shore-line. A regatta course extends along its whole length to Diversey Avenue, the northern limits of the park. When it is completed, which will be sometime during this year, the commissioners will have added to the park 100 acres of land, and given to Chicago the finest regatta course in the world. The sea-wall will be continued to a point opposite Graceland Cemetery. The park will be connected with the new boulevard at three different points. There will be land connection at the north and south ends of the park, and a bridge at a point opposite Webster Avenue. To the east of the regatta course an avenue of trees is to be planted, and from it down to the water's edge will be a sloping lawn decorated in the highest style of the landscape gardener's art. The sandy beach now lying to the west, between the Lake Shore Drive and the regatta course, will be cultivated and become a part of the park. The canal will be about 200 feet wide, and will extend to the northern limits of the park. At the ends it will be widened to 350 feet, to give the boats an opportunity to turn. Between its sloping grassy banks, shaded by avenues of elms and brightened by flower plats, this placid stream will wind its sinuous course; and its bosom will be ruffled, from time to time, by the flashing blades of the best oarsmen. Many other improvements are contemplated for this part of the city, which will eventually make the Lake Shore Drive and Lincoln Park the most famous pleasure grounds in the world.

MICHIGAN AVENUE BOULEVARD

Commences at Jackson Street, and extends south for about three and one-fourth miles to Thirty-fifth Street. It is 100 feet wide, and is completed its entire length. It is a fashionable drive, and runs through one of the richest residence sections of the South Side.

THIRTY-FIFTH STREET BOULEVARD

Commences at the south end of Michigan Avenue Boulevard and extends eastward about one-third of a mile, where it connects with Grand Boulevard. It is sixty-six feet wide, and is completed its entire length.

GRAND BOULEVARD

Connects with Thirty-fifth Street Boulevard at its eastern terminus and extends two miles directly south, where it enters the northwestern corner of Washington Park. It is 189 feet wide; its entire length is bordered with grass strips bearing double rows of trees. Roadways thirty-three feet wide flank it on either side—the one on the east being for traffic, and that on the west for equestrians. These are also bordered by grass strips and a single row of trees. There are many handsome residences along the boulevard, and in pleasant weather it is thronged with pleasure seekers.

OAKWOOD BOULEVARD

Connects Grand Boulevard and Drexel Boulevard at Thirty-ninth Street. It is 100 feet wide, and completed.

DREXEL BOULEVARD

Is a gem in the Boulevard system. It commences at the east end of Oakwood Boulevard, and, running south parallel with Grand Boulevard to Fifty-second Street, turns east for one block, and enters Washington Park one square south of its northern boundary. It is 200 feet wide and 1.48 miles long, and has 3.05 miles of completed driveways. There is a broad central strip throughout the entire length, planted with trees and shrubbery, and ornamented with sinuous walks and grass plats and beds and borders of flowers and foliage plants in various designs. At Fifty-first Street stands the splendid fountain donated by the Messrs. Drexel of Philadelphia, in honor of whom the boulevard was named. Along either side of the central space is a broad driveway as level and smooth as a floor, and thronged on pleasant evenings with vehicles containing representatives of the wealth and fashion of the city, many of them occupants of the handsome villas along the boulevard, or owners of others that are being erected there. Drexel Boulevard was modeled after Avenue l'Impératrice, Paris, and with the highest order of taste in design and of skill in execution, nothing has been omitted that could add to its attractiveness. It is conceded that it surpasses its prototype.

GARFIELD BOULEVARD

Is similar in design to Grand Boulevard, having a broad central driveway with a row of trees and grass plats and shrubbery on either side, outside of which are roadways for traffic and for equestrian exercise, the whole plan being laid within a lane of elms. It is 200 feet wide, and has a total length of three and one-half miles. It leaves Washington Park at Fifty-fifth Street, and extends west along the line of that street to Gage Park.

WESTERN AVENUE BOULEVARD

Is also planned on a similar scale and of kindred design with Grand Boulevard. It is 200 feet wide, and runs directly north from Gage Park to the Illinois and Michigan Canal, a distance of nearly three miles. It also forms a part of other boulevards which now connect the South Side and West Side parks.

DOUGLAS BOULEVARD,

L-shaped, 250 feet in width and one and three-fourths miles in length, connects Douglas and Garfield Parks, entering the former from the west and the latter from the south. Its plan is essentially the same as that of Central Boulevard. Improvements are constantly being made, and Douglas promises to become one of the most fashionable and popular boulevards on the West Side.

CENTRAL BOULEVARD

Constitutes the connecting link between Garfield and Humboldt Parks. It is a little over a mile and a half in length, and has an average width of 250 feet. The completed driveway, thirty-eight feet wide, is bordered on either side by a slender lawn, with a "bridle path" running along within its outer edge, and fringed with rows of elms. The viaduct arching the tracks of the Chicago, Milwaukee & St. Paul Railway affords a good view of the surrounding country.

HUMBOLDT BOULEVARD

Connects Humboldt Park with Diversey Avenue, which leads to Lincoln Park and the Lake Shore Drive, thus completing the circuit. The boulevard proper is 250 feet in width; but it embraces in its plan Palmer Place, 400x1750 feet, and Logan Square, some 400x800 feet. Its total length is about three miles.

WASHINGTON BOULEVARD

Extends from Halstead Street through Union Park to Garfield Park, a distance of three and one-fourth miles. From Ashland Avenue west it is lined by handsome residences and gay lawns, shaded by beautiful trees. It is 100 feet wide and is a favorite driveway, especially with those living on the West Side.

ASHLAND BOULEVARD

Extends from Washington Boulevard south to the boulevard extensions of West Twelfth Street, thus connecting Douglas and Union Parks. It has many elegant mansions and some of the handsomest churches in the city. It is paved with asphaltum, and is the most perfect drive in the city.

The City's Thoroughfares.

STREETS, AVENUES, BRIDGES, VIADUCTS AND TUNNELS.

It has been an almost impossible task for the city to keep pace in its facilities for intramural transit with the growth of its population. The outlying suburbs which a few years ago were nothing but stretches of bare prairie lands have become populous districts, and the question of constant and rapid transportation with the business centers for the inhabitants has been and is still a serious one. Yet no other city in America to-day can boast of so many miles of street railway. Cable and horse car lines penetrate in every direction to the most remote corners of the city; suburban trains on many of the railroads run almost constantly, and two different lines of elevated railroad are now being built. And yet, with all these advantages, there is much justice in the demands of the citizens in many quarters for quicker transportation. The bulk of the city's business, both wholesale and retail, is done within the confines of Polk Street on the south, the river on the west and north, and the Lake on the east. This is in extent not more than three-quarters by one-half miles. When it is taken into consideration that Chicago extends over an area of 178 square miles, it will readily be seen how difficult it is to transport the great mass of people required to do the enormous business transacted here, to and from this small territory. While no other city is so well prepared to handle a great mass of people, there is no other that has so much demanded of it. The working people of Chicago are not content to live in close, ill-ventilated tenements in or near the heart of the city, but seek homes on the

FLOWER BED

DREXEL MONUMENT AND SUN DIAL

THE ELEPHANT

DREXEL BOULEVARD.

prairies beyond the smoke and dust of trade, where their children may romp on the grass and they themselves may, between their hours of labor, breathe the fresh air and catch a glimpse of blue sky.

Chicago is twenty-four miles long by ten miles wide, and has nearly a thousand miles of streets, more than one-third of which are paved. The names of the principal streets generally indicate their origin. Many of them are named for the Presidents and others who were prominent in the nation or State; the names of people more or less conspicuously connected with the history of Chicago, of the surrounding States, and other equally obvious sources, contributed to the nomenclature. The names of the Presidents and leading statesmen of the country will be readily recognized. Clark Street was christened in honor of Gen. George Rogers Clark, of Kentucky, who acquired military fame in the early contests with the French and Indians. Fifth Avenue was originally named in honor of Captain Wells, who was one of the victims of the Indian massacre in 1812, and that portion of the street which lies in the North Division still retains the name. Ann Street was named after a daughter of the venerable Philo Carpenter; Augusta after another daughter, and so on of many other names of women. In this respect Chicago has shown no lack of gallantry.

The city is laid out in rectangular lines, with the exception of several streets, which were constructed on the routes of the old plank roads, and which consequently radiate to the northwest and southwest. The principal business streets of the city lie on the South Side. South Water Street, which lies next to and parallel with the main river, is largely devoted to the produce commission business. It is always almost impassable from the number of trucks, vans and carts which throng it and the boxes. of produce which incumber its sidewalks. Here are brought and distributed daily the various products of the market garden, orchard, field and stream.

State Street is the great shopping street of the city, and on any fair afternoon it can be seen thronged with pedestrians and carriages, and presenting a scene of gaytey, wealth and beauty such as is paralleled only on Regent Street, London, or some of the more notable boulevards in Paris. It was originally much narrower, and was widened to its present handsome and attractive proportions by moving the houses back along a stretch of three miles. Michigan Avenue, Wabash Avenue and State Street, near the river, are all given up to wholesale houses. Michigan Avenue, a few blocks from the river, loses its identity in Michigan Avenue Boulevard (see chapter on " Parks and Boulevards"), the extire extension of which is a favorite residence street, as are also Prairie, Calumet, Indiana and other avenues, containing residences which are palaces in their cost and architectural design and finish. The South Side cable car system covers State Street, Wabash Avenue, Cottage Grove Avenue, and with its horse-car connections penetrates to the remotest confines of the South Side. Archer Avenue, branching from State Street between Nineteenth and Twentieth Streets, takes a southwesterly direction, crosses a branch of the Chicago River, and extends beyond the city limits. It has horse cars, and resembles, in the character of its buildings, shops, people, etc., Blue Island and Milwaukee Avenues on the West Side.

Madison Street is the great east and west thoroughfare of Chicago. The street is well paved from the Lake to Garfield Park, a distance of more than four miles. The street is almost entirely devoted to wholesale and retail business, and one of the most animated in the city. It has a line of cable cars, and is the direct route to Garfield Park, the Chicago Driving Park and the Northwestern Railroad machine shops. Randolph and Lake Streets, running parallel with Madison, are also main business thoroughfares, and each has a line of horse cars, while an elevated railroad is in course of construction above Lake Street. Monroe and Adams Streets, also running parallel with Madison Street, are, east of the river, entirely in the wholesale district ; from the river west to Halstead Street, manufacturing is the principal industry. Farther west they are flanked on either side by beautiful residences. Ogden Avenue, beginning in Union Park, runs in a southwesterly direction, passing through Douglas Park, and ending at Twenty-second Street, near the city limits. It has a line of cable cars, is well paved, and has become one of the principal business thoroughfares of the West Side.

From Lake Street south and Halstead Street east to the river is a manufacturing district. Here the great machinery, steam engine, boiler and kindred iron-working concerns are located. Halstead Street, which is reached on Madison Street some five blocks west from the river, is one of the longest streets in the city. It extends in almost a straight line from Lincoln Park to the Union Stock Yards. It has a line of horse cars running its entire length. Retail business flourishes on Halstead Street. At certain hours of the day it is almost as animated as the more aristocratic State Street across the river. Its buildings are not of the best, however, and give the street a somewhat dingy appearance. Its population is mostly foreign. Blue Island Avenue is another great West Side business thoroughfare. It branches from Halstead Street at the latter's junction with Harrison Street, running in a southwesterly direction through the great lumber districts. Foreigners, mostly German and Irish, have full possession of Blue Island Avenue; and, while an immense amount of business is transacted here, its buildings are poor and unpretentious. Milwaukee Avenue, beginning at the river and Lake Street, extends in a northwesterly direction away beyond the city limits. This street was formerly one of the plank roads that connected early Chicago with the country. It is now the home of the Swede, the German, the Norwegian and the Italian. It is known as Dinnerpail Avenue from the great number of working people who go back and forth in its street cars to their daily work in the city.

On the North Side, Clark Street is the leading business street, being occupied mainly by the smaller retail stores. It extends northward beyond Lincoln Park, and is a great thoroughfare. The streets lying near and parallel with the river are largely used by manufacturing establishments and commission houses engaged in handling hides, leather, wool, etc. The preferred residence streets are LaSalle and Dearborn Avenues, Rush, State and Pine Streets, some of the residences being very elegant and artistic in architectural and other ornamentation. Chicago Avenue, from North Clark Street west to the river; Division Street, from North Clark to Clyborne Avenue; Clyborne Avenue, which here has its beginning and extends in a northwesterly direction to the city limits; and Larrabee Street, running north and south, are all business thoroughfares. They traverse a section of the city inhabited almost wholly by a foreign population—Scandinavian, German, etc.

The residences on the streets referred to as residence streets are generally built of superior materials. Red pressed brick is much used, but stone is the favorite. Of the latter there are many kinds, all varying in color, so that there is nowhere any sameness in the character of the coloring. There is a restful diversity in the forms of the houses on the older streets; each building, having had an independent owner, was built according to his tastes and desires. Block-building has become more fashionable of late, and in many quarters of the newer city whole rows of buildings, each the counterpart of its neighbor, tire the vision with their unbroken monotony. The various materials used in the construction of residence buildings in Chicago add much to their attractiveness. Beside the Joliet limestone, milky white at first, after exposure a rich, soft cream color, is the deep, rich brown of a sandstone from Lake Superior, or the close-grained dark gray of the Buena Vista quarries. A dozen other kinds of material, including the cheerful cream-colored pressed brick of Milwaukee, afford infinite variety of pleasing effects. The churches are generally constructed of rough-dressed limestone of a dark gray, which is a color eminently in harmony with their purpose. The winds blowing alternately from the Lake and from the land do much toward freeing the city of smoke, so that these richly-colored building materials are rarely obscured by stains, and the streets present always the striking effects flowing from the warm, bright, sympathetic colors.

THE BRIDGES.

One of the most interesting questions of intermural transit is the question of bridges. The Chicago river is a navigable stream, and the amount of shipping from its docks yearly is astounding. The river separates two portions of the city, principally given up to residences, from another portion, in which the most of the business is transacted. To destroy the shipping by closing up the river is not to be thought of. To form some plan whereby travel from one portion of the city to the other will not be inter-rupted is quite as important to the average citizen, however, as that boats should come and go through the heart of the city to his detriment. Thus far nothing better than the swinging bridge has been devised, and these governed by a wise ordinance which keeps them closed between the hours of seven and eight o'clock morning, and six and seven o'clock evening, although the occasion of many annoying delays and much complaint, are mod-erately successful. Forty-five bridges in all span the Chicago River. Nearly all are swinging bridges and many of them are operated by steam. Those which have been built recently are splendid steel structures, some of them having four tracks, besides the railed walks for foot passengers. The Rush Street bridge is notable as having the longest draw in the world. Dearborn Clark and Wells Streets have each been supplied of late with new bridges of beautiful architectural design and the most modern improvements. The Adams Street bridge is a marvel of en-gineering skill. Although two feet three inches lower at the east end than at the west end, it is reversible and its great bulk, 259 feet in length by 57 feet in width, swings noiselessly round on its center truss, without the least friction, one end taking the place of the other as neatly and compactly as though there were no laws of levels and pitches and grades whatsoever. There is a new bridge being built at Madison Street which, it is promised, will be the handsomest structure of the kind in Chicago.

VIADUCTS.

The many railroads centering in Chicago and their numerous intersection with streets are a constant menace to travel. Grade crossings are the rule, and despite gates and other devices thrown about them for the protection of life, accidents are frequent and disastrous. Engineers have long sought to overcome this diffi-culty, but nothing practical has as yet been proposed. Wherever it is possible the city has insisted on railroads erecting viaducts at the most dangerous crossings. There are now thirty-five of these in the city. The one at Twelfth Street is much the longest and finest. It extends from Clark Street to Wabash Avenue above the tracks of the Atchison, Topeka and Santa Fe Railroad Company. It is over a half mile in length and cost $210,000.

TUNNELS.

There are three tunnels under the Chicago River. Two of them, the Washington Street tunnel and the La Salle Street tunnel, were built by the city for the use of teams and pedestrians. They never became popular and were finally disposed of to the cable companies of the North and West Sides. The Washington Street tunnel, which was the first one built, was completed in 1869 at a cost of over $500,000. Its total length is 1,608 feet. The La Salle Street tunnel was completed July 1, 1871, at a total cost of $566,276.48. Its total length is 1,854 feet. The West Side cable system demanded the use of another underground passage and the company secured the right to build one between Jackson and Van Buren Streets. It will have, when completed, two sections, one for the lines south of Madison Street, and the other for those north of it. The southern shaft was completed early in this year, and the other is progressing rapidly in that direction.

MILEAGE OF STREETS.

The total number of miles laid out in streets in the city of Chicago is 2,235.71 miles. There are over fifty miles of boulevards and about two miles of viaducts, making in all about 2,290 miles, the greater portion of which will be paved before the close of 1892.

SEWERAGE SYSTEM.

One of the most difficult problems which has presented itself to the city has been the problem of sewerage. The city is so nearly on a plane with the lake, and extends over such a wide tract of country that nature lent little assistance in the disposal of the city's sewerage. Expert engineering has, however, overcome all difficulties. The Illinois and Michigan Canal has been utilized to good purpose. Immense pumping works at different points on the river cause a continual current from the lake to flow *up* the stream and out through this canal to the Illinois River. A ship canal is to be built, connecting Lake Michigan with the Mississippi River. It will have a channel 160 feet wide and eighteen feet deep, with a current flowing two and a half miles an hour. The cost of this immense waterway is estimated at $20,-000,000. This will give Chicago an excellent sewerage system, and also furnish means for water transportation direct with the Mississippi Valley and the Gulf of Mexico.

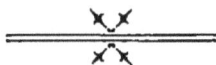

Intramural Transit.

CABLE CARS AND THEIR CONNECTIONS, SUBURBAN TRAINS, ELEVATED ROADS, CARETTE LINES.

The City Railway or Intramural Service of Chicago embraces horse cars, cable, electric and elevated railways. They all start from the business center of the city and radiate in all directions to its farthest limits. The street car systems, operating horse and cable lines, are under the control of three great companies, viz: The Chicago City Railway Company, which operates the lines in the South Division; the West Chicago City Railway Company, which operates the lines in the West Division, and the North Chicago Street Railroad Company, which operates the lines on the North Division of the city. The Chicago Passenger Railway Company, which has a large system of horse car lines on the West Side, is practically under control of the West Chicago City Railway Company. The North and West Chicago street car systems are under one management, Mr. Charles T. Yerkes being president of both companies. The South Chicago City Railway Company is an independent line. Chicago has over 400 miles of street railway, including sidings and switches, and the different lines move on an average over half a million persons every day. Taking into consideration the difficulties to be encountered, the service of the Chicago City railways is excellent. Many diffi-

culties, which at first it seemed impossible to overcome, have
been conquered, the utilizing of the tunnels has brought the different divisions of the city into uninterrupted communication,
and with the addition of the elevated roads, which are now being
constructed, and the great number of suburban trains which the
steam railways run back and forth almost constantly, Chicago
will soon be in condition to handle a population as large as the
city of London without delay or friction.

STEAM RAILROAD SERVICE.

The principal railroads with terminals in Chicago operate a
line of suburban trains, which are a great accommodation to that
portion of the population living at a distance from the city's business center, and the number of passengers which they move
yearly is enormous.   They have a system of commutation tickets
which brings the cost of transportation anywhere in the city
limits to from five to seven cents, and the fare to suburban towns
beyond is quite as low in proportion to distance.   The Illinois
Central suburban trains are said to carry more passengers than
any suburban line in the world.   Over 15,000,000 passengers were
accommodated on this line during 1890, and the number for '91
promises to be increased by at least a quarter.   The Chicago &
North-Western, the Chicago, Milwaukee & St. Paul, the Chicago
Rock Island & Pacific, the Chicago, Burlington & Quincy, the
Wisconsin Central, the Northern Pacific, the Grand Trunk, the
Eastern Illinois, and the Michigan Central, all of which have
depots in the business center of the city, do a heavy suburban
business.   Were it not for the accommodations furnished by these
and other lines of steam railway, the cable and horse car lines
would be unable to meet the demands of intermural transit, and
as it is there are times in the day when they are badly overcrowded.

SOUTH SIDE CABLE SYSTEM.

The first cable car system to be started in Chicago was that of
the South Side.   This was opened to the public in 1882.   It now
operates 152 miles of track and 1,250 cars.   Its annual revenue is
three and one-half millions; its cars have an average speed of ten

GRAND BOULEVARD.

·miles an hour, and it moves each day more than a hundred and fifty thousand people. It has a wonderfully perfect system—an accident, or even a delay being of rare occurrence. It is remarkable, too, for the harmonious manner in which its affairs are conducted. During its eighteen years of existence it has never had a strike on its lines, or any difficulty with its employes which was not peaceably adjusted. Cars on all its lines pass at the junction of State and Madison Streets, where passengers may select their car, which is plainly lettered along the top, for any point desired on the South Side. Transfer checks are given for cross lines, whether horse or cable, and only one fare is required for the whole distance.

NORTH CHICAGO STREET RAILROAD COMPANY.

The North Side cable car system, with its horse car connections, pretty extensively covers that division of the city. It is well equipped with new cars, and its machinery is the best that could be produced at the time of its construction. Its lines all run through the La Salle Street tunnel, at the entrance of which on Randolph Street cars can be taken for almost any point on the North Side. The route of each car is plainly marked along the top of the car. Conductors give transfers for cross lines at one fare for the trip. The loop on the South Side runs on La Salle Street to Monroe Street, thence to Dearborn Street, thence to Randolph Street, thence to the tunnel on La Salle Street. Cars may be taken at any one of the crossings within this radius for the North Side and no extra fare is charged. This system moves about 200,000 passengers daily.

WEST CHICAGO STREET RAILROAD COMPANY.

This is by far the greatest cable system of the city, and when completed will operate more miles of road than any other company in the world. The horse car lines of the Chicago Passenger Railway are also under its direction, and form a part of its wonderful system which extends over three-fourths of the territory occupied by Chicago. Its capital stock is $10,000,000. The gross receipts of the company for 1890 were $3,663,381, and operating expenses $2,202,767, leaving a net income to the company of $1,460,613. It traveled during this time 12,215,903 miles, and carried 75,152,694 passengers, the average cost of each passenger being 2.93 cents. Many miles of cable have been added during the first half of 1891, and the system now moves on an average of 300,000 persons daily. It reaches the South Side by way of tunnels under the river. Its loop at the present writing extends no farther south than Fifth Avenue, but arrangements have been completed with the Chicago City Railway Company for the partial use of State Street, and the loop is to be immediately extended to that thoroughfare. Cars can then be taken at State and Madison for any point on the West Side, as well as the South, which will much facilitate travel. There are two distinct lines in the West Side cable system, one running directly west on Madison Street, with branches covering the southwestern portion of the city; the other running northwest on Milwaukee Avenue to the city's confines. Both lines connect with the down town loop, and the cars for each line are distinctly marked. Three distinct power-houses are required for the operation of these lines, and all are supplied with the latest and most improved machinery and appliances. The principal power-house is located at Madison and Rockwell Streets (West Side). This is 210x225 feet, and is supplied with two engines of 1,200 horse-power each. One is kept going day and night, moving the Madison Street cars; the other is kept in reserve in case of accident. West of Fortieth Street the cars move at the rate of fourteen miles an hour; east of that ten miles an hour is maintained. There is also a Corliss engine in the power-house for the purpose of reversing the cars at Rockwell Street when it becomes necessary. The power-house is of itself an attractive structure. It is lighted by electricity, and surmounted by a large smokestack 175 feet high.

The Milwaukee Avenue line is in operation quite similar to that of Madison Street. Two Corliss engines of 1,200 horse-power each supply the force necessary to move the long line of cars from Jefferson and Washington Streets to Armitage Avenue, in the extreme northwestern part of the city. The speed maintained on this line is about the same as that on Madison Street.

The third ower-house is located at Jefferson and Washington

Streets, where also are the offices of the company. Two 500 horse-power Wetherell-Corliss engines are stationed here to supply the power needed to operate the Washington Street tunnel loop. The cars of both the Madison Street and Milwaukee Avenue lines are here delivered to the loop-cable, and by it are drawn through the tunnel around the loop and returned again to their respective cables at this point. The tunnel is brightly lighted by electricity. There is also an electric signal system in operation by which conductor or gripman may communicate with the power-house offices at any time. By this means they are enabled to keep the tracks clear or stop the machinery at once in case of accident. The officers of the company are: President, Charles T. Yerkes; directors, Charles T. Yerkes, W. L. Elkins, J. B. Parsons, R. C. Crawford, David R. Fraser.

Several other transmural companies are formed, and several different lines projected. The Calumet Electric Road is to extend from the South Chicago Rolling Mills by way of Eighty-ninth Street, Mackinaw Avenue, Harbor Avenue, Ninety-third Street and Stony Island Avenue to Ninety-fifth Street. This company will employ the Rae system of overhead wires. Instead of the Thompson-Houston and Sprague systems, which require two small motors for each car, the Rae system employs but one. A speed of from fifteen to twenty miles an hour is secured with entire safety. A part of this system is already in operation, and many new lines projected. These lines, where they do not come in conflict with the city ordinance forbidding overhead wires, are sure to become popular on account of the cheapness and simplicity of their construction and operation.

ELEVATED ROADS.

Construction of the Lake Street elevated railroad, the super-structure of which has been built from Canal Street, near the river, to Union Park, is now at a standstill, owing to some legal complications. There is, however, little doubt but that the road will be finally completed. So far as built it is a substantial structure. It will have two tracks, and in operation will be similar to the New York elevated roads. If it could secure a terminal on the South Side its extension to the city limits would no doubt be speedily accomplished. Another elevated railroad is projected along Milwaukee Avenue, and still another to occupy Randolph Street. Incorporation papers have been granted to companies having these lines in view, but their construction is not at present beyond doubt.

SOUTH SIDE "L" ROAD.

This is an elevated railroad running from Van Buren Street over the alley between State Street and Wabash Avenue to the city's southern limits. The superstructure is already up the greater portion of the way, and the work will progress as fast as the ground can be cleared. This will be one of the most complete elevated roads in the world. The stations are exceedingly neat and attractive. The rails are of solid steel of the best quality, weighing ninety pounds to the yard. An improved joint gives a smooth surface to the top surface of the rails, and that clicking sound so familiar to trávellers on railroads will be entirely abolished. This line, which will be finished and in operation, will lead direct from the business portion of the city to the World's Columbian Exposition at Jackson Park, and will no doubt be a favorite route for visitors at the Fair.

CARETTE LINES.

· The carette is of recent importation to Chicago, but it has already become quite a favorite with the great crowd of office workers which pours from the doors of the business blocks in the city at the closing hour, to overflow horse-car, grip-car and suburban train. The carette is built much on the style of the street car, with the exception that it is mounted on wheels like those of the omnibus, but lower. It is drawn by horses and runs on regular lines as the street cars do. Those in Chicago are the property of the Russell Street Carette Company, with offices at 148 South Green Street. The lines run over Madison, Adams and Rush Streets, from Ashland Avenue to Lincoln Park. About forty cars are at present in the service. The route of the cars is circular, and covers a portion of each division of the city. It is by far the most comfortable conveyance yet introduced to meet the demands of travel on streets without tracks. While it has a much greater capacity than the omnibus, it is much easier of movement, and can discharge and take on passengers with greater facility. Twenty persons can be seated comfortably on the inside, and there is room for at least three more on the seat in front, which is quite as popular as the front seat in the grip-car. Each car has a conductor and driver; and the manner of conduct is much the same as the street car. The carette is a useful and a popular addition to the different lines in operation for intramural transit.

The Railroads.

THEIR EARLY HISTORY—LOCATION OF CENTRAL DEPOTS—SUBURBAN TOWNS, AND HOW TO REACH THEM.

It is a curious fact that for many years after Chicago had become a prosperous city waterways were considered of more importance than railroad lines. It was not until a short railroad line, from Chicago to Galena, had been constructed and put in operation, that the business men of the city awoke to a full realization of the importance of overland transportation. During those earlier years all the energies of Chicago were directed toward the construction of a great canal that was to connect Lake Michigan with the Mississippi River. This, it was urged, would be adequate to bring to Chicago the farm products of the Mississippi Valley and at the same time give Chicago direct communication with the seaboard by way of "the Father of Waters," and the Gulf of Mexico. The attention of Chicago was directed toward the south and west and a more direct route with the Atlantic on the east than that already furnished by the chain of the Great Lakes was not considered of importance. The first railroad projected out of Chicago was the Galena & Chicago Union. This was chartered in January, 1837, with an authorized capital of $100,000.

The charter contemplated propulsion either by steam or animal power. The survey was scarcely begun, however, before the panic of 1837 swept over the country, paralyzing business in all its branches, and the Galena & Chicago Union, with many another promising enterprise, was abandoned. It was revived ten years later, and after a three years' struggle was completed. The first railroad engine ever operated in Chicago was brought to the city by way of Lake Michigan. This was in October, 1847. It was named the " Pioneer," and immediately put to work on the Galena line. This engine is still in existence, the property of the Northwestern Railway Company.

In 1837 the State of Illinois attempted the construction of the Illinois & Michigan Canal, together with some 1,300 miles of railroad. This gigantic enterprise fell to pieces of its own weight. Even the magnificent Chicago of to-day, with its million and a quarter population and incalculable riches, finds the construction of such a canal as was then contemplated a difficult matter, although assisted by the state. What a spirit of enterprise must have stirred the hearts of those early settlers to embark in such a venture. Perhaps, could the panic have been averted, the scheme would have been successful and the Henepin Canal, which has given rise to so much congressional oratory in the late congresses, might have been a fact, and Mississippi steamboats be now touching prows with the great lake steamers in the harbors of Chicago.

With the completion of the Chicago & Galena Railroad the importance of overland transportation became manifest, and other lines were rapidly constructed. In February, 1852, the Lake Shore & Michigan Southern (then the Michigan Southern & Indiana Northern) entered the city. This gave Chicago her first railroad communication with the East. This line was closely followed by the Michigan Central. The Chicago & Northwestern, the Chicago, Burlington & Quincy, the Chicago, Rock Island & Pacific, the Pittsburgh, Fort Wayne & Chicago, and several minor lines soon after had terminals in the city. Since that time the growth of Chicago's railroad interests is without parallel in the world's history. Every great railroad in the United States has either a terminal here or is directly connected with the city arrangement with a friendly line. Twenty-six independent lines now center in the city. Several union passenger depots of magnificent proportions and beautiful architecture adorn the central portion of the city, while some, the exclusive property of one company, are no less imposing.

It would be an impossibility for all these lines to secure the track room necessary to receive and deliver freight to the numerous warehouses, docks and manufactories which are everywhere in the city. This difficulty has been overcome by a system of belt railroads, which completely encircle Chicago, crossing every railroad centering here. These lines are for the use of all alike, and furnish ready and direct access to any point of shipping.

Thus the products of a factory on any line of road are easily transferred to any of the other lines, and raw materials from every part of the country delivered at any warehouse or manufactory in the city without change of cars. The first belt road built was at no point more than four miles from the center of the city. It proved so successful that similar ones were put in operation with a wider radius, the one having the greatest circumference being distant twenty to forty miles from the city's center. These lines have caused many manufacturing towns to spring up on the outskirts of the city, some of which have had a surprising growth and are now handsome cities. The right of way has been secured for a new belt line to operate in connection with the World's Fair, which will greatly facilitate the handling of exhibits and at the same time furnish all railroad companies equal opportunities for the transportation of freight to and from the Columbian exposition.

The passenger depots of the principal railroads centering in Chicago are located near the business center of the city, and the greater number of these companies do a large suburban business. The roads that make a specialty of suburban traffic and their central depots are as follows:

Atchison, Topeka & Santa Fe.—Central depot Polk Street and Third Avenue. Take State Street cable line or Dearborn Street horse car line.

Baltimore & Ohio.—Grand Central Depot, Fifth Avenue and Harrison Street. Take Van Buren Street cars.

Chicago & Erie.—Central depot Polk Street and Third Avenue. Take State Street cable or Dearborn Street horse car line.

Chicago & Alton.—Central depot Canal and Adams Streets, West Side. Take cars going west on Adams, Van Buren or Madison Streets. Within easy walking distance of business center.

Chicago & Eastern Illinois.—Central depot Polk Street and Third Avenue. Take State Street cable or Dearborn Street horse car line.

Chicago & Grand Trunk.—Central depot Polk Street and Third Avenue. Take State Street cable or Dearborn Street horse car line.

Chicago & Northern Pacific.—Central depot Fifth Avenue and Harrison Street. Take Van Buren Street cars going west from State or south from Madison Streets, or Harrison Street line.

Chicago & North-Western.—Central depot Wells and Kinzie Streets, North Side. Take Dearborn, State, or Wells Street car going north. Within easy walking distance of business center.

Chicago, Burlington & Quincy.—Central depot Canal and Adam Streets, West Side. Take Adam, Van Buren or Madison Street car going west. Within easy walking distance of business center.

Chicago, Milwaukee & St. Paul.—Central depot Canal and Adams Streets, West Side. Take Adams, Van Buren or Madison Street car going west. Only a short distance from business center.

Chicago, Rock Island & Pacific.—Central depot Van Buren and Sherman Streets. Take cars on Clark Street or Fifth Avenue going south. Within easy walking distance of business center.

Chicago, St. Louis & Pittsburgh.—Central depot Canal and Adams Streets, West Side. Take Adams, Van Buren or Madison Street car going west. Within easy walking distance of business center.

Chicago, St. Paul & Kansas City.—Central depot Harrison Street and Fifth Avenue. Take Van Buren Street cars going west from State or south from Madison Street, or Harrison Street line.

Cleveland, Cincinnati, Chicago & St. Louis ("The Big 4").—

Central depot foot of Lake Street. Within easy walking distance of business center.

Illinois Central.—Central depot foot of Lake Street. Within easy walking distance of business center.

Lake Shore & Michigan Southern.—Central depot Van Buren and Sherman Streets. Take cars on Clark Street or Fifth Avenue going south. Within easy walking distance of business center.

Louisville, New Albany & Chicago ("Monon Route").—Central depot Polk Street and Third Avenue. Take State Street cable or Dearborn Street car line.

Michigan Central.—Central depot foot of Lake Street. Within easy walking distance of business center.

Pittsburgh, Fort Wayne & Chicago.—Central depot Canal and Adams Streets, West Side. Take Adams, Van Buren or Madison Street car line going west. Within easy walking distance of business center.

Wabash.—Central depot Polk Street and Third Avenue. Take State Street cable or Dearborn Street horse car line.

Wisconsin Central.—(Now a part of the Chicago & Northern Pacific system).—Central Depot, Fifth Avenue and Harrison Street. Take Van Buren Street cars at State and Madison or Adams Street cars at State and Adams streets.

These roads furnish such excellent opportunities for reaching the city at all hours that many beautiful suburban towns have grown up for fifty miles out along these lines. They are generally of pleasing appearance and have most of the conveniences of the city, with the added advantages of pure air, wide shady streets, attractive flower gardens and restful lawns. Below we give a list of the largest and most attractive suburbs.

ARGYLE PARK.

Situated on the Evanston division of the Chicago, Milwaukee & St. Paul R. R. It is distant from the City Hall five and a half miles. It is a beautiful suburb with wide avenues and macadamized streets.

AUBURN PARK.

This is one of the prettiest of suburbs. It is situated on the Chicago, Rock Island & Pacific R. R., nine miles from the city hall. It has a population of 4,500. Many of Chicago's wealthiest and most influential citizens have residences here. Its sewerage and drainage systems are of the best and it has every modern convenience that can add to the health and comfort of its residents.

AUSTIN.

A delightful suburb on the Galena division of the Chicago & Northwestern Railway, but six and a half miles from the City Hall. Population, 4,600. Large elms, oaks and cottonwoods are plentifully planted along the streets and about the lawns. There are pretty parks with flower plats and fountains. Its architecture is diversified and beautiful. An electric street railway furnishes its inhabitants cheap and quick transportation.

BLUE ISLAND.

Among the oldest of Chicago's suburban towns. Located on the Chicago, Rock Island & Pacific Railroad, sixteen miles from the City Hall.

BRIGHTON PARK.

Located on the Chicago, St. Louis & Pittsburgh, and the Chicago and Alton Railroads. It is but seven and a half miles from the City Hall, and while having all the advantages of rural life is yet near enough to the city's center to afford the conveniences of a city residence.

BURLINGTON HEIGHTS.

Seventy-two and a half miles from the City Hall on the Chicago & Northern Pacific Railroad.

CHELTENHAM BEACH.

A pleasure resort, on the shore of Lake Michigan, twelve miles south of the City Hall. Take Illinois Central trains. It has a large hotel and restaurant, a large exhibition hall, and an immense amphitheater for Pyrotechnic display.

DAUPHIN PARK.

A beautiful town convenient to the World's Columbian Exposition grounds. The Illinois Central, the Michigan Central, the Chicago, Rock Island & Pacific, the Atlantic & Pacific, the Western Indiana and the New Albany railroads come together here. It has beautiful groves, splendid avenues, well paved streets and splendid residences, water works, electric lights and all modern conveniencies.

DEERING.

Situated on the Milwaukee division of the Chicago & Northwestern Railway. Location of the Deering Harvester Works. A manufacturing suburb.

DELEVAN LAKE.

Located about thirty-eight miles from Chicago on the Wisconsin Central and the Northwestern railroads. This beautiful suburb surrounds a lake three miles in length by two in breadth. Its cottages are the summer homes of many of Chicago's leading people. Natural groves adorn the sloping shores of the lake. There is a large family hotel and many handsome dwellings, pleasant drives and secluded walks. Numerous boat houses furnish boats for pleasure and fishing parties, and several private yachts and small steamers animate the scene. It is fast becoming a favorite summer resort.

EDGEWATER.

Situated on the Evanston division of the Chicago, Milwaukee & St. Paul Railroad, seven and a half miles from the City Hall. It is charmingly situated just north of the city limits, on a gently sloping eminence overlooking Lake Michigan. The town was originally laid out in a natural forest of beech, birch and maple. Only enough of these were removed to allow space for avenues and buildings, leaving the town itself buried in a wilderness of

foliage. It is the most charming suburb of Chicago. The residences are all of modern architecture, elegant in design, solid in
construction and rich in furnishings. Between the spreading
branches of the trees a fine view of the lake is presented. Its
short distance from the city, together with its many natural
charms, make it a favorite residence for the wealthiest citizens.

EVANSTON.

Situated on the Milwaukee division of the Chicago & Northwestern Railway and on the Evanston division of the Chicago,
Milwaukee & St. Paul Railroad, on the shore of Lake Michigan,
twelve miles north of the City Hall. During the summer season
small lake steamers ply between Evanston and Chicago. Trains
run at intervals of a few minutes, morning and evening, and hourly
during the day. Depots at Wells and Kenzie, North Side, or
Canal and Adams Streets, West Side. Steamers at foot of Monroe Street. The town was named for Dr. John Evans, of Chicago,
who early took a deep interest in its affairs and gave freely of his
wealth to establish those institutions of learning and culture
which have given Evanston a national reputation. Its population
is now about 9,000. Nothing could be more in keeping with the
nature of the inhabitants than the town itself. Art and culture
bow sedately to you from the long avenues of stately oaks and
elms. Culture and art look with the serene eyes of satisfied
contentment from the trim, well kept lawns and regularly designed flower gardens. Art and culture reach out their taper
finger tips from residences, sculptured like temples, pillared like
palaces. Evanston is the Athens of our suburbs. The centre
and heart of learning. If Chicago in general has not yet brushed
the dust that comes with money-getting from its garments, the
little city of Evanston can be said to have done so. White and
clean, with the atmosphere of learning continually about her she
looks serenely out over the blue waters of the lake, a fitting goddess of that splendid city just below, which is destined during
the next half century to become the literary center of America.
Evanston is celebrated for its educational institutions, its churches,
its high social advantages, and the cultured character of its inhabi-

tants. A great many of its residents are distinguished in literature and the names of a number are familiar to the English
speaking nations.

Chicago is proud of Evanston. Proud of the Northwestern
University which has, in a little more than two decades of actual
life, won its way to the front rank of the country's educational
institutions. The residents of Evanston are a highly educated,
refined, pure minded people. While they are among Chicago's
wealthiest citizens, they are also among the most liberal, charitable and progressive of her population. The University, has no
doubt, influenced the tastes and habits of Evanston to a great
degree. It has also sent into the world many graduates whose
names have since become household words. The grounds about
the university buildings are cultivated as a park. There are several
splendid churches, among which the recently erected Episcopal
and Catholic edifices are noticeable. The Evanston life saving
crew has won enviable fame for its many brave and self-sacrificing
acts. Evanston has a free circulating library and a paper, *The
Index,* published weekly.

FOX LAKE.

This is one of the most popular of the many summer resorts
contiguous to Chicago. It is located on the Wisconsin division
of the Chicago & Northwestern Railway, and is distant from the
city fifty-one miles. It has many villas to which the wealthier
residents of Chicago retire with their families during the summer
season. The lake is well supplied with pleasure boats and the
disciple of Isaac Walton may here indulge in his favorite pastime
with pleasing results. Many social clubs, the members of which
have their homes in Chicago, have club houses here with all the
accessories for sport and pastime. Trains leave at short intervals
for Fox Lake from the Northwestern depot at Wells and Kenzie
Streets (North Side) and the Chicago and Northern Pacific at fifth
Avenue and Harrison Street.

GENEVA.

This delightful suburban resort is more familiarly known as
Geneva Lake. It is about thirty-five miles from Chicago on the

Galena division of the Chicago & Northwestern Railway. Around this beautiful lake many people of wealth have laid out and cultivated grounds until they bloom in joyous beauty. Pretty cottages peep from nests of fir and pine, while the more ambitious oak and pine tower aloft and cast their umbrageous shade over pleasant walks and drives. No more delightful place for a few days rest and recreation could be suggested.

HINSDALE.

This pretty suburb was one of the first to become popular and many business men of the city have long made their homes within its borders. It is situated on the Chicago, Burlington & Quincy Railroad about fifteen miles from the Central Depot in the city. Like most of the suburbs of Chicago it has a wealth of shade trees of the handsomest varieties. Its streets are well paved and numerous roads leading far into the country are bordered with rows of elm and oak. Oak Forest Cemetery is near this place. The residents of Hinsdale are ambitious only that the homelike features of their place may not be disturbed, and the manufacturer who would erect noisy mills and polute their pure air with the smoke of industry finds no sympathy here. It is located on one of the most elevated spots about the city and commands a very fine view of Chicago with its outlying villages.

LAKE FOREST.

Situated on the shore of Lake Michigan, twenty-eight and a half miles north of the City Hall. It is reached by the Milwaukee division of the Chicago & Northwestern Railway (depot, Kenzie and Wells Street, North Side). It is on the line of the Sheridan Drive from Lincoln Park to Waukegan. Its surroundings are picturesque and romantic. Many Indian legends connected with the early settlement of Chicago are located in this vicinity. The Lake Forest University is located here. The native forest still stands in all its grandeur along the bluff overlooking the lake. The wild magnificence, which must have at one time held court in this forest, has been but partially tamed by the hand of civilization. Beautiful residences stand in the shadow of trees centuries old and the lake beats a wild dirge at the foot of the cliffs which have given them back a sullen defiance for ages. When the Sheridan Drive shall have been completed this will be one of the most interesting points along its entire course.

MAYWOOD.

A manufacturing town situated on the Galena division of the Chicago & Northwestern Railway, ten miles from the City Hall. From an altitude of seventy-five feet above Lake Michigan and twenty-five feet above the Desplaines River, which runs along its eastern borders, it overlooks the country for miles around. It was originally prairie ground, but many years of settlement have given it a magnificent grove of trees, which grow along the banks of the winding river in luxurious profusion. It is quite wealthy in itself, and has first-class educational institutions, handsome churches and many attractive social features.

MORGAN PARK.

So named from its founder, Thomas Morgan, who took up a homestead where the town is located in 1844. It is thirteen miles from the City Hall, on the Chicago, Rock Island & Pacific Railroad. It has the Mount Vernon Military Academy, the Morgan Park (Baptist) Theological Seminary and the Morgan Park Female Seminary. Two artesian wells supply the town with the purest water. It is elevated far above the surrounding country, and the view from its highest point is superb. To the north and east lie South Chicago, Englewood, Washington Heights and Fernwood. To the east Pullman, Kensington and Roseland come into view, away to the south and east winds the tree embowered Calumet River, and the villages of Riverdale and Gano, while rising silently out of the west are those beautiful homes of the friend to whom we have said the last good-bye—Mounts Olivet, Hope and Greenwood.

OAK PARK.

Located on the Galena division of the Chicago & Northwestern Railway. This beautiful suburb is almost entirely in the hands of Chicago's most successful business men. It is distant but twenty minutes ride from the Wells Street depot, and affords the best possible advantages for a suburban dwelling. No prettier spot could be selected for a town. Its elevation affords it the best possible sewerage. The ground is broken into gentle undulation, and its close proximity to the center of trade makes a home for the business man here most desirable. Its founders were men of means, to whom a beautiful home with pleasant surroundings, was, after a day spent in the city's turmoil, held an added delight. Almost every dwelling in the confines of Oak Park gives evidence of wealth, taste and refinement. The streets are well paved and kept clean. There is an abundance of shade trees. The dwellings are set well back from the street, and well kept lawns and flower gardens smile on every hand. They have a complete system of water-works and perfect drainage.

WAUKESHA.

Located on the Galena division of the Chicago & Northwestern Railway. Distant from Chicago 104 miles. The waters from the springs of Waukesha have become known the world over for their wonderful curative properties. Their fame has also contributed to make this pretty Wisconsin village one of the most popular of northern summer resorts.

WILMETTE

Located on the Sheridan Road, twelve miles from the City Hall. It is reached by the Milwaukee division of the Chicago & Northwestern road. A pretty suburb, and sure to become popular on account of its location.

WINNETKA.

Located on the Milwaukee division of the Chicago & Northwestern Railway, eighteen miles from the City Hall. The Sheridan Road runs directly through Winnetka, and since steps have been taken to complete that famous drive, it, like all the suburbs which it touches, has improved rapidly. It has the advantages of

CONSERVATORY, GARFIELD PARK.

a natural forest and the lake breezes. The name is Indian, and means "beautiful place," which is very appropriate for this natural strip of woodland, with its cultivated lawns and tasteful dwellings by the side of the lake that "sings the whole day long."

WOODLAND.

A beautiful suburb on the Illinois Central Railroad about nine miles from the City Hall. Its location near the grounds selected for the Columbian Exposition has added greatly to its importance. It is almost surrounded by parks. Jackson Park on the east, Washington Driving Park on the west, with Oakland Cemetery, which is as beautiful as any park could be, on the south. Many handsome buildings for the accommodation of the World's Fair visitors are contemplated in this attractive suburb. It is but twenty-five minutes ride from the city, and those who bring their families to spend several weeks at the Exposition will find here a quiet spot after "the cares that infest the day" to get the rest which a down town hotel could not furnish.

Lake Michigan.

Beautiful Lake Michigan! Thy body is sapphire and thy robes are emerald and gold. The brooch at thy throat is set with a million sunbeams and thy bosom is as the bosom of an innocent maiden in the arms of her lover. Two generations of men have exhausted their energies designing and constructing decorations for thee, and thy limbs are weighted with the glories of their handiwork. And chiefest of these is Chicago.

There can be nothing finer than a view of this city on a clear day from the deck of a steamer a few miles out from shore. For nearly thirty miles it sweeps a beautiful crescent about the lake, its hundreds of lofty spires flashing in the sunlight; its grand piles of parti-colored granite structures cooling their brows in the drifting clouds. At the head of that liquid chain of linked seas, which form a grand internal and international waterway, Lake Michigan is of as much importance to the commerce as she is necessary to the sequent beauties of the country. For many years Lake Michigan was the only commercial highway from the great northwest to the Atlantic seaboard. The numerous railroads of later years have robbed her of a goodly share of the enormous traffic which is hers by natural right. But nevertheless her ships carry an immense amount of merchandise, in despite of fierce railroad competition. And if swifter emissaries have despoiled her of the dead and senseless freight, no invention of man will ever construct a car so palatial or an engine so swift as to furnish for the quick and sentient a trip so enjoyable as that afforded by a well equipped steamer taking its undulating way through the singing waters.

Several new boats, elegant in design and finish, with a speed of twenty miles an hour, have been launched lately at Chicago. These became at once popular with the traveling public, so much so that they are unable to accommodate one half of the business offered. The coming year several new boats will be launched and the lake carrying trade greatly increased.

The Graham & Morton Company have three steamers plying constantly between Chicago and St. Joe and Benton Harbor. The finest of these is the New Chicago, a double deck screw steamer capable of accommodating five hundred passengers. It is a handsome vessel with a speed of twenty miles an hour. The interior decorations are of mahogany and rosewood. The furniture is upholstered in silk plush, the carpets are elegant brussels, and the staterooms large and well furnished. The steamer is lighted by incandescent lights.

The Goodrich line, which sends its ships as far as Buffalo, has also several first-class steamers afloat. The Virginia, which was but recently launched, is one of the finest screw steamers in the world. While not as large as the ocean steamers, it is more elegant in its appointments and richer and more elaborate in finish. It is now engaged between Chicago and Milwaukee, making the round trip every twenty-four hours. This company has also several other splendid vessels in course of preparation.

Chicago Harbor.

The government harbor is being constantly improved and will eventually be one of the largest, safest and most sheltered harbors in the world. The harbor proper covers an area of 270 acres with communicating slips along the Lake front covering about 200 acres more, making in all 470 acres. In addition to this the river for several miles inward has a depth sufficient to float the largest lake vessels, giving safe anchorage to innumerable craft. A great breakwater, erected at enormous expense, runs parallel with the shore at a distance of three-quarters of a mile. It is 5,436 feet in length and rises ten feet above the surface of the Lake. A wide smooth pavement will extend along the top on the Lake side, affording a delightful promenade. Other piers are in course of construction, both to the north and south of the river's mouth, which will give protection to vessels entering the river and also afford excellent boating privileges. The sea wall and breakwater now being built along the Lake shore will form a regatta course which will be unequalled. Many small excursion boats ply constantly between these piers and the city. Many more will be added for the accommodation of World's Fair passengers, and these, with the improvements now going forward, will give to Chicago Harbor a gay and animated appearance.

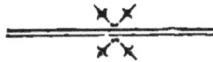

Public Buildings.

POST OFFICE AND CUSTOM HOUSE.

The Post-office and Custom-House occupies the square bounded by Dearborn Street on the East, Jackson Street on the South, Clark Street on the West and Adams Street on the North. This building upon which a half million dollars was expended was never satisfactory either from an architectural or a practical point of view. Even in its earlier days its arrangement was unsatisfactory for the transaction of the Government business and postal needs of the city has since far out-grown the building's capacity. The uneven settlement of the structure has caused accidents to the walls which arouse alarm, and the Government is being urged to erect a new building in its place. Nothing further than an appropriation of $50,000 for the purpose of repairs has been secured, but it is the opinion of experts that the building must at no distant day be torn down or it will fall of its own accord.

THE GOVERNMENT APPRAISERS BUILDING.

The building, which is used for storage and office purposes by the Government appraisers, stands at the north corner of Harrison and Sherman Streets, with a frontage on both streets. The principle entrance is on Harrison Street. From foundation to roof the structure has been built with a view to solidity and strength, and the contractors claim that it cannot be sufficiently over-loaded with merchandise to affect its stability in the least. It is likewise fire-proof and braced and anchored throughout.

The building which is constructed of Connecticut brown stone, beams and girders of steel, consists of eight stories and basement. The height is 125 feet. The Sherman Street frontage is eighty-five feet and that on Harrison Street sixty-five feet. In architectural style the exterior is modern. But little attempt has been made at carving, although there is sufficient to relieve the exterior from plainness, and render it pleasing to the eye. Around the building is a forty-foot driveway, permitting ease of access to the freight-doors on all sides.

The interior finish is simple but neat and in keeping with the outward solid appearance. White oak, highly polished, is used exclusively for woodwork, excepting for flooring in office and storage rooms, where yellow pine is substituted. In the corridors tiling is utilized for floors, and the walls here and around the stairways are of imported enameled brick. The plastering is all laid on fire-proofing. Iron stairways to the left of the main entrance and one passenger elevator furnish people the means of entrance and exit. Two large freight elevators are also provided for the handling of merchandise.

In the basement is located the heating apparatus. The four floors above contain offices, but goods will be stored on these floors as well as those where no partitions have been made for office rooms. The windows are provided with plate glass and protected by steel shutters.

The construction was commenced in the spring of 1889. The contract price is \$218,000, not including heating plant and elevators. These will bring the total cost close to \$240,000.

THE INTER-STATE EXPOSITION BUILDING.

No other building in Chicago is so familiar to the people of the country as the Inter-state Exposition Building. Beneath its spacious roof, year after year, have been exhibited the rich products of field, forest and mine, together with the ingenious and useful contrivances of man, from the tiny puzzle-maker to the mammoth thresher. The hum of machinery softened by the music of playing fountains, has filled the air, while people of every state and nation touched elbows about the display stands. Here too the voice of Conkling, and Garfield, and Logan have been heard in impassioned oratory. High ambitions have been crushed and modest worth exalted in the numerous conventions, national and state, religious and secular, that have been held within its walls. There is some talk of its being removed so as to give the citizens residing on Michigan Avenue, at this point, an unobstructed view of the lake ; but it would seem, a structure so useful, and which is so rich in association should remain untouched, at least, until the conclusion of the World's Fair. The building is nearly 800 feet in length, by 240 feet in width. It has three lofty towers, and its roof is supported without the aid of pillar or column. The view of the entire interior is thus unobstructed. It will readily accomodate 20,000 people.

BOARD OF TRADE.

The Chicago Board of Trade is perhaps the best known, and most influential commercial organization in the world. No other institution of its kind in existence exerts so great an influence over the welfare of mankind. The traffic in bread stuffs, everywhere

is practically regulated by it.   The transactions of the London Exchange, the Bourse of Paris, or the Stock Exchange of New York
are of far less importance to humanity in general, than are those
of the Board of Trade of Chicago.   It has a membership of 2,000
shrewd, energetic, and enterprising men, and in its great building
at the foot of La Salle Street, fortunes are made and lost with
almost every tick of the clock.   To be a member of this great commercial body is considered one of the greatest honors to be won in
the field of commerce, and a disreputable transaction, or a contract repudiated is sure to bring odium upon the operator and
place him beyond the pale of speculation with his fellows for all
time.

The volume of regular business transacted by this body for the
year, runs into the billions, and the speculative business of the
board as indicated by the clearing house reports for the last year,
shows the amazing increase of 31,000,000 over those of 1889.

. This organization was founded in 1850, and was incorporated
with thirteen subscribers.   For many years they transacted business
in the old Chamber of Commerce Building at the corner of La
Salle and Washington Streets.   It now occupies a beautiful new
building at the foot of La Salle Street, near the Grand Pacific
Hotel.

The structure is of granite, unique in design, and covers a space
of 225 by 174 feet.   It is surmounted by a tower, tapering into a
pinnacle 322 feet above the pavement.   Upon its extreme point
glistens a metallic weather vane, the largest in the world, in the
shape of a lake schooner, fifteen feet in length, with rigging in
proportion.   From the street below it looks no larger than a toy
ship.

The building is massive in proportion and from the look-out
balcony which surrounds the tower a fine view of the city is obtained.   The first floor of the building is given up to private offices, telegraph offices, etc.

The great exchange hall occupies a space of 174 by 155
feet, and is eighty feet high, with a glass ceiling 70 by 80 feet.
Within this chamber a large five story block might be placed with
ease.

The decorations of the interior are elaborate and elegant.

Above the main floor two galleries are erected, one for the invited guests, and the other for the general public, open business hours. Here the visitor may gain a perfect view of the operators on the floor, hear the hasty and inarticulate utterances of the excited operators, and view a scene impossible to describe and still more impossible for the average visitor to understand.

THE ART INSTITUTE.

No finer exposition of modern architecture can be found in the city than that presented by the Art Institute building. The eye lingers on this structure with a restful pleasure. The material used is a brown stone. The building, while of much smaller dimensions than its near neighbor the Auditorium, attracts quite as much attention and applause. It is located on the corner of Michigan Avenue and Van Buren Streets, looking across the boulevard to the lake beyond, plashed by white sails and dotted by small steamers.

This admirable institution owes its birth and origin to a few liberal minded men of Chicago, in whom the love of the beautiful had outlived the struggle for gold. These gentlemen not only contributed liberally of their means to construct the building, but have since lent their influence and judgment to the school, which is rapidly becoming prominent among the first of its kind in America. Even its founders were unprepared for the advance which Chicago has made in the direction of art during the last ten years. The building which they supposed would answer the requirements of its patrons for half a century at least, is already proving inadequate for its uses, and will be disposed of that a larger one may be built. The original cost of the Institute building and grounds was about $275,000. Many priceless pictures hang upon its walls, either loaned or donated. The value of the collection of art now on exhibition at the Institute is said to be more than $6,000,000. The Institute is open to visitors every day and evening.

The Chicago Art School is carried on in the Art Institute building. This school has already graduated pupils whose work has won them an enviable reputation, and whose personality will

help hasten the time, nor far distant, when Chicago will become
the literary and art center of America.   In the Art School are the
following classes :   Costumed Life Class, Nude Life Class, Painting from Still Life, Classes in the Antique, Modeling, Perspective,
Saturday Sketching Class, Artistic Anatomy, Ornamental Designing, a class intended for children and teachers called the
Saturday Class, with hours from 10 to 12 a. m., Evening Life and
Antique Classes, Architectural Class, Class Lectures on Antique
Sculpture, and Composition Class.   Regular school hours are from
9 a. m. to 4 p. m.   The Fall term begins September 29, and
closes December 20.   Winter term from December 29 to March
21.   Spring term March 23 to June 13.   Pupils may enter the
Elementary Class at any time without examination.   Tuition
fees are reasonable, the object of the Art Institute being to maintain a school of art in Chicago which shall do honor to the city
and cultivate in its citizens a love for this most refining and en-
nobling of the arts.

THE CHICAGO SOCIETY OF ARTISTS.

This society, which was organized but little more than three
years ago, is now in a flourishing condition.   The rooms of the
society are on the seventh floor of the new Athenæm building,
16 to 26 Van Buren Street.   These rooms were designed expressly for this society, and are not only beautiful in their
appointments, but afford the best possible lights both for painting and displaying pictures.   Many fine compositions of local
artists are on exhibition here, and a visitor to these rooms will be
well repaid.

THE AUDITORIUM.

The fame of this magnificent structure has already gone forth
to all the land.   The eloquent Chauncey M. Depew said of it,
that having seen all the grand and noted buildings in the world,
the grandest of them was the Auditorium of Chicago.   It has
at least no rival on the American continent.   The eye cannot take
in its collossal dimensions from any point of view other than the
deck of a steamer a mile or so out from shore.   Seen from such a

THE AUDITORIUM.

point of vantage its grandeur becomes apparent. It dwarfs all other objects in the view. Could this building have been placed on an elevation, the world could not offer another work of man so stupendous. It has a total street frontage of ·710 feet. The main building is 145 feet high, and the great tower, which has the dimensions of an ordinary office building, is 125, making a total height of 270 feet. The tower is 70 by 41 feet, which is about one-fifth the area covered by the foundations. The first two stories are granite, laid in mighty blocks, some of which weigh over twenty tons. The remaining stories are of building stone. Colossal granite pillars support the magnificent arches which form the entrances on Michigan Avenue, Congress Street and Wabash Avenue. The weight of the entire building is 1,100,000 tons, and yet so intelligently was the foundations laid that the building in settling has never disturbed the walls to the line of a hair. Taking into consideration the unstable condition of the soil on which Chicago is built, this is a most wonderful feat of engineering. The interior of the Auditorium corresponds in richness with its outward proportions. Very little wood entered into its construction. Iron and brick were used for the coarser work, terra cotta and marble where finish was demanded. The building contains $600,000 worth of iron work, 800,000 square feet of terra cotta, 175,000 square feet of wire lath, 60,000 square feet of plate glass, twenty-five miles of gas and water pipes, 230 miles of elastic wires and cable, 10,000 electric lights, eleven dynamos, thirteen electric motors and other necessary appliances in proportion. There were 50,000 square feet of Italian marble used in laying the mosaic floors. These floors contain 50,000,000 pieces of marble, each piece being put in by hand. The walls in the public part of the building are mostly finished in old gold and terra cotta.

The Auditorium comprises within itself a grand opera house, a magnificent hotel, a mammoth office building, and a tower of observation, which overlooks the entire city. The world cannot point to another such pile of magnificence, usefulness and beauty, and yet it was begun and completed in a little more than two years' time, an unrivaled example of modern enterprise and engineering.

To Mr. Ferdinand W. Peck is due the credit of originating the enterprise which has given to Chicago the finest assembly hall in the world. There are about 300 citizens interested in the enterprise. The first shovel full of earth thrown in preparation of the Auditorium's construction was on January 20, 1887.

During that year 250,000 tons of granite, necessary to the construction of the two first stories, were brought from Maine and Minnesota, and the corner stone was laid in September of that year. These two stories were enroofed in time for holding the Republican convention in the building in the following June. Twelve thousand people tested the capacity of the hall on that occasion, and when Harrison was nominated the delegates went back to their respective States to tell their constituants of the wonderful building which Chicago had built in almost a night. On October 2, 1888, the cope stone on the tower's top was laid by the masons with impressive ceremonies, and on December 9, 1889, less than three years after the earth was broken on its site, occurred the grand opening, at which were present the President of the United States, many State governors, with dignitaries and scientists, orators and musicians famous everywhere. It was a red letter day for Chicago and the monument to her industry, enterprise and achievement looks grandly down upon every visitor who moves along the beautiful boulevard of Michigan Avenue.

THE MASONIC TEMPLE.

The Masonic Temple is located at the corner of State and Randolph Streets. It has a frontage on the former street of 170 and on the latter of 114 feet. When finished it will be twenty stories high, towering in the air 265 feet above the street. It is built in the modern style of architecture, a harmonious blending of the ancient and medieval forms. Wisconsin granite is used in the construction of the first three stories, above that a gray fire brick. The facades, arches and supporting pillars are all massive in appearance and add greatly to the rythmic grandeur of the whole structure. When finished it will divide honors with the Auditorium. The building of such a temple was never dreamed of by any organization before. To the late Norman T. Gazette, who was tireless in his endeavors to secure the means for such an enterprise, the city is to a great extent indebted. It is a monument worthy of his ardor for the order and his enthusiastic belief in the final completion of the edifice.

A magnificent interior court will extend from the first floor to the roof, its sides faced with differently shaded marble. On the east side of this court a magnificent bronze staircase will rise to the topmost floor. The floors will be mosaic, the walls marble and onyx and wherever wood is used it will be old oak highly wrought and polished. Fourteen passenger elevators running from basement to roof will make individual trips every three minutes. In the basement will be a grand café. Several of the floors will be given up to shops or booths, a unique idea and one entirely new to this city. The sixteenth, seventeenth, eighteenth, nineteenth and twentieth stories will be sacred to masonry and furnished with magnificent splendor. There will be a great drill hall, blue lodge rooms, rooms for the consistories, the commanderies, a fine banquet hall and handsomely furnished parlors. The Apollo Commandery, of which the founders of this temple are members, will occupy an entire floor. This is one of the largest and wealthiest commanderies in the order.

THE TEMPERANCE TABERNACLE.

This temple is being built by the W. C. T. U. and will be one of the handsomest buildings in the city. The building is 190 by 90 feet and will be eleven stories high, and will cost when completed about $1,100,000. The architecture is modern and strikingly original. The materials of the first two stories are of a dun-colored granite, delicately veined with pink. The remaining stories will be of Anderson fire brick. The building has a look of solid grandeur, and is by far the handsomest building of all the handsome buildings that line La Salle Street. For ten stories the building retreats in a well-defined line from perpendicular. The roof, which begins at the tenth story, is broken into turrets. Thus the three upper stories form a pleasing contrast to the more massive walls below. From the center of the turrets the building will be surmounted by a statue of a woman kneeling in prayer. Three banks will have their offices on the first floor. Here also

will be Willard Hall, so named for Miss Frances Willard, so long
prominent as a worker and lecturer in the temperance field.
Eight thousand people can be seated in the audience room, and
the galleries will hold perhaps as many more. A wide hall on
Monroe Street will give entrance to the auditorium. The windows of this hall will be memorial windows; a fountain will play
continually in the center of the ampitheatre, while from exalted
niches will look benignly down the marble busts of those who
labored through life unceasingly for the temperance cause. The
building will be devoted principally to offices, the rent of which
will be expended in temperance work.

CHAMBER OF COMMERCE BUILDING.

This handsome building stands on the site of the old Chamber
of Commerce, in which the Board of Trade operated for several
years previously to moving into their own building at the foot of
La Salle. The new Chamber of Commerce is built of light gray
faced stone; the style of architecture adopted gives the building
a light and airy appearance very pleasing to the eye. This impression is hightened by the appearance of the interior, which is
finished in Italian marble. The Chamber of Commerce is strictly
an office building; five hundred light and commodious offices
sweep round the great court which rises from the mosaic floor of
the first story to the mammoth skylight which covers the twelfth
story far above. Up the south end of the court climbs a bronze
staircase. There are a dozen elevators in the building which take
one to the top floor in a little more than a minute's time.
Through the great stretch of glass, which forms the roof above the
court, a mellow light streams in, and the offices on every floor extending, as they do, from the court to the outside of the building,
are always light and well ventilated. A town of two thousand
persons could find lodgment in the building. There is, perhaps,
as much business transacted every day in the Chamber of Commerce Building as is transacted in any one of several state
capitals.

THE ROOKERY.

The Rookery is located at the corner of Monroe and La Salle Streets. The curious name it bears was originally given to a rambling brick ruin, put up hastily after the great fire, and used for years thereafter as the City Hall. Some clever wag gave to this tumble-down shell the title of "The Rookery," and so apt a title clung to it until it was torn away to make room for the superb structure which took its place and its name as well. And so what was originally coined as a term of contempt or derision has come to signify all that is rich and splendid in architectural construction. Among all the costly buildings which lift their heads high above the smoke and noise of the city, there is none that, for rugged strength of outline or splendor of decoration, can compare with the Rookery. Its floors are of the richest mosaic; its walls of the most spotless marble; its stairways broad and curving as those of a king's palace; and all its decorations of that massive style which inspires the admiration of the meanest mind and stirs to awe the soul of greatness. The Rookery cost $1,500,000. The building has six hundred magnificent offices, each finished with the same rich care and elegance which marks the building throughout. There are two groups of elevators, one at the Monroe Street entrance and one at the La Salle Street entrance, running continually. Thirty-five hundred persons are occupied in the building during business hours.

THE MARSHALL FIELD BUILDING.

Between the lines made by Adams, Franklin, Quincy Streets and Fifth Avenue stands one of the grandest monuments to the business talent of one man that the world can show. The building covers the entire square of ground. It is built entirely of red granite, many of the stones in the first story weighing more than twenty tons each. If Marshall Field & Co. do the biggest dry goods business in the world, they have certainly the finest building to do it in. The architect who planned this building, conceived the idea of using the lightest kind of pine for the interior of the building, so that in case of fire it would burn out quickly and leave the walls intact. Iron girders, while they are not inflammable, once they become heated, warp and twist to such a degree that the walls which they were put in to support are ruined by them. Marshall Field's building, if it should take fire, would, so far as the walls are concerned, be but little damaged. This great structure was built in less than two years. It is said to be the largest mercantile house in the world. No mark anywhere on the walls of the building informs the passers-by what the magnificent structure is used for or to whom it belongs. At the Adams Street entrance a small brass plate, let into a stone on one side of the arch, bears the simple announcement, " Marshall Field & Co." Thus it is to be known.

THE ARMORY.

Take Wabash Avenue Cable Cars to Sixteenth Street.

The First Regiment, I. N. G., was organized twenty-one years ago. At its first meeting in August, 1874, forty-eight men were enrolled. It now has an enrollment of 530 men. During the troubled times of 1875 when the Relief and Aid Society was threatened by a mob, it did good service, and again in 1886, when previously to the Haymarket riots the destruction of the city was threatened by strikers, this regiment was instrumental in checking the riotous demonstrations at the Union Stock Yards and other places in the city. For several years the regiment has had headquarters on the Lake front adjoining the Exposition building. A few years ago several patriotic citizens began the work of raising a fund for the purpose of building an armory which should in some measure correspond with the strength and comliness of the gallant First, and the massive stone structure at the northeast corner of Sixteenth Street and Michigan Avenue is the result. The building, which is built of stone in massive blocks, is 64 by 174 feet, and would prove a formidable structure in case of siege. It has at once a grand and war-like appearance. The walls are thirty-five feet high, above which rise massive battlements crowned with turrets. The entrance is a great arched doorway through which a full company abreast might march. The windows are guarded by steel bars. The interior is richly finished in stone, brick, iron and heavy oak. The drill hall occupies the entire space on the first floor. Stairways lead from the first floor to the visitors' gallery. The quarters of the field and staff officers are on the second floor. There are company quarters and squad drill rooms above. There are comfortable quarters for non-commissioned officers, orderlies and veterans; also a drum corps room and a gymnasium. On the first floor is a banquet hall, 30 by 50 feet, elegantly finished in old dark oak. The First Regiment, I. N. G., have the largest and most complete militia building in America.

OTHER BUILDINGS OF INTEREST.

To give a detailed description of all the noted buildings which have been built in this city during the last ten years would require much more space than this little book allows. Almost all the great buildings which are the result of the prosperity and growth of this city are substantial, rich and convenient beyond precedent. Story after story has been added to their height, as the ground increased in price, until one is no more surprised to hear of a twenty-story building than he would have been a few years ago at the mention of one six stories high. Among the most attractive buildings in the business center of the city are:

Home Insurance Building.—Located at 205 La Salle Street, near the Board of Trade.

The Tacoma Building.—Located at the corner of Madison and La Salle Streets. One of the first high buildings to be built.

The Owings Building.—Located at the corner of Adams and Dearborn Streets. Interesting for its great height and its peculiar style of architecture.

Manhattan Building.—Located on Dearborn street near the Post-office. A beautiful office building sixteen stories high. A little farther south on this street are

The Monon Building, a splendid twelve-story structure;

The Caxton, a new fire-proof office building of twelve stories in height; it is built of terra cotta and pressed brick. From the eastern windows on the upper floors, one can have a glorious view of the lake. This is one of the most attractive office buildings in the city. Many of the buildings now being built in the city will be from sixteen to eighteen stories in height ; all are built of stone, fire-proof brick, and iron, and as near fire-proof as it is possible for buildings to be.

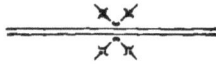

Theatres and Amusements.

Whoso may come to Chicago, from whatever part of the world, will find theatres quite as grand and amusements quite as praiseworthy as those he left behind him.   While Chicago theatrical managers may not be able to boast of two and three "runs" for a single play, they can truly say that in no city of the world are there more beautiful theatres ; neither is there any other city where plays are better staged and mounted.   Every great foreign company coming to this country visits Chicago, where they are sure of large and appreciative audiences.   The round of amusements for any season will compare favorably with those of London, Paris or Berlin.   Many plays which have won popular favor have had their first hearing in Chicago.   The long series of Arabian Nights entertainments, which have become universal favors, were all Chicago productions.   The architectural beauty of the Chicago theatres and their elegant interior furnishings have been warmly praised by notable personages from foreign lands, and even the citizen of this wonderful city by the inland sea, who is satisfied with nothing that does not border on the impossible, is fain to give his approval of the splendid play-houses of Chicago.

Beside the regular theatres there are numerous other amusement halls and places of interest, where the visitor may find pleasure and instruction.   That strangers may have no difficulty in finding such places as they may select, we give under this head a list and short description of those most likely to prove attractive.

ALHAMBRA THEATRE.

Located at the corner of State Street and Archer Avenue. Take State Street cable car. The Alhambra is a handsome

MASONIC TEMPLE.

theatre with a seating capacity of twenty-five hundred. The interior is finished in restful shades of salmon intermingled with a delicate pink. It is modern in construction and provided with numerous and roomy exits. The stage is forty-five feet deep, twenty-five feet wide at the front. It is one of a circle of theatres under the management of H. R. Jacobs.

AUDITORIUM THEATRE.

Located on Wabash Avenue and Congress Street. Take Wabash Avenue or Cottage Grove Avenue cable cars. The magnificent proportions of this theatre, which is a part of the great Auditorium building, has never been equalled. The main object of the projectors of the Auditorium was to give Chicago a theatre in which might be produced the works of the masters of song and story, and at such prices of admission that the toiler as well as the millionaire might feast his soul on the glorious harmonies of Wagner and Beethoven. A theatre alone large enough for such a purpose would necessitate an expenditure which could promise no adequate return for the investment. The genius of Mr. Fred. W. Peck suggested a mammoth building of which the theatre would be but a part, and from which the combined returns would give the stockholders a liberal dividend. The idea was adopted and the result has proved the wisdom of its author. As a consequence Chicago has the largest, grandest and most complete amusement hall in the world. The best orators, singers, actors and artists of this and foreign countries have pronounced in its favor. The acoustic properties of the Auditorium theatre are perfect. The main floor and galleries have a seating capacity of 4,050. Aside from this there are forty boxes, supplied with luxurious chairs and sofas and richly hung in delicate tints of finest plush. The second balcony and gallery can be shut down on occasion, reducing the size of the theatre about one-half. More than 5,000 incandescent lights illumine the house and stage. The interior is finished in soft dull gold delicately shaded. The orchestra accommodates one hundred musicians.

The stage is large enough to accommodate a chorus of 500 voices. It is sixty-nine feet deep and ninety-eight feet wide,

7

There are 6,862 square feet of available stage room. Stage changes are made by the use of hydraulic machinery by the simple movement of a lever. Grand opera, oratorios and tragedy find here a fitting home. One of the largest organs in the world, and said to be the most perfect musical instrument ever built, is located in a compartment behind the north wall. It contains 7,193 pipes and swell, and is divided into seven parts, viz.: great, pedal, swell, choir, echo, solo and stage. There is no musical effect but what may be produced from this grand instrument.

The great political conventions find the Auditorium Theatre well adapted to their needs, and the central location of Chicago, its splendid hotel accommodations and its delightful climate make it the most popular convention city in America.

BATTLE OF GETTYSBURG PANORAMA.

Located on the northeast corner of Wabash Avenue and Panorama Place. Take Wabash or Cottage Grove Avenue cars. An historical representation of one of the great battles of the Civil War. From a central elevation you view the contending armies in the full heat of strife. Look where you may you see wide stretches of country dotted by small groves, with fields of golden grain between. Here are regiments with broken ranks in hand to hand conflict. There are battalions in battle array moving steadily on to the scene of conflict. The smoke of cannon and the flash of steel are all about you. The wounded, the dying and the dead are scattered about the field. You are in the midst of black-browed war with all its attendant horrors and its heroic inspirations. Open day and evening.

CASINO.

(Formerly the Eden Musee.) Located on Wabash Avenue near Adams Street. Take Wabash or Cottage Grove Avenue cable cars. There are four floors given up to the exhibition of wax works, historical paintings, etc., etc. On the fifth floor is a large amusement hall where a high class variety performance is given afternoon and evening. Ices, creams and cooling drinks are also served here. The Casino is open day and evening. Lyman B. Glover, business manager. Admission twenty-five cents and fifty cents.

CENTRAL MUSIC HALL.

Centrally located at the Corner of Randolph and State Streets. A popular lecture and concert hall with a seating capacity of 2,000. Of late years it has become famous as the place in which Prof. David Swing delivers his eloquent Sunday morning lectures. It has a grand concert organ, a ꞏroomy stage, but no scenery. Some of the greatest singers and lecturers have appeared upon this stage.

CHICAGO OPERA HOUSE.

Centrally located at the corner of Washington and Clark Streets. J. W. Norton & Co., proprietors. David Henderson, manager. One of the most popular theaters in the city. Seating capacity, 2,100. While tragedy and grand opera have occasionally held the boards at this theater it is virtually the home of comedy. Light operas and spectacular plays have here their most complete representation. A few seasons ago Mr. Henderson inaugurated a series of summer performances founded on the Arabian Nights. These beautiful entertainments were the product of Chicago authors and have proved very popular both at home and on the road. The best of modern comedies are presented at the Chicago Opera House. The theatre is absolutely fire-proof. Its interior is elegant. Plays are mounted here with unsurpassed splendor. No theatre in Chicago has a better patronage. Admission prices are 50, 75, $1.00 and $1.50. Boxes, $10, $12 and $15.

COLUMBIA THEATRE.

Centrally located near the corner of Monroe and Dearborn Streets. Proprietors and managers, Al. Hayman and Will J. Davis. For several years after it was first opened the Columbia theatre proved an unfortunate enterprise. Jack Haverly, then in the height of his popularity, was its first manager. Reverse of fortune soon after compelled him to give it up. Several other well known theatrical men afterward attempted its management but with disastrous results. Under the supervision of Messrs. Hayman and Davis, however, it at once stepped into popularity, and is to-day a favorite place of amusement with a steady and liberal patronage. The theatre is one of the largest and handsomest in the city. It has a seating capacity of 2,400. The stage is large, its settings first class and the acoustics of the house of the first order. Admission 50, 75, $1.00, $1.50. Boxes $10, $12 and $15.

CRITERION THEATRE.

Located at the corner of Sedgwick and Division Streets, North Side. Take Sedgwick Street car on North Side cable line. A favorite resort for the residents of North Chicago. Seating capacity, 1,800.

EPSTEIN'S NEW DIME MUSEUM.

Located on Randolph Street near Clark. A museum of curi‧osities, wax works, electric contrivances and natural human and animal freaks. A variety performance is given in the theatre every hour. Admission, 10 cents.

GRAND OPERA HOUSE.

Centrally located on Clark Street opposite the Court-House. Harry L. Hamlin, manager. Where the Grand Opera House stands has been amusement ground since the city was in its infancy. A public hall first occupied this ground. Afterwards the Colosseum, a variety, concert and beer hall, stood here. In 1878 this was transformed into a vaudeville theater and christened "Hamlin's." Two years later it was again reconstructed into its present beautiful proportions and given the name of the Grand Opera House. The trend of this theatre is toward the modern drama. Several worthy productions of American dramatists have had their initial performance at this house. The seating capacity of the Grand is about 1,700. The plays presented are invariably well mounted and the cleanest and best dramas of the American school are oftenest seen at this theatre. Admission 50, 75, $1.00 and $1.50. Boxes $10 and $15.

HALSTEAD STREET OPERA HOUSE.

Located at the corner of Halstead and Harrison Streets. Take South Halstead or Blue Island Avenue cars. Popular prices.

HAVLIN'S THEATRE.

Located on Wabash Avenue between Eighteenth and Twentieth Streets. Take Wabash Avenue cable line. John A. Havlin, lessee. J. S. Hutton, manager. This is a new and pretty theatre located near a populous resident district. Standard plays are given here with first class companies to interpret them. The house has a seating capacity of about 2,000, and is finished with all the richness and beauty of its down-town rivals.

HAYMARKET THEATRE.

Located on Madison Street near Halstead, West Side; Will J. Davis, manager. Take Madison Street cable line. One of the largest and handsomest theatres in the country. Its seating capacity is 2,406. It has a stage ninety feet deep with a procenium opening of forty-eight feet. The interior of the building is handsomely decorated in color, something between old gold and salmon. Everything about the Haymarket is constructed on a grand and liberal scale. The foyer occupies as much room as the amphitheatre of some theatres. It is enlivened by a fountain and decorated by numerous statues. Aside from the Auditorium no other theatre in the city can compare with it in dimensions. Every part of the stage is visible from any seat in the auditorium. The best companies are constantly presenting here the best plays. Much of the Haymarket's success is no doubt due to the management of Mr. Davis, whose natural ability and years of experience well qualify him to select such amusements as are likely to please the patrons of his theatre. Admission 15, 25, 50, 75, and $1.00. Turkish chairs, $1.50. Boxes, $5.00 to $10.00.

HOOLEY'S THEATRE.

Centrally located on Randolph Street near La Salle, opposite City Hall. Richard M. Hooley, proprietor. Harry Powers, business manager. This beautiful temple of the muses was opened by Mr. Hooley on the 17th day of October, 1872, and with the single exception of one brief season, when J. H. Haverly gained control and gave it his name, it has born the name of the veteran manager who controls it to-day. Hooley's Theatre is the synonym of all that is best and noblest in the drama. Here the standard companies of London and New York bring the good old comedies and rare dramas of the best playrights of the past and present, and here assemble the wisest and wittiest of Chicago's amusement lovers to hear them. The house seats an audience of about 1,500. Everything about the theatre is rich and tasteful and the comfort of his patrons is one of the first cares of "Uncle Dick" Hooley. Admission, 50, 75, $1.00 and $1.50. Boxes, $10 and $15.

H. R. JACOBS' ACADEMY.

Located on Haistead Street, near West Madison Street. Take Madison Street cable cars. One of several theatres in this city under the control of H. R. Jacobs. A pretty theatre, seating about 1,800 people. It has a medium sized stage, with first-class scenery. The plays presented here are mostly light comedies, or the better class of vaudeville attractions. Admission, 25, 50 and 75 cents.

H. R. JACOBS' CLARK STREET THEATRE.

Located on North Clark Street, near the bridge; five minutes' walk from the Court-House; vaudeville and light comedy; popular prices of admission.

JACOB LITTS' STANDARD THEATRE.

Located on Halstead and Jackson Streets, West Side. Take South Halstead or Van Buren street cars. Light comedy and burlesque. Popular prices.

KOHL & MIDDLETON'S SOUTH SIDE DIME MUSEUM.

Located on South Clark Street, near Madison. Curiosities and hourly stage performance.

LIBBY PRISON MUSEUM.

Located on Wabash Avenue, near Sixteenth Street. Take Wabash Avenue cable cars. Here enclosed within a massive wall, surmounted by turrets at regular intervals, is the original Libby Prison, brought from Richmond, Virginia, and rebuilt exactly as it originally stood, even to each separate brick. Aside from this famous war relic, there is a war museum in which are stored thousands of mementoes of the battle fields, as well as state papers and other documents that have a bearing on the "late unpleasantness." There are pictures in oil of Abraham Lincoln and Mrs. Lincoln, as well as those of the famous Union and Confederate generals. Many other rare and curious relics of historic value may be seen here. Open day and evening. Admission, 50 cents, children half price.

LYCEUM THEATRE.

Located on Desplanes Street, between Madison and Washington Streets, West Side. Ten minutes' walk from the Court-House. T. L. Grenier, proprietor. First class variety. Admission popular prices.

McVICKER'S THEATRE.

Located on the west side of Madison Street, between State and Dearborn Streets. Only a few minutes walk from the principal hotels. Horace McVicker, manager. This is the most historic place of amusement standing in Chicago. It was built by J. H. McVicker in the early history of the city. It has been twice destroyed by fire to rise each time more beautiful than before. It is now one of the handsomest theatres in the world. For years after the public began to neglect the dramas enriched by time and the genius of author and actor for two hundred years and turn with the spirit of the age to the more frivolous

productions of the day, J. H. McVicker fought against the
innovation. An actor of the old school himself, he could not
understand why Hamlet, and Richard the Third, and Bob Acres
and fat but witty Jack Falstaff should be superseded by senti-
mental everyday fellows in store clothes who fell in love with
their wife's chambermaid, or giggling acrobats whose only hold
upon the public was a local gag. His stock company was the
last to go, and he is still an unbeliever in the "star system." At
this theatre you will always find a first-class company and generally a good play. The house of itself is an attraction. Everything about it speaks of taste and refinement. The house will seat
about 2,100 people. Its stage is large and the stage settings
always rich and in keeping with the play. Admission, 50, 75,
$1.00, $1.50. Boxes the same as the other first-class theatres.

NEW WINDSOR THEATRE.

Located at North Clark and Division Streets. Take North
Clark Street cable car, marked Lincoln Park. M. B. Leavitt,
manager. Bruno Kennicott, assistant manager. The New
Windsor is quite as handsome as any of its down town rivals. It
has a seating capacity of 2,000, a stage 50 by 70 feet. The very
best of stage settings are used in mounting plays at the Windsor.
It is the center of a rich and populous resident district and has
always a good patronage. Admission, 35, 50, 75, $1.00.

THE PANORAMA OF NIAGARA FALLS.

Situated at the corner of Wabash Avenue and Hubbard
Court. This is the monster painting that had such a successful
run in London, England, coming straight to this city from there.
It was painted by the celebrated French artist, Paul Philippo-
teaux. It is fifty feet in height and 410 feet in circumference,
while four tons of paint are spread on the canvas. The point of
view is the top of the old museum on the Canada side, and the two
great falls, Goat Island, the Maid of the Mist, Suspension Bridge,
and all the other well known Niagara features, are portrayed with
a realism and accuracy of detail that is almost startling. Two
dioramas by the same artist are shown without extra charge to

WOMAN'S TEMPLE.

visitors. They are a very good view of the Whirlpool rapids and a highly colored Southern scene—Cotton Picking on the Mississippi. The exhibition is well worth a visit from all strangers. Open daily and Sundays 10 to 10.

PARK THEATRE.

Located on State Street, between Harrison and Congress Streets. Take State Street cable line. John D. Long, manager. Variety; popular prices.

PEOPLE'S THEATRE.

Situated on the east side of State Street, between Harrison and Congress Streets. Jo. Baylies, lessee and manager; Joseph J. Oliver, business manager. Take State Street cable line. A pretty theatre of medium capacity, in which the lighter dramas and farce comedies have representation. Admission, 15, 25, 35 and 50 cents.

WEBER MUSIC HALL.

Situated on the corner of Wabash Avenue and Adams Street. Short walk from the down town hotels. Charles C. Curtis, manager. A small, but pretty hall with stage, but no scenery. High class concerts are frequently given here.

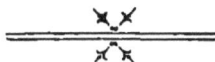

Public and Private Charities.

Chicago is no less ambitious in her charities than in her pursuit of wealth. Organizations for the relief of the poor and the distressed are numerous, and institutions for the care of the sick and suffering rise on every hand. Hospitals, dispensaries, homes, asylums, covering every form of suffering, and relieving every age, from the infant in swaddling clothes, to the old and feeble tottering on the verge of eternity find ready support from citizens, who, if as the world charges, are zealous in the collection of gold, are also liberal in bestowing it on worthy objects.

THE CHICAGO RELIEF AND AID SOCIETY

Is an organization which has stood the test of years and brought succor and sustenance to thousands. Directly after the great fire of 1871, when the city lay in ruins and two-thirds of the city's population were without homes and many without food or clothing, this society did a work which will cause it to be remembered while a generous impulse stirs the heart of humanity. During those weeks of terrible suffering and anguish the members of this noble organization took scarcely time for sleep. Of the millions in money and provisions which flowed into the city from a kindly world, they handled the greater part, and long after the rush which followed immediate want had subsided, the committees of this society continued to collect and distribute donations among the city's unfortunate, left penniless by the flames. In the three years following the fire they expended nearly five millions of dollars. The society was organized by a special act of Legislature in 1857. It is located on La Salle Street, between Randolph and Lake Streets. It owns the building in which it operates. All degrees of poverty and suffering find a kindly friend and a helpful benefactor in this society. During the year 1890 it received 13,565 applications for relief; about one-half of these were approved and relief furnished. The cash donations during this time amounted to $31,583, all of which was expended in worthy charities. Carloads of clothing, tools and food are distributed annually through this channel. There is no more worthy relief organization. The officers are: President, C. H. S. Mixer; treasurer, H. W. King; secretary, W. H. Hubbard; general superintendent, Rev. C. G. Truesdell; directors meet the first Saturdays of every month. The society has branch offices as follows: Southern office, 2207 Michigan Avenue; telephone 8531. Northern office, 624 North Clark; telephone 3415. Western office, Monroe, corner Ogden Avenue; telephone 4721.

ARMOUR'S MISSION.

Situated at the corner of Armour Avenue and Thirty-third Street. Take State Street cable line. A training and Sunday School for the children of the poor. Over 2,500 children find their way into the Sunday School. There is a kindergarten which will accommodate 200 pupils. The training school takes care of as many more. A free dispensary in the building treats forty to fifty patients daily. There are over 2,000 pupils enrolled in the different departments. Visitors are gladly welcomed.

BUREAU OF JUSTICE.

Office at 149 La Salle Street. An organization for the protection of the honest unfortunate who fall under the ban of the law and are unable to secure legal advice or council. It also assists laborers to collect their wage claims where they are dishonestly withheld. It is a deserving organization and well merits the aid it receives.

CHICAGO CHILDREN'S HOSPITAL.

Located at 214 Humboldt Boulevard. A sanitarium built directly over the waters of Lake Michigan where the poor and destitute and the infirm and crippled children of the city may find cool and pleasant quarters during July and August. It is an offshoot from the Fresh Air Fund.

"CHICAGO DAILY NEWS" FRESH AIR FUND.

A fund collected by the *Daily News* for the purpose of taking care of the sick children and invalids among the poor and giving them at least one week in the country during the hot summer months. The *News* itself contributes largely to this charity. From 8,000 to 10,000 sick children and adults have the benefit of pure air for at least two months of the year. A sanitarium is established every summer on the South Side at the foot of Twenty-second Street sufficiently large to accommodate at least 500 babies. There is also a kindergarten for the older children.

CHICAGO HOSPITAL FOR WOMEN AND CHILDREN.

Located at the corner of Paulina and West Adams Streets.

CHICAGO ORPHAN ASYLUM.

Located at 2228 Michigan Avenue.

CHICAGO NURSERY AND HALF-ORPHAN ASYLUM.

Located at 855 North Halstead Street.

ERRING WOMAN'S REFUGE.

Located at Indiana Avenue and Thirty-first Street. Take Indiana Avenue cars. The object of this charity is the relief, protection, care and reformation of repentant erring women. It is a noble work and has accomplished much good.

THE FOUNDLING'S HOME.

Located on Wood Street just south of Madison Street, West Side. Take Madison Street cable line. The Foundling's Home is on one of the most noted of Chicago's numerous charities. To Dr. George E. Shipman belongs the credit of its establishment. It was first opened in 1874 at 54 South Green Street. Its growth was so rapid as to necessitate a removal to larger quarters before three months had gone by, and a building was secured at the corner of Randolph and Sangamon Streets. In May, 1872, the Chicago Relief and Aid Society donated $10,000 to the charity and the Orphan's Home was immediately incorporated and work commenced on the building which it now occupies. The original building was cruciform in shape, forty by sixty feet, three stories high, with an attic and basement. A new wing has been added, sixty-two by forty feet, five stories high, and connected with the main building by an annex. In the building there are nine dormitories and eight hospital rooms. There are also rooms for the superintendent and family, lady assistants, etc. More than one hundred inmates may be accommodated and the home is generally full. Many of these little waifs find good homes in Christian families. Quite a number are returned to their parents, some, too delicate to brave a world unto which they have no well defined claim, find rest in unbroken slumber. About $7,000 per annum is required to pay the expenses of the Home, and this sum is all raised by private contributions. It is a most worthy charity and well deserving of the most liberal support.

GOOD SAMARITAN SOCIETY.

Located at 15 Lincoln Avenue, North Side. Take Clark Street cable car marked "Lincoln Avenue." An industrial home for worthy women and girls. Supported by voluntary contributions.

HOLY FAMILY ORPHAN ASYLUM.

Located at Holt and Division Streets. A Catholic institution. Sister Mary Subowidzka, Superior.

HOME FOR INCURABLES.

Located on Ellis Avenue and Fifty-sixth Streets. Take Cottage Grove Avenue cable line. F. D. Mitchell, superintendent; Miss Libbie S. Ainsworth, matron; Dr. William P. Goldsmith and Dr. John H. Wilson, attending physicians. The buildings together with the surrounding grounds are the gift of the late Mrs. Clarissa C. Peck. The building is a five story structure with wings, capable of accommodating 125 patients. The best of care is taken to have everything as bright and cheerful as possible about the Home. Lawns with shade trees and swinging hammocks invite the weary. There are reading rooms, a smoking room, and upon every floor a cosy parlor. The institution is self supporting.

HOME FOR SELF-SUPPORTING WOMEN.

Located at 275 and 277 Indiana Street, North Side. Take Indiana Street car. Women and girls whether they be employed or not may here find a home and assistance in securing work.

HOME FOR UNEMPLOYED GIRLS.

Situated at 189 Huron Street, North Side. Take North Market Street car. Girls out of work are cared for here until they secure employment.

HOME FOR WORKING WOMEN.

Located at 189 East Huron Street, North Side. Take Clark Street cable line. A quiet, well kept and orderly place where women and girls in need receive shelter and assistance.

HOME FOR THE FRIENDLESS.

Located at 1926 Wabash Avenue. Take Wabash Avenue cable line. A non-sectarian hospital for the friendless poor. A school for children is connected with it. There are generally 200 inmates in the Home. All classes of the worthy poor are here fed, protected and encouraged.

HOME FOR THE AGED OF THE LITTLE SISTERS OF THE POOR.

Located at the corner of Throop and Harrison Streets. A home for destitute men and women over sixty years old, and who are of good moral character.

HOUSE OF THE GOOD SHEPHERD.

Located at the corner of North Market and Hurlbut Streets. An asylum for women and female children. It is under the charge of the Sisters of the Good Shepherd.

HOME FOR INCURABLES.

Located at the corner of Racine and Fullerton Avenues. The name indicates the mission of this charity.

NEWS-BOYS' AND BOOT-BLACKS' HOME.

Located at 1418 Wabash Avenue. Take Wabash Avenue cable line. A most interesting and worthy charity. Food and shelter are never denied to a boy who applies, and for a very small sum he may have a permanent home in the building. There is a night school four evenings in the week. Clean clothing is given to the needy upon his first entrance and if he proves worthy he is pretty certain to find friends to advance him to better things than selling papers and blacking boots. Donations of cast off clothing are very acceptable to the managers.

OLD PEOPLES' HOME.

Located on Indiana Avenue near Thirty-ninth Street. A commodius brick building with a capacity of eighty inmates. Only old ladies of good moral character who have resided in Chicago for two years are admitted.

SCHOOL FOR DEAF AND DUMB.

Located at 409 May Street, West Side. Take Harrison Street cars. This charity owes its being to the personal efforts and support of the Ephpheta Society, of which Mrs. John Cudahy is president. There are four experienced teachers in the school, and an average of fifty pupils. An interesting and noble work.

SERVITE SISTERS' INDUSTRIAL HOME.

Located at 1326 West Van Buren Street. Take West Madison Street cable line. An industrial home for girls who are without homes, or who wish to better their condition. It is under the supervision of the Servite Sisters of Mary.

SOLDIERS' HOME FUND.

A fund which had its nucleus in a great sanitary fair held in Chicago during the war for the benefit of disabled soldiers. There is now something over $70,000 in the fund and the income from this is distributed among the needy survivors of the Union army residing in Chicago. This fund is disbursed every Saturday by Mrs. L. H. Bristol at the rooms of the Chicago Relief and Aid Society.

WAIF'S MISSION.

Located at 44 State Street, Taylor E. Daniels, superintendent. This is one of the grandest works of charity that was ever inaugurated, and deserves the hearty support of every generous hearted man. Boys abandoned by their parents to find a living in the streets as best they may, are sought out and brought into the mission by Superintendent Daniels, who is never weary with well doing. A hundred thousand free meals a year, fifteen thousand free beds, five thousand free baths, twelve hundred hair cuts, and ten thousand garments given away. Think of the misery averted, the hunger stayed, the hopes kindled in despairing hearts by this work. Every Sunday afternoon a liberal dinner is spread in the Armory at the foot of Monroe Street. and from five hundred to a thousand waifs march adown the tables and are filled. There are services with much singing in which they all join lustily. There is a movement on foot to build suitable mission quarters where a great training school, night schools, etc., may be carried on.

YOUNG MEN'S CHRISTIAN ASSOCIATION.

Central rooms located in the building of the Association at 148 Madison Street. The rooms of the Y. M. C. A. are handsomely furnished with an eye to comfort and convenience as well as beauty. There is a large reading room where the leading newspapers and periodicals are on file ; a splendid library and a gymnasium. Lectures, receptions, concerts and a high class of amusements are given during the fall and winter season. Active and associate membership tickets may be secured by any reputable male over 16 years of age at a cost of $5.00 a year. Boys between the ages of twelve and sixteen are admitted as juniors at $3.00 per annum. A membership ticket entitles the holder to the privileges of the gymnasium, physical instruction. baths, summer athletics, and outing clubs. There are gospel meetings, training classes, Bible classes, prayer meetings and teachers' meetings. There are several branches of the Y. M. C. A. in different parts of the city which contain the leading features of the main building.

THE ROOKERY AND BOARD OF TRADE.

In addition to the charities mentioned there are many more quite as worthy organized societies that are as yet unable to build or rent a building. The home of their president or secretary is the headquarters of the association. A world of charitable work is accomplished every year through these agencies. Then there are the church societies and missions, hundreds of them engaged in making life a little smoother for the unfortunate.

Churches and Religious Institutions.

Since its early settlement as a frontier town, Chicago has shown a deep interest in religious matters, and the growth of its churches and religious institutions has kept pace with its secular interest. A visitor to the city will be at once impressed with the number and magnificence of its church edifices; its numerous and commodious church hospitals and the learning and eloquence of its divines. Gentile and Jew, Protestant and Catholic strive in worthy emulation to outdo one another in the splendor of their tabernacles, the music of their choirs, and the wisdom of their preachers, pastors and bishops. To give a detailed description of the prominent church edifices of Chicago would require more space than is commensurate with the size of this book. The most we can hope to do is to enumerate the most popular churches, ministers and preachers of the different denominations with their respective locations. The visitor, however, may feel assured that whatever one of them he may select to attend he will find it spiritually, artistically and ethically pleasurable.

The leading churches of the West Side are found principally along Washington and Ashland boulevards or around Jefferson and Union parks. Two of the oldest churches in the city, the Centenary Methodist and the Second Baptist, are located on Monroe and Morgan streets. On the North Side they lie principally in the district north of Ontario and east of Clark Streets; many of them on Dearborn Avenue. On the South Side are many splen-

8

did church edifices. The district east of State Street and south of Twenty-second Street is rich with them. Wabash Avenue, Indiana Avenue and State Street have some of the handsomest church buildings in America. The different cable car lines run from the center of the city directly to the localities mentioned. For the North Side take Clark Street cable line; for the West Side take Madison street cable line; for the South Side, State or Wabash Avenue cable line.

   The Central Independent Church, in which Prof. Swing preaches, holds morning services in Central Music Hall at the corner of State and Washington Streets, while the no less popular Dr. Thomas, whose church is styled the Peoples' Church, preaches to his flock in McVicker's Theatre at the same hour.

   The popular ministers, whose eloquence and advanced and liberal teaching have brought into prominence are: Prof. David Swing, Central Church, Central Music Hall, State and Randolph Streets; Dr. H. W. Thomas, Peoples' Church, McVicker's Theatre, Madison Street, near State Street; Simon J. Mac-Pherson, Second Presbyterian Church, Michigan Boulevard and Twentieth Street; F. J. Brobst, Westminster Presbyterian, Peoria and Jackson Streets; F. W. Gunsaulus, Plymouth Congregational, Michigan Avenue, near Twenty-sixth Street; Rabbi E. G. Hirsch, Sinai Congregation, Indiana Avenue and Twenty-first Street; Dr. John H. Barrows, First Presbyterian, Indiana Avenue and Twenty-first Street; H. H. Barbour, Belden Avenue Methodist Church, Belden Avenue and Halstead Street; Dr. P. S. Hensen, First Baptist Church, South Park Avenue and Thirty-first Street; Dr. George C. Lorimer, Emanuel Baptist Church, Michigan Avenue, near Twenty-third Street; Dr. W. M. Lawrence, Second Baptist Church, Morgan and Monroe Streets; Dr. E. P. Goodwin, First Congregational Church, Washington Boulevard and Ann Street; Dr. F. A. Noble, Union Park Congregational, Washington Boulevard and Ashland Avenue; Rt. Rev. William E. McLaren, Episcopal Cathedral, Washington Boulevard and Peoria Street; Rev. Dr. Clinton Locke, Grace Episcopol Church, 1445 Wabash Avenue; Rt. Rev. Charles E. Cheney, Christ's Episcopal Church, Michigan Avenue and Twenty-fourth Street; Rt. Rev. Samuel Fallows, St. Paul's Episcopal, Adams Street and

Winchester Avenue; J. P. Brushingham, Ada Street M. E. Church, Ada Street, between Lake and Fulton Streets: Robert McIntyre, Grace M. E. Church, cor. La Salle Avenue and Locust Street; Dr. William Fawcett, Park Avenue M. E. Church, Park Avenue, cor. Roby Street; Frank M. Bristol, Trinity M. E. Church, Indiana Avenue, near Twenty-fourth Street; Dr. W. T. Meloy, First United Presbyterian Church, Monroe and Paulina Streets; Dr. M. W. Stryker, Fourth Presbyterian Church, Rush and Superior Streets; Dr. John L. Wilhrow, Third Presbyterian Church, Ashland Boulevard and Ogden Avenue; Jenkins Lloyd Jones, All Soul's Church, Oakwood Boulevard and Langley Avenue; T. G. Milsted, Unity Church, Dearborn Avenue and Walton place; J. Colman Adams, St. Paul's Unitarian Church, Prairie Avenue and Thirtieth Street. The St. James Reformed Episcopal Church, located at the corner of Cass and Huron Streets, North Side, has a chime of bells and a boy choir of sixty voices. The Grace Episcopal Church, 1445 Wabash Avenue, has also a boy choir, which under the instruction of Prof. Rooney, has become famous. It is to this choir that Blatchford Kavenaugh, the wonderful boy soprano, belongs. There is scarcely a church of note in the city that has not one or more superior voices to lead the singing, while great organs under the hands of masters fill the edifices with solemn and rapturous harmonies.

The Schools.

There are 205 public schools in Chicago with an average attendance of 146,000. Of these 194 are graded schools and eleven are high schools. Aside from this there are 50,000 pupils in private schools, the greater number of which are connected with some one of the societies. There are 2,842 teachers employed in the public schools and 1,164 in the parochial or sectarian institutions. There are in addition to these several schools in which are taught the higher branches of learning. A fair estimate would place the whole number of young men, woman and children in attendance at some one or other of these branches of learning, at not less than 250,000. The public school buildings are generally splendid structures of brick and stone, situated in the center of a square, away from other buildings so that pupils may not be deprived of light and air. Dúring the year 1889–1890 Cook County collected for school purposes from all sources $4,164,308, and paid out in salaries, for school buildings and other expenses, $3,787,-222. There was, according to the last census, but 2,635 persons in Cook County unable to read and write. Chicago is perhaps the most cosmopolitan city in the world. It has a greater per cent. of foreign population than any other American city. With this fact in view, it is surprising to find so large a number of pupils in its schools and the small number of illiterate persons in the county. It is a glorious thing to contemplate a country governed by a race of people to whom has been given a hundred years of such educational advantages. The America of 2092 will be governed by such a people.

The Cemeteries.

The burial places of Chicago are beautifully located and handsomely kept. Miles from the restless city, in the midst of solitude they lie, amidst clumps of evergreen, trailing roses and lilies waxen white.

ROSEHILL CEMETERY.

This is the largest of the cemeteries. It is located six and one half miles from the City Hall on the Milwaukee division of the Chicago & Northwestern Railway. Depot at foot of Wells Street, North Side. There are five hundred acres in this cemetery. The ground is a rolling upland, carefully and artistically cultivated. It rises gently from the level prairie which surrounds it, and from whatever point of approach presents a charming view. The main entrance to the grounds is through a castellated stone structure which contains a chapel arranged for funeral services. Macadamized walks and drives wind about through the grounds, sometimes under an avenue of trees, sometimes in the broad glare of the sun. The cemetery is watered from an artesian well 2,279 feet deep. Slender lakes stretch like ribbons of liquid silver between extensive flower-plats upon which the landscape gardener has expended his best gifts. There are spacious greenhouses and conservatories for the propagation of plants and flowers. The cemetery has many costly tombs and graceful monuments. To the west of the grounds stands a memorial shaft erected to General Edward Geenfield Ransom, whose career as a soldier took him through the battles of Charleston, Mo., Fort Donelson, Shiloh, Corinth, Champion Hills, Miss., Vicksburgh, to meet death at Pleasant Hill, La., almost at the close of the war. Another monument marks the grave of Geo. S. Bangs, the originator of the United States fast-mail service. The Soldiers' monument at the head of the main avenue is a handsome and costly structure. A pleasant carriage drive reaches Rosehill by the way of the Lake Shore Drive, Lincoln Park and Graceland Cemetery.

CALVARY CEMETRY.

The principal Roman Catholic burying ground of the city, situated ten miles north of the City Hall on the Milwaukee division of the Chicago & Northwestern Railway. Depot at the foot of Wells Street, North Side. Also Evanston division of the Chicago, Milwaukee & St. Paul Railway; Union Depot, Canal and Madison streets. It lies on the Sheridan Road, and the carriage drive which reaches it over this thoroughfare, together with the Lake Shore Drive and Lincoln Park, is charming. The cemetery is adorned by natural and ornamental shade trees, well kept flower-plats and smooth winding drives and walks. There have been over 30,000 interments in Calvary Cemetery since its consecration in 1861.

GRACELAND CEMETERY.

Located six miles north of the City Hall on North Clark Street. Take train on the Evanston division of the Chicago, Mil-

waukee & St. Paul Railway, Union Depot, Canal and Madison
Streets, for Buena Park Station. Also reached by way of the
Lake Shore Drive, through Lincoln Park and Lake View. The
cemetery grounds are maintained by the interest on a fund collected from the sale of lots. The grounds are as beautiful as care
and art can make them. The avenues, drives and walks are per-
féctly macadamized, and the lawns and flower-plats are kept fresh
and fragrant by a free use of perfect waterworks. Living springs
form charming lakes in which the rarest specimens of water
flowers flourish.

Graceland Cemetery is said to be one of the most beautiful
burial places in the country. Many names which the city holds
dear from long association mark the grassy mounds in this hal-
lowed spot. The remains of John Kinzie, the "Father of Chicago," after several disinterments, have here at last a final
resting place. Other members of his family sleep at his side or
near him. To one familiar with the early history of Chicago
Graceland Cemetery is like the remembrance of stirring acts from
a half forgotten drama.

OAKWOODS CEMETERY.

A beautiful cemetery of two hundred acres in the southwestern part of the city. Take Illinois Central Railroad, foot of Randolph or Van Buren Streets, or Cottage Grove Avenue cable line.
Rosehill, Graceland and Oakwoods cemeteries are the principal
Protestant burying places of Chicago. Each of them has a
pleasant location and delightful surroundings. The natural solem-
nity of a city of the dead is softened and tempered by the bloom
and fragrance of flowers, the music of swaying boughs, and the
graceful shade of well kept groves of oak, maple, elm and ever-
greens. The remaining cemeteries of the city are located as
follows:

AUSHE MAARIV CEMETERY.

North Clark Street and Belmont Avenue, on Evanston division of the Chicago, Milwaukee & St. Paul Railroad; also reached
by North Clark Street cable line.

AUSTRO-HUNGARIAN CEMETERY.

Located at Waldheim, ten miles from the City Hall on the Chicago and Northern Pacific Railroad. Depot at Harrison Street and Fifth Avenue.

B'NAI SHILOM CEMETERY.

Located on North Clark Street and Graceland Avenue. Take North Clark Street cable line, or Evanston division of Chicago, Milwaukee & St. Paul Railroad.

CHEBRA GEMILATH CHASADIM UBIKAR CHOLIM CEMETERY.

Located on North Clark Street near Graceland Cemetery. [See Graceland Cemetery.]

CHEBRA KADISHA UBIKAR CHOLIM CEMETERY.

Located on North Clark Street, south of Graceland Cemetery. [See Graceland Cemetery.]

CONCORDIA CEMETERY.

Located about nine miles west of the City Hall on Madison Street, besides the Desplaines river. [See Forest Home Cemetery.]

FOREST HOME CEMETERY.

Located about nine miles west of the City Hall, on Madison Street, on the bank of the Desplaines river. Take train on the Chicago & Northern Pacific Railroad. Depot at Harrison and Fifth Avenue.

GERMAN LUTHERAN CEMETERY.

Take North Clark Street cable cars to southeast corner of Graceland Avenue.

MOUNT GREENWOOD CEMETERY.

Located near Morgan Park, fourteen miles south of the City Hall. Take trains at the Van Buren Street Depot, via Chicago, Rock Island & Pacific Railway.

MOUNT OLIVE CEMETERY.

Located at the suburb of Dunning, nine miles west of the City Hall, on the Chicago, Milwaukee & St. Paul Railroad. A beautiful cemetery, the burying-place of Scandinavian families.

OHAVEY SCHOLOM CEMETERY.

Located at Oakwoods, Sixty-seventh Street and Cottage Grove Avenue. [See Oakwoods Cemetery.]

WALDHEIM CEMETERY.

Located west from the City Hall, ten miles, on the Chicago & Northern Pacific Railroad. Depot at Harrison Street and Fifth Avenue. Funeral train leaves daily at 12:01 P. M. In this cemetery are buried the Anarchists who were executed for participation in the Haymarket plot.

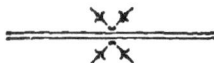

The Libraries.

The first successful effort toward establishing a public library in Chicago was made by the Young Men's Christian Association soon after its permanent organization in 1841. Up to 1871 it had accumulated some 16,000 volumes which were swept away in the great fire. Since that time, for some reason, this association has made no attempt to establish a library of its own. The Historical Society, which had also a respectable number of volumes destroyed at the same time, has been more persevering and has to-day more than 150,000 volumes of books and a rich store of manuscript relating to the early traditions of Illinois as well as a large collection of autograph letters of men famous in the history of our country.

THE PUBLIC LIBRARY.

The Public Library is located on the third floor of the City Hall. Here will be found one of the largest collections of books for general reading in the United States. This library circulates more books than the library of any other city in the country. It is under the supervision of Fred. H. Hild, whose wide knowledge of books and keen intelligence has enabled him to add greatly to the useful and interesting volumes.

At the present rate of increase the Chicago Public Library will, before the end of the century, be one of the largest circulating libraries in the world. The manner of securing books of reference is very simple. Upon application a slip is furnished you on which you write the name of the book required, which upon presentation to any one of the clerks is immediately furnished you. If you desire to refer to a book on any subject and are ignorant of its name or author you write on the slip Pooles Index which contains a complete list of books written upon every subject. Books of reference are not allowed taken from the rooms. To secure a book for home reading an application must be made out in your name, signed by some citizen of Chicago. If this be accepted, you are furnished with a card which upon presentation entitles you to one book every two weeks.

NEWBERRY LIBRARY.

This library, which is now located on the northwest corner of Oak and State Streets, will during the coming year be moved into its own building now in course of construction at the southeast corner of the streets mentioned. The building will be three hundred feet long and sixty feet wide. It will rank among the finest buildings in the city for beauty of architecture and elaborate finish. A million volumes will find resting place in its spacious rooms. The Newberry Library circulates none of its books. They are used for reference only. It is open to all alike and when the new building is finished every accommodation possible will be furnished visitors in pursuit of knowledge. The library was founded by Walter L. Newberry, an early settler of Chicago, who resided on the North Side. His endowment consisted of real

estate worth at the time of his death some two millions of dollars.
The property has since increased in value to nearly double that
sum, and the income from this vast amount makes possible the
establishment in Chicago one of the most complete reference libraries in the world.

JOHN CRERAR LIBRARY.

When John Crerar died in Chicago in 1890, he bequeathed
from his large fortune more than $2,000,000 worth of property
for " the creation, maintenance and endowment of a free public
library to be called ' The John Crerar Library,' and to be located
in the city of Chicago, Illinois ; a preference being given to the
South Division of the city, inasmuch as the Newberry Library
will be located in the North Division. I direct that my executors
and trustee cause an act of incorporation under the laws of Illinois to be procured to carry out the purposes of this bequest, and
I request that Norman Williams be made the first president thereof,
and that in addition to my executors and trustees the following
named friends of mine will act as the first board of directors in such
corporation and aid and assist my executors and trustees therein,
namely: Marshal Field, E. W. Blatchford, T. B. Blackstone,
Robert T. Lincoln, Henry W. Bishop, Edward G. Mason, Albert
Keep, Edson Keith, Simon J. McPherson, John M. Clark and
George A. Armour, or their survivors. I desire the building to be
tasteful, substantial and fire-proof, and that a sufficient fund be
reserved over and above the cost of its construction to provide,
maintain and support a library for all times. I desire the books
and periodicals selected with a view to create and sustain a healthy
moral and Christian sentiment in the community, and that all
nastiness and immorality be excluded. I do not mean by this
that there shall not be anything but hymn books and sermons,
but I mean that * * * and all skeptical trash and works of
questionable moral tone shall never be found in this library. I
want its atmosphere that of Christian refinement and its aim and
object the building up of character, and I rest content that the
friends I have named will carry out my wishes in these particu-
lars." When the provisions of this will shall have been carried out
this library will be second to none in the city.

ARMOUR MISSION LIBRARY.

A free circulating library located in the Armour Mission at Thirty-third and Butterfield Streets.

CHICAGO ATHENÆUM LIBRARY.

A library for the use of the members of the Chicago Athenæum, in the building of the society located on the south side of Van Buren Street, between Wabash and Michigan Avenues. Open week-days from 8 A. M. to 9 P. M.

CHICAGO HISTORICAL SOCIETY LIBRARY.

Located at 142 Dearborn Avenue, North Side. Here are collected the most interesting historical volumes as well as the writings and correspondence of men prominent in the history of our country. Open daily from 9 A. M. to 5 P. M. Take North Clark Street cable line.

UNION CATHOLIC LIBRARY.

This library, conducted by the Catholic Library Association, is located at 94 Dearborn Street. It has a collection of 28,000 volumes. The rooms, which will accommodate four hundred persons, are pleasant and comfortably furnished. Open from 12 M. to 6 P. M. week-days, and 3 to 6 P. M. Sundays.

The Hotels.

DESCRIPTION OF THE PRINCIPAL AMERICAN AND EUROPEAN HOTELS—THEIR LOCATION, AND HOW TO REACH THEM.

Perhaps no city in the world has so many really magnificent hotels as Chicago. Certainly no other city of its size begins to compare with it in this regard. There are almost two thousand buildings in the city which are wholly or in part given up to the hotel business. Other splendid buildings for hotel purposes are being rapidly built and before the time arrives for the World's Columbian Exposition to open, there will be ample accommodations for a population double the city's present population. All of the better hotels have either been built or remodeled during the last decade, and possess all the modern improvements which tend to the comfort and safety of guests. Fire proof hotels covering half a square and lifting their cornices twelve stories in the air, are no unusual sight in Chicago. Visitors may here find ready accommodations at prices to suit their purse or their inclination.

AUDITORIUM HOTEL.

Elsewhere in this book we have described the wonderful building which under one roof and within its four walls contains the finest opera house in the new world ; a numberless list of offices where gather enough people every business day to form a good sized town ; the tower at its top from which you may gain a birdseye view of the whole city, and on a clear day when the wind is right look sixty miles across the lake to where Old St. Joseph lifts her fruit-crowned hills. Situated almost in the heart of the business district, its massive front towering over the lake and ready to catch the cooling winds fresh from its dancing waters, the Auditorium Hotel offers to the tourist all the advantages of regal splendor combined with natures' charms. It has 400 guest rooms furnished with tasteful elegance, while many of them are rich with decorations. The house is sumptuously furnished throughout. The dining room, which is 175 feet long, and culinary department, are on the top floor, an arrangement which will recommend itself to the reader at a glance. The banquet hall has been pronounced without a rival. Mosaic floors, delicately carved pillars and costly fittings give to the rotunda an oriental appearance. The hotel is managed by the Auditorium Hotel Company, composed of J. H. Breslin of New York, president; H. R. Southgate, vice-president and manager.

GRAND PACIFIC HOTEL.

Located on Clark, Jackson and La Salle Streets, near the center of the city, but a short walk from the principal depots and places of amusement. Across the street from the Clark Street entrance stands the Post-office and the Custom-house. Near the La Salle Street entrance, directly opposite is the Board of Trade building, the Rialto and many more of the handsomest office buildings of which Chicago can boast. The famous Rookery is not a stone's throw away. Two blocks distant is the mammoth wholesale house of Marshall Field & Co., with its great structure of brown granite covering an entire square. The Grand Pacific has long been the headquarters of the Republican party as the Palmer House has been the headquarters of Democracy. When the national delegates assemble to nominate a president the flags of the respective parties are always displayed after this fashion. The total frontage of the Grand Pacific Hotel is about eleven hundred feet and the building covers quite an acre and a half of ground. Its accommodations have recently been increased by the addition of 100 rooms, making a total of 500 guest rooms. The managers of the Grand Pacific have always avoided anything bordering on display in the finishing or furniture of the house. Everything about the hotel is richly solid and subdued. Messrs. Drake and Parker have been so long before the public as hotel proprietors that the memory of man knoweth not the day of their advent. Their acquaintances are legion and the Grand Pacific will never loose in popularity while they continue in the management of its affairs.

THE WELLINGTON.

The Wellington is a six-story and basement stone structure located on the northeast corner of Wabash Avenue and Jackson Street, within one block of the lake front, at the head of the Grand Boulevard system, and only four blocks from the Board of Trade, Post-office and business center. The exterior of the building is handsome and imposing, but it is not until one inspects the interior that he fully appreciates the advantages possessed by the hotel. One of the first impressions received on entering is the refined taste with which everything appears to have been selected. The main corridor and entrance has walls of rich mahogany, ceilings arched gracefully and artistically panelled, and a floor and wainscoting of marble.

To the left of the corridor is situated a handsome, spacious apartment, the wainscoting of which is in mahogany eight feet deep, in which elegant mirrors are set. The furniture is mahogany and the floor is tiled. This room is devoted to a café for gentlemen. On the right of the entrance is another room of the same size used as a café for ladies and gentlemen. This room is finished in old ivory, exhibits a wealth of mirrors, the floor is richly carpeted and the furniture is of handsome mahogany. Both of these rooms are lighted by a profusion of electric lights, so placed, however, as to afford a mellow agreeable light, being in rows at the top of the wainscoting and in circles around the capitals of the columns.

The cuisine of the Wellington is unsurpassed, the cafés supplying the very best of viands and delicacies prepared in the most perfect manner.

Birch and mahogany are the woods in which are finished the ladies' entrance and waiting room, the latter being also beautifully furnished and exquisitely decorated. The gentlemen's room is finished in oak, the furniture being of like material. The floor is marble, and a handsome oak mantel enhances the elegant effect.

The main stairway and passenger elevator land on the parlor floor at the grand promenade, luxuriously furnished, and lighted from a large covered court extending to the roof, with balconies surrounding it on every floor. The grand promenade and hallways on this floor are decorated in the style of the First Empire. The scheme of the decoration is superbly carried out. On this floor are suits of grand parlors, several family suits, dining-rooms so arranged that they can be converted into one room to accommodate eighty or more persons. There are also here a separate dining-room, as well as a club-room and committee-room, each of large size.

The rooms of the Wellington are so laid out that patrons may procure almost any kind desired, either single, alcove, or in suits

CHAMBER OF COMMERCE.

of two or five, and with or without stationary bowls and private baths. Every room is furnished and decorated in the most attractive manner. The furniture throughout is of mahogany, antique oak or cherry. Several of the rooms are supplied with handsome writing desks, fully equipped with writing materials. Every room in the building has gas as well as electricity for lighting, and is also furnished with steam heat. On every floor there are four public bath rooms, for the use of such guests as prefer rooms without connecting bathrooms. These latter—some of which are as large as ordinary rooms—have porcelain-lined tubs, steam heat and electric light, and are finished in hard wood.

Every hall is richly carpeted and is lighted by electricity and gas and heated by steam. All the carpets throughout the house are velvet, Wilton and moquette. It is conducted on the European plan. The proprietors, Messrs. Gage & Wheeler, are gentlemen known all over the land as men of integrity and ability, and it is they who have already placed the Wellington among the very first of America's grand hotels.

THE RICHELIEU.

The Richelieu Hotel is located on Michigan Boulevard, between Jackson and Van Buren Streets. The Richelieu is composed of four separate and distinct buildings, making it absolutely safe to life in case of fire, and is so arranged that guests can walk from one building to the other from each story, as occasion may require. The Richelieu is patronized by people of great wealth, well-to-do persons of culture and refinement. It is one of the most perfectly appointed and elegant hotels in America.

Mr. Bemis, in opening this beautiful house to the public, did more than inaugurate an inn—he dedicated a home. There is not one room from the lowest to the topmost floor that is not like a beautiful apartment in a sumptuous house. The walls are decorated with the finest works of art, the beds are as delicious resting places and as daintily equipped as any couch of rest in the palace of a millionaire.

It is said that the Richelieu combines the ease of boarding with the content and order of a well-ordered and beautiful home.

It is magnificently furnished and appointed from top to bottom, with choice paintings decorating the walls, and the furnishing of each bedroom in the house is such that it can during the daytime be converted into a cozy, charming parlor. The furnishing is complete and in keeping with the luxurious comfort and elegance that are found in every portion of the house, and its china and glassware are unequalled.

THE LELAND.

The Leland Hotel is located on the corner of Michigan Boulevard and Jackson Street facing the Lake Front Park which may yet become a part of the site of the World's Columbian Exposition. It is within easy walking distance of the principal depots and places of amusement. When the new extension to the Leland is completed it will make this the gem of Chicago hotels. It commands a magnificent view of Lake Michigan, and the famous Boulevard Drive. The interior furnishings are elegant. The name itself has always been the synonym for excellence in the hotel line, and it is safe to say that the Lelands are really the princes of hoteldom in America. Warren F. Leland is the proprietor of the Chicago hostelry bearing his name. He gives it his personal supervision, and the guest has the choice of both the American and European plans. The building is fire-proof.

PALMER HOUSE.

The Palmer House, on the southeast corner of State and Monroe Streets, is one of the most centrally located hotels in the city. It has a frontage on State Street, Monroe Street and Wabash Ave., and covers one-half the entire square. It is nine stories high, has 708 rooms, and can accommodate 2,500 guests. The building is fire-proof, and one of the handsomest structures in the city. The Palmer House is conducted on both the American and the European plans.

The grand rotunda is thronged every evening by commercial people, with whom the hotel is very popular. Before it was completed, the original structure was destroyed in the great fire of 1871. The ashes were scarcely cold before work was commenced on it again and continued for a great part of the time night and day until its completion in 1873, when it was formally opened. Potter Palmer, the proprietor, is one of the familiar figures in Chicago history. He has always taken an active part in public benefactions. His residence on the Lake Shore Drive is a veritable castle.

SHERMAN HOUSE.

The Sherman House is located on the northwest corner of Clark and Randolph Streets, directly opposite the Court-house. It is one of the oldest and most popular hotels in the city. It was named after Francis C. Sherman, the first mayor of Chicago, who in an early day had a blacksmith shop on the present site of the hotel. About three years ago the interior of the hotel was remodeled; the rotunda enlarged and beautified, until now it presents an appearance quite as attractive as that of the more modern hotel buildings. J. Irving Pierce, the proprietor, has for many years been identified with the hotel life of Chicago, and the patrons of his hotel are made up mostly from those who make regular visits to the city at intervals of from one to three months, and who find here a homelike welcome.

TREMONT HOUSE.

The Tremont House is located at the corner of Lake and Dearborn Streets, near that quarter of the city given up to the wholesale business of groceries, hardware, etc. It has a patronage similar to that of the Sherman House. The building is of stone, massive in appearance and attractive from its somewhat antiquated style of architecture. During the year of 1890 the entire interior of the house was remodeled at a cost of $50,000. The rotunda, which before was dark, is now one of the lighest and handsomest in the city. The rooms are all large and elegantly furnished; the great dining hall, which is almost square, has lofty ceilings handsomely frescoed; the service is quiet, genteel, and obliging. Messrs. Hurlburt & Eden are the proprietors.

CHICAGO HOTEL.

The new Chicago Hotel, now being built at the corner of Dearborn and Adams streets, will when finished add another to the

9

many wonders of this wonderful city. The building will be built entirely of stone, brick and steel, and will be sixteen stories high. The exterior will present the handsomest features of modern architecture and the interior finished in marble and mosaic of the costliest designs. It will be conducted on the American and European plans.

SARATOGA HOTEL.

The Saratoga Hotel is located on the east side of Dearborn Street, Nos. 155–161, near to the centre of business, railroad terminals, and amusements. It is a European hotel of the first class. A restaurant is attached to the hotel, and guests, if they desire it, may be served with meals in their rooms. The house is furnished in the best style. Office on the ground floor.

ATLANTIC HOTEL.

The Atlantic Hotel is located on the corner of Van Buren and Sherman Streets, directly opposite the Chicago, Rock Island & Pacific and Michigan Central depot. It is a well-kept hotel with medium charges. Being so near the wholesale district, it is a favorite with country merchants, grain and stock men. The house is well furnished and the table excellent. Cummings Bros., proprietors.

BRIGGS HOUSE.

The Briggs House, located on the corner of Fifth Avenue and Randolph Street, has long been a landmark in Chicago. It was one of the first large hotels built in the city, and for many years was among the best hotel buildings in the city. The grander modern structures have overshadowed it, but it still holds a place in popular favor. Charges are moderate. Frank Upham, proprietor.

BURKE'S EUROPEAN HOTEL.

Located on the south side of Madison Street, between La Salle and Clarke Streets. Strictly European. The Chicago Oyster House, a restaurant directly underneath, furnishes convenient dining facilities.

CLIFTON HOUSE.

The Clifton House, conducted on the American plan, is located on Monroe Street and Wabash Avenue, directly opposite the Palmer House. It is convenient to cable lines, amusements, etc. The house contains 250 well furnished rooms.

COMMERCIAL HOTEL.

Located on the corner of Lake and Dearborn Streets. American plan. Respectable and well managed. Rates, $2.00 per day and upward.

CONTINENTAL HOTEL.

Located on Wabash Avenue and Madison Street, in the business center. American plan. Very popular with country shoppers and merchant buyers. Rates moderate. Mrs. Hannah Collins, proprietress.

GAULT HOUSE.

Located on West Madison and Clinton Streets. The leading hotel on the West Side. American plan. Very convenient to Union depot. This is one of the popular hotels with travelers and families. Rates, $2.00 and upward. Rogers & Fall, proprietors.

GORE'S HOTEL.

Located at 266–274 South Clark Street. American or European plans. A splendid fire-proof building, handsomely furnished and centrally located. Gore & Heffron, proprietors.

HOTEL BREVOORT.

Located on the north side of Madison, between La Salle and Clark Streets. Strictly European. One of the best known hotels in the city. It is popular with travelers and merchant-buyers, being situated close to the wholesale and retail districts. George N. Hubbard, proprietor.

HOTEL DREXEL

Located at 3956 Drexel Boulevard, near the entrance to Washington Park and contiguous to the grounds of the World's Columbian Exposition. A family hotel of high standing.

HOTEL GRACE.

Located on Clarke and Jackson Streets, opposite the Postoffice. European plan. A well furnished, high-class house. Edward Grace, proprietor.

HOTEL WOODRUFF.

Located on Wabash Avenue and Twenty-first Street. A first-class family hotel, beautifully situated in a resident part of the city. The hotel has 100 rooms. Rates, $3 to $4 per day. J. W. Boardman & Co., proprietors.

HYDE PARK HOTEL.

Located at Lake Avenue and Fifty-first Street, convenient to the South parks. One of the largest and best furnished hotels in the city. Winter & Milligan, proprietors.

SOUTHERN HOTEL.

The Southern Hotel, located on Wabash Avenue and Twenty-second Street, is first-class in its appointments. The South Side cable line runs directly by the hotel, making it convenient for guests to reach any part of the city. E. A. Bacheldor, proprietor.

VIRGINIA HOTEL.

The Virginia Hotel, located at 78 Rush Street, on the North Side, is a splendid new structure in the modern style. It is finished in the highest style of art. Its rooms are elegantly furnished and the best of everything served at table.

Hundreds of other hotels, both on the American and European plan, are scattered over the city, and the visitor in Chicago cannot fail to find such accommodations as he desires in any quarter of the city. We have attempted to make mention of those only which are the most prominent and are best calculated by their location and surroundings to please the tourist and traveler.

National Banks.

AMERICAN NATIONAL BANK.

Located at 185 Dearborn Street. A. W. Irwin, president; A. L. Dewar, cashier.

ATLAS NATIONAL BANK.

Located at the southwest corner of La Salle and Washington Streets. C. D. Guannis, president; S. W. Stone, cashier.

CHICAGO NATIONAL BANK.

Located at the southwest corner of Dearborn and Monroe Streets. John R. Walsh, president; William Cox, cashier.

COLUMBIA NATIONAL BANK.

Located at the northwest corner of La Salle and Quincy Streets. L. Everingham, president; Zimri Dwiggins, cashier.

COMMERCIAL NATIONAL BANK.

Located at southeast corner of Dearborn and Monroe Streets. Henry F. Eames, president; John B. Meyer, cashier.

CONTINENTAL NATIONAL BANK.

John C. Black, president; Douglas Hoyt, cashier.

DROVERS' NATIONAL BANK.

Located at 4207 South Halstead Street. S. Brintnall, president; W. H. Brintnall, cashier.

ENGLEWOOD NATIONAL BANK.

Located at Englewood, Chicago. J. R. Embrew, president;
W. E. Brown, assistant cashier.

FIRST NATIONAL BANK.

Located at the northeast corner of Dearborn and Monroe
Streets. Samuel M. Nickerson, president; H. R. Symonds,
cashier.

FORT DEARBORN NATIONAL BANK.

Located at 187–189 Dearborn Street. H. M. Hibbard, president; Peter Dudley, cashier.

GLOBE NATIONAL BANK.

Located at the northwest corner of Jackson and La Salle
Streets. Oscar D. Wetherell, president; D. A. Moulton, cashier.

HIDE AND LEATHER NATIONAL BANK.

Located on the southeast corner of La Salle and Madison
Streets. Charles F. Grey, president; D. L. Forest, assistant
cashier.

HOME NATIONAL BANK.

Located at 184 West Washington Street. Albert M. Billings,
president; Henry H. Blake, cashier.

LINCOLN NATIONAL BANK.

Located at 59 North Clark Street. V. C. Price, president; E.
S. Noyes, cashier.

MERCHANTS' NATIONAL BANK.

Located at 80 and 82 La Salle Street. J. C. Blair, president;
John C. Neeley, cashier.

METROPOLITAN NATIONAL BANK.

Located at the northwest corner of La Salle and Madison Streets. E. G. Keith, president; W. D. Preston, cashier.

NATIONAL BANK OF AMERICA.

Located at the northwest corner of La Salle and Madison Streets. Isaac G. Lombard, president; Edward B. Lathrop, cashier.

NATIONAL BANK OF ILLINOIS.

Located at 115 Dearborn Street. Geo. E. Schneider, president; A. H. Hammond, cashier.

NATIONAL LIVE STOCK BANK.

Located at Union Stock Yards, Chicago. Levi P. Doud, president; Roswell Z. Herrick, cashier.

NORTHWESTERN NATIONAL BANK.

Located at 217 La Salle Street. Ebenezer Buckingham, president; Fredrick W. Gookin, cashier.

OAKLAND NATIONAL BANK.

Located at 3961 Cottage Grove Avenue. H. P. Taylor, president; J. J. Knight, cashier.

UNION NATIONAL BANK.

Located at northeast corner of La Salle and Adams Street. J. P. Odell, president; W. C. Oakley, cashier.

PRAIRIE STATE NATIONAL BANK.

Located at 110 West Washington Street. James W. Scoville, president; George Zan Zandt, cashier.

State and Private Banks.

AMERICAN TRUST AND SAVINGS BANK.

Located in the Owens Building, Dearborn and Adams Streets. G. B. Shaw, president; J. R. Chapman, cashier.

BANK OF MONTREAL.

Located at 226 La Salle Street. William Muro, manager.

CENTRAL TRUST AND SAVINGS BANK.

Located at 172 Washington Street. William Holgate, president; Charles Sparre, cashier.

CHEMICAL TRUST AND SAVINGS BANK.

Located at 85 Dearborn Street. Adlai T. Ewing, president; A. J. Howe, assistant cashier.

CHICAGO TRUST AND SAVINGS BANK.

Located at the northeast corner of Washington and Clark Streets. D. H. Tolman, president; P. E. Jennison, cashier.

COMMERCIAL LOAN AND TRUST COMPANY.

Located at 115–117 La Salle Street. James B. Hobbs, president; Charles C. Reed, cashier.

CORN EXCHANGE BANK.

Located in the Rookery Building, at the corner of Adams and La Salle Streets. Charles L. Hutchinson, president; Frank W. Smith, cashier.

DIME SAVINGS BANK.

Strictly a savings bank. Located at 104–106 Washington Street. Samuel G. Bailey, president; J. W. Converse, teller; William Kelsey Reed, treasurer.

FARMERS' TRUST COMPANY.

Located at 112 Dearborn Street. R. Sayer, president; Josiah L. Lombard, vice-president and treasurer.

GLOBE SAVINGS BANK.

Located at 225 Dearborn Street. Charles W. Spalding, president; H. Stuart Derby, cashier.

HIBERNIAN BANKING ASSOCIATION.

Located at the southwest corner of Clark and Lake Streets. John V. Clark, president; H. B. Dox, cashier.

ILLINOIS TRUST AND SAVINGS BANK.

Located in the Rookery Building, southeast corner of La Salle and Adams Streets. John J. Mitchell, president; James S. Gibbs, cashier.

INTERNATIONAL BANK.

Located at 110 La Salle Street. Francis A. Hoffman, president; Rudolph Schloesser, cashier.

MERCHANTS' LOAN AND TRUST COMPANY.

Located at the southeast corner of Washington and Dearborn Streets. John W. Doane, president; Frank C. Osborne, cashier.

NORTHERN TRUST COMPANY.

Located at 217 La Salle Street. Byron S. Smith, President; Arthur Huntley, cashier.

PRAIRIE STATE AND SAVINGS BANK.

Located at 45 South Desplaines Street. Charles B. Scoville, president; George Woodland, cashier.

PULLMAN LOAN AND SAVINGS COMPANY.

Located at 1 Arcade Building, Pullman. George M. Pullman, president; Edward F. Bryant, secretary.

SCHAFFNER AND COMPANY, BANKERS.

Located at the southwest corner of Dearborn and Madison Streets. Herman Schaffner and A. G. Becker, managers.

SECURITY LOAN AND SAVINGS BANK.

Located at 127 La Salle Street. E. R. Walker, president; D. Rankin, cashier.

STATE BANK OF CHICAGO.

Located at the northeast corner of La Salle and Lake Streets. H. A. Haugan, president; John R. Lindgren, cashier.

UNION TRUST COMPANY.

Located at 133 Dearborn Street.

WEST SIDE BANK.

Located at 102 Madison Street. Noble C. Shumway, cashier.

Inebriate Asylums.

Sufferers from alcoholic poison or inebriety are treated at the following institutions:

ALEXIAN BROTHERS' HOSPITAL.

Located at 539–569 North Clark Street. Take North Market Street car.

DR. CHARLES W. EARL'S PRIVATE ASYLUM.

Located at 553 Washington Boulevard (West Side). Take Madison Street cable line.

MERCY HOSPITAL.

Located at Calumet Avenue and Twenty-sixth Street. Take Cottage Grove Avenue car.

ST. JOSEPH'S HOSPITAL.

Located on Garfield Avenue and Burling Street, near North Halstead Street. Take Garfield Avenue or North Halstead car.

INSTITUTIONS FOR THE CURE OF INEBRIETY.

The institutions mentioned above give hospital treatment alone. Those which follow accept patients only who will conform to their rules and treatment for a permanent cure of the disease. These are:

THE MARTHA WASHINGTON HOME.

(Exclusively for females.) Located at Graceland and Western Avenues. Take Chicago & Northwestern train at Wells Street depot, North Side, for Culyer Station, near Ravenswood.

The institution is in charge of Mary F. Felt, matron, but is under the supervision of the Board of Directors of the Washingtonian Home. No person is admitted to the Martha Washington Home without first making application to the committee of admission of the Washington Home Association. Residents of Cook County who are unable to pay charges may be admitted free on recommendation of the committee. The regular charges are $10 per week. Strict rules are in force regarding the behavior of the patients, and the breaking of any of these is cause for discharge from the Home. There are generally from fifteen to twenty inmates at the institution. One hundred and fifty patients were treated at this institution during the year 1890. Moral lessons are given daily; and the atmosphere of the place is Christian-like and kindly.

THE WASHINGTONIAN HOME.

The Washingtonian Home is located at the junction of Madi-. son Street and Ogden Avenue, West Side. Take Madison Street cable line.

This is one of the oldest and best known inebriate asylums in the country. It receives $20,000 per year from the city, and in return accepts such patients as are sent to it by the courts free of charge, providing they are not former patients. All other patients are required to pay from $10 to $15 per week, according to room assigned them. The institution is under the immediate supervision of Superintendent Daniel Wilkins and Mrs. Daniel Wilkins, matron. The patients are required to religiously obey all the rules and regulations of the institution under pain of expulsion. Religious services are held in the chapel every morning, and lectures of an hour in length given during the day. No patient may leave the Home without permission. Good, healthful food is furnished, and each patient after the three first days in the institution is assigned a separate room. There is no attempt at medical treatment, unless the patient be suffering from some disorder other than alcoholism. The moral tone of his surroundings and the lessons he learns from seeing the sufferings of others are the means by which his cure is to be effected. Since the establishment of the Home, in 1863, there have been 13,000 persons treated at the Washingtonian Home. Just how many of this number received permanent benefit there are no means of knowing, but that quite a percentage have never returned to their former habits is claimed by the directors of the institution. There are generally from ninety to one hundred patients in the Home. The Home received during the year 1890 $48,140.87 and disbursed $50,830.93.

THE LESLIE E. KEELEY INSTITUTE.

The Leslie E. Keeley Institute for the cure of inebriety, dipsomania and opium habits, is located at Dwight, Illinois, seventy-two miles distant from Chicago. Take Chicago & Alton train at Union depot, Madison and Canal Streets, West Side.

This institution is conducted on a principle entirely new to

DOUGLAS MONUMENT.

reformatories. Here the habit is considered a disease and treated as such. There is no confinement of the patients, but each is allowed his full liberty. Neither is the patient deprived at once of the stimulant he has been in the habit of using. Medicine is given internally and hypodermically, and the patient soon tires of his drug or liquor and voluntarily throws it away. There have been over seven thousand patients treated at Dwight since the cure was put in operation, and it is stated on good authority that only five per cent. have failed of receiving a cure. The drug used is the bi-chloride of gold, and the formula of its decoction is a discovery of Dr. Leslie E. Keeley's.

Gentlemen's and Social Clubs.

ARGO CLUB.

The Argo Club is a semi-aquatic organization. Its club house is situated at the extreme eastern end of the Illinois Centrel Pier, directly over the Lake. The building is shaped like the body of a three-deck steamer, and the windows resemble port holes. Taken all together is very much in harmony with its surroundings. The interior is elegant and there is a kitchen and storeroom in the hold. The main saloon is on the first deck above. Another deck is furnished with state rooms while the hurricane deck at the top furnishes a delightful promenade and lounging place fanned by the lake breezes. The whole is furnished sumptuously. The club numbers about one hundred members.

CALUMET CLUB.

The Calumet is located at the corner of Michigan Avenue and Twentieth Street and is reached by the Wabash Avenue cable line. It occupies an entire building four stories high fronting on both the above named streets. On the first floor are the offices, the grand hall and drawing rooms, café and billiard room. The second floor is devoted to card rooms and a large dancing hall which may be easily converted into a theatre. The third floor furnishes private apartments, and on the top floor are the dining rooms and kitchen. To preserve the early history of Illinois and the city of Chicago is one of the chief aims of this organization. Its Roster contains the names of many of the leading men of the South Side as well as those of noted statesmen and scholars of Illinois. Once a year it gives a reception to old settlers and these gatherings have become historic.

THE CHICAGO CLUB.

This is one of the oldest and most exclusive clubs of the city. It has a handsome club house on the north side of Monroe Street between State Street and Wabash Avenue. The Chicago Club is an outgrowth of the old Dearborn Club, which was among the first organizations of the kind in the city. The building now occupied by the club was built soon after the great fire of 1871. The interior is finished with a quiet elegance which accords well with the substantial character of its members. The membership is limited to 450 residents and 150 non-residents. Admission fee, $3.00. Dues, $80, payable semi-annually.

IROQUOIS CLUB.

The Iroquois Club is distinctly Democratic in politics. Its club rooms at 110 Monroe Street in the Columbia Theatre building are headquarters for the great leaders of the State and city Democracy. No man is at home here who is not a devoted adherent to the Jeffersonian principals. The club rooms are spacious and furnished with comfortable elegance. No club in the world entertains its guests more sumptuously than than the Iroquois. In politics it is a power that is felt in all municipal, State and general elections. The club was organized in 1881 and has now about five hundred members.

UNION LEAGUE CLUB.

The Union League Club is located on Jackson Street and Fourth Avenue, directly opposite the south of front Post Office Square. This club, which was organized in 1879, is patriotic in its aims, and purposes the promotion "by moral, social and political influence the equality of citizenship, the freedom of speech, the purity of the ballot, and loyalty to the Federal Government." It declares for honesty in the administration of public affairs and the conviction and punishment of public officials guilty of betraying their trusts. Although the majority of the club are undoubtedly in sympathy with the Republican party, yet the organization is conducted on strictly non-partisan principles. The club house is a splendid structure: the interior decorations elegant and artistic, and the different departments furnished with princely magnificence. It has a goodly library and an art gallery filled with rare and costly paintings, sculpture and bric-a-brac. The Union League Club is foremost in all great public enterprises which tend to advance Chicago in the eyes of the world, and will contribute largely toward the entertainment of distinguished guests to the World's Columbian Exposition.

UNION CLUB.

The Union Club is situated on Washington Place and Dearborn Avenue, North Side. Take North State Street cars or Clark Street cable line. The wealthiest and most aristocratic club on the North Side. The club house building is among the handsomest of the many handsome structures in this part of the city. Whatever art could suggest in decoration, or money purchase for comfort, are here. The club is strictly a social one and very exclusive as to its membership, which is restricted to 600. Its admission fee is $100 and its annual dues $60.

CHICAGO WOMAN'S CLUB.

The Chicago Woman's Club is an outgrowth of the Fortnightly Club, of which Mrs. Caroline M. Brown was the prime mover. It was organized in 1870, and although one of the distinctly specified aims of the Woman's Club was, from the beginning, philan-thropic work, during the first seven years of its existence it was devoted almost exclusively to literary effort and the theoretical study of reformatory and philanthropic work. In the winter of 1883, however, it was decided that the club should enter upon practical work, and since that time an unselfish battle has been persistently carried on by the club in the muddy pool of moral and political abuses. It was instrumental in founding the " Protective Agency for Women and Children" and in securing funds for its conduct during the first few years of its existence. It established and operates a free kindergarten, the use of a room in the Brighton School being allowed them for that purpose. It was active in securing the en-forcement of the compulsory education law and in providing clothing for destitute children who could not otherwise attend school. The Industrial Art Association owes its existence to the Woman's Club, which has been successfully introduced into the different mission schools of the city. One of the most impor-. tant financial undertakings of the Woman's Club was the raising by the efforts of individual members of $40,000 for the Industrial School for Boys located at Glenwood.

THE CHICAGO ELECTRIC CLUB.

The Chicago Electric Club is composed of electricians and those connected with electric pursuits. Its rooms at 103 Adams Street are very handsomely fitted up. There are reception rooms for members and their friends of both sexes. The club has its own dining hall, billiard and card rooms and a pleasant audience room for club meetings decorated with works of art, paintings and bric-a-brac. There is also a music room with piano and other instru-ments. The names of some of the members are well known in European circles as well as in our own county.

THE ILLINOIS CLUB.

The Illinois Club is the fashionable social organization of the West Side, its membership being composed principally of promi-nent business men who are residents of that section of the city.

The club was organized in April, 1878, and occupies a two-story stone front mansion at 154 South Ashland Avenue, one of the finest of the West Side thoroughfares. The furnishing throughout—billiard, card and reading rooms, parlors and all other apartments—is both elegant and substantial; the decoration is of a highly artistic order. The walls are hung with many choice works of art from the most noted studios of Europe and America. The receptions and musicales given by the club are delightful entertainments, and the club house is thronged with representatives of the world of fashion on such occasions. The membership fee is $100, and the annual dues $40.

THE FORTNIGHTLY CLUB OF CHICAGO.

The Fortnightly Club of Chicago meets on the first and third Fridays of each month at 2:30 P. M. at Art Institute, Michigan Avenue and Van Buren Street. It was originally organized as a Woman's Club in 1873 by Mrs. Kate Newell Doggett, but is now devoted to social intercourse and intellectual culture. A thorough knowledge of the subject to be treated at each meeting is necessary. Each writer has a year in which to master the subject she is to present. The work of the club for the year is divided into two courses, the continuous course of study and the miscellaneous course. A committee of five members takes charge of the continuous course which is represented by a paper at one of the two meetings that occur each month, and another committee of the same number directs the miscellaneous course, which presents a paper on the alternate day. At each of the meetings a discussion under appointed leaders follows the paper. Tea and cake are served and a delightful social hour closes the meeting. The membership of "The Fortnightly of Chicago" is limited to 175. The initiation fee and also the yearly dues are $12. The officers are: President, Mrs. Charles D. Hamill; vice-presidents, Mrs. Otto H. Matz and Mrs. H. M. Wilmarth; corresponding secretary, Mrs. Henry B. Stone; recording secretary, Mr. F. H. Gardiner; treasurer, Mrs. B. F. Ayer.

10

HARVARD UNIVERSITY CLUB.

This club is composed of graduates of Harvard University who are residents of Chicago. It has no club house but gives an annual entertainment and banquet at the Auditorium Hotel, where it entertains the graduates and officers of the Harvard University.

HYDE PARK SUBURBAN CLUB.

The Hyde Park Suburban Club is located at the corner of Washington Avenue and Fifty-first Street in Hyde Park Center. Take Illinois Central train, foot of Randolph or Van Buren Streets. Officers, President, Judge Van H. Higgins; vice-president, B. F. Ray; secretary, W. P. Griswold; treasurer, C. A. Mallory; directors, Hamilton B. Bogue, L. P. Harvey, Charles H. Hunt, William H. Kerr, W. V. O'Brien, W. L. Pearce, Barton Sewell, A. W. Wheeler and Geo. L. Warner. The club has a handsome building, well fitted for pleasure and comfort. It is strictly a gentlemen's club and nothing is neglected which could add to the æsthetic or animal nature of its members. A neat café, billiard room, card rooms, art gallery, and a spacious reception hall, all finished in antique oak, make a handsome interior. The building was designed and built for the special purposes of this club. It was dedicated in 1890.

IRISH AMERICAN CLUB.

The Irish American Club was organized May, 1880, with a charter membership of 100. It has pleasant quarters at 40 Dearborn Street. The club is officered as follows: President, M. B. Harley; vice-president, Thomas H. Cannon; financial secretary, John B. Heanley; secretary, Joseph J. Duffy; treasurer. N. D. Laughlin. Admission fee, $25. Annual dues, $20. This club is strictly non-partisan and non-sectarian, and is composed of some of the leading Irishmen and Irish Americans in the city. The club rooms are handsomely fitted up. Receptions are fre quently given. ·

THE LAKESIDE CLUB.

Located on Indiana Avenue, between Thirty-first and Thirty-second Streets. Take Indiana Avenue car, via Wabash cable line. The club house, a modern building of brick and stone, containing three stories and a basement, is owned by the organization. The billiard room, café, bowling alley, private supper room and dining room, capable of seating 400 guests, are located in the basement; on the first floor are the ladies' and gentlemen's parlors and reception room, drawing rooms, and an assembly and dancing room fifty-five feet wide by one hundred feet long; in the second story are the card rooms and gymnasium; in the third story are private rooms and servants' apartments. Admission fee, $50; annual dues $40.

THE KENWOOD CLUB.

The Kenwood Club is located at Forty-seventh Street and Lake Avenue, Kenwood. Take Illinois Central train at Randolph or Van Buren Street depot. It is a social and family club and ladies and other members of the family are entitled to privileges. A bowling alley, dining-room and kitchen are in the basement; the hall, office, reception and dancing hall are on the first floor; on the second floor are the card rooms, billiard room, reading room, library, ladies' and gentlemen's dressing rooms, etc. The officers are: Edwin F. Bayley, president; William S. Seaverns, vice-president; Charles B. Vankirk, second vice-president; Harry B. Black, treasurer; Charles C. Whittiker, secretary. The board of directors is composed of C. B. Bouton, John S. Belden, William T. Brown, Ed. R. Woodle, W. T. Whetmore, T. S. Fauntleroy, J. Frank Aldrich and F. H. McClure. Admission fee $100; annual dues, $40.

THE EVANSTON COUNTRY CLUB.

This is a summer social organization of the suburb of Evanston. The club house is situated in the midst of beautiful grounds, on Hinman Avenue and Clark Street, close to Lake Michigan and is known as the "Shelter." The club gives frequent receptions, band concerts, boating parties, etc., during the season. The mem-

bership is about 300 equally divided between ladies and gentlemen.
The officers are: President, Marshall M. Kirkman; vice-presidents, William E. Stockton and Frank Elliott; treasurer, Nicho-
las J. Iglehart; secretary. Edwin F. Brown. The directorate is
composed of twenty ladies and eleven gentlemen. The badge of
the club, a four-leaf clover, is worn by many of Chicago's prominent business men.

THE LA SALLE CLUB.

The La Salle is prominent among the wealthy and aristocratic
West Side social organizations. It is located at 252 Monroe
Street and is easily reached by the Madison Street cable line.
The club house is a marble front building with a frontage of 125
feet and a depth of ninety-five feet. A recent addition of 48 by 125
feet gives the club roomy quarters. In the basement are the lunch
room, café, cigar stand, gymnasium and bowling alley. A large
hall, two parlors, a reading room, and a billiard room occupy the
first floor; on the second floor is a large assembly hall and several
card rooms; private apartments and the servants' quarters occupy
the upper story. The admission fee is $50 and annual dues $20.

NEWSBOYS' CLUB.

The Newsboys' Club is located in the Imperial building, 252–
260 South Clark Street. It has pleasant rooms, a library of about
600 volumes, games and amusements. The members are quite as
proud of their quarters as their more wealthy neighbors. Good
character is the essential recommendation to membership in this
club. Its officers are: Miss J. P. Miller, president; Miss Sands,
vice-president; Miss Rutherford, recording secretary; Miss Old-
ham, corresponding secretary; Miss Barker, treasurer, and Misses
Pearson and Miss Castle, librarians.

THE STANDARD CLUB.

The Standard Club is located on Michigan Avenue and Thir-
teenth Street. Take Wabash Avenue cable line. The leading
Hebrew club of the city. It was organized in 1869 and occupies

one of the most elegant and complete club houses in Chicago. In the basement are the bowling alleys, gymnasium, etc.; on the first floor are the parlors, library, café, billiard room, etc.; on the second floor are ladies' parlors and retiring rooms, and three dining rooms; on the third floor is the assembly and ball room, with theatrical appointments. The club is richly furnished. Its membership is limited to three hundred and fifty. Admission fee, $100; annual dues, $80. Officers: President, Joseph Spiegel; vice-president, M. Bensinger : treasurer, Abr. G. Becker; financial secretary, Bernard Mergentheim; recording secretary, N. Greenefelder. Directors: M. Selz, M. Hirsh, H. Nathan, J. R. Wineman, A. M. Snydacker, N. J. Schmaltz, H. Elson, M. Born, Adolph Loeb, H. Hepner.

THE SUNSET CLUB.

The Sunset Club is an association of professional and business men, which meets periodically for the purpose of discussing some question of current interest and listening to the reading of papers on important national or local subjects by members of the club.

THE WAH NAH TON CLUB.

The Wah Nah Ton Club is a Chicago Democratic club, something after the style of the Tammany of New York City. Committees: At large—General John C. Black, Allen C. Durborow, Jr., John P. Hopkins, J. W. Richards, William H. Barnum, William J. English, William C. Walsh, Henry T. Murray, M. J. Kearney, Benjamin F. Ely, Henry P. Fleming, John S. Cooper, Robert J. Smith, James S. Thomas, Jacob Stainer, Owen Murray, N. A. Cremer, Frank E. Kennedy. Wards—Harry Wilkinson, John C. Schubert, Charles Kern, William Best, Daniel Corkery, Edward Burke, W. E. McCarthy, William Loeffler, Edward Cullerton, Patrick McMahon, John A. King, James Bradley, Rodger C. Sullivan, H. Olaf Hanson, John Lonergan, Victor Bardonski, William H. Ford, William J. Major, John Powers, W. H. Larkin, George Kersten, James H. Farrell, William H. Lyman, Fred

Greisheimer, Harry Geohegan, Michael Fitzgerald, W. J. Florence, Thomas Kelley, Thomas Gahan, John Fitzgerald, Jesse Sherwood, C. S. Darrow, Dr. J. J. Larkin, F. J. Gaulter.

THE PRESS CLUB OF CHICAGO.

The Press Club of Chicago was organized and incorporated in January, 1880, for the purpose of securing a closer intimacy among members of the journalistic profession in Chicago, and affording them a place of rest and recreation during their unemployed hours. The club rooms are located at 131 Clark Street. The club membership is limited to 250. It has now about 240 members. It is the only unmixed newspaper club in the country. Nobody is eligible to membership who has not been for at least one year prior to his application, connected in a literary capacity with a Chicago newspaper, or who shall not have been engaged in purely literary work for the same length of time. The rooms occupy the entire third floor of the building, and a pleasant café and ladies reception room on the second floor. The club contemplates building a club house of its own in the near future. The last Saturday night in each month is termed "Fourth Night," and is devoted to a reception of the members of the club, their friends, and ladies. Twice each year there is a grand benefit performance in some leading place of amusement, the proceeds of which go to the building fund. Some of the best operatic, dramatical and oratorical talent of both continents has appeared at these entertainments. The membership fee is $25; the annual dues, $20. The club has the portrait of each president done in oil at the close of his term. F. B. Wilkie, one of the main organizers of the club, was its first president. The present officers are: President, William A. Taylor, the *Herald*; first vice-president, Thomas R. Weddell, *Inter-Ocean:* second vice-president, A. T. Packard, Railroad News Bureau; third vice-president, Oliver E. Moody, *Morning News*; recording secretary, William M. Glenn, *Tribune*; financial secretary, Sam. T. Clover, *Herald*; treasurer, Melville E. Stone; directors, Kirk LaShelle, *Evening Post;* John J. Lane, *Mail*; John E. Wilkie, *Tribune*; R. C. Jacobsen, *Hide and Leather*; W. T. C. Hyde, *Times.*

THE PHŒNIX CLUB.

The Phœnix Club is located at Thirty-first Street and Calumet Avenue. Take Cottage Grove Avenue cars. It is composed of young men of Hebrew lineage. The club rooms were secured for five years, and $5,000 has been expended in remodeling and building. There are two large parlors, a library, dining-room, billiard hall, smoking room, and all the requisites of a first-class social club. Card playing and any form of gambling are positively prohibited. Officers: Milton A. Strauss, president; A. J. Briersdorf, vice-president; D. L. Frank, secretary; E. Lowenstein, assistant secretary; and L. A. Nathan, treasurer.

PARK CLUB OF HYDE PARK.

This club was organized in 1868 as a family club. It is located on Rosalie Court, Hyde Park Center. Take Cottage Grove Avenue cable line, or Illinois Central train at Randolph or Van Buren Streets to South Park station. It occupies a handsome building four stories in height. On the first floor are the ladies' reception room, café and hall; on the second floor are the billiard room, card rooms and director's room; the upper room is thrown into an assembly room with boudoirs, etc. The basement is given up to bowling allies, pool room and janitor's rooms. The club has splendid verandas, which make it a most attractive resort in the summer. Admission fee, $50; annual dues, $25.

THE UNIVERSITY CLUB.

The University Club is located in the University building on Dearborn Street and Calhoun Place. Its members are graduates of the various colleges and universities. The entire building above the fourth floor is occupied by the University Club. The apartments are richly and tastefully furnished. There are reception rooms, parlors, billiard room, card rooms, etc., and all the comforts of a modern club house.

THE WASHINGTON PARK CLUB.

This popular club is situated at South Park Avenue and Sixty-first Street. Take Cottage Grove Avenue cable line. It was organized in 1883. It has a commodious Club house, within easy access of the Washington Club racing park, south of Washington Park. It is a combination of the higher class of sporting, country and city clubs, members of nearly all the other leading clubs being connected with it. The club house is handsomely fitted up for the comfort of the members and the ladies of the members' families. Following are the officers for 1891 : President, George Henry Wheeler ; vice-presidents, Samuel W. Allerton, Albert S. Gage, Charles Schwartz, Columbus R. Cummings ; treasurer, John R. Walsh ; secretary, John E. Brewster ; assistant secretary, James F. Howard ; executive committee, the president, the vice-presidents, the treasurer, *ex-officio,* Charles D. Hamill, John Dupee, Jr., Arthur J. Caton, Henry J. McFarland, Thomas Murdoch, J. Henry Norton, John B. Carson ; property committee, John Duyee, Jr., Charles D. Hamill, John B. Carson . house committee, Charles Schwartz, Charles D. Hamill, J. Henry Norton ; racing stewards, Albert S. Gage, Samuel H. Sweet, Henry J. McFarland, John Dupee, Jr., John E. Brewster ; board of directors for 1891, Nathaniel K. Fairbank, Norman B. Ream, Samuel W. Allerton, James W. Oakley, Columbus R. Cummings, Charles J. Barnes, John R. Walsh, J. Henry Norton, Albert S. Gage, Samuel H. Sweet, Henry J. McFarland, George H. Wheeler, Thomas Murdoch, Charles J. Singer,. James B. Goodman, John Dupee, Jr., Wirt D. Walker, John H. McAvoy, John B. Carson, Thomas Cratty, Arthur J. Caton, Charles Schwartz, Charles D. Hamill, John E. Brewster. The admission fee is $150 ; annual dues, $40.

THE WHITE CHAPEL CLUB.

This is one of the most unique clubs in the country and is as widely known as the famous Clover Club of Philadelphia. The club rooms are located in the rear of 122 La Salle Street, fronting on Whitechapel Court. It is a purely social club and its members are men of marked ability in the professional or literary field. This is the test of eligibility. Residents of Chicago are permitted

WASHINGTON PARK, DERBY DAY, 1891.

to visit the club rooms on Saturday, and inspect the extremely unique decorations, when vouched for by a member of the club. It is customary, once a month, to hold a social meeting called a "Symposium," to which guests are invited by the club and by individual members. The initiation fee is $25, and one objection from any member bars an applicant from admission. President, Chas. G. Seymour; corresponding secretary, Hugh Blake Williams, M. D.; financial secretary, Willard C. Thompson; treasurer, Henry Kosters; board of directors for 1889–90, Dr. Frank W. Reilly, Sidney P. Browne, Frederick F. Thompson, Will P. MacHenry, George A. Babbitt, Opie P. Read, Dana L. Hubbard, and Horace Taylor.

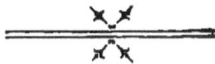

The Daily Newspapers.

The history of the newspapers of Chicago is quite as wonderful as the history of its trade and commerce, its massive buildings or its magnificent parks and boulevards. The daily papers of Chicago rival those of New York in every feature. Individual genius, without which no great American paper was ever established, marks the utterances and shapes the policies of each of the leading dailies of this city. Their opinions on subjects pertaining to the affairs of the nation have as much to do with shaping the policy of political parties as the utterances of the journals of the country's metropolis.

Chicago has twenty-four dailies, 260 weeklies, thirty-six monthlies, five bi-monthlies, and fourteen quarterlies. According to the report of the postmaster-general, the quantity of newspapers mailed at Chicago during the year 1890 equaled the combined amounts mailed at Boston, Cincinnati, Buffalo, Baltimore, and New Orleans. Twenty million pounds of serial matter was mailed for distribution by publishers of this city during the last year. This amount does not include the great number of daily papers distributed throughout the city by carriers and sold on the street by newsboys. The following are the leading daily publications:

THE CHICAGO TRIBUNE.

When Chicago was little more than a village the Chicago Tribune was founded. Its first number was issued on the 10th day
of June, 1847, from a little room in the third story on Lake Street.
To-day, from a handsome building of its own on the southeast
corner of Madison and Dearborn Streets, it sends forth more than
90,000 papers every day: its editorials are quoted in every civilized
country, and its influence second to no newspaper in the United
States.

The founders of the Chicago Tribune were James Kelly, John
E. Wheeler, Joseph K. C. Forrest and Thomas A. Stewart. The
history of the paper from that time until 1854 is one of trials.
The town of Chicago was in its swaddling clothes; people were
poor; facilities for gathering news were few, and oftentimes there
were none at all. In 1854, two important events in the history of
the Tribune had occurred. One was the issuing of a tri-weekly,
the other the publication of Associated Press dispatches, which
association the Tribune assisted in organizing, and of which it remains a member.

Up to this time several changes had taken place in the pro-
prietary interests and management of the Tribune. It was about
this time that Mr. Joseph Medill, now editor-in-chief and principal owner, came to Chicago from Cleveland, O., and purchased an
interest in the Tribune. In 1855 he became managing editor and
business manager and organized a staff. It was at this time that
the Chicago Tribune commenced to assume the features of a
metropolitan daily newspaper. The old press, previously operated
by hand, was removed to make room for a steam-power press.
From that day until the present, the standing question in the
Tribune office has been, "How can we get more presses and faster
to reach the daily increasing circulation?" In 1858 the Tribune
absorbed the Democratic Press of this city, and for a while the
paper was issued as the Press and Tribune.

In 1860 the name of the paper was restored, and in 1861, under an act of the legislature, the Tribune Company was incorporated with a capital of $200,000, the principal stockholders being

J. L. Scripps, William Bross, Charles H. Ray, Joseph Medill, and Alfred Cowles.

Mr. Medill became editor-in-chief in 1873, and has had the controlling interest since. It is under his administration that the paper has reached its present extraordinary success. In 1871 occurred the fire which forms one of the pages of the world's history. On the night of the 8th of October in that year, one-half of the Tribune had been printed. [This was before the present system of printing an entire paper at once was known.] The facts, incidents and other data of the fire had been written and sent to the composing room. But before the hour of going to press the flames had reached the Tribune buildings and driven out every occupant, and a few minutes later the building was in ruins.

Mr. Medill at once procured a temporary building on Canal Street, near Randolph, and the paper was issued from there Wednesday morning, two days after the fire, with a very full account of the greatest fire in the history of conflagrations.

In exactly one year from that date the Tribune had completed its present building and moved into it. It required something more than money to accomplish these wonders. This something the Tribune still retains, and it is that which has caused the daily circulation to travel upward from 2,240 in 1855 to more than 90,000 in 1891, and which has made it one of the greatest advertising mediums in the whole country.

It is not necessary to enlarge upon the history of the Tribune. The project of the World's Columbian Exposition was in part one of the suggestions of its editor, and to its completeness he has contributed most valuable service and counsel.

THE CHICAGO TIMES.

The Chicago Times was founded in the early part of 1854, the first number being issued January 10 of that year. Its original proprietors were James W. Sheahan, Daniel Cameron and William Price. Sheahan was a young law student in Washington, D. C., supporting himself by reporting the proceedings of Congress for the New York *Herald* and writing newspaper articles on various topics. Stephen A. Douglass became impressed with his journalistic ability and urged him to go to Chicago and become the editor of a new paper. Douglass was anxious for the establishment of a paper which would support his views in the contest over the Kansas-Nebraska Bill, then at its height. So in the midst of this great political storm the Chicago Times began its career.

The paper soon began to attract attention, for Sheahan was a most vigorous and forcible writer, but the business management of the concern allowed it to become entangled in financial embarassments and in 1860 it passed into the hands of Cyrus H. McCormick, of reaper fame.

Mr. McCormick found that the talents which had made him rich as a manufacturer of farm implements were not adapted to running a newspaper successfully and he soon became tired of the business, and in 1861 he sold it to Wilbur F. Storey, who had just disposed of the Detroit *Free Press*. Mr. Storey found the affairs of The Times in a rather unpromising shape but he put his last dollar into its coffers and by the force of his great energy, his imperious and invincible will, his audacity and uncompromising aggressiveness, soon put the paper on a paying basis and it was not long until the Chicago Times was one of the best known and most widely read papers in America.

The career of Wilbur F. Storey is a part of the history of the country in the crucial era of its existence. Perhaps with one exception he is the most striking figure in the annals of American journalism. He was the leading force in the West, if not in the country, in developing the daily newspaper into the marvelous gatherer and purveyor of intelligence that it is. The amazing prodigality with which he poured into every corner of the earth money to build up the facilities of his paper for obtaining the news appalled his conservative contemporaries, but like bread cast upon the waters it returned a hundred fold and it was soon found that the golden stream had changed its course and was flowing back. Riches and greatness were the recompense for those years of tremendous energy and tireless effort.

Mr. Storey's fearless persistence in criticising the government during the war led to an attempt by Gen. Burnside to suppress the sheet by a military order, but this was countermanded by President Lincoln and the paper never missed an issue. About 1877 Mr. Storey's health began to fail and he gradually relinquished the active management of his paper. After a physical decline extending over several years he died in 1884.

The Times passed through the various stages incident to property involved in the settlement of a great estate, embarrassed by the contentions of rival claimants and subjected to expensive litigation. It emerged from this to become again involved in a legal controversy concerning its ownership which at this writing (August, 1891), has just been happily settled by a sweeping decision in the federal court which clears away all dispute and leaves the paper free and unhampered.

The fortunes of the paper are now in the hands of Joseph R. Dunlop, editor-in-chief, and Herman J. Huiskamp, head of the business management. Mr. Huiskamp is president of the Chicago Times Company and Mr. Dunlop secretary. These gentlemen bring to their present positions the prestige and potency of success already achieved in life and their active presence at the head of the Times is rapidly placing the paper on its old footing as one of the great newspapers of the world. Mr. Huiskamp before forming his connection with the Times had amassed a fortune in another business enterprise, and Mr. Dunlop has long been conspicuous among the leading journalists of the country.

The Times is an independent Democratic paper, but, as in the days of Storey, it steadily refuses to become the organ of any faction or of any man. Its editor's instructions to his subordinates are: " Print the news and be fair."

THE INTER OCEAN.

The Inter Ocean came into the newspaper field nineteen years ago to satisfy a want manifest to many people in Chicago and the Northwest. The judgment of its founder, the late J. Young Scammon, was confirmed by the support it received from the people, and the rank it took among the leading papers of the country. The competition it encountered from powerful rivals was intense, but it flew the Republican banner, true blue, and won with the

people. A newly established newspaper requires money, and
this one was no exception to the rule. The great financial panic
in 1873, as a supplement to the fires of '71 and '72 that had re_
duced Chicago to ashes, seriously sapped the fortune of Mr.
Scammon. After a varying struggle of two years, in October,
1875, the Inter Ocean was sold, under the foreclosure of a mort-
gage held by Dr. O. W. Nixon, to the Inter Ocean Pub_
lishing Company, a corporation organized especially for publishing it. Then Hon. F. W. Palmer, who was editor of the paper, was
president of the new corporation, and William Penn Nixon, secretary and treasurer. In 1876 Mr. Palmer resigned his position
both as editor of the paper and president of the company. Dr.
O. W. Nixon was made president of the corporation and William
Penn Nixon became editor and general manager, and has since
continued to discharge his laborious dual duties with wonderful
success, as is attested by the growth and power of the paper
under his direction. A few months ago H. H. Kohlsaat, one of
the most successful and enterprising young business men that
Chicago has produced purchased a controlling interest in the
Inter Ocean, and has now assumed the business management as
publisher. William Penn Nixon continues in editorial charge of
the paper that he has established upon sound and patriotic principles, making the Inter Ocean a newspaper in the highest and
best sense of the word. The Inter Ocean has not always been a
great financial success, but through its large circulation has made
itself an influential power. At a low estimate its various editions
have not less than a half a million readers.

A little over a year ago the paper forsook its modest, overcrowded quarters on Madison Street, and moved into its new home,
a commanding seven-story structure on the northwest corner of
Madison and Dearborn Streets. (This corner was purchased by
Mr. Kohlsaat in 1890 at the then phenomenal price of $7,500 per
front foot.) Walter Scott, one of the fathers of the perfecting
press, made a number of his inventions while foreman of the
printing department of the Inter Ocean, and it was due to him
that this paper was the first newspaper in the world to be cut,
folded and pasted without rehandling after leaving the press. It
was the first paper in the West to secure direct cable service from

Europe, and it was the pioneer in adopting electricity as the motive power to run its presses and stereotyping machinery.

An exchange once remarked of this paper: "Among those papers which commend themselves to thinking men for their unflinching advocacy of human rights, their correct position, and their merits, the Inter Ocean is pre-eminent."

THE CHICAGO HERALD.

On the south side of Washington Street, between La Salle Street and Fifth Avenue, stands a building which, though not prominent on account of its size, yet nevertheless attracts the attention of all who come within its vicinity to the exclusion of, in some respects, more pretentious surroundings. Though but six stories high and in the center of a block it possesses an individuality which arrests the interests and commands the admiration of the beholder. Three massive granite arches form an imposing substructure from which rises to a gable surmounted by a tall flagstaff the handsome terra-cotta front. At the base of the flagstaff stands out in bold relief the large bronze figure of a mediæval herald, while within arched recesses above the fourth story windows sculptured figures in bas-relief represent various stages of progress in the art of printing. Statue and figures are highly artistic, and reflect great credit upon the gifted sculptor, Johannes Gelert, whose work they are. A glance reveals the structure as a newspaper building, the new home of the Chicago Herald.

With a frontage of sixty-one feet it runs back one hundred and seventy feet to the alley, while from the ground to the apex of the gable the distance is one hundred and twenty feet. Passing through the entrance the visitor finds himself within a room sixty by sixty, somewhat resembling a large hotel rotunda —the most commodious and artistically decorated newspaper business office in the United States. It richly repays a visit. A gallery to the left in the rear overlooks the press-room in the base ment where ten Scott-Potter web perfecting presses stand in a straight line. An electric light plant in the basement provides for the illumination of the entire building with both arc and incandescent lights. Elevators upon the right side of the business office

lead to the leased offices on the second, third and fourth floors, and
to the editorial floor and the composing and stereotyping rooms
above. Abundant light is furnished by a court sixty by thirty
upon the east side of the building. The composing room upon
the sixth floor (with its high ceiling, perfect ventilation and walls
of white glazed brick) is such an one as has never been seen before. The building throughout is supplied with every possible
convenience for the comfort of employés and tenants, and every
attainable facility for the production of a newspaper. It is said
to be the most complete newspaper structure which has yet been
erected. The marvelous success of the Herald has been achieved
within a single decade. Its existence for several years after its
birth was a struggle, but the ability and industry of its founder
and publisher, James W. Scott, soon started the tide of success
which has given it the largest morning circulation in Chicago and
made it one of the most profitable newspapers of the country.
Democratic but independent in politics, it is recognized as the
most influential exponent of Democracy in the West. The paper
is owned by the Chicago Herald Company, of which James W.
Scott and John R. Walsh are the principal stockholders. H. W.
Seymour has charge of the editorial page, and W. A. Taylor is
news editor.

THE DAILY NEWS.

The Daily News was founded in December, 1875. It has
three distinct publications: the Morning News, the Noon News
and the Evening News. The combined circulation of these editions is 220,000 to 200,000, daily. It is owned by the Chicago Daily
News Company, Victor E. Lawson, editor and publisher. The
News was founded by Melville E. Stone, Percy R. Miggy and
William E. Doughter. Both the latter named gentleman retired
during the first year, Mr. Victor Lawson securing the principal
stock, and Mr. Stone becoming editor. Later he became part
owner of the paper. In 1888 Mr. Stone retired from the paper
and Mr. Lawson, who had from the first year of the existence of
the News been its publisher, took complete management of its
affairs.

Much of the wonderful success achieved by the News is no

doubt due to the ability and genius of Mr. Lawson. The Daily News gives the gist of domestic and foreign news in a condensed form. Its editorials are crisp and forceful, and it boldly strikes at public abuses regardless of party. The Daily News has an equipment of four Hoe quadruple inserting presses with a combined capacity of 160,000 eight-page papers an hour. It has a force of 316 people at work in the different departments, and its numerous editions and extras gives employment to thousands of newsboys during the whole day. Its offices, press and publication rooms are at 123 Fifth Avenue.

ILLINOIS STAATS ZEITUNG.

The Illinois Staats Zeitung is a German daily morning paper. Its office of publication is on the northeast corner of Washington Street and Fifth Avenue. The founder of the Staats Zeitung was Robert Hoeffgen, in 1848. It was issued as a weekly, and the proprietor wrote his own matter, solicited advertisements, set his own type and worked off the paper from the press. Having done this he took the papers on his arm and went about delivering them to his subscribers.

Dr. Helmuth, Arnold Voss, Herman Kriege, edited the paper in turn. In 1851 George Schneider became connected with the paper and it was changed into a daily. It was an ardent supporter of Abraham Lincoln in the memorable Lincoln–Douglass campaign. No paper did more for the success of Mr. Lincoln than did the Illinois Staats Zeitung. The influence of the Illinois Staats Zeitung is felt in the Common Council, the Legislature, and in political campaigns, National or State, as well as in all local elections. More than once it has been opposed by the entire Anglo-American press, but yet has carried the day. In 1861 William Rapp became the editor of the Illinois Staats Zeitung. In the same year Mr. Lawrence Brentano bought out Mr. Hoeffgen's interest and assumed the editorial management. In the fall of that year Mr. Geo. Schneider sold his interest to Mr. A. C. Hesing. Messrs. Brentano and Hesing were associated together until 1867, when Mr. A. C. Hesing purchased Mr. Brentano's interest. In this year Mr. Herman Raster assumed the editorial

11

management, which position he filled with great honor until his
death in Germany in August, 1891. The fire of 1871 claimed the
Illinois Staats Zeitung as one of its victims. Its loss was total,
yet is was among the first of the Chicago dailies to appear, which
it did within forty-eight hours after the fire had ceased. On the
10th of March, 1872, its present magnificent structure was com
pleted and occupied. The cost of the same, with machinery,
presses, etc., amounted to nearly $300,000. The Illinois Staats
Zeitung of to-day is among the German newspapers second only
to the New York *Staats Zeitung* in wealth and circulation, while
in ability, in power and in influence it is not equaled, much less
surpassed, by any German newspaper of the United States. The
combined circulation of the editions of the Illinois Staats Zeitung
amount to over 97,000, being larger than that of any German
newspaper published west of the Allegheny Mountains.

THE CHICAGO EVENING POST.

The Chicago Evening Post, whose first number was issued on
Tuesday, April 29, 1890, assumed from the start a place and
clientage of its own. It is a newspaper of eight pages, complete
in all departments. James W. Scott is the president of the company
which publishes it; Cornelius McAuliff is managing editor, Mont-
gomery B. Gibbs, city editor, and Clinton Collier, business manager.

On Saturday, January 24, 1891, it abandoned its temporary
office and moved into its own new and commodious quarters, the
Evening Post Building, 164 and 166 Washington Street, a handsome, modern structure specially constructed for its own occupancy.
This, within nine months of its foundation, was not the least of the
achievements of the new paper. The building has a frontage of
40 feet on Washington Street and extends 175 feet back to Calhoun Place, having light on three sides and from a roomy court.
The counting room and publication offices occupy the ground
floor and the editorial rooms the upper floors. In the basement
are six Scott presses with a capacity of 15,000 an hour. Each
department is equipped with the most modern devices for speed,
accuracy and convenience. The Evening Post is independent in

FLORAL GLOBE, WASHINGTON PARK.

politics as in all other things. It is pre-eminently a newspaper.
Direct wires connect its office with bureaus in Washington, New
York and other news centers, and carry day by day a larger telegraph service than ever was attempted by an afternoon paper
before.

The Evening Post is, specially aside from its news features,
noted for the fullness and accuracy of its commercial and financial
reports, its intelligence of society and women ; its art, musical
and theatrical features, its sporting intelligence, and for its wealth
of literary and miscellaneous matter. Its numerous illustrations
are easily among the first daily papers of the world. They find a
handsome setting in the typographical beauties of the paper's well
printed pages. In spite of a continually increasing pressure upon
its columns by advertisers, the Evening Post has refused to exceed its limit of eight pages. In that space its finds room to give
a daily summary of the affairs of the world, in form at once complete and readable. The appreciation of Chicago people for such
service is attested by the growing circulation of the Evening Post,
which one year after its birth exceeded that of any other paper
in Chicago, with the possible exception of two.

THE CHICAGO EVENING JOURNAL.

The Evening Journal is the oldest of Chicago newspapers.
William Stewart was its founder, and its first number was issued
April 9, 1839. In 1841 it was sold to the late Judge Buckner
S. Morris. Its publication was discontinued in the fall of 1842,
and a month later the Express was started as its successor. In
1844 the Express was sold to a stock company and started anew
as the Journal. A few months later the paper passed into the
hands of Richard L. Wilson, its editor, and was established on a
firm basis as an organ of the Whig party. At the demise of the
Whig party the Journal became a Republican paper, and has since
that time continually upheld the principles of that party.

In December, 1856, Richard Wilson died, and Charles Wilson,
who was associated with him in the publication of the Journal,
became sole proprietor of the paper. He was appointed secretary
of the American legation at London under President Lincoln, and

during his absence the affairs of the Journal were in charge of his brother, John L. Wilson. Andrew Shuman was editor. During the stirring years of the Civil War the Journal grew rapidly in circulation and influence. The fire of 1871 swept away the Journal office and consumed all its books and papers. With an enterprise worthy of Chicago, the proprietors rented a job office on the West Side that had escaped the flames, and that evening the paper appeared as usual, not having missed a number. In March, 1875, Charles L. Wilson died and the greater part of the stock of the Journal went to his wife and daughter. Andrew Shuman was made president of the company, and continued to control the editorial policy of the paper, with Henry W. Farrar, Mrs. Wilson's brother, as secretary, treasurer and business manager. On the 1st of March, 1880, the company leased the newspaper establishment to Andrew Shuman and John R. Wilson, a nephew of the late proprietor. This partnership was continued until January 1, 1883, at which time John R. Wilson obtained control of a majority of the stock, the officers then being Andrew Shuman, president; W. K. Sullivan, secretary, and John R. Wilson, treasurer. On Gov. Shuman's death, in May, 1890, W. K. Sullivan was elected president and John R. Wilson secretary and treasurer.

The Evening Journal is published at 161 Dearborn Street. It is conservative in all its statements, and is looked upon as one of the most reliable newspapers in the country. Its support comes from the more conservative element of the Republican party.

THE CHICAGO GLOBE.

The Chicago Daily Globe was founded in 1887 by Charles R. Dennett, Andrew Matteson, and A. L. Paterson, of the old Times' staff under the Storey management, and Horace A. Hurlbut, A. T. Ewing, and Walter C. Newberry. On August 7, 1890, it passed into the hands of the present management, with Harry Wilkinson as publisher and editor.

From an early day under the new management the paper began to thrive and to take a prominent place among its older contemporaries. It was bold and aggressive in the discussion of political questions; and an eloquent representative of the Democratic party in Chicago and Illinois. It championed the cause of labor, and many prominent labor organizations voted it their official organ. It is now the only daily paper that gives special attention to the cause of the workingman. While its circulation includes people in all walks, it counts as its constituents what is commonly called the middle class.

The management of the Daily Globe now consists of Harry Wilkinson, publisher and editor; E. E. Wood, business manager; Charles D. Almy, managing editor; Harry L. Beach, city editor. The stock is $250,000; the bonds are all redeemed and the indebtedness is entirely cancelled

THE FREIE PRESSE.

The Freie Presse is a German Republican newspaper published at 90 and 94 Fifth Avenue. It is edited by Richard Michaelis, and is a widely circulated and influential newspaper. Like the News, it publishes several editions daily. It has also weekly and Sunday editions, the latter under the name of *Anheim*, a splendid publication.

THE ABENDPOST.

The Abendpost, a German daily published at one cent per copy, was established in 1889, and has a present circulation of 32,000. It is entirely independent in politics. Its principal circulation is in the city. It has commodious offices at 187 Washington Street. It is published by the Abendpost Company, Fritz Glogauer, president and treasurer, Julius Goldzier, secretary.

GOODALE'S DAILY SUN.

This is a bright daily newspaper published at the Union Stock Yards. Its columns are devoted to the news of special interest to stock dealers and shippers. Harvey L. Goodall is publisher and proprietor.

THE CHICAGO MAIL.

The offices of the Chicago Evening Mail are located at the northwest corner of Washington Street and Fifth Avenue. It is published by the Chicago Mail Company. It was originally the Chicago Press, founded by F. O. Bunnell in 1882. When it became the property of Messrs. Stevens & Dillingham, the name was changed to the Evening Mail. Mr. Frank Hatton and Mr. Clinton Snowdon bought the property in 1885 and gave it the title of the Chicago Mail. In 1887 it was again sold to the Chicago Mail Co., James J. West being the principal stockholder. It was originally a Democratic paper; Messrs. Hatton & Snowdon made it Republican. It is now Democratic in politics.

THE WEEKLY PRESS.

Among the most prominent of the weekly publications are the following:

AMERICA.

America is published at 182 Monroe Street, by the Slason-Thompson Co. It is an illustrated weekly of the highest class. Its editorials are strong, vigorous, and American in every sense. Its cartoons, mostly the work of T. H. Powers, are strikingly original in conception, and drawn with a boldness of outline and freedom in handling which promise a bright future for this young artist. The literature of America is of a high order, and this journal is certain to gain a place in the front rank of our best political and literary publications.

THE ARKANSAW TRAVELER.

The Arkansaw Traveler is one of the widest quoted and best known publications in the country. The genius of its editor, Mr. Opie P. Read, has given the paper an international reputation. It is published at 182 Monroe Street, Opie P. Read, editor; Ed. R. Pritchard, associate editor; P. D. Benham, business manager.

THE CITIZEN.

The Citizen is the leading Irish Nationalist publication of Chicago. It is edited by John F. Finerty. The Citizen is a journal of high literary merit. It has a wide circulation and exerts a powerful influence on many questions of national importance.

FIGARO.

Location of publication office, 170 Madison Street.   A popular society journal of the higher class.   It is ably edited and has
firmly established itself as the organ of society people on all
sides of the city.

GRAPHIC.

Published at the southeast corner of Dearborn and Monroe
Streets.   An illustrated weekly.   George P. Englehard, editor.
The Graphic was the first illustrated weekly newspaper of a general and literary character to secure a foothold in Chicago, although
many such enterprises have been started here.   It is skillfully
managed, well edited, and its illustrations are not only very creditable but are frequently superior to any which appear in the illustrated papers of the East.

INLAND ARCHITECT.

Publication office, 19 Tribune Building.   Artistically one of
the handsomest newspapers printed in the United States.   It is
edited with ability, and every issue is remarkable for some feature
of more than ordinary merit.

THE PRESTO.

The Presto is a weekly journal devoted to the interests of
music in general.   Its business office and composing rooms are in
the Como Block, 323–325 Dearborn Street.   Mr. Frank Abbott is
editor and manager.   The Presto was originally started in Des
Moines, Iowa, in 1884, but removed to Chicago in June, 1888,
when it was a monthly paper; shortly after it became a semi-
monthly, and in the spring of '91 again changed to a weekly
paper.   It is an intelligent and reliable authority on musical matters.

SATURDAY EVENING HERALD.

The Saturday Evening Herald is the recognized organ of polite
society, and authority upon all matters of a social nature.   It was
founded in 1875 by George M. McConnel, Lyman B. Glover and

John M. Dandy.   In 1880 Messrs. Glover and Dandy purchased the interest of Major McConnel, and the firm was known as Glover & Dandy until 1884, when a stock company was formed, Judge E. R. Paige becoming a stockholder.   In 1886 John M. Dandy purchased the interest of Mr. Glover, assuming the editorial and business management of the paper.   The Saturday Evening Herald has a wide and influential circulation among the best families of this city and its suburban towns.   It is a clean, wholesome and readable paper, free from sensationalism and the offensive features peculiar to many so-called society journals, and is held in high esteem by the public and the press.   The offices of the Herald are located in the Grand Opera House, No. 89 Clark Street.

Some of the other periodicals of prominence are The Advance, 155 La Salle Street; American Contractor, 110 Randolph Street; American Engineer, 232 La Salle Street; American Field, 243 State Street; American Israelite, 320 Dearborn Street; American Jeweler, 351 Dearborn Street; Canadian American, 328 Dearborn Street; Catholic Home, 415 Dearborn Street; Catholic Pilot, 81 Randolph Street; Chicago Dry Goods Reporter, 167 Adams Street; Chicago Eagle, 9 Times Building; Chicago Legal News, 87 Clark Street; Chicago Sporting Journal, 125 Clark Street; Chicago Sportsman, 12 Sherman Street; Drovers' Journal, Union Stock Yards; Electric Age, 35 Commercial Bank Building; Electrical Engineer, 225 Dearborn Street: Electrical Review, 163 Randolph Street; Farm, Field and Stockman, 12 Times Building; Farm Implement News, 325 Dearborn Street; Farmer's Review, 215 Dearborn Street; Farmer's Voice, 328–334 Dearborn Street; German American Miller, 35 Clark Street; Horseman, 323 Dearborn Street; Illustrated American, 142 Dearborn Street; Independent, 88 Fifth Avenue; Industrial American, 110 Dearborn Street; Industrial World, 53 La Salle Street; Interior, 69 Dearborn Street; Iron Age, 59 Dearborn Street; Legal Adviser, 76 Fifth Avenue; Le Combat, 441 Centre Avenue; L'Italia, 348 Clark Street; Living Church, 162 Washington Street; Lumber Trade Journal, 94 La Salle Street; Merchant Traveler, 225 Dearborn Street; Musical World, 145 Wabash Avenue; National Builder, 185 Dearborn Street; National Live Stock Journal, 230 Rialto Building; National Weekly, 359 Dearborn Street; De Nederlander, 545 Blue

Island Avenue; Norden, 369 Milwaukee Avenue; Northwestern
Christian Advocate, 57 Washington Street; Northwestern Lum-
berman, 325 Dearborn Street; Occident, 154 Lake Street; Open
Court, 175 La Salle Street; Orange Judd Farmer, 226 La Salle
Street; Prairie Farmer, 168 Adams Street; Railway Age, 205 La
Salle Street; Real Estate and Building Journal, 163 Washington
Street; Sporting Journal, 125 Clark Street; Svenska Kuriren, 26
North Clark Street; The Universalist, 59 Dearborn Street; Union
Signal, 161 La Salle Street.

Hack, Cab and 'Bus Fares.

The traveler coming into Chicago on any train will be approached by one of Parmelee's agents with transfer checks for
baggage. These he will give in exchange for your railroad checks,
and your baggage will be transferred to any other depot or delivered at the hotel you may name within the old limits of the
city. The legal charge for this is fifty cents for one trunk and
twenty-five cents apiece for each additional piece of baggage. For
fifty cents additional he will furnish you with a ticket of the omnibus line, which will transfer you to any depot, or to any one of
the down-town hotels.

Uniformed agents are stationed in every depot whose duty it
is to direct passengers to their destination. Outside of each depot
are carriage, hack, hansom, cab and coupé stands. The fares of
these conveyances are regulated by ordinance. To avoid difficulty the traveler should be particular to make arrangements with
the driver before entering the vehicle. If an overcharge is demanded the fact should be reported to the police. The legal
rates are as follows:

RATES OF CARRIAGE FARE.

For conveying one or two passengers from one railroad depot to another railroad depot......................$1.00
For conveying one or two passengers not exceeding one
mile.. 1.00

For conveying one or two passengers any distance over one
mile and less than two miles $1.50
For each additional passenger of the same party or family.. .50
For conveying one or two passengers in said city any distance
exceeding two miles.............................. 2.00
For each additional passenger of the same family or party.. .50

For conveying children between five and fourteen years of
age, half of the above price may be charged for like distances, but
for children under five years of age no charge shall be made, *provided*, that the distance from any railroad depot, steamboat landing or hotel to any other railroad depot, steamboat landing or
hotel, shall, in all cases, be estimated as not exceeding one mile.

For the use by day of any hackney coach, or other vehicle
drawn by two horses or other animals, with one or more
passengers, per day $8.00

For the use of any such carriage or vehicle by the hour with
one or more passengers, with the privilege of going from place to
place and stopping as often as may be required, as follows:

For the first hour..................................... $2.00
For each additional hour or part of an hour 1.00

Every passenger shall be allowed to have conveyed upon such
vehicle, without charge, his ordinary traveling baggage, not exceeding in any case one trunk and twenty-five pounds of other
baggage. For every additional package, where the whole weight
of baggage is over 100 pounds, if conveyed to any place within
the city limits, the owner or driver shall be permitted to charge
· fifteen cents.

RATES OF COUPE FARE.

The prices or rates of fare to be asked or demanded by the
owners or drivers of cabs, or other vehicles drawn by one horse or
other animal for the conveyance of passengers for hire, are as
follows:

One mile or fraction thereof, for each passenger for the first
mile.. $0.25

One mile or fraction thereof, for any distance after first mile,
  for one or more passengers........................... .25
For the first hour..................................... .75
For each quarter hour additional after first hour........... .20

All such vehicles shall be under the direction of the passenger, from the time he or she call said vehicle until the same is discharged, and will be paid for accordingly.

In the case of a vehicle being engaged by the hour, and discharged at a distance from its stand, the owner or driver shall have the right to charge for the time necessary to return to such stand.

For service outside of city limits, and in the parks, for the
  first hour $1.00
For each quarter hour after the first hour................ .25

Every passenger shall be allowed to have conveyed upon such vehicle, without charge, his ordinary traveling baggage, not exceeding in any case, one trunk and twenty-five pounds of other baggage. For every additional package, where the whole weight of baggage is over 100 pounds, if conveyed to any place within the city limits, the owner or driver shall be permitted to charge fifteen cents.

TABLE SHOWING THE DISTANCE FROM

CHICAGO TO PRINCIPAL CITIES.

CITIES.	Miles.	CITIES.	Miles.
Albany, N. Y.	821	Jackson, Mich.	210
Altoona, Pa	585	Jacksonville, Fla.	1,171
Ashland, Wis.	434	Jersey City, N. J.	911
Atlanta, Ga.	853	Joliet, Ill.	40
Auburn, N. Y.	682	Kalamazoo, Mich.	142
Aurora, Ill.	45	Kansas City, Mo.	458
Baltimore, Md.	854	Keokuk, Ia.	338
Battle Creek, Mich.	175	Kokomo, Ind	139
Bay City, Mich.	316	La Crosse, Wis.	277
Birmingham, Ala.	651	La Fayette, Ind.	120
Boston, Mass	1,150	Lexington, Ky.	373
Buffalo, N. Y.	536	Lincoln, Nebr	541
Burlington, Ia.	206	Logansport, Ind	117
Butte City, Mont.	1,642	London, Ont	397
Canton, Ohio	367	Louisville, Ky	318
Cedar Rapids, Ia	219	Madison, Wis.	129
Chattanooga, Tenn	593	Mansfield, O	293
Cincinnati, O	294	Memphis, Tenn.	544
Cleveland, O.	339	Milwaukee, Wis.	85
Columbus, O.	314	Minneapolis, Minn.	410
Concord, N. H.	1,096	Mobile, Ala.	860
City of Mexico	2,600	Montgomery, Ala.	747
Council Bluffs, Ia.	488	Montreal, Can.	842
Davenport, Ia.	183	Nashville, Tenn.	442
Dayton, O.	265	Newark, O.	347
Denver, Colo	1,025	Newark, N. J.	903
Des Moines, Iowa	358	New Albany, Ind.	317
Detroit, Mich.	285	New Haven, Conn	988
Dubuque, Ia.	172	New Orleans, La.	915
Duluth, Minn.	505	New York, N. Y.	911
Eau Claire, Wis.	312	Oil City, Pa.	497
Elgin, Ill.	36	Omaha, Nebr.	492
Elizabeth, N. J.	898	Oshkosh, Wis.	156
Elmira, N. Y.	697	Patterson, N. J.	954
Evansville, Ind.	287	Pekin, Ill.	160
Fargo, N. Dak.	718	Peoria, Ill.	160
Ft. Wayne, Ind.	152	Philadelphia, Pa.	822
Hannibal, Mo.	313	Pittsburg, Pa.	539
Hamilton, O	269	Port Huron, Mich.	335
Hamilton, Ont.	473	Portland, Me.	1,255
Helena, Mont.	1,569	Providence, R. I.	1,098
Hot Springs, Ark.	777	Pueblo, Col.	1,153
Indianapolis, Ind.	184	Quebec, Can.	1,009

Cities.	Miles.	Cities.	Miles.
Quincy, Ill	263	St. Louis, Mo.............	282
Racine, Wis	62	St. Paul, Minn....	399
Richmond, Ind	224	Steubenville, O..	464
Rochester, N. Y...........	604	Syracuse, N. Y.	684
Rockford, Ill	83	Terre Haute, Ind.........	178
Rock Island, Ill....	181	Toledo, O.	243
Salt Lake City, Utah.......	1,806	Topeka, Kans	559
Saginaw, Mich.....	303	Troy, N. Y..............	840
San Antonio, Tex	988	Utica, N. Y......	733
San Francisco, Cal....	2,450	Vancouver, B. C	2,350
Sandusky, O..............	291	Vicksburgh, Miss.	776
Santa Fé, N. Mex.........	853	Washington, D. C..... ...	811
Scranton, Pa.......	813	Watertown, N. Y.........	'751
Sioux City, Ia	515	Winona, Minn............	297
Sioux Falls, S. Dak	631	Wheeling, W. Va.........	468
South Bend, Ind...........	86	Worcester, Mass..........	985
Springfield, Ill	185	Youngstown, O..........	473
Springfield, Mass.........	931	Zanesville, O............	385
St. Joseph, Mo......	469		

COLUMBUS.

Air, America.

Columbus, thee we sing;
Let now thy spirit wing
 Its radiant flight
From realms unknown to shine
O'er all where all is thine—
The bays of Fame we twine
 For thee to-night.

With lofty purpose thou
Didst thy frail bark endow
 With Jesus' grace;
And lo! the world around
By liberty is crowned—
Columbia! Freedom's ground
 For every race.

Thy consecrated clay
We pile cloud-high to-day
 With grateful bloom;
Thy name and worth are told
In sunny clime and cold;
The new world and the old
 Kneel by thy tomb.

CHARLES EUGENE BANKS.

* Written by request of the World's Fair Commissioners and sung at a banquet given by them in honor of the World's Fair Ambassadors at the Palmer House, Chicago, September 29, 1891.

THOMAS W. PALMER,
President National World's Fair Commission.

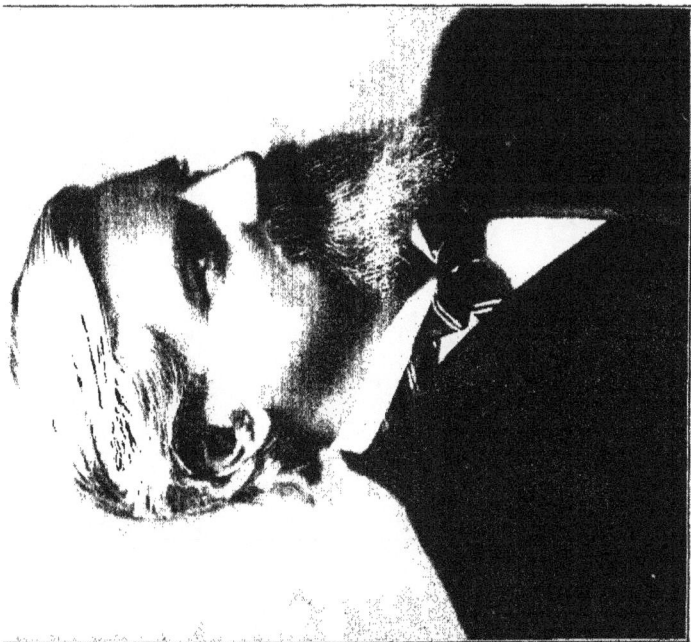

GEORGE R. DAVIS,
Director-General.

THE WORLD'S COLUMBIAN EXPOSITION.

Guide to the Grounds and Buildings, with Full Description of Each.

HE World's Columbian Exposition will mark a new era in the progress of civilization. No event in the past meant so much to the people of its time. Where is it written that the nations of the earth assembled at one place in honor of one man? Not only will the peoples of every country mingle together in the beautiful grounds dedicated to this exposition in Chicago, but they will bring with them the richest products of every clime. The useful, the curious and the beautiful will be there in magnificent display. Whatever movable thing the world has that can please the eye, delight the ear, or instruct the mind will find its way to this splendid celebration.

The honor of having first suggested the idea of holding a World's Fair to celebrate the four hundredth anniversary of the discovery of the New World by Columbus is claimed by many, and it is not easy to positively assign the honor to any one. However, about six years ago, Mr. E. George Mason, of Chicago, sent a communication to the annual meeting of the Directors of the Chicago Exposition Co., suggesting the advisability of celebrating in some proper way the four hundredth anniversary of the discovery of America. After some discussion the matter was allowed to drop.

Subsequently in various newspapers throughout the country the question of such a celebration was occasionally mentioned

and discussed. About two years ago the discussion became
general, and Joseph Medill, of Chicago, very actively fostered
the idea.

It was immediately taken up by the whole country, and
shortly thereafter a hot rivalry sprang up among the various
cities for the honor of providing a site for a great World's Fair,
to be held in 1892. Under the stimulus of this rivalry the
project began to assume greater and more magnificent proportions, and when the question came up for decision in the National
Congress it was found best to provide for a great International
Universal Exposition, to be held during the summer of 1893,
the date of the discovery of America, October 12, 1492, to be
celebrated by appropriate ceremonies.

The act of Congress, which definitely selected Chicago as the
city in which the Exposition should be held and which fixed the
dates of the celebration to be held in 1892 and of the formal opening and closing of the Exposition in 1893. was approved by the
President of the United States April 25, 1890.

The act provides that :

WHEREAS, It is fit and appropriate that the four hundredth anniversary
of the discovery of America be commemorated by an exhibition of the resources
of the United States of America, their development, and of the progress of civilization in the New World; and

WHEREAS, Such an exhibition should be of a national and international
character, so that not only the people of our Union and this continent, but
those of all nations as well, can participate, and should therefore have the sanction of the Congress of the United States :   Therefore,

*Be it enacted by the Senate and House of Representatives of the United
States of America in Congress assembled,*   That an exhibition of arts, industries, manufactures, and products of the soil, mine, and sea shall be inaugurated
in the year eighteen hundred and ninety-two, in the city of Chicago, in the
State of Illinois, as hereinafter provided.

After providing for the appointment of a National Commission,
Section 5 of the act recites :

That said commission be empowered in its discretion to accept for the
purpose of the World's Columbian Exposition such site as may be selected and
offered and such plans and specifications of buildings to be erected for such
purpose at the expense of and tendered by the corporation organized under
the laws of the State of Illinois, known as "The World's Exposition of eighteen

hundred and ninety-two." *Provided*, That said site so tendered and the buildings proposed to be erected thereon shall be deemed by said commission adequate to the purpose of said exposition : *And Provided*, That said commission shall be satisfied that the said corporation has an actual bona fide and valid subscription to its capital stock which will secure the payment of at least five millions of dollars, of which not less than five hundred thousand dollars shall have been paid in, and that the further sum of five million dollars, making in all ten million dollars, will be provided by said corporation in ample time for its needful use during the prosecution of the work for the complete preparation for said exposition.

Sections 8 to 11 inclusive provide :

That the President is hereby empowered and directed to hold a naval review in New York Harbor, in April eighteen hundred and ninety-three, and to extend to foreign nations an invitation to send ships of war to join the United States Navy in rendezvous at Hampton Roads and proceed thence to said review.

SEC. 9. That said commission shall provide for the dedication of the buildings of the World's Columbian Exposition in said city of Chicago on the twelfth day of October, eighteen hundred and ninety-two, with appropriate ceremonies, and said exposition shall be open to visitors not later than the first day of May, eighteen hundred and ninety-three, and shall be closed at such a time as the commission may determine, but not later than the thirtieth day of October thereafter.

SEC. 10. That whenever the President of the United States shall be notified by the commission that provision has been made for the grounds and buildings for the uses herein provided for, and there has also been filed with him by the said corporation, known as "The World's Exposition of eighteen hundred and ninety-two," satisfactory proof that a sum not less than ten million dollars, to be used and expended for the purposes of the exposition herein authorized, has in fact been raised or provided for by subscription or other legally binding means, he shall be authorized, through the Department of State, to make proclamation of the same, setting forth the time at which the exposition will open and close, and the place at which it will be held ; and he shall communicate to the diplomatic representatives of foreign nations copies of the same, together with such regulations as may be adopted by the commission, for publication in their respective countries, and he shall, in behalf of the Government and people, invite foreign nations to take part in the said exposition and appoint representatives thereto.

SEC. 11. That all articles which shall be imported from foreign countries for the sole purpose of exhibition at said exposition, upon which there shall be a tariff or customs duty, shall be admitted free of payment of duty, customs fees, or charges under such regulations as the Secretary of the Treasury shall prescribe ; but it shall be lawful at any time during the exhibition to sell for delivery at the close of the exposition any goods or property imported for and actually on exhibition in the exposition buildings or on its grounds, subject to such regulations for the security of the revenue and for the collection of the import duties as the Secretary of the Treasury shall prescribe: *Provided*, That all such articles when sold or withdrawn for consumption in the United States shall be subject to the duty, if any, imposed upon such articles by the revenue laws in force at the date of importation, and all penalties prescribed by law shall be applied and enforced against such articles, and against the persons who may be guilty of any illegal sale or withdrawal.

In accordance with the provisions of Section 5, the task of raising the required $5,000,000 was proceeded with. Pending the action of Congress prominent citizens of Chicago had formed the Exposition Company and invited subscriptions at the rate of $10 per share. The responses were quick and generous, and 29,374 shareholders subscribed $5,467,350. The legislature of the State authorized the city of Chicago to bond itself for $5,000,000 in aid of the Fair, the bonds to be available as soon as $3,000,000 of the capital stock had been paid in.

In view of these facts the President of the United States issued the following proclamation, December 24, 1890:

By the President of the United States of America:

A PROCLAMATION.

WHEREAS, Satisfactory proof has been presented to me that provision has been made for adequate grounds and buildings for the uses of the World's Columbian Exposition, and that a sum not less than $10,000,000, to be used and expended for the purposes of said Exposition, has been provided in accordance with the conditions and requirements of Section 10 of an Act entitled "An Act to provide for celebrating the four hundredth anniversary of the discovery of America by Christopher Columbus by holding an International Exhibition of arts, industries, manufactures and the products of the soil, mine and sea, in the city of Chicago, in the State of Illinois," approved April 25, 1890.

Now, THEREFORE, I, Benjamin Harrison, President of the United States, by virtue of the authority vested in me by said Act, do hereby declare and proclaim that such International Exhibition will be opened on the first day of May, in the year eighteen hundred and ninety-three, in the city of Chicago, in the State of Illinois, and will not be closed before the last Thursday in October of the same year.

And in the name of the Government and of the People of the United States, I do hereby invite all the nations of the earth to take part in the commemoration of an event that is pre-eminent in human history and of lasting interest to mankind by appointing representatives thereto, and sending such exhibits to the

World's Columbian Exposition as will most fitly and fully illustrate their resources, their industries and their progress in civilization.

IN TESTIMONY WHEREOF I have hereunto set my hand and caused the
seal of the United States to be affixed.

Done at the city of Washington this twenty-fourth day of December, in the
year of our Lord one thousand eight hundred and ninety, and the Independence of the United States the one hundred and fifteenth.

By the President: BENJ. HARRISON.

    JAMES G. BLAINE, *Secretary of State.*

The management of the World's Columbian Exposition includes four organizations:

  1. National Commission (authorized by Act of Congress).

  2. World's Columbian Exposition (organized under laws of the State of
Illinois).

  3. Board of Lady managers (authorized by Act of Congress).

  4. World's Congress Auxiliary.

The National Commission, which is a supervisory body, is
composed of eight commissioners-at-large, with alternates appointed by the President, and two commissioners and two alternates from each State and Territory and the District of Columbia,
appointed by the President on nomination of their respective
Governors. This commission has held four sessions, and has now
practically delegated its authority to eight of its members who
constitute a Board of Reference and Control, and who act with a
similar number selected from the World's Columbian Exposition.

The World's Columbian Exposition, as its corporate name
reads, is composed of forty-five citizens of Chicago, elected annually by the stockholders of the organization. To this body falls
the duty of raising the necessary funds and of the active management of the Exposition. Its committees supervise the various
departments into which the work has been divided.

The Board of Lady Managers is composed of two members,
with alternates, from each State and Territory and nine from the
city of Chicago. It has supervision of women's participation in
the Exposition and of whatever exhibits of women's work may
be made.

The World's Congress Auxiliary is organized to provide for
and facilitate the holding of a series of congresses of thinkers, or

to supplement the exposition that will be made of the material progress of the world by a portrayal of the achievements in science, literature, education, government, jurisprudence, morals, charity, art, religion and other branches of mental activity.

The Director-General is the chief executive officer of the Exposition, and the work is divided into the following great departments:

A—Agriculture, Food and Food Products, Farming Machinery and Appliances.

B—Viticulture, Horticulture and Floriculture.

C—Live Stock, Domestic and Wild Animals.

D—Fish, Fisheries, Fish Products and Apparatus of Fishing.

E—Mines, Mining and Metallurgy.

F—Machinery.

G—Transportation Exhibits—Railways, Vessels, Vehicles.

H—Manufactures.

J—Electricity and Electrical Appliances.

K—Fine Arts—Pictorial, Plastic and Decorative.

L—Liberal Arts, Education, Engineering, Public Works, Architecture, Music and the Drama.

M—Ethnology, Archæology, Progress of Labor and Invention—Isolated and Collective Exhibits.

N—Forestry and Forest Products.

O—Publicity and Promotion.

P—Foreign Affairs.

DIRECTORY OF THE EXPOSITION.

Following are the chief officers of the Exposition Executive:

DIRECTOR-GENERAL—George R. Davis.

NATIONAL COMMISSION—President, Thomas W. Palmer; Vice-Presidents, Thomas W. Waller, M. H. de Young, D. B. Penn, G. W. Allen, Alex. B. Andrews; Secretary, John T. Dickinson.

WORLD'S COLUMBIAN EXPOSITION—President, W. T. Baker; Vice-Presidents, Thomas B. Bryan, Potter Palmer; Secretary, J. A. Kingwell; Solicitor-General, Benjamin Butterworth; Treasurer, A. F. Seeberger; Auditor, W. K. Ackerman; Chief of Construction, D. H. Burnham.

JOINT BOARD OF REFERENCE AND CONTROL—From the Commission,

Thos. W. Palmer, Michigan, President; James A. McKenzie, Kentucky; Geo. V. Massey, Delaware; William Lindsay, Kentucky; Michael H. de Young, California; Thos. M. Waller, Connecticut; Elijah B. Martindale, Indiana; J. W. St. Clair, West Virginia. From the Directors, Lyman J. Gage, presidents Thos. B. Bryan, Potter Palmer, Ferd. W. Peck, Edward T. Jeffrey, Edwin Walker, Frederick S. Winston, W. T. Baker.

CHIEFS OF DEPARTMENTS—
   Publicity and Promotion, M. P. Handy.
   Agriculture, W. T. Buchanan.
   Installation, Joseph Hirst.
   Electricity, Prof. John P. Barrett.
   Ethnology, Prof. F. W. Putnam.
   Fish and Fisheries, Capt. J. W. Collins.
   Fine Arts, Halsey C. Ives.
   Traffic Manager, E. E. Jaycox.
   Consulting Engineer, A. Gotleib.
   Consulting Landscape Architect, F. L. Olmstead.

BOARD OF ARCHITECTS—
   R. M. Hunt, New York, Chairman.
   Geo. B. Post, New York.
   McKim, Mead & White, New York.
   Peabody & Stearns, Boston.
   Van Burnt & Howe, Kansas City.
   W. L. B. Jenny, Chicago.
   S. S. Beeman, Chicago.
   Alder & Sullivan, Chicago.
   Henry Ives Cobb, Chicago.
   Burling & Whitehouse, Chicago.
   Holabird & Roche, Chicago.

BOARD OF LADY MANAGERS—
   President, Mrs. Bertha H. Palmer.
   Secretary, Mrs. Susan Gale Cooke.

WORLD'S CONGRESS AUXILIARY—
   President, Charles C. Bouner.
   Vice-President, Thomas B. Bryan.
   Secretary, Benjamin Butterworth.
   Treasurer, Lyman J. Gage.

Lyman J. Gage, of the First National Bank, the most solid financial institution of its kind west of New York, was president of the Exposition Company during its first year. In his report, made April 1, 1891, he presented the following estimate of the company's resources and expected expenditures, adding that he regarded his estimate of the resources a conservative one and that of the expenditures liberal beyond expectation:

RESOURCES.

Available as required from stock...........................	$ 5,000,000
From the city of Chicago................................	5,000,000
	10,000,000
Prospectively available from gate receipts................	7,000,000
From concessions and privileges........................	1,000,000
From salvage...	3,000,000
	$21,000,000

ESTIMATED EXPENDITURES.

For grounds and buildings.........................	$12,766,890
For administration......	3,308,563
For operating expenses, May to November, 1893...........	1,550,000
	$17,625,453

A fuller statement, however, of the amount of money which will be expended on the World's Columbian Exposition begins to reveal the enormous scope of the project. The various states of the Union have made appropriations of money to be expended in buildings and special exhibits as follows:

Arizona...	$ 25,000
California..	300,000
Colorado...	100,000
Connecticut..	25,000
Delaware...	10,000
Idaho..	20,000
Illinois...	800,000
Indiana	75,000
Iowa...	50,000
Maine..	40,000
Massachusetts...	75,000
Michigan	100,000
Minnesota..............................:................	50,000
Missouri	150,000
Montana..	50,000
Nebraska...	50,000
New Hampshire...	25,000
New Jersey...	20,000
New Mexico..	25,000
North Carolina...	25,000
North Dakota...	25,000

STATE APPROPRIATIONS—*Continued.*

Ohio...$ 100,000
Pennsylvania 300,000
Rhode Island 25,000
Vermont.............. 15,000
Washington.. 100,000
West Virginia... 40,000
Wisconsin... 65,000
Wyoming 30,000

$3,070,000

Several of the States above named will certainly appropriate additional sums.   Those which have not, will no doubt, each and all, appropriate sums of equal average, aggregating probably six million dollars.

This will be further increased by liberal sums from many cities, counties, corporations, manufacturers, etc., etc., to a grand total of upwards of ten millions of dollars.

The assurances of co-operation by foreign powers are ample, and place beyond question the international character of the Exposition.   Up to June 15, 1891, formal and official acceptances were received from France, Great Britain, Germany, Spain, Japan, China, Mexico, Peru, Honduras, Salvador, Costa Rica, U. S. of Colombia, Cuba, Guatemala, Jamaica, Venezuela, Dominican Republic, Turkey, Denmark.

At the same time positive, although not official, assurances of acceptance had been received from Egypt, Morocco, Nicaragua, Ecuador, Brazil, Hayti, British Columbia, etc., etc.   Estimates only can be made of the amount that will be expended by these countries, but the most conservative estimates yet made indicate that the money to be expended from all quarters at the Fair will approach $40,000,000.

Money having thus been secured in unparalleled amount it became imperative that both the site and the buildings to be erected should also surpass in grandeur and magnitude, all previous Expositions.   In this connection the following table is of interest. It is to be noted that the estimates for the World's Columbian Exposition are made on a most conservative basis:

COMPARATIVE TABLE OF WORLD'S FAIRS.

Where Held and Year.	Site, Acreage.	Square Feet Under Roof.	No. of Exhibi- tors.	No. of Admis- sions.	No. of Days Open.	Receipts.	Guarantee.	Cost.
London, 1851.	21½	700,000	17,000	6,039,195	144	$1,780,000	English Government.	....
Paris, 1855,	24½	1,866,000	22,000	5,162,330	200	644,100	French Government.	$5,000,000
London, 1862,	23½	1,291,800	28,653	6,211,103	121	1,644,260	English Government.	2,300,000
Paris, 1867,	87	3,371,904	52,000	10,200,000	217	2,103,675	French Government.	....
Vienna, 1873,	280	....	42,000	7,254,687	186	....	$4,500,000	7,850,000
Phila., 1876,	236	1,688,858	30,864	9,910,996	159	3,813,724	2,500,000	....
Paris, 1878,	100	1,858,778	40,366	16,032,725	191	2,531,650	....	....
Paris, 1889,	173	1,000,000	55,000	28,149,353	183	8,300,000	3,600,000	6,500,000
Chicago, 1893,	1,037	5,000,000	......	....	179	....	26,500,000	....

The Chicago guarantee as estimated above is made up as follows:

Resources of local corporation	$21,000,000
Government appropriation	1,500,000
The States, already voted	1,775,000
The States, to be voted	1,225,000
Cities and trades	1,000,000
Total	$26,500,000

The Exposition site is a magnificent one. No World's Fair ever had one surpassing it. It embraces Jackson and Washington

M. P. HANDY,
Chief Department of Publicity and Promotion,

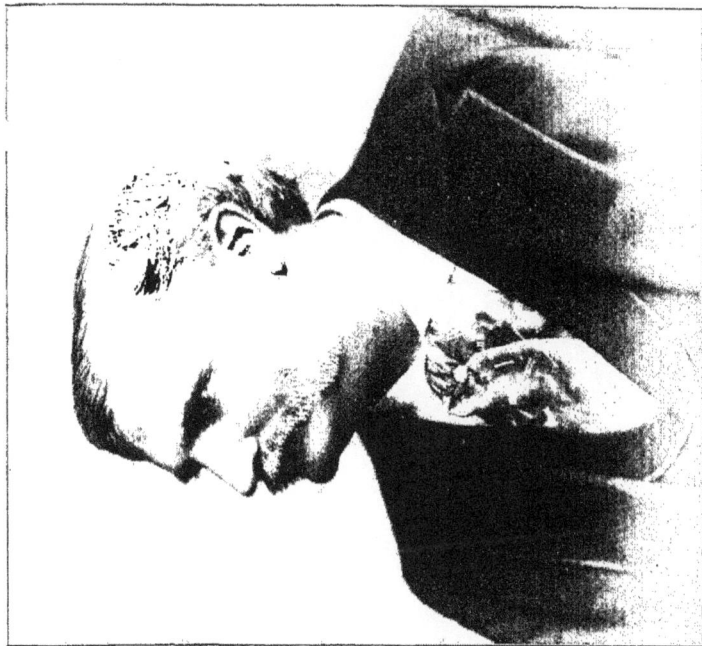

BENJAMIN BUTTERWORTH,
Solicitor-General,

Parks and Midway Plaisance, a strip 600 feet wide connecting
the two—in all 1,037 acres. Jackson Park, where nearly all of the
Exposition buildings will be, is beautifully situated on Lake Michigan, having a lake frontage of two miles, and embraces 586 acres.
Washington Park has 371 acres and Midway Plaisance 80 acres.
Upon these parks, previous to their selection as the World's Fair
site, $4,000,000 was spent in laying out the grounds and beautify-
ing them by lawns, flower-beds, etc. The Exposition Company
will spend more than a million in their further preparation. The
contract for grading and for excavating lagoons alone was let for
$397,000. These parks are connected with the center of the city
and with the general park and boulevard system by more than
thirty-five miles of boulevards from 100 to 300 feet in width. The
projected improvements at Jackson Park include additional walks,
driveways, lagoons, fountains, statuary, lake piers, etc.

More than a thousand men, scores of teams and several huge
steam dredgers have for some time been at work in Jackson Park
making the necessary changes of grades, excavating the lagoons
and raising the terrace sites for the buildings. This part of the
work is nearly finished. More than nine hundred thousand cubic
yards of earth had to be moved. All specifications for iron and
wood work have been completed. Working plans of most of the
chief buildings are finished and the work of construction is well
under way.

Properly preceding any description in detail of the Exposition
buildings may be given something in the way of general explana-
tion of the appearance of the Exposition site and palaces as they
will appear in 1893. The following quotations from President
Gage's report covering this may be considered authentic:

"The ground is being prepared for a system of lagoons and
canals from 100 to 300 feet wide, which, with the broad, grassy terraces leading down to them, will pass the principal buildings, inclose a wooded island 1,800 feet long, and form a circuit of three
miles, navigable by pleasure boats.

"These canals, which will be crossed by many bridges,' will
connect with the lake at two points; one at the southern limit of
the present improved portion of the park and the other more than
half a mile farther south, at the great main court of the Exposi-

tion. At this point, extending eastward into the lake 1,200 feet, will be piers which will afford a landing-place for the lake steamers, and enclose a harbor for the picturesque little pleasure boats of all epochs and nations, which will carry passengers along the canals, stopping at numerous landing-places.

" This harbor will be bounded on the east, far out in the lake, by the long columned façade of the Casino, in whose free spaces crowds of men and women, protected by its ceiling of gay awnings, can look east to the lake and west to the long vista between the main edifices as far as the gilded dome of the Administration Building. The first notable object in this vista will be the colossal statue of Liberty rising out of the lagoon at the point where it enters the land, protected by moles, which will carry sculptured columns emblematic of the thirteen original states of our Union. Beyond this, beyond the first of many bridges, will lie a broad basin from which grassy terraces and broad walks will lead, on the north, to the south elevation of the enormous Main Building; and on the south to the structure dedicated to agriculture.

" The Main Building, extending northwestward a third of a mile, will be devoted to manufactures and liberal arts, and will receive from all nations the rich products of modern workmanship. Recalling architecturally the period of the classic revival, it has the vivacity, the emphatic joyousness of that awakening epoch. The long, low lines of its sloping roof, supported by rows of arches, will be relieved by a central dome over the great main entrance, and emblematic statuary and floating banners will add to its festive character.

" The north elevation of the classic edifice devoted to agriculture will show a long arcade behind corinthian columns supporting a series of triple arches and three low graceful domes. Liberally adorned with sculpture and enriched with color, this building by its simplicity, refinement and grace, will be idyllically expressive of pastoral serenity and peace. At its noble entrance a statue of Ceres will offer hospitality to the fruits of the earth. Behind it, at the south, sixty-three acres of land will be reserved for the live-stock exhibit.

" The lofty octagonal dome of the Administration Building forms the central point of the architectural scheme. Rising from the columned stories of its square base 250 feet into the air, it will stand in the center of a spacious open plaza, adorned with statuary and fountains, with flower-beds and terraces, sloping at the east down to the main lagoon. North of the piaza will be the two buildings devoted to mines and electricity, the latter bristling with points and pinnacles as if to entrap from the air the intangible element whose achievements it will display.

"South of the plaza will be Machinery Hall, with its powerhouse at the southeast corner. A subway at the west will pass under the terminal railway loop of the Illinois Central Road to the circular machinery annex within. North of this railway loop, and along the western limit of the park, will be the Transportation Building. Still farther north, lying west of the north branch of the lagoon at the point where it incloses the wooded island, will extend the long, shining surfaces and the gracefully curving roof of the crystal palace of horticulture. Following the lagoon northward, one will pass the Women s Building, and eastward will reach the island devoted to the novel and interesting fisheries exhibit, shown in an effective, low-roofed Romanesque structure, flanked by two vast circular aquaria, in which the spectator can look upward through the clear waters and study the creatures of ocean and river. This building will be directly west of the northern opening of the system of lagoons into Lake Michigan, and in a straight line with the Government Building and the Main Building, which extend along the lake shore to the southeast.

"North of the lagoon which bounds this fisheries island lies the present improved portion of Jackson Park, which will be reserved for the buildings of States and of foreign governments. The Illinois Building will occupy a commanding position here, its classic dome being visible over the long lagoon from the central plaza. Along the Midway Plaisance will be placed a number of special exhibits, like the historical series of human dwellings, reproductions of famous streets, etc., and it is probable that some of these may overflow into Washington Park."

ADMINISTRATION BUILDING.

The gem and crown of the Exposition buildings will be the Administration Building. It will be located at the west end of the great court, in the southern part of the site, looking eastward, at the rear of which will be the railroad loop and the great passenger depot. The first object which will attract visitors on reaching the grounds will be the gilded dome of this great building. To the south of the Administration Building will be the Machinery Hall, and across the great court in front will be the Agricultural Building to the south and the Manufacturers' Building to the northeast.

This great building, the Administration Building, will be the only one besides the Electrical Building that will cost as much as $650,000. The architect is Richard M. Hunt, of New York, president of the American Institute of Architects, to whose established reputation it will be a memorable addition. It will cover an area of 250 square feet, and consist of four pavilions, 84 feet square, one at each end of the four angles of the square of the plan and connected by a great central dome 120 feet in diameter and 220 feet in height, leaving at the center of each façade a recess 82 feet wide, within which will be one of the grand entrances to the building. The general design is in the style of the French renaissance, and it will be a dignified and beautiful specimen of architecture, as befits its position and purpose among the various structures by which it will be surrounded.

Externally, the design may be divided in its height into three principal stages. The first stage consists of the four pavilions, corresponding in height with the various buildings grouped about it, which are about sixty-five feet high. The second stage, which is of the same height, is a continuation of the central rotunda, 175 feet square, surrounded on all sides by an open colonnade of noble proportions, it being twenty feet wide and forty feet high, with columns four feet in diameter. This colonnade is reached by staircases and elevators from the four principal halls, and is interrupted at the angles by corner pavilions, crowned with domes and groups of statuary. The third stage consists of the base of the great dome, thirty feet in height and octagonal in form, and the dome itself, rising in graceful lines, richly ornamented with heavily molded ribs and sculptural panels, and having a large skylight of glass to light the interior. At each angle of the octagonal base are large sculptured eagles, and among the springing lines are panels with rich garlands. This great dome will be gilded, and, asserting itself grandly at the end of the long vistas which open up in every direction, across the lagoons and between the neighboring palatial buildings, will form a fitting crown to the first and second stages.

The four great entrances, one on each side of the building, will be 50 feet wide and 50 feet high, deeply recessed and covered by semicircular arched vaults, richly covered. In the rear of these arches will be the entrance doors, and above them great screens of glass, giving light to the central rotunda. Across the face of these screens, at the level of the office door, will be galleries of communication between the different pavilions. On each side of these entrances, and in the entrant angles of the corner pavilions, groups of statuary, of an appropriate and emblematic character, will be placed. The interior features of the building will even exceed in beauty and splendor those of the exterior. Between every two of the grand entrances, and connecting the intervening pavilion with the great rotunda, is a hall, or loggia, 30 feet square, giving access to the offices and provided with broad, circular stairways and swift-running elevators. Internally, the rotunda is octagonal in form, the first story being composed of eight enormous arched openings corresponding in size to the arches of the great entrances. Above these arches is a frieze 27 feet in width, the panels of which are filled with tablets borne by figures carved in low relief and covered with commemorative inscriptions. The principal story of the rotunda is crowned with a richly decorated cornice, on the shelving top of which is a continuous balcony on the same level as the colonnade outside and from which can be viewed the vast interior. Above the balcony is the second story 50 feet in height. The walls are embellished with plasters, between which a frieze of windows is placed, giving light to the rotunda from the rear wall of the surrounding colonnade. From the top of the cornice of this story rises the interior dome, 200 feet from the floor, and in the center is an opening 50 feet in diameter, transmitting light from the exterior dome overhead. The under side of the dome is enriched with deep panelings, richly molded, and the panels are filled with

sculpture in low relief, and immense paintings, rep-esenting the
Arts and Sciences. In size this rotunda will rival if not surpass
the celebrated domes of a similar character in the world.

As to the uses of the administration building, each of the corner pavilions, which are four stories in height, will be divided into
large and small offices for the various departments of the administration and lobbies and toilet rooms. The ground floor contains,
in one pavilion, the fire and police departments, with cells for the
detention of prisoners ; in a second pavilion the offices of ambu-
lance service, the physician and pharmacy, the foreign department and the information bureau ; in the third pavilion the post-
office and a bank, and in the fourth the offices of public comfort
and a restaurant. The second, third and fourth stories will contain the board rooms, the committee rooms, the rooms of the
Director-General, of the department of publicity and promotion
and of the World's Columbian Commission.

ART INSTITUTE ON THE LAKE FRONT.

After it was definitely decided to hold the Exposition in
Jackson Park the World's Fair Commissioners set about forming
some plan whereby a certain portion of the art features of the
Exposition might have a place in the city proper. The present
Art Institute being already too small to accommodate its rapidly
increasing classes, it was proposed to its directors that if they
could dispose of their present building the World's Fair Commissioners would join them in erecting a structure suitable to
their requirements, the building to be used by the Exposition
while the Fair lasted, after which it should become the property
of the Art Institute. Such a plan has been perfected, and a
splendid granite structure in the Italian Renaissance style,
340 by 180 feet, will be erected on the site of the old Chicago Ex
position building. Shepley, Rutan & Cooledge, of Boston, were
the fortunate designers, their plans for a building having been
accepted by both the World's Fair Commissioners and the Art
Institute Directors. In this building the World's Congress
auxiliaries will hold their conferences. This will be of great

advantage to the members of these congresses, giving them ample halls for discussion and display in the heart of the city, and when the great show is over Chicago will have at least one building left made memorable by occupation of a part of the great Columbian Exposition.

The rapidly developing taste for art in its purest forms which is manifest in Chicago will in the new art building find a fitting place of expression. Already designers, sculptors and artists in oil and crayon, born and reared in Chicago, are making a name for themselves both at home and abroad. Several of the graduates of the present art school have been honored in recent exhibitions, and many are not only in the enjoyment of that pleasure which comes from recognition of merit but are in possession of a handsome competence, the direct result of their work. It has long been the fashion in eastern circles to ridicule Chicago as the home of the sordid money-getter, the soulless real estate speculator, and the unenlightened and unregenerate packer of pork. This may have been true of the Chicago of a decade ago, but the city to-day counts among its residents some of the most liberal patrons of art in the world—men who love art for art's sake and do not hesitate to pay liberally for any production having merit, no matter who the artist may be.

ART PALACE.

Grecian-Ionic in style, the Fine Arts' Building is a pure type of the most refined classic architecture. The building is oblong, and is 500 by 320 feet, intersected north, east, south, and west by a great nave and transept 100 feet wide and 70 feet high, at the intersection of which is a great done 60 feet in diameter. The building is 125 feet to the top of the dome, which is surmounted by a colossal statue of the type of famous figures of Winged Victory. The transept has a clear space through the center of 60 feet, being lighted entirely from above.

On either side are galleries 20 feet wide and 24 feet above the floor. The collections of sculpture are displayed on the main floor of the nave and transept, and on the walls both of the ground floor and of the galleries are ample areas for displaying the paintings and sculptured panels in relief. The corners made by the crossing of the nave and transept are filled with small picture galleries.

Around the entire building are galleries 40 feet wide, forming a continuous promenade around the classic structure. Between the promenade and the naves are smaller rooms devoted to private collections of paintings and the collections of the various art schools. On either side of the main building, and connected with it by handsome corridors, are very large annexes, which are also utilized by various art exhibits.

The main building is entered by four great portals, richly ornamented with architectural sculpture, and approached by broad flights of steps. The walls of the loggia of the colonnades are highly decorated with mural paintings, illustrating the history and progress of the arts. The frieze of the exterior walls and the pediments of the principal entrances are ornamented with sculptures and portraits in bas-relief of the masters of ancient art.

The general tone or color is light gray stone.

The construction, although of a temporary character, is necessarily fire-roof. The main walls are of solid brick, covered with "staff," architecturally ornamented, while the roof, floors, and galleries are of iron.

All light is supplied through glass sky-lights in iron frames.

The building is located beautifully in the northern portion of the Park, with the south front facing the lagoon. It is separated from the lagoon by beautiful terraces, ornamented with balustrades, with an immense flight of steps leading down .from the main portal to the lagoon, where there is a landing for boats. The north front faces the wide lawn and the group of State buildings. The immediate neighborhood of the building is ornamented with groups of statues, replica ornaments of classic art, such as the Choriagic monument, the "Cave of the Winds," and other beautiful examples of Grecian art. The ornamentation also includes statues of heroic and life-size proportions.

This building cost between $500,000 and $600,000.

The Art Palace was planned in the Exposition's Construction

MRS. POTTER PALMER.
President Board of Lady Managers.

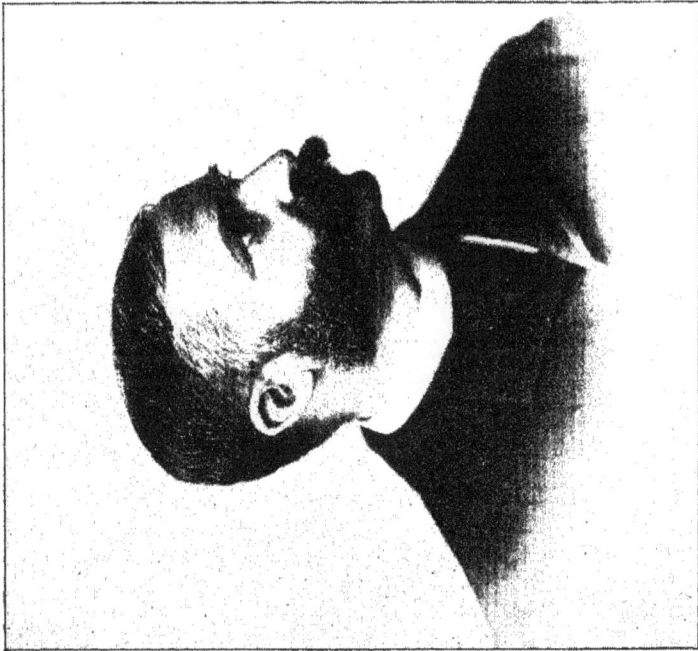

W. T. BAKER,
President World's Columbian Exposition.

Bureau, under the eye of Chief of Construction D. H. Burnham, and the details worked out by Chief Designer P. B. Atwood.

The outline plan was left by the late consulting architect, George W. Root.

AGRICULTURAL BUILDING.

One of the most magnificent structures raised for the Exposition is the Agricultural Building, of which McKim, Meade & White, of New York, are the architects. The style of architecture is classic renaissance. This building is put up very near the shore of Lake Michigan, and is almost surrounded by the lagoons that lead into the Park from the Lake. The building is 500 by 800 feet, its longest dimensions being east and west. The north line of the building is almost on a line with the Pier extending into the Lake, on which heroic columns, emblematic of the Thirteen Original States, are raised. A lagoon stretches out along this entire front of the building. The east front looks out into a harbor which affords refuge for numerous pleasure craft.

The entire west exposure of the building faces a branch of the lagoon that extends along the north side. With these picturesque surroundings as an inspiration, the architects have brought out designs that have been pronounced all but faultless. For a single-story building the design is bold and heroic. The general cornice line is 65 feet above grade. On either side of the main entrance are mammoth Corinthian pillars, 50 feet high and 5 feet in diameter. On each corner and from the center of the building pavilions are reared, the center one being 144 feet square. The corner pavilions are connected by curtains, forming a continuous arcade around the top of the building. The main entrance leads through an opening 64 feet wide into a vestibule, from which entrance is had to the rotunda, 100 feet in diameter. This is surmounted by a mammoth glass dome, 130 feet high. All through the main vestibule statuary has been designed, illustrative of the agricultural industry. Similar designs are grouped about all of the grand entrances in the most elaborate manner. The corner pavilions are surmounted by domes 96 feet high, and above these tower groups of statuary. The design for these

13

domes is that of three women, of herculean proportions, supporting a mammoth globe.

To the southward of the Agricultural Building is a spacious
structure devoted chiefly to a Live Stock and Agricultural
Assembly Hall. This building is conveniently near one of the
stations of the elevated railway. It is a very handsome building, and was designed to be the common meeting point for all
persons interested in live stock and agricultural pursuits. On
the first floor, near the main entrance to the building, is located
a bureau of information, in charge of attendants, who furnish
visitors with all necessary information in regard to the Assembly
Hall and the main Agricultural Building, as well as other features of the Exposition. This floor also contains suitable
committee and other rooms for the different live stock associations of every character, where such associations can meet
and have their secretaries in constant attendance, thus affording
this important industry ample headquarters near the Live Stock
exhibit and the Agricultural Building. On this floor there are
also large and handsomely equipped waiting-rooms for ladies,
lounging-rooms for gentlemen, and ample toilet facilities. Broad
stairways lead from the first floor into the assembly-room, which
has a seating capacity of 1,500. This assembly-room furnishes
facilities for lectures, delivered by gentlemen eminent in their
special fields of work, embracing every interest connected with
live stock, agriculture, and allied industries.

Such a building was never erected at any exposition, and its
construction here shows that the Board of Directors purposed
affording every desirable facility that they could furnish to aid
the great live stock and agricultural interests.

Close by the Agricultural Building and its Annex are buildings for the Forestry and Dairy exhibits. These measure, respectively, 200 by 500 and 95 by 200 feet. In the Forestry Building the visitor may see a very extensive exhibit illustrating forestry resources and products. In the Dairy Building he may be
a pupil of a dairy school, scientifically conducted, and may watch
the tests which will determine the respective merits of different
breeds of cattle as milk producers.

The Agricultural Building covers more than nine acres, and

its Annex about 3.5 acres. The Forestry and Dairy Buildings together cover about three acres. The Live Stock buildings, which will, of course, be of inexpensive construction, cover about thirty acres. All of these structures together cost nearly $1,000,-000 and afford most extensive and gratifying provision for showing and subserving the agricultural and allied interests.

DAIRY BUILDING.

The Dairy Building, by reason of the exceptionally novel and interesting exhibits it will contain, is quite sure to be regarded with great favor by World's Fair visitors in general, while by agriculturists it will be considered one of the most useful and attractive features of the whole Exposition. It was designed to contain not only a complete exhibit of dairy products, but also a Dairy School, in connection with which will be conducted a series of tests for determining the relative merits of different breeds of dairy cattle as milk and butter producers.

The building stands near the lake shore in the southeastern part of the park, and close by the general live-stock exhibit. It covers approximately half an acre, measuring 95 by 200 feet; is two stories high and cost $30,000. In design it is of quiet exterior. On the first floor, besides office headquarters, there is in front a large open space devoted to exhibits of butter, and farther back an operating-room, 25 by 100 feet, in which the Model Dairy will be conducted. On two sides of this room are amphitheater seats capable of accommodating 400 spectators. Under these seats are refrigerators and cold-storage rooms for the care of the dairy products. The operating-room, which extends to the roof, has on three sides a gallery where the cheese exhibits will be placed. The rest of the second story is devoted to a café, which opens on a balcony overlooking the lake.

The Dairy School, it is believed, will be most instructive and valuable to agriculturists. Its plan was first proposed by the Columbian Dairy Association, an organization formed with the express purpose of insuring the success of the dairy exhibit at the Fair, and has been widely approved by dairy associations throughout the country. The school will include a contest between both herds and individuals of the chief breeds of dairy cattle, with a view of ascertaining the respective merits of each in milk-giving and butter-producing. Each herd will be charged each day with the food consumed, accurately weighed, and will be credited with the milk and butter produced. Manufacturers of dairy utensils and appliances gladly offer to furnish all that will be required in their line. Spectators will be able to obtain an excellent view of the processes in all their stages. The tests and all details of management will be under rules prepared by a committee composed of one member from each of the dairy cattle associations in the United States, three from the Columbian Dairy Association, three from the Agricultural Colleges and U. S. Experimental Stations and one from the manufacturers of dairy utensils. The school will continue through a definite period, probably three or four months, and each participating herd will be represented by the same number of cows. The results of this test and of the exhibition which will be made of the latest and most advanced scientific methods known in connection with the feeding and care of cattle, the treatment of milk and the production of butter and cheese, cannot fail to be of great and lasting benefit to the dairy interests of this country. These interests, it is scarcely necessary to state, are of enormous importance and extent, and, indeed, are scarcely surpassed by any other branch of industry in respect of the amount of money invested. It cannot be doubted that the Exposition Dairy School will cause a more economic and scientific management of the dairy interests of the entire country and consequently a greater return from the capital and labor invested.

ELECTRICAL BUILDING.

The Electrical Building, the seat of perhaps the most novel and brilliant exhibit in the whole Exposition, is 345 feet wide and 700 feet long, the major axis running north and south. The south front is on the great Quadrangle or Court ; the north front faces the lagoon ; the east front is opposite the Manufactures Building, and the west faces the Mines Building.

The general scheme of the plan is based upon a longitudinal

nave 115 feet wide and 114 feet high, crossed in the middle by a transept of the same width and height. The nave and the transept have a pitched roof, with a range of skylights at the bottom of the pitch, and clearstory windows. The rest of the building is covered with a flat roof, averaging 62 feet in height, and provided with skylights.

The second story is composed of a series of galleries connected across the nave by two bridges, with access by four grand staircases. The area of the galleries in the second story is 118,546 square feet, or 2.7 acres.

The exterior walls of this building are composed of a continuous Corinthian order of pilasters, 3 feet 6 inches wide and 42 feet high, supporting a full entablature, and resting upon a stylobate 8 feet 6 inches. The total height of the walls from the grade outside is 68 feet 6 inches.

The north pavilion is placed between the two great apsidal or semicircular projections of the building ; it is flanked by two towers 195 feet high. The central feature is a great semicircular window, above which, 102 feet from the ground, is a colonnade forming an open loggia or gallery, commanding a view over the lagoon and all the north portion of the grounds.

The east and west central pavilions are composed of two towers 168 feet high. In front of these two pavilions there is a great portico composed of the Corinthian order, with full columns.

The south pavilion is a hemicycle or niche 78 feet in diameter and 103 feet high. The opening of the niche is framed by a semicircular arch, which is crowned by a gable or pediment, with smaller gables on the returns, and surmounted by an attic, the whole reaching the height of 142 feet. In the center of this niche, upon a lofty pedestal, is a colossal statue of Franklin, whose illustrious name intimately connects the early history of the Republic with one of the most important discoveries in the phenomena of electricity.

At each of the four corners of the building there is a pavilion, above which rises a light open spire or tower, 169 feet high. Intermediate between these corner pavilions and the central pavilions on the east and west sides, there is a subordinate pavilion bearing a low, square dome upon an open lantern. There are thus ten spires and four domes. The entablature of the great Corinthian order breaks around each of the pilasters of the four fronts, and above each pilaster in the Attic order is a pedestal bearing a lofty mast for the display of banners by day and electric lights by night. Of these masts there are in all fifty-four.

The first story of the building is indicated in these façades between the great pilasters of the Corinthian order, by a subordinate Ionic order, with full columns and pilasters, forming an open screen in front of the windows.

The Electricity Building has an open portico extending along the whole of the south façade, the lower, or Ionic order, forming an open screen in front of it. The various subordinate pavilions are treated with windows and balconies. The details of the exterior orders are richly decorated, and the pediments, friezes, panels and spandrils have received a decoration of figures in relief, with architectural motifs, the general tendency of which is to illustrate the purposes of the building.

The appearance of the exterior is that of marble, but the walls of the hemicycle and of the various porticos and loggia are highly enriched with color, the pilasters in these places being decorated with scagliola, and the capitals with metallic effects in bronze.

In the design of this building, it was proposed by the architects to so devise its details and general outlines, that they might be capable of providing an electric illumination by night on a scale hitherto unknown, the flagstaffs, the open porticos, and the towers, especially, being arranged with this in view. Van Brunt & Howe, of Kansas City, are the architects. The cost is $375,000.

It was proposed that the hemicycle or niche, which forms the south porch, should have either a great chandelier or crown of lights suspended from the center of the half dome, or should be provided with electric lights masked behind the triumphal arch which forms the opening of the niche.

FISHERIES BUILDING.

This building will be 1,100 feet long and 200 feet wide. It is built upon a curved island, and conforms in shape to this. The general design of the building is Spanish Romanesque, and its general effect is exquisitely light and pleasing. The two polygonal wings are to serve as aquarials. The three domes of this building are to be of the same color and general effect as that of the Administration Building; and the artists in charge of the color scheme of the whole Exposition have planned to use these two widely separated domes as the color accents of the whole scheme.

While the extreme dimensions of the building are very large, yet the structure is so laid out that the general effect is rather of delicacy than of the grandeur to be expected from the mere statement of dimensions. It is composed of three parts, a main building 365 feet long and 165 feet wide, and two polygonal buildings each 133 feet 6 inches in diameter, connected with the main structure by two curved arcades.

The main building is provided with two great entrances in the centers of the long sides. These entrances are by pavilions 102 feet long, projecting 41 feet beyond the line of the main building, and flanked at each corner with circular towers. The great pediment over the south or chief entrance is filled with sculpture, the subject being a scene of whale fishing. The angles are surmounted by statues representing fishers casting the spear, throwing the handline, and holding the finny prey.

The quadrangular first story is surmounted by a great circular story capped by a conical roof. A graceful open turret crowns this roof and four smaller towers spring from and surround the base.

The general design of the whole structure is Roman in masses, with all the details worked out in a realistic manner after various fish and marine forms. Thus the double row of engaged columns which form the exterior face of the building have capitals which are formed of a thousand varied groupings of marine forms, while the delicate open work of the gallery railings display as many different fishes.

The circular story is surrounded by a broad exterior gallery, and the four flanking towers of the entrances and the four smaller towers of the central roof terminate in open turrets, from all of which views of every part of the grounds can be obtained.

The materials of construction are wood, iron and steel, "staff" and glass. The roofs will be covered with glazed Spanish tiles, and the general coloring of the building will be at once soft and brilliant, as befits the grace of the architectural lines.

The main entrance leads past the broad winding stairs which give access to the turrets of the flanking towers into a wide vestibule and thence to the main floor of the building. All of the floors will be of asphalt concrete, and the floor of the second story is disposed as a gallery, leaving the interior open to the great elliptical ceiling of the dome far overhead. This ceiling will be enriched with brilliant frescoes. The wide gallery of the second story will permit visitors to have a general view of the principal part of the exhibits. From this gallery the summits of the four smaller towers of the roof are reached by winding stairs.

The two curved arcades leading to the aquarial exhibit on the east and the angling exhibit on the west are open to the air, and are provided with wide staircases on both of their sides, thus adding four means of access to the various parts of the building.

The two circular buildings, in one of which will be installed the angling exhibit and in the other the aquarials, are precisely similar in size and exterior appearance. They are not in reality circular, but polygons of many sides. The result is that the severity of the simple curve is obviated by a succession of obtuse angles, which lend grace and lightness to the general design. The western building is perfectly plain within, as in it the varied exhibit of angling appliances is to be placed. The aquarials will be found in the eastern building, and there is little doubt but that this will be one of the chief points of interest of the whole Exposition.

In the center will be a circular basin 30 feet in diameter, in the middle of which will rise a towering mass of rockwork. From clefts and crevices in this rockwork miniature cascades will ripple down to the masses of reeds, rushes and ornamental semiaquatic plants in the basin, amid which will be seen gorgeously brilliant fishes disporting. Around this basin there will be a circular wall 16 feet wide, reached by two broad entrances. These entrances pass through the inner series of tanks. The larger section of these tanks will be devoted to fresh-water fishes, the smaller to those from salt water. This series contains the tanks of greatest capacity. They will have vertical sides, as they will be inspected from both sides, and the bottom will be rounded. They will vary in capacity from 7,000 to 17,000 gallons each. The sea-water for the marine fishes will be secured by evaporating the necessary quantity at the United States Fish Commission Station at Wood's Holl, Mass., to one-fifth its bulk, thus reducing both quantity and weight for transportation about 80 per cent. The fresh water required to restore it to its proper density will be supplied from Lake Michigan. From this same source will be drawn all the fresh water needed. In transporting the marine specimens from the coast to Chicago, about 3,000 gallons of pure sea-water will be brought on each trip.

Surrounding these great tanks, which will be about 7 feet wide, there will be a second annular walk 16 feet wide. This walk will be vaulted over and the walls above the clear glass fronts of the tanks will be made of stained glass, so that all of the light will perforce come through the tanks. Around the outer circumference of the walk will be placed the second series of tanks. These will be somewhat smaller than those in the inner series, ranging from 750 to 1,500 gallons each in capacity. The entire length of the glass fronts of the aquaria will be about 575 feet, or over 3,000 square feet of surface. The panorama presented will be one of surpassing interest and beauty, and the whole exhibit will rival the greatest permanent aquaria of the world, not only in size but in the number and character of the specimens displayed. Thus it is already known that Dr. Ladislao Neeto, the director of the National Museum at Rio Janeiro, Brazil, and who organized the magnificent exhibit of Brazil in the fishery exposition at Berlin, proposes to send a much more complete exhibit to Chicago in 1893.

The total water capacity of the aquarium, exclusive of two huge reservoirs which are to be placed in the main structure, will be 18,725 cubic feet or about 140,000 gallons. This will weigh 1,192,425 pounds, or almost 600 tons. Of this amount about 40,000 gallons will be devoted to the marine exhibit. In the entire salt water circulation, including reservoirs, there will be about 80,000 gallons. The pumping and distributing plant for the marine aquarium will be constructed of vulcanite. The pumps will be in duplicate, and will each have a capacity of 3,000 gallons per hour.

It is the intention of the State Fish Commission of the different States to make provision for a comprehensive exhibit of native and·cultivated live fish, with hatcheries, appliances and equipments for transportation, models of fishways in use, etc. Each State will have its special exhibit, and in addition to this there will be a large Government display of shell and sea-fish. The coast States will send especially large displays.

Of all the exhibits to be made by the United States Government, the most interesting will be that of the Fish Commission. Up to the present time no comprehensive display has ever been made of the fauna belonging to this country. It is intended that such an exhibition shall be made in Chicago. This ought to be interesting in consideration merely of the fact that fishing was the earliest industry of the New World, dating from the period of the discovery of America by Columbus. The Commission proposes to exhibit alive in aquaria the principal forms of fishes and invertebrates of both oceans, the Gulf of Mexico, the Great Lakes, and the inland rivers, with particular reference to those which have commercial value.

Not only will marine creatures of all sorts be shown, but the finny denizens of the streams also, and likewise the whitefish, the catfish, the big pickerel, and the huge sturgeons of the interior waters. Such a task will necessarily be of great magnitude, inasmuch as the labor and skill required to fetch the fishes in good condition from points so remote, over thousands of miles of railway, must be enormous and of the very highest order. It has been announced hitherto that such an exhibition was impossible, but thanks to modern devices and the discoveries of the Fish Commission, no serious difficulties are anticipated. The marine fishes will be captured off the coast and forwarded alive by rail, in tanks filled with sea-water, to Chicago. Not only on the Atlantic seaboard, but on the Pacific likewise, the vessels of the Commission will devote attention to this work. They will secure the scaly captives in seines, select such desirable ones as are caught in the pound nets of the fishermen, and take them in tanks ashore,

EXCAVATING AT JACKSON PARK FOR EXPOSITION SITE.

where they will be shipped to the Exposition. The tanks utilized for transportation will be of sufficient size not to crowd the occupants, and provided with a device for circulating and aerating the water.

The main structure will contain a full and complete exhibit of all the various appliances used in the fishing industry in all countries and in all times, while the special department of angling will have the whole of the west wing for its exhibit. It is the intention of the Department of Fish and Fisheries to make the exhibits of foreign nations as large as possible, and thus far there is every reason to believe that the highest degree of success in this direction will be attained.

Captain Joseph W. Collins, chief of the department, was appointed to that position on February 13, 1891, having been selected for his eminent fitness for the work to be performed. He has had wide experience in exposition matters, and is probably the best informed man regarding fishery expositions and their conduct to be found in the country.

FORESTRY BUILDING.

The Forestry Building is, in appearance, perhaps, the most unique of all the Exposition structures. Its dimensions are 200 by 500 feet. To a remarkable degree its architecture is of the rustic order. On all four sides of the building is a veranda, supporting the roof of which is a colonnade consisting of a series of columns composed of three tree-trunks, each 25 feet in length, one of them from 16 to 20 inches in diameter and the others smaller. All of these trunks are left in their natural state with bark undisturbed. They are contributed by the different States and Territories of the Union and by foreign countries, each furnishing specimens of its most characteristic trees. The sides of the building are constructed of slabs with the bark removed. The window frames are treated in the same rustic manner as is the rest of the building. The main entrance is elaborately finished in different kinds of wood, the material and workmanship being contributed by the wood-workers of the world. The other entrances are finished artistically to represent the woods of different countries and regions. The roof is thatched with tan bark and other barks. The interior of the building is finished in various woods in a way to show their beautiful graining, susceptibility to polish, etc. The visitor can make no mistake as to the kinds of tree-trunks which form the colonnade, for he will see upon each one a tablet upon which are inscribed the common and scientific name, the State or country from which the trunk was contributed and other pertinent information, such as the approximate quantity of such timber in the region whence it came. Surmounting the cornice of the veranda and extending all around the building are numerous flagstaffs bearing the colors, coats-of-arms, etc., of the Nations and States represented in the exhibits inside.

The Forestry Building contains a most varied exhibition of forest products in general—the most complete which could be gathered together. It contains logs and sections of trees, worked lumber in the form of shingles, flooring, casing, etc. There are shown here dye woods and barks, mosses, galls, abnormal woody products, lichens, vegetable substances used for bedding and upholstery; gums, resins, vegetable ivory, cocoanut-shells, gourds, wood pulp, rattan, willowware and woodenware generally, such as pails, tubs, brooms, etc. There is also an exceedingly interesting monographic display by the different States, in which their characteristic woods are most effectively and beautifully shown.

The Forestry Building was designed by P. B. Atwood, Chief Designer in the Exposition's Construction Department, and cost about $100,000. Chief Buchanan, of the Exposition's Department of Agriculture, is entitled to the lion's share of credit for the existence of this exceedingly novel and attractive building and display. As Acting Forestry Chief he induced the Directory to make the necessary appropriation of money, and he devoted much time and energy in effecting the erection of the building and the collection of the exhibit. The structure has a delightful site near the lake shore in the southeastern portion of the grounds. In itself and in the exhibits it contains it illustrates the forestry wealth of the world and particularly of the United States. No forestry display was ever made before which approached this in extent or completeness.

THE SAW-MILL EXHIBIT.

In response to a very general desire on the part of the manufacturers of lumber and saw-mill plants, arrangements were made, through Chief Buchanan's efforts, to show several complete saw-mills in operation. This exhibit is in connection with that of Forestry, and it is entirely distinct from the displays of saw-mill and wood-working machinery, which are installed in the Machinery Building. Four saw-mill plants are installed, occupying altogether a building measuring 125 by 300 feet.

The building is plainly constructed, costing only about $35,-000, but affords ample facilities for a competitive display of saw-mill plants and the latest improvements in connection with the same. Exhibitors of saw-mill plants in this building bear the expense of installing and operating them. One-half of the building is two stories high, to accommodate bands and gangs and to provide also a gallery from· which visitors may view the working of the machinery to good advantage and without danger.

This exhibit is a very novel and interesting one, as well as instructive to those who desire to witness the workings of the latest and most approved saw-mill machinery.

GOVERNMENT BUILDING.

Delightfully located near the lake shore, south of the main lagoon and of the area reserved for the Foreign Nations and the several States, and east of the Woman's Building and of Midway Plaisance, is the Government Exhibit Building. The buildings of England, Germany, and Mexico are near by to the northward. The Government Building was designed by Architect Windrim, now succeeded by W. J. Edbrooke. It is classic in style, and bears a strong resemblance to the National Museum and other Government buildings at Washington. It covers an area of 350 by 420 feet; is constructed of iron, brick, and glass, and cost $400,000. Its leading architectural feature is a central octagonal dome 120 feet in diameter and 150 feet high, the floor of which will be kept free from exhibits. The building fronts to the west, and connects on the north, by a bridge over the lagoon, with the building of the Fisheries Exhibit.

The south half of the Government Building is devoted to the exhibits of the Post-Office Department, Treasury Department, War Department, and Department of Agriculture. The north half is devoted to the exhibits of the Fisheries Commission, Smithsonian Institution, and Interior Department. The State Department exhibit extends from the rotunda to the east end, and that of the Department of Justice from the rotunda to the west end of the building. The allotment of space for the several department exhibits is: War Department, 23,000 square feet; Treasury, 10,500 square feet; Agriculture, 23,250 square feet; Interior, 24,000 square feet; Post Office, 9,000 square feet; Fishery, 20,000 square feet, and Smithsonian Institution, balance of space.

The Treasury Department exhibit is in charge of Assistant Secretary Nettleton. He matured the plans whereby the Mint, the Coast, and the Geodetic Survey, the Supervising Architect of the Treasury, the Bureau of Engraving and Printing, the Bureau of Statistics, the Life-Saving Board, the Light-House Board, and the Marine Hospital, all have made exhibits.

The authorities of the Mint show not only a complete group of the coins made by the United States, but a large number of the coins of foreign countries.

The Supervising Architect of the Treasury shows a number of photographs of all of the public buildings of the Capital. These include not only the buildings but also the parks and reservations.

The Bureau of Engraving and Printing shows many new bills under framing. These include a sample of every bill of every denomination that the United States Government now authorizes as money.

A Life-Saving Station is built and equipped with every appliance, and a regular crew goes through all life-saving maneuvers.

Perhaps the most interesting exhibit of the whole Treasury Department is that by the Coast Survey. It includes a huge map of the United States, about 400 feet square, or about the size of a block of city property. This is accurately constructed of plaster of paris, and is placed horizontally on the Exposition grounds with a huge covering erected over it, with galleries and pathways on the inside to allow the visitors to "walk over the whole United States" without touching it. This model is built on a scale showing the exact height of mountains, the depth of the rivers, and the curvature of the earth.

The Quartermaster's Department shows lay-figure officers and men of all grades in the army, mounted and on foot, fully equipped in the uniform of their rank and service.

Aside from these there are nineteen figures, showing the uniforms worn during the Revolutionary War and the War of 1812, and thirty-one figures showing the uniforms in the Mexican War. A novel exhibit is that of a telephone as used on the battle-field. The heliograph, which practically annihilates distance in the matter of talking, is shown in full operation. All means of army telegraphing and signaling with the batteries, lines, cables, bombs, torches, and so forth, are shown with great elaborateness.

Captain Whipple, of the Ordnance Department, developed the plan for an exhibit of huge guns and explosives. At certain hours of the day there are regular battery drills and loading and firing of pieces. Many of the guns used are the finest of their kind in the world.

The exhibit of the Medical Bureau occupies a hospital built especially for its use, operated by a corps of hospital nurses and doctors.

HALL OF MINES AND MINING.

Located at the southern extremity of the western lagoon or lake, and between the Electricity and Transportation Buildings, is the Mines and Mining Building. The architect of this building, which is 700 feet long by 350 wide, is S. S. Beman, of Chicago. Its architecture has its inspiration in early Italian renaissance, with which sufficient liberty is taken to invest the building with the animation that should characterize a great general Exposition. There is a decided French spirit pervading the exterior design, but it is kept well subordinated. In plan it is simple and straightforward, embracing on the ground floor spacious vestibules, restaurants, toilet rooms, etc. On each of the four sides of the building are placed the entrances, those of the north and south fronts being the most spacious and prominent. To the right and left of each entrance, inside, start broad flights of easy stairs leading to the galleries. The galleries are 60 feet wide and 25 feet high from the ground floor, and are lighted on the sides by large windows, and from above by a high clearstory extending around the building.

The main fronts look southward on the great Central Court, and northward on the western and middle lakes, and an island gorgeous with flowers. These principal fronts display enormous arched entrances, richly embellished with sculptural decorations, emblematic of mining and its allied industries. At each end of these fronts are large, square pavilions, surmounted by low domes, which mark the four corners of the building, and are lighted by large arched windows extending through the galleries.

Between the main entrance and the pavilions are richly decorated arcades, forming an open loggia on the ground floor and a deeply recessed promenade on the gallery floor level, which commands a fine view of the lakes and islands to the northward and the great Central Court on the south. These covered promenades' are each 25 feet wide and 230 feet long, and from them is had access to the building at numerous points. These loggias on the first floor are faced with marbles of different kinds and hues, which will be considered part of the Mining Exhibit, and so utilized as to have marketable value at the close of the Exposition. The loggia ceilings will be heavily coffered, and richly decorated in plaster and color. The ornamentation is massed at the prominent points of the façade. The exterior presents a massive, though graceful appearance.

The main fronts are 65 feet high from ground to top of cornice, and the main central entrances are 90 feet to apex of pediment. The long sides of the building are treated in a simpler manner than the main fronts; large segmental windows extend through the galleries and are placed between the broad piers, affording an abundance of light to the space beneath the galleries.

The two-storied portion of the building, of which the gallery forms the upper part, extends entirely around the structure, and is 60 feet wide.

The great interior space thus inclosed is one story high, 630 feet long and 230 feet wide, with an extreme height of 100 feet at center and 47 feet at sides, and is spanned by steel cantilever roof trusses supported on steel columns placed 65 feet apart longitudinally, and 115 feet and 57 feet 6 inches transversely, thus leaving clear space in center of building 630 feet long and 115 feet wide, with two side divisions, each 57 feet 6 inches wide and 630 feet long, leaving the central space incumbered with only 16 supporting steel posts. The cantilevers are of pin connection to facilitate erection. The inner and higher ends of the cantilevers are 46 feet apart and the space between them is spanned by riveted steel trusses with an elliptical chord.

These trusses are designed so as to form a clearstory 12 feet high, with vertical sash extending the entire length of central space—630 feet ; this space terminating at each end with a great glass gable setting back 60 feet from front ends of building. The wide spacings of the cantilever necessitated an extensive system of longitudinal perlines of the riveted-lattice type. A great portion of the roof is covered with glass. It may be of interest to state that the cantilever system as applied to roofs has not been used heretofore on so large a scale.

The exterior of this building, like that of all the others, will be made of "staff," similar to that used in facing the recent Paris Exposition buildings. The cost of the Mines Building is $260,000.

HORTICULTURAL BUILDING.

Immediately south of the entrance to Jackson Park from the Midway Plaisance, and facing east on the lagoon, is the Horticultural Building. In front is a flower terrace for outside exhibits, including tanks for Nymphæa and the Victoria Regia. The front of the terrace, with its low parapet between large vases, borders the water, and at its center forms a boat landing.

The building is 1,000 feet long, with an extreme width of 250 feet. The plan is a central pavilion with two end pavilions, each connected with the central one by front and rear curtains, forming two interior courts, each 88 by 270 feet. These courts are beautifully decorated in color and planted with ornamental shrubs and flowers. The center pavilion is roofed by a crystal dome 187 feet in diameter and 113 feet high, under which are exhibited the tallest palms, bamboos, and tree ferns that can be procured. There are galleries in each of the pavilions. The galleries of the end pavilions are designed for cafés, the situation and the surroundings being particularly adapted to recreation and refreshment. These cafés are surrounded by an arcade on three sides, from which charming views of the grounds can be obtained.

In this building are exhibited all the varieties of flowers, plants, vines, seeds, horticultural implements, etc. Those exhibits requiring sunshine and light are shown in the rear curtains, where the roof is entirely of glass and not too far removed from the plants. The front curtains and space under the galleries are designed for exhibits that require only the ordinary amount of light. Provision is made to heat such parts as require it.

The exterior of the building is in "staff," tinted in a soft warm buff, color being reserved for the interior and the courts. The cost of this building was about $300,000.

ILLINOIS STATE BUILDING.

The Illinois Building at the World's Columbian Exposition is by far the most pretentious of those erected by the several States of the Union. Being in a sense the host at the Exposition it was deemed not only proper but requisite that Illinois should make such appropriation and provide such a building as would enable her to perform creditably the duties of that office. The State appropriated $800,000.

Situated on a high terrace, in one of the most favored spots in Jackson Park, the Illinois Building commands, for nearly a mile to the southward, a view of the beautiful waterway which encircles the great island and extends to the buildings for Electricity and Mines, while to the northward across a branch of the lagoon is presented the imposing façade of the Palace of Fine Arts. To the westward are the California Building and those of several other States, and to the eastward the buildings of a number of the foreign nations. The building in the main is 160 feet wide by 450 feet long. On the north, Memorial Hall forms a wing 50 by

75 feet, and on the south another wing 75 by 123 feet and three stories high accommodates the executive offices; and, in the third story, two public halls. The side walls are 47 feet high, while the south wing is 72 feet and the ends 54 feet. Surmounting the building at the center a fine dome, 72 feet in diameter, rises to a height of 235 feet. The building is constructed almost wholly of Illinois material—wood, stone, brick and steel—and is covered with " staff " artistically treated. The grand entrance faces the waterway to the south, while at the west and north ends are others scarcely less imposing. In front of the entrances are beautiful terraces with balustrades, statues, fountains, flowers and stone steps leading down to the roadways and lagoon landings.

The building is embellished with fine carving and statuary. It is thoroughly lighted; first, from the side windows, which are placed about fourteen feet above the floor to permit cases to be placed against the walls; second, with skylights placed in the flat roof of the side aisles; and, third, with continuous skylights on the ridge of a pitched roof or nave. Ventilation is provided for through windows placed a story above the flat-aisle roof and the foot of the sloping roof over the nave. The interior of the structure is appropriately and beautifully ornamented.

Memorial Hall, which is fire-proof, has a gallery encircling it, and contains a large and interesting collection of relics and trophies of the war and other periods, all owned by the State. There are also spacious galleries from which an excellent survey of the main exhibit hall may be taken. One feature of the Illinois Building which is sure to attract much attention consists of five model common school-rooms, of high grade, fully equipped and furnished under the direction of the State Superintendent of Public Instruction. Here may be seen an illustration of the methods and results of educational work as pursued in the normal universities, the public, technical and art schools, and the high schools of the State; an exhibit by the University of Illinois of the equipment, methods of instruction and achievements of that institution in its several departments, and an exhibit of the educational and industrial work as conducted in the State charitable institutions.

There are no competitive exhibits in the Illinois Building. These are distributed in their proper places in the several Exposition structures. The Illinois building contains a " collective departmental exhibit for the State, which shall illustrate its natural resources, together with the methods employed and results accomplished by the State in its municipal capacity through its several departments, boards, commissions, bureaus and other agencies in the work of promoting the moral, educational and material welfare of its inhabitants so far as such methods and results are susceptible of exhibition." There are also collections, correctly classified and labeled, illustrating the natural history and archæology of the State ; an exhibition by the State Fish Commission of native and cultivated live fish, with hatchery and appliances and equipments for transportation, models of fishways in use; a special collection of the cultivated products in the several branches of agriculture ; architectural drawings (with elevations) of every public building erected and now used or maintained in whole or in part by the State; also maps, charts, diagrams and tables conveying full and accurate information relative to Illinois and its resources. The topographical maps of the State are sure to claim much attention. To the women of Illinois was granted $80,000, or one-tenth of the entire appropriation, and also one-tenth of the space in the building. The visitor will doubtless be intensely interested in observing how creditably the women of the State have improved the exceptional opportunity thus afforded them. The Illinois building was designed by W. W. Boyington & Co., Chicago, and cost $250,000.

THE MANUFACTURES BUILDING.

The Building for Manufactures and Liberal Arts is the leviathan of the Exposition Buildings and is by far the largest Exposition building ever erected or contemplated. It lies on the shore of Lake Michigan, on what might be called the central eastern portion of the Exposition Grounds. It is rectangular in form, its greatest dimension being north and south. It covers an area of 1,687 by 787 feet, or thirty and one-half acres. It is simple in form, comprising an immense hall in the center, surrounded by a nave and two galleries. The Central Hall is 1,280 feet long by 380 feet wide, and is roofed by a single arched span without a supporting column. This hall is surrounded by a gallery 20 feet from the floor and 67 feet wide, which gallery overlaps the floor of the hall 21 feet. Outside of this gallery is a nave 108 feet wide and 97 feet high. Surrounding the nave is a gallery, also 20 feet from the floor, and 50 feet wide, which extends to the building line. All told, there is in this immense building a total floor space of 44 acres. Its architecture is severely classic, and it is richly ornamented in the exterior. The feature of this building is its Central Hall with its immense arched roof. The largest similar structure in existence is the Jersey City Railway Depot, which is 600 feet long and 250 feet wide.

The steel trusses in the roof of this Central Hall, which occupies less than half the area of the building, weigh 10,000,000 pounds, or 5,000 tons. There are 22 of the main trusses, each one weighing 245,000 pounds.

These trusses are 14 feet wide at the base and 10 feet wide at the apex of the roof, and are on pile foundations, each truss being supported by a group of 25 piles driven 35 feet into the clay — one of the best building foundations in the world. Each of these foundations is capped with 5,000 feet of 14 by 14 inch timbers. To give some adequate idea of the immense amount of steel in the roof of this single room, it may be stated that in the great Brooklyn Bridge there is a total of 3,600 tons of iron and steel, while in the still greater St. Louis Bridge there are 5,600 tons of iron and steel.

The height of this roof is not an insignificant factor, although the immense area covered by the building will necessarily dwarf its height. The apex of the roof of the Central Hall is 245½ feet from the ground, or 3½ feet higher than the tower of the celebrated Auditorium Building in Chicago. This room or Central Hall has a clear height from floor to roof of 201 feet, which height would inclose the ordinary ten-story building. In the structural iron work of the nave and galleries there are 1,700,000 pounds of iron, so that the total of iron and steel work in the roof of this great building aggregates 5,850 tons. Only by comparison can any idea be obtained of the vastness of this building. It is four times as large as the Roman Colosseum, where history informs us 80,000 Romans were accustomed to gather at one time to see Christians devoured by tigers. St. Peter's Cathedral in Rome is the largest church structure in the world. It is so large that 10,000 people present within its walls at one time give no impression of a crowd. It is so large that although it is never heated its temperature never changes. It is so large that any church in America would be lost inside of it, and it is authoritatively stated that the largest church in Chicago could be placed within its vestibule, and yet three such church structures could be placed on the floor of the Manufactures Building. Perhaps the one structure on earth that brings with it an idea of vastness is the great Egyptian pyramid Cheops. This immense mass is 746 feet square at the base and 450 feet high, and yet, granted that it is of solid stone, it could be taken down and its material piled up in Central Hall of the Manufactures Building. It might be of interest to those up in base-ball parlance that six games of outdoor base-ball could be played at one time on the floor of this building, with the assurance that if the ball was batted at any time out of the limit of its field it would insure the batsman a home run. It is 20 times larger in area than the Auditorium Building, the most notable of the big buildings in Chicago, and, shorn of their towers, six Auditorium Buildings could be placed inside the Central Hall of the Manufactures Building. A thousand residences, 25 by 50 feet in size, could be placed on the floor of this building. The standing army of Russia could mass on this floor, and the entire population of the city of St. Louis could sit in chairs upon it. It will be lighted by electricity, and over 35,000 lights will be required. A city in extent, it will be lighted as a city. Its aisles—some 20 miles in extent—will be laid out as streets, and lighted by ornamental lamp-posts, of the usual height, bearing shielded arc lights. The exhibits will be illuminated with incandescent lights. Structural lighting will be effected by groups of arc lights, hung in the area of space between the exhibits and the roof.

In the loggias and galleries of the building 16 large cafés and 76 dining rooms will be operated.

There will enter into the construction of this building over

MACHINERY HALL.

1,300 car-loads of material—including, in the principal items, 17,000,000 feet of lumber, and 5,850 tons of iron and steel. Ten car-loads of nails will be required, and 41 cars of glass will spread over its 10 acres of skylight in the roof.

Work is now in progress on the structure. The foundations are in and the floor is nearly completed. There will be in the floor and foundations 7,000,000 feet of lumber.

The floor is absorbing 210 car-loads of pine, and five car-loads of nails are required to fasten it to the joists. Its contracted cost is $1,500,000. It will be ready for occupancy at the time of the Dedication Ceremonies in October of '92, at which time the great Central Hall will be arranged to seat 70,000 people. The architect of this gigantic building, Mr. Geo. B. Post, of New York, has been remarkably successful in giving architectural symmetry to its immense proportions, and his work will stand as one of the marvels of the Exposition and of the world.

MACHINERY HALL.

Machinery Hall, of which Peabody & Stearns, of Boston, are the architects, has been pronounced by many architects second only to the Administration Building in the magnificence of its appearance. This building measures 850 by 500 feet, and, with the Machinery Annex and Power House, cost about $1,200,000. It is located at the extreme south end of the Park, midway between the shore of Lake Michigan and the west line of the Park. It is just south of the Administration Building, and west and across a lagoon from the Agricultural Building. The building is spanned by three arched trusses and the interior presents the appearance of three railroad train-houses, side by side, surrounded on all of the four sides by a gallery 50 feet wide. The trusses are built separately, so that they can be taken down and sold for use as railroad train-houses. In each of the long naves there is an elevated traveling crane running from end to end of the building, for the purpose of moving machinery. These platforms are built so that visitors may view from them the exhibits beneath. The power for this building is supplied from a power-house adjoining the south side of the building.

All of the buildings on the great plaza are designed with a view to make a grand background for display, and, in order to conform to the general richness of the court and add to the striking appearance, the two façades of the Machinery Hall on the court are rich with colonnades and other features. The design follows classical models throughout, the detail being followed from the renaissance of Seville and other Spanish towns, as being appropriate to a Columbian celebration. An arcade on the first story admits passage around the building under cover, and, as in all the other buildings, the exterior is of "staff" colored to an attractive tone; the ceilings are enriched with strong color. A colonnade with a cafe at either end covers the space between Machinery and Agricultural Halls, and in the center of this colonnade is an archway leading to the Cattle Exhibit. From this portico there extends a view nearly a mile in length down the lagoon, and an obelisk and fountain in the lagoon form the southern point of this vista.

Machinery Annex adjoins the Hall on the west, covering about five acres, and increasing the length of the main building to about 1,400 feet, thus making it next in size to the great Manufactures Building.

NAVAL EXHIBIT.

Unique among the other exhibits is that made by the United States Navy Department. It is in a structure which, to all outward appearance, is a faithful, full-sized model of one of the new coast-line battleships designed by the Bureau of Construction and Repairs of the Navy Department, and now being built at a cost of about $3,000,000 each by Cramp & Son, Philadelphia, and the Union Iron Works, San Francisco. This imitation battleship of 1893 is erected on piling on the Lake front in the northeast portion of Jackson Park. It is surrounded by water and has the appearance of being moored to a wharf. The structure has all the fittings that belong to the actual ship, such as guns, turrets, torpedo tubes, torpedo nets and booms, with boats, anchors, chain cables, davits, awnings, and deck fittings, together with all appliances for working the same. Officers, seamen, mechanics and marines are detailed by the Navy Department during the Exposition, and the discipline and mode of life on our naval vessels are completely shown. The detail of men is not, however, as great as the complement of the actual ship. The crew give certain drills, especially boat, torpedo and gun drills, as in a vessel of war.

The dimensions of the structure are those of the actual battle-ship, to-wit: length, 348 feet; width, amidships, 69 feet 3 inches; and from the water line to the top of the main deck, 12 feet. Centrally placed on this deck is a superstructure 8 feet high, with a hammock berthing on the same 7 feet high, and above these are the bridge, chart-house, and the boats.

At the forward end of the superstructure there is a cone-shaped tower, called the "military mast," near the top of which are placed two circular "tops" as receptacles for sharpshooters. Rapid-firing guns are mounted in each of these tops. The height from the water line to the summit of this military mast is 76 feet, and above is placed a flagstaff for signaling.

The battery mounted comprises four 13-inch breech-loading rifle-cannon; eight 8-inch breech-loading rifle-cannon; four 6-inch breech-loading rifle-cannon; twenty 6-pounder rapid-firing guns; six 1-pound rapid-firing guns; two Gatling guns, and six torpedo tubes or torpedo guns. All of these are placed and mounted, respectively, as in the genuine battleship.

The superstructure shows the cabins, staterooms, lavatories, lactrines, mess-rooms, galley and fittings, mess-table for crew, lockers, berthings, etc.; also the manner in which officers and enlisted men live, according to the rules of the Navy. On the superstructure deck and bridge is shown the manner in which the rapid-firing guns, search lights, boats, etc., are handled. The entrance to the conning-tower is from the deck, in which are all appurtenances that the captain has at his disposal when taking the ship into battle and during the progress of a fight at sea.

An electric light plant is installed and provision made for heating with steam. On the berth deck are shown the various fittings pertaining to the hull, machinery, and ordnance; ordnance imple-ments, including electrical devices, gun-carriage motors and range finders; models showing typical ships of the past and present; samples of the provisions, clothing, stores, and supplies, bunting, flags, etc.; in short, the thousand and one things that go to make up the outfit of a man-of-war.

The traditional costumes of the sailors of the Navy from 1775 to 1848 are shown by men dressed in those costumes.

On the starboard side of the ship is shown the torpedo protection net, stretching the entire length of the vessel. Steam launches and cutters ride at the booms, and all the outward appearance of a real ship of war is imitated.

Nothing of the kind has ever before been attempted at a World's Fair. The cost of this curious and original structure is about $100,000.

THE TRANSPORTATION BUILDING.

Forming the northern architectural Court of the Exposition is a group of edifices of which the Transportation Building is one. It is situated at the southern end of the west flank and lies between the Horticultural and the Mines Buildings. Facing eastward, it commands a view of the floral island and an extensive branch of the lagoon.

The Transportation Building is exquisitely refined and simple in architectural treatment, although it is very rich and elaborate in detail. In style it savors much of the Romanesque, although to the initiated the manner in which it is designed on axial lines and the solicitude shown for fine proportions and subtle relation of parts to each other, will at once suggest the methods of composition followed at the Ecole des Beaux Arts.

Viewed from the lagoon, the cupola of the Transportation Building forms the effective southwest accent of the quadrangle, while from the cupola itself, reached by eight elevators, the Northern Court, the most beautiful effect of the entire Exposition, may be seen in all its glory.

The main entrance to the Transportation Building consists of an immense single-arch enriched to an extraordinary degree with carvings, bas-reliefs and mural paintings, the entire feature forming a rich and beautiful, yet quiet, color climax, for it is treated in leaf and is called the golden door.

The remainder of the architectural composition falls into a just relation of contrast with the highly wrought entrance, and is duly quiet and modest, though very broad in treatment. It consists of a continuous arcade with subordinated colonnade and entablature. Numerous minor entrances are from time to time pierced in the walls, and with them are grouped terraces, seats, drinking fountains and statues.

The interior of the building is treated much after the manner of a Roman basilica, with broad nave and aisles. The roof is therefore in three divisions; the middle one rises much higher than the others, and its walls are pierced to form a beautiful arcaded clearstory. The cupola, placed exactly in the center of the building and rising 165 feet above the ground, is reached by eight elevators. These elevators of themselves naturally form a part of the Transportation exhibit, and as they also carry passengers to galleries at various stages of height, a fine view of the interior of the building may easily be obtained. The main galleries of this building, because of the abundant elevator facilities, prove quite accessible to visitors.

The main building of the Transportation exhibit measures 960 feet front by 250 feet deep. From this extends westward to Stony Island avenue an enormous annex, covering about nine acres. This is one story only in height. In it may be seen the more bulky exhibits. Along the central avenue or nave the visitor may see facing each other scores of locomotive engines, highly polished, and rendering the perspective effect exceedingly novel and striking. Add to the effect of the exhibits the architectural impression given by a long vista of richly ornamented colonnades, and it may easily be seen that the interior of the Transportation Building is one of the most impressive of the Exposition.

The Transportation exhibits naturally include everything, of whatsoever name or sort, devoted to the purpose of transportation, and range from a baby carriage to a mogul engine, from a cash conveyor to a balloon or carrier pigeon. Technically, this exhibit includes everything comprised in Class G of the Official Classification. The Transportation Building cost about $300,000. Adler & Sullivan, of Chicago, are the architects.

WOMAN'S BUILDING.

Encompassed by luxuriant shrubs and beds of fragrant flowers, like a white silhouette against a background of old and stately oaks, is seen the Woman's Building, situated in the northwestern part of the Park, separated by a generous distance from the Horticultural Building on the one side and the Illinois State Building on the other, and facing the great lagoon with the Flowery Island as a vista—a more beautiful site could not have been selected for this daintily designed building.

Among a great number of sketches submitted in competition for this building by women from all over the land, it did not take the President of the Board of Lady Managers, Mrs. Potter Palmer, long, with her exquisite taste, to decide upon her choice. She quickly discovered in the sketch submitted by Miss Sophia G. Hayden, that harmony of grouping and gracefulness of details which indicate the architectural scholar, and to her was awarded the first prize of a thousand dollars, and also the execution of the design. The second and third prizes were given respectively to Miss Lois L. Howe, of Boston and Miss Laura Hayes, of Chicago, both fully deserving the honors conferred upon them.

Miss Hayden, who was a pupil in the architectural class in the School of Technology, in Boston, and graduated with high honors, immediately went to Chicago, and personally made the plans and elevations for the building.

Directly in front of the building the lagoon takes the form of a bay, about 400 feet in width. From the center of this bay a grand landing and staircase leads to a terrace six feet above the water. Crossing this terrace other staircases give access to the ground, four feet above, on which, about 100 feet back, the

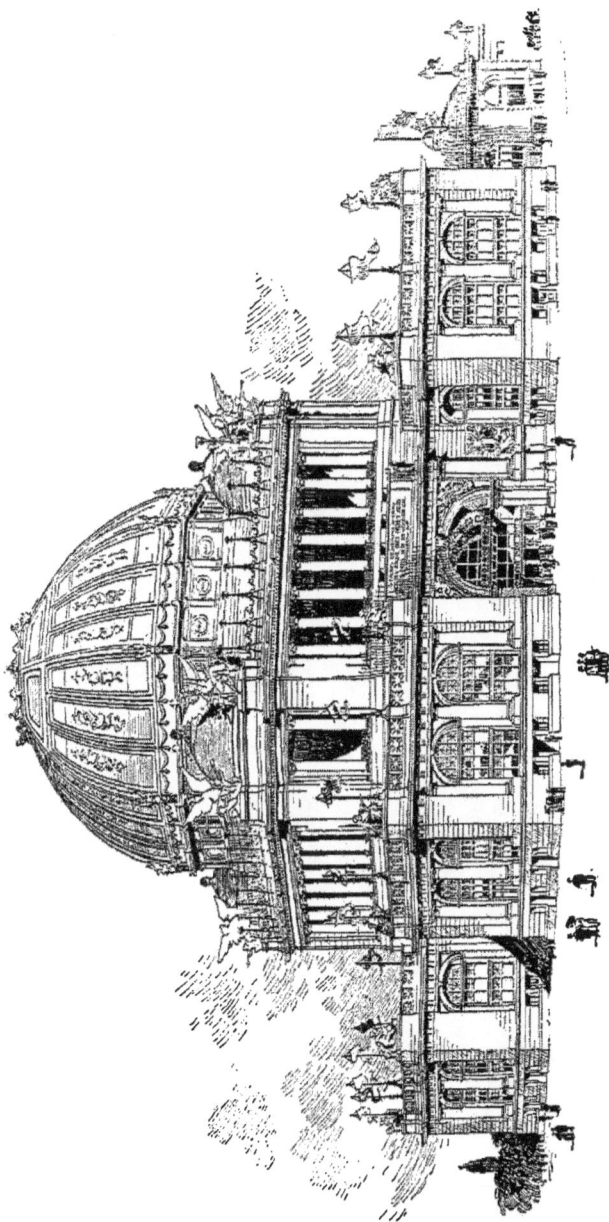

ADMINISTRATION BUILDING.

building is situated. The first terrace is designed in artistic flower beds and low shrubs, forming, together with the creamy-white balustrades rising from the water's edge, and also in front of the second terrace, a charming foreground for the fine edifice. The principal façade has an extreme length of 400 feet, the depth of the building being half this distance. Italian renaissance is the style selected. Its delicacy of lines is well adapted to represent this temple for the fair sex.

The main grouping consists of a center pavilion flanked at each end with corner pavilions connected in the first story by open arcades in the curtains, forming a shady promenade the whole length of the structure. The first story is raised about ten feet from the ground line, and a wide staircase leads to the center pavilion. This pavilion, forming the main triple-arch entrance with an open colonnade in the second story, is finished with a low and beautifully proportioned pediment enriched with a highly elaborate bas-relief. The corner pavilions, being like the rest of the building, two stories high, with a total elevation of 60 feet, have each an open colonnade added above the main cornice. Here are located the Hanging Gardens, and also the committee rooms of the Board of Lady Managers.

A lobby 40 feet wide leads into the open rotunda 70 x 65 feet, reaching through the height of the building and protected by a richly ornamented skylight. This rotunda is surrounded by a two-story open arcade, as delicate and chaste in design as the exterior, the whole having a thoroughly Italian court-yard effect, admitting abundance of light to all rooms facing this interior space. On the first floor, on each side of the main entrance, and occupying the entire space of curtains, are located, on the left hand, a model hospital; on the right a model kindergarten, each occupying 80 x 60 feet.

The whole floor of the south pavilion is devoted to the retrospective exhibit; the one on the north to reform work and charity organization. Each of these floors is 80x200 feet. The curtain opposite the main front contains the Library, Bureau of Information, records, etc.

In the second story above the main entrance and curtains, are located ladies' parlors, committee-rooms and dressing-rooms, all leading to the open balcony in front, and commanding a splendid panorama of almost the entire ground. The whole second floor of the north pavilion incloses the great assembly-room and club-room. The first of these is provided with an elevated stage for the accommodation of speakers. The south pavilion contains the model kitchen, refreshment rooms, reception-rooms, etc.

The building is encased with " staff," the same material used on the rest of the buildings, and as it stands with its mellow, decorated walls bathed in the bright sunshine, the women of the country are justly proud of the result.

STAFF.

The buildings for exposition purposes will all be covered by staff, a composition which was first used in the Paris Exposition. Thirty thousand tons or 2,000 car-loads of this material will be required to face the main structures. Staff will also be used in the construction of statuary. This curious material is composed chiefly of powdered gypsum, the other constituents being alumnia, glycerine and dextrine. These are mixed with water without heat and the mixture is then cast in molds in any shape desired and allowed to harden. The natural color is a murky white, but other colors are secured by external washes so as to give the buildings a varied appearance. To prevent brittleness the material is cast around a coarse cloth, bagging or oakum. The casts are shallow—about one-half inch thick. They may be in any shape or form—in imitation of cut stone, rock, faced stone or mouldings of the most delicate designs. For the lower portions of the walls the material is mixed with cement, which makes it hard. Staff is impervious to water and is a permanent building material, although the cost is less than one-tenth of that of marble or granite.

Aside from the cost of the great buildings which will be not far from $7,000,000, the following are among the sums which have been or will be spent in preparation of the Exposition grounds : Grading and filling, $450,000 ; landscape gardening, $323,500 ; viaducts and bridges, $125,000 ; piers, $70,000 ; water-way improvements, $225,000 ; railways, $500,000 ; steam plant,

$800,000 ; electric lighting, $1,500,000 ; statuary, $100,000 ; vases, lamps, etc., $50,000; lake front adornment, $200,000 ; water supply and sewerage, $600,000 ; other expenses, $1,000,000 ; total $5,943,500. The total expense of organization, administration and operation of the Exposition is estimated at nearly $5,000,000. This takes no account of the sums to be spent by the government. the States or foreign nations.

Making the Exposition International.

The World's Columbian Exposition will be the ninth in the series of world's expositions. London, Paris, Vienna, have had their exposition. America had one in Philadelphia. All of these places were well known. Their history reaches far back into the past. Even Philadelphia is an old city compared to Chicago. It is known all over the civilized world. Its name, like those of the great capitals of Europe, was linked with the history of commerce, industry, and invention long before it was thought of for the Centennial Exposition.

Not so in the case of Chicago. Few people outside of the United States knew there was such a city, till twenty years ago the world at large was startled by the intelligence of a great conflagration, a disaster that swept away property amounting to hundreds of millions of dollars, in a region popularly supposed to be a wilderness. Together with the news of this calamity there came, for the first time, the report that a great city was rising on the shore of Lake Michigan, the commercial capital of an empire beyond the supposed boundaries of civilization, wider in extent, more varied in natural opportunities, than any of the great empires of history.

But the Chicago of 1871 was but a little hamlet compared to the Chicago of to-day. The empire whose possibilities were then brought under the observation of the civilized world has developed to an extent then entirely unexpected, and, at present, but little understood outside of the limits of the United States. Chicago is to-day the second city of America in point of population, the first in point of promise of continued substantial growth. Most of the commerce of Chicago, however, was until recently confined to this continent. Only within a few years did Chicago enter, and as it entered, conquer the markets of the world. The European continued to deal with New York and other seaport cities, remaining ignorant of the fact that these cities drew their supplies, their life blood, from the great West via Chicago. The average European heard little or nothing about Chicago since the great fire. He retained the idea that was created at that time and knew nothing of the existence of a city of palaces in the center of the North American continent.

When the World's Columbian Exposition was located in Chicago it did not receive the impetus that was given to previous expositions held in London, Paris, or Vienna. As far as foreign countries were concerned, it became necessary first to inform them what Chicago was. This implied information with regard to the Western section of the United States, for the two are inseparable.

This great handicap has been successfully overcome, and once overcome, the eyes of Europeans were opened to the wonders of·this western world. The effect was instantaneous and miraculous. The curtain was suddenly raised upon unknown wonder lands, and the fact once established to the conviction of the skeptical European mind that the claims made in behalf of Chicago were amply borne out by the facts, they became ready to believe almost anything. So great was the amazement at the revelation of unknown wonders that thereafter it was difficult to protect Europeans·from imposition by charlatans, for credulity took the place of skepticism.

It is not too much to say that in certain countries, at least, the feeling for the World's Columbian Exposition falls little short of enthusiasm.

It is true that much of the opposition which appeared at the outset still remains and may affect the representation of some foreign countries at the Exposition. Without any intention of discussing the merits of the tariff laws of the United States the fact cannot be denied that those laws have had the effect of deterring many merchants who would otherwise have attended the Exposition, from making any notable effort to be represented. Naturally this feeling extended to government circles and caused the invitation issued by the President of the United States to be received more coolly than would have been the case had the commercial interests of those countries felt that they could freely export their goods to the United States.

But even this, the weightiest of all objections raised against participation in our exposition, was at last overcome, in part at least. Most of the governments of civilized nations have decided to be represented and have appointed commissioners to take charge of the exhibit.

The course which this branch of the exposition work pursued may be outlined as follows:

An official invitation was issued by President Harrison and transmitted to foreign governments through the usual channels of diplomatic intercourse. In due course of time the acceptances or declinations were returned in the same manner and communicated by the State Department to the Director-General of the Exposition. The foreign government would, then, select its commissioners to manage its section of the Exposition. These commissioners placed themselves in communication with the Director-General and the Department of Foreign Affairs and received printed rules and regulations for the government of foreign exhibits together with the rules issued by the Treasury Department for the admission free of duty of goods intended for exhibition. Upon receipt of this information the commissioners began to "work up" the exposition in their respective countries with varying results.

Official interest in the Exposition was somewhat slack in many countries as to the objects of the exposition and more particularly the provisions made to carry out these objects were not understood. Semi-official statements contained in the foreign press were of little value to government circles and could not be taken into consideration as a basis for official action. In order to meet this difficulty a commission of representatives of the Exposition was sent abroad, consisting of A. G. Bullock of Massachusetts and Judge Wm. Lindsay of Kentucky, members of the United States Commission for the Exposition; Ferd. W. Peck and Benjamin Butterworth, members of the local directory, and M. P. Handy, chief of the department of Publicity and Promo-

15

tion. This commission spent' two months in Europe and established communication with official circles as well as with
commercial and industrial bodies whose opinion would be apt
to influence official action and whose members would, in most
cases, become the actual exhibitors. Returning home this commission brought with it some of the commissioners appointed
by foreign governments and entertained them in Chicago long
enough to permit them to gain a full insight into the plans of
the exposition as well as to propound their own demands and
make selections of space and location for their respective exhibits.
In this manner the closest relations were at once established with
the countries so represented.

The first commission to Europe visited England, France,
Germany, Austria-Hungary, Denmark, Sweden, Belgium and
Holland. It became necessary to send another commission to
visit the countries that had been omitted. This commission
started early in December and consisted of Vice-president T. B.
Bryan and Director H. N. Higinbotham. The commission will
be supplemented by the addition of two other men later on.
They were sent to visit Spain and Portugal, Italy, Greece,
Turkey, the Balkan States, Russia, Egypt, Tripoli, Algiers,
Morocco, and if time permitted, the Orient as well.

While these commissions were received with uniform courtesy
and distinction, official interest in the exposition assumed widely
differing forms and degrees. Great Britain took but a lukewarm
interest at first, but has been waking up of late. The interest of
France was little more than perfunctory and such as was required
by international courtesy. The opposition remains strong in
that country and if a good exhibit is to be secured it will require
much hard work. On the other hand, Germany has shown a
most remarkable interest. It is the personal desire of the
emperor that a most brilliant showing be made, the commissioner appointed is working like a beaver, traveling all over the
country lecturing and laboring with commercial organizations
and large manufacturers, and all but two or three industries have
resolved to be splendidly represented. In a similar manner
Austria displays a most gratifying interest. Russia likewise
promises to be magnificently represented. The Scandinavian

countries and Denmark follow in the same line. Germany has selected space for a separate government building.

The instructions to foreign commissions issued by the Department of Foreign Affairs were as follows:

GENERAL REGULATIONS FOR FOREIGN EXHIBITORS.

1. The Exhibition will be held on the shore of Lake Michigan, in the City of Chicago, and will be opened on the first day of May, 1893, and closed on the 30th day of October following.

2. All governments have been invited to appoint commissions for the purpose of organizing their departments of the Exhibition. The Director-General should be notified of the appointment of such foreign commissions as soon as the appointment is made.

Diagrams of the buildings and grounds will be furnished to the foreign commissions on or before January 1, 1892, indicating the localities to be occupied by each nation, subject, however, to revision and readjustment.

3. Applications for space and negotiations relative thereto must be conducted with the commission of the country where the article is produced.

4. Foreign commissions are requested to notify the Director-General not later than June 1, 1892, whether they desire any increase or diminution of the space offered them, and the amount.

5. Before November 1, 1892, the foreign commissions must furnish the Director-General with approximate plans showing the manner of allotting the space assigned to them, and also with lists of their exhibitors and other information necessary for the preparation of the official catalogue.

Products brought into the United States at the ports of Portland, Me.; Boston, Mass.; New York, N. Y.; Philadelphia, Penn.; Baltimore, Md.; Norfolk, Va.; Newport News, Va.; Key West, Fla.; Mobile, Ala.; New Orleans, La.; Galveston, Texas; San Francisco, Cal.; Port Townsend, Wash.; Portland, Ore.; Port Huron, Mich.; Detroit, Mich., and Chicago, Ill., or at any other port of entry, intended for display at the International Exhibition, will be allowed to go forward to the Exhibition buildings, under proper supervision of custom officers, without examination at such ports of original entry, and at the close of the Exhibition will be allowed to go forward to the port from which they are to be exported. No duties will be levied upon such goods unless entered for consumption in the United States.

6. The transportation, receiving, unpacking, and arranging of the products for exhibition will be at the expense of the exhibitor.

7. The installation of heavy articles requiring special foundations or adjustment should, by special arrangement, begin as soon as the progress of the work upon the buildings will permit. The general reception of articles at the Exhibition buildings will commence on November 1, 1892, and no articles will be admitted after April 10, 1893.

NOTE.—Weight of single article limited to 30,000 pounds.

8. Space assigned to foreign commissions and not occupied on the 10th day of April, 1893, will revert to the Director-General for reassignment.

9. If products are intended for competition it must be so stated by the exhibitor; if not, they will be excluded from the examination by the international juries.

10. An Official Catalogue will be published in English, French, German, and Spanish. The sale of catalogues is reserved to the World's Columbian Exposition,

11. Foreign commissions may publish catalogues of their respective sections.

12. Exhibitors will not be charged for space.

A limited quantity of steam and water power will be supplied gratuitously. The quantity of each will be settled definitely at the time of the allotment of space. Any power required by the exhibitor in excess of that allowed will be furnished by the World's Columbian Exposition at a fixed price. Demands for such excess of power must also be settled at the time of the allotment of space.

13. Exhibitors must provide at their own cost all show-cases, shelving, counters, fittings, etc., which they may require, and all countershafts, with their pulleys, belting, etc., for the transmission of power from the main shafts in the building where the exhibit is located. All arrangements of articles and decorations must be in conformity with the general plan adopted by the Director-General.

NOTE.—The general plan requires all decorations, signs, etc., to be in harmony with the dignity and magnitude of the magnificent exhibition, and the Director-General is empowered to secure this result.

The World's Columbian Exposition will take precautions for the safe preservation of all objects in the Exhibition; but it will in no way be responsible for damage or loss of any kind, or for accidents by fire, or otherwise, however originating.

NOTE.—A thoroughly equipped fire department will protect the buildings and exhibits, and a large police force will maintain order. The entire Exposition grounds will be under the immediate supervision of the City of Chicago and of the State of Illinois. A guard equal to any possible contingency is thus provided; the municipal authority being upheld, if necessary, by the State troops, and the State, by the army of the United States, so that no apprehension need arise as to losses resulting from lawlessness.

14. Favorable facilities will be arranged by which exhibitors or foreign commissions may insure their own goods.

NOTE.—Special care has been taken to render everything about the Exposition as nearly fireproof as possible, and it is reasonably certain that the rates of insurance will not be excessive, but, on the contrary, very reasonable. Exhibitors may insure in any company, foreign or domestic. Arrangements will be made with English, French, German, and American companies to fix uniform or special rates on exhibits and buildings, so that no advantage will be taken of any exhibitor who wishes to insure his goods.

Foreign commissions may employ watchmen of their own choice to guard their goods during the hours the Exhibition is open to the public, subject to the rules and regulations of the Exposition.

15. Foreign commissions, or such agents as they may designate, shall be responsible for the receiving, unpacking, and arrangement of objects, as well as for

the removal at the close of the Exposition; but no person shall be permitted to act as such agent until he can give to the Director-General written evidence of his having been approved by the proper commission.

16. Each package must be addressed, "To the Commission (name of country) at the World's Columbian Exposition, Chicago, United States of America," and should have at least two labels affixed to different, but not opposite sides, of each case, and give the following information:

17. (1) The country from which it comes; (2) Name of firm of the exhibitor; (3) Residence of the exhibitor; (4) Department to which objects belong; (5) Total number of packages sent by that exhibitor ; (6) Serial number of that particular package.

18. Within each package should be a list of all objects.

19. If no authorized person is at hand to receive goods on their arrival at the Exposition buildings, they will be removed without delay and stored at the risk and cost of whomsoever it may concern.

20. Articles that are in any way dangerous or offensive, also patent nostrums and empirical preparations, whose ingredients are concealed, will not be admitted.

21. The removal of goods on exhibition will not be permitted prior to the close of the Exhibition.

NOTE.—Articles on exhibition in competition may be sold under special permit.

22. Sketches, drawings, photographs, or other reproductions of articles exhibited will only be allowed upon the joint assent of the exhibitor and the Director-General ; but views of portions of the building may be made upon the Director-General's sanction.

23. Immediately after the close of the Exhibition, exhibitors shall remove their effects, and complete such removal before January 1, 1894 ; goods then remaining will be removed and sold for expenses, or otherwise disposed of under the direction of the World's Columbian Exposition.

24. Each person who becomes an exhibitor thereby acknowledges and agrees to be governed by the rules and regulations established for the government of the Exhibition.

Special regulations will be issued concerning the exhibition of fine arts, awards, the organization of the international juries, and sales of special articles within the buildings, and on other points not touched upon in these preliminary instructions.

25. All communications concerning the Exhibition will be addressed to the Director-General, World's Columbian Exposition, Chicago, Illinois, U. S. A.

The management reserves the right to explain or amend these regulations, whenever it may be deemed necessary for the interest of the Exhibition.

WALKER FEARN,   GEORGE R. DAVIS,
Chief, Department of Foreign Affairs.   *Director-General.*

The United States Treasury Department has issued rules to carry out the intentions of the law authorizing the Exposition, which provide:

"That all articles which shall be imported from foreign countries for the sole purpose of exhibition at said Exposition, upon which there shall be a tariff or customs duty, shall be admitted free of payment of duty, custom fees, or charges, under such regulation as the Secretary of the Treasury shall prescribe; but it shall be lawful at any time during the exhibition to sell, for delivery at the close of the Exposition, any goods or property imported for and actually on exhibition in the Exposition buildings or on its grounds, subject to such regulations for the security of the revenue and for the collection of the import duties as the Secretary of the Treasury shall prescribe: *provided*, That all such articles, when sold or withdrawn for consumption in the United States, shall be subject to the duty, if any, imposed upon such articles by the revenue laws in force at the date of importation, and all penalties prescribed by the law shall be applied and enforced against such articles and against the persons who may be guilty of any illegal sale or withdrawal."

In addition to the commissions sent abroad some of the departments have had special emissaries in Europe for the purpose of interesting their particular branches of art, science and industry in the exposition.   Halcey C. Ives, chief of the department of Fine Arts, has been in Europe for months.   His reception was superb.   He visited Paris during the salon and secured many promises to exhibit.   He went to Berlin during the international art exposition last Summer and made a favorable impression.   In Vienna he aroused so much enthusiasm that it was resolved to postpone until 1894 an art exposition which had been planned for 1892.   In Copenhagen also he was eminently successful.   J. Allan Hornsby, secretary of the department of electricity, visited the great electrotechnic exposition at Frankfort. His reception was a marvel of consideration.   Arriving late he expressed a desire to be permitted to inspect the exposition after it was closed and the directory resolved to keep it open two weeks beyond the closing time, in order to afford him an opportunity to study it.

The official representation of the exposition in the Latin-American countries was undertaken by the State Department with the advice and instructions of the Director-General.   Officers of the army and navy were assigned to this work according to their personal fitness for the various tasks.   These men have been engaged in Central and South America since January, 1891, and the results so far have been eminently satisfactory.   The commissioner to the West Indies, Frederick Ober, has secured many relics from the time of Columbus which will prove very attractive.

The Asiatic countries have not yet shown any great degree of interest with the exception of Japan. This enterprising nation was among the first to accept the official invitation of the United States and appropriated a large amount of money for its exhibit, which is expected to be one of the most attractive of the entire Exposition.

The official work with foreign governments was materially assisted by another branch of work, which, while emanating directly from the Exposition authorities was directed to unofficial channels, namely the newspapers and publishers abroad. Information regarding the World's Columbian Exposition, about Chicago and the United States in general was sent out to thousands of newspapers in such a way as to make it readable and interesting from other points of view than those of the manufacturer or merchant or the government commissioner. Matters that were thought to be interesting to the average reader were sent out free of charge with a request to publish the same, and the request meeting with much favor the World's Columbian Exposition was constantly kept before the foreign reader in some form or other. It is believed that this work did more to create a public sentiment favorable to the Exposition than could have been accomplished by any official action. The articles were prepared in the language of the countries they were sent to and written by men thoroughly conversant with the spirit of the respective nation and knowing what kind of reading matter would be best calculated to awaken interest.

The following table contains the nations that have accepted the invitation to take part in the Exposition, with the appropriations made to carry out this acceptance, so far as they are known :

Argentine Republic	$100,000	Costa Rica	100,000
Austria-Hungary	147,000	Denmark	......
Belgium	......	Danish West Indies	10,000
Bolivia	150,000	Ecuador	125,000
Brazil	550,000	France	400,000
China	......	Algeria	......
Chile	100,000	French Guiana	......
Columbia	100,000	Germany	215,000

Great Britain.	125,000	Mexico	750,000
Barbadoes	......	Dutch Guiana	6.000
British Columbia	......	" West Indies	10,000
" Guiana.	20,000	Nicaragua	31,000
" Honduras	7,000	Orange Free State	......
Cape Colony	25,000	Paraguay	......
Ceylon	40,000	Persia	......
Jamaica	10,000	Peru	140,000
New South Wales	......	Russia	......
New Zealand	27,000	Salvador	30,000
Trinidad	15,000	San Domingo	......
Queensland	......	Siam.	......
Guatemala	120,000	Spain	......
Hayti	...	Cuba.	25,000
Honduras	20,000	Porto Rico	......
Hawaiian Islands	.. ...	Turkey	......
Japan	700,000	Uruguay	......
Korea	......	Venezuela	......
Madagascar	......	Zanzibar	......

The Netherlands and Egypt have declined to take part.
The subjoined list gives the names of foreign commissioners as far as appointed, in some cases the name of the president alone being given where the list is long.

BELGIUM—President, Mr. Vercruysse; Commissioner-General, Mr. Alfred Simonis; 1st Vice President, Mr. Slingeneyer; 2nd Vice President, Mr. Hovine; Secretary-General, Mr. Amelin.

BRAZIL—Commissioners, Lieut. Com. J. Cordeiro da Graça (appointed to accompany Capt. Rodgers and assist his work.) Lieut. Antonio de Barros Barrete (appointed to accompany Lieut. Sawyer and assist his work.) *State of Rio de Janeiro*—Lieut. Gov. A. Getulio das Neves, President. *State of Maranhao*—Dr. Tarquino Lopez, President. *State of Minas Geraes*—Dr. Francisco Luiz de Veiga, President. *State of Para*—Baron de Marajo, President.

COSTA RICA—Enrique Pittier, Chairman, Geo. K. Cherrie; Adolfo Tonduz; Luis Chable.

GUATEMALA—Dr. Don Gustavo E. Guzman; Dr. Leon Rosenthal; Don Ignacio Solis.

HONDURAS—Dr. R. Fritzgartener.

NICARAGUA—Don Antonio Salaverri.

SALVADOR—Dr. Esteban Castro (Sub-Secretary of Fomento), President; Dr. H. Prowe; General D. Juan Canas; Dr. D. Dario Gonzales; Dr. D. Carlos Renson.

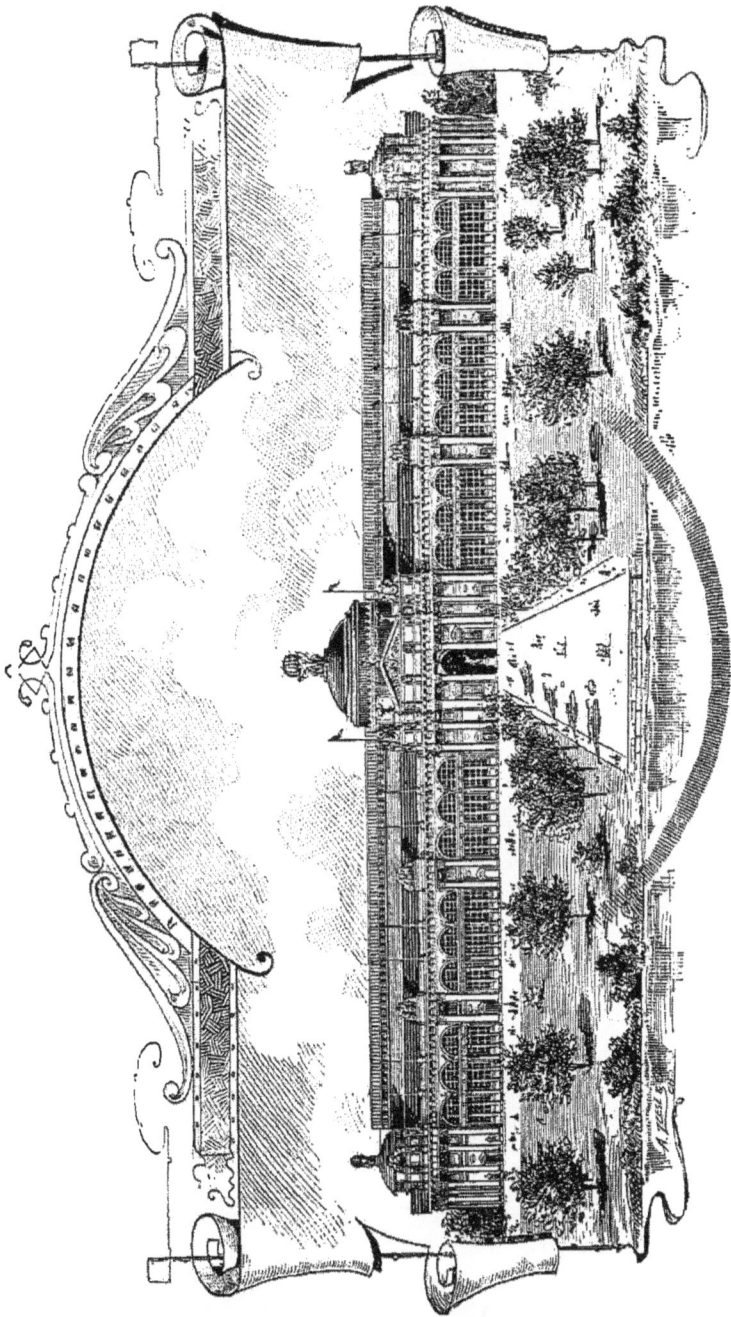

AGRICULTURAL BUILDING.

CHINA—Resident Agent at Shanghai, The Customs Taotai at Shanghai; The Chinese Legation in Washington.

COLUMBIA—Sr. Don Carlos Martinez Silva; Sr. Don Salvador Camacho Roldan; Sr. Don Vicente Restrepo; Sr. Don Gonzalo Ramos Ruitz.

DENMARK—Dr. Emil Meyer.

ECUADOR—Dr. Eduardo Arosemena,. President; Senor Don Jose Nicolas Vacas; Senor Vincente Pallores Penafiel; Senor Juan Abel Echeveria; Senor Teofilo Saenz; Senor Luis Felipe Carlos; Senor Amadeo Tobar; Gen. Jose Maria Placido Caamano, Chief Commissioner.

FRANCE—His Excellency the Minister of Commerce.

GERMANY—The Honorable Privy Councillor Wermuth.

GREAT BRITAIN—The Council of the Society of Arts. Sir Henry Trueman Wood, Secretary. *New South Wales.* Executive Commissioner, Dr. Renwick; Wm. M. Millary, President.

BRITISH GUIANA—Royal Agricultural and Commercial Society, B. Howell Jones, President.

BRITISH HONDURAS—Hon. John T. Phillips (Appointed Chairman Exposition Committee) Frederick Gahne, Esq.; J. M. Currie, Esq.; W. S. Marshall, Esq.; J. M. Moir, Esq.; Sydney Cuthbert, Esq.; F. Fisher, Esq.

CAPE COLONY—L. Wiener, M. L. A.

JAMAICA—Lieut. Col. C. J. Ward, C. M. G.

TRINIDAD—Henry Fowler, Esq., Colonial Secretary, appointed Chairman of Preliminary Exposition Committee.

JAPAN—His Excellency Munimitsu, Minister of State for Agriculture and Commerce, President; Mr. Kicutaro Yanagiya, Secretary to the Ministry of Agriculture and Commerce; Mr. Nobuakira Yamataka, Director of the Sections of Industry and Art in the Imperial Museum; Mr. Kiujokaze Ashiwara, Secretary to the Ministry of Agriculture and Commerce; Mr. Takashi Hara, Private Secretary to the Minister of State for Agriculture and Commerce; Mr. Seiichi Tejima, Director of the Tokio Technological School. *Tokio, Japan.*

KOREA—Mr. Ye Wan Yong, *Seoul, Korea.*

DUTCH WEST INDIES.—J. H. R. Beaujon; D. Gaerste, Wz.; M. B. Gorsira, Pz.; D. A. D. Jesurun; Ed. I. Van Leer, L. L. D.; E. S. L. Maduro; J. E. Van der Meulen, Jr.; R. M. Ribbins; Lieut. M. J. Selhorst; J. B. Van der Linde Schetborgh.

PARAGUAY—Dr. Jose S. Decoud; Dr. Don Benjamin Aceval; Dr. Don Hector Velasquez; Dr. Don Guillermo Stewart; Dr. Don Emilio Hassler; Don Ricardo Brugada; Don Ricardo Mendes Goncalvez; Don Emilio Aceval; Don Pedro Miranda; Don Pacifico de Vargas; Don Geronimo Percira Gazal; Don Pedro V. Gill; Don Daniel Anisitz; Don Noberto Molinas; Don Enrique Mangel; Don Leon Boussiron; Don Luis Von

Strate; Don Esteban Mendiondon; Don Alfredo Bolttner; Don Antonio
Pecci; Don Pedro Rufinelli; Don Santiago Scharer; Don Carlon von
Gulich.

PERSIA—·Hon. E. Spencer Pratt, Commissioner General; M. Octave Dia-
mante, Secretary General.

PERU—Don Eduaido Habich; Don Eulogio Dalgado; Don Ricardo Palma;
Don Ricardo Rossel; Don Eugenio Larraburey Unanue; Don Federico
Elmore; Don Ernesto Malinouski; Don Samuel Palacios; Don Gabino
Pacheco Zegarra.

RUSSIA—His Excellency Privy-Councillor Behr.

CUBA—Excmo. Sr. D. Antonio C. Telleria, President.

The products of every industry of every land will be seen at
the World's Fair, together with the wonderful works and resources of our own country. In fact, the most noticeable feature
of the preliminary work of the World's Columbian Exposition is
the unprecedented interest displayed by foreign nations. Never
before in the history of a great historical and industrial enterprise has the outside world responded with such promptitude
and marked unanimity. It is a rational enthusiasm, too, for the
event to be commemorated is of world-wide importance and
interest far surpassing the centenary of a single nation. It is in
honor of the discovery of a new world, and 400 years of a new
era and a new civilization: It is to demonstrate the grandeur of
the New World, who people it, how it is governed, who owns it,
what it has contributed to wealth, science, art, and the progress
of civilization! The United States is but one of the nineteen
republics of the New World which Columbus discovered, and a
correct understanding of its achievements and possibilities requires a grouping together of the products of the various nations
of the three Americas.

The total land area of all America is over 15,000,000 square
miles. This immense territory is controlled partly by independent American republics and partly by European colonies. In
North America, exclusive of Mexico, the United States controls
one-half and Great Britain the other half. The area of the
United States and Alaska is in round numbers 3,600,000 square
miles, while Great Britain has in her Canadian and other North
America possessions 3,400,000 square miles.

Of American republics there are two in North America, five in Central America, ten in South America, and two in the West Indies. Of European colonies on the continent, there are one in North America, one in Central America, and three in South America. Of the forty principal West India islands, Great Britain controls fifteen, France five, Holland six, Denmark three, and Sweden one. The total population of these various republics and colonies is, in round numbers, 125,000,000.

The facts relating to the material development, progress, and wealth of the New World are still more significant, and illustrate what America has to exhibit in 1893, and why its several nations are making such elaborate preparations for the coming event. It has already constructed 200,000 miles of railways, as against 170,000 miles of the rest of the world. It has during the last 400 years produced $6,200,000,000 in silver, as against $1,180,000,000 of the rest of the world. During the last fifty years the total gold product was $5,950,000,000 in value, while that of the outside world was but $1,290,000,000. The public debt is $2,500,000,000, or only one-tenth of that of the whole world. The total wealth of the New World has never been estimated, but that of one of our republics—the United States—is now about $62,500,000,000. The grain crop of this single republic for the year 1891 is estimated at about 3,500,000,000 bushels.

These are but illustrations of the material wonders of the new world which Columbus discovered, but they are sufficient to show why the American republics and colonies are so intensely earnest in preparing for the coming Exposition, and why the nations of the Old World are also responding with marked unanimity. All of the American republics, nineteen in number, have accepted the invitation to join in the Exposition. Of the various States of the United States, forty-nine have already provided appropriations and all others will, and in 1893 the shores of Lake Michigan will present the most magnificent display of the world's wealth and genius ever dreamed of by man. It is not probable that any commercial nation of the world will fail to be an active participant.

Government of the Exposition.

The World's Columbian Exposition is an entertainment given to the world by the United States government in celebration of the discovery of America and the progress of humanity. The big show is produced by a firm of two partners—the "World's Columbian Commission," and the "World's Columbian Exposition." The former is national in its character, being created by Act of Congress. Its members are appointed by the President and its officers are elected by the commission. The other member of the firm is local in its character, being a stock company, organized and operating under the laws of Illinois, its officers being elected by the stockholders.

When the United States government decided to give its entertainment, the citizens of Chicago virtually said, "Give your entertainment in our city, and we will furnish the grounds and buildings for it. We will pay all the expenses of its production and assume the financial loss or profit, as the case may be."

The government creates and produces the entertainment. The Chicago company furnishes the site and pays the expenses. The "World's Columbian Commission" puts on the drama of Human Progress, engages the company, and fixes the date of the performance. The "World's Columbian Exposition" builds the playhouse, furnishes, lights and heats it, equips the stage with machinery and scenery, pays the advertising bills and the salaries of the performers, engages the ushers and ticket sellers and takes in the cash.

While in theory the two bodies occupy separate spheres in the production of the fair, practically, every specific act of the Chicago corporation is under the supervision of the National Commission, and the government, through its commission, is primarily responsible for the success or failure of the fair. The Chicago corporation, in theory, has no original or exclusive powers. It can do nothing without the approval of the National Commission, while that body is responsible to Congress. As crystalized in the act of Congress, the National commission has the exclusive power to allot space to exhibitors; to classify and install exhibits; to determine the plan and scope of the Exposition; to appoint judges and examiners; to award premiums, and to have general charge of all intercourse with exhibitors and foreign nations.

The Chicago corporation has the collateral power of furnishing grounds and buildings for the fair, the national body having power to accept or reject the site and the plans for the buildings. Even after having accepted the site and building plans, which has been done, the power of the commission, in this connection, is not exhausted, and it can at any time reconsider its action. This has been done in one notable instance. Plans for the Manufactures Buildings were accepted, the Exposition company let the contracts for its erection, and work was begun. At the instance of the national commission the plans were radically changed, and the original cost of the building almost doubled.

The Illinois corporation has the power to prescribe all rules and regulations affecting the rights and privileges of exhibitors and the public during the continuance of the fair, outside of the exclusive powers of the commission enumerated above; but all such rules and regulations are subject to modification by a majority of the commission. It is a matter of open history that these lines were not followed in the early conduct of the business of the fair. In its construction of its powers, the Chicago corporation encroached upon the domain of the national commission. The controversies arising led to the appointment of a joint conference committee, to determine the powers and duties of the two bodies. This committee laid out the plan of procedure now in practice. The work of the Exposition is divided into 15 departments, each department having a chief officer, who generally directs the business of that department, under the control of the Director-General of all the departments—George R. Davis. The salaries of these officers are fixed by the Director-General, and paid by the Chicago company, as well as the expenses of the departments. The salary of the Director-General and his clerk-hire is paid by the national commission. The Chicago body has the power to discontinue the appropriation for any one or more of these departments at any time it sees fit. To insure harmony, a board of reference and control was created, consisting of eight members from each body, to which all matters of difference are referred, and whose action thereon is final.

None of the original or exclusive powers of the national commission are vitiated by this compact or constitution, and one of the most important of these to the public is the exclusive power of allotment of space to exhibitors. No authority but Director-General Davis and his department chiefs can allot space for or install an article for exhibition at the fair. The Chicago corporation has no power in this direction. It has developed in the correspondence with would-be exhibitors that many of them are in doubt on this point. In the preparation of the grounds and buildings it has become necessary to supply a vast amount of machinery for the service of the Exposition. It is the province of the Chicago corporation to supply the power to drive the machinery; to light the grounds and buildings, to furnish water, etc., and to effect this, engines, boilers, pumps, dynamos, etc., must be installed in the buildings. The Chicago corporation, however, can make no contracts for the competitive exhibition of any article. The construction department of the Exposition company can fur-. nish such service machinery as it desires, but space must be allotted it by the Director-General.

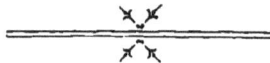

World's Congresses.

A peculiar organization has been formed to be operated in connection with the World's Columbian Exposition, which like many other features of the Exposition is as novel as it is promising of good results. The purpose is to realize to the fullest extent the educational possibilties of such an aggregation of the best and most advanced products of the human mind from all over the world. The remarkable educational power of such an exhibition has been recognized fully on previous occasions, but no plan was discovered to exploit all these advantages to their extreme limit.

The World's Congress Auxiliary to the World's Columbian

Exposition has for its object the exploitation of the Exposition in this direction. It is nothing less than to bring together the greatest minds in all branches of industry, art, and science.

Congresses will be held and all imaginable subjects be discussed by those best able to give valuable opinions on them. There is to be no distinction or favoritism ; all varieties of thought will have equal rights and equal opportunities to have them expressed. The secretary of the Auxiliary, C. C. Bonney, thus expresses the objects of the organization :

To promote the holding of appropriate conventions during the World's Columbian Exposition of 1893, for the consideration of the living questions in all the departments of human progress; and in addition thereto a Union Congress for each department, under the direction of the Auxiliary, in which the important results accomplished will be set forth by the most eminent representatives who can attend, thus securing freedom and independence of separate organizations, and union and harmony in presenting to the world the higher achievements of mankind; while the people who will come to the Exposition may enjoy the privilege of seeing and hearing many of the distinguished leaders with whose name they have become familar. The Auxiliary has no jurisdiction over any exhibit of material things, but will deal exclusively with conventions of persons and their proceedings, with the aim of promoting, by fraternal action, the progress, prosperity, unity, peace and happiness of the world. It is hoped that the Congresses will result in a series of permanent world-wide fraternities of very great practical value.

The controlling purpose of the Auxiliary will be to bring all of the departments of progress into harmonious relation with each other, to the end that the utmost attainable completeness and unity may characterize the World's Congresses of 1893, without materially impairing the distinctive characteristics of the various contributions to the marvelous progress of the nineteenth century. Differing religious denominations, temperance societies, schools of medicine, and other organizations will work in harmony to secure a result in which all are alike interested, and to obtain which the Auxiliary will endeavor to exercise the highest impartiality and justice. It will aim to secure a presentation of the best aspect of every sincere and commendable effort to attain a result beneficial to mankind, leaving the comparative merits of competing institutions to the judgment of the enlightened world.

A number of committees have been appointed to attend to the various branches of this work. Honorary membership in these committees has been conferred on many persons well known in the literary and scientific worlds. Acceptances have been received from the following :

The Hon. Jas. G. Blaine, United States Secretary of State, Washington, D. C.

The Rev. Phillips Brooks. Boston.

Dr. John S. Billings, U. S. A., Washington, D. C.

The Hon. Thomas M. Cooley, Inter-State Commerce Commission.

Hon. George William Curtis, New York.

Dr. James B. Angell, LL.D., Ann Arbor, Michigan, President Michigan University.

Prof. H. P. Armsby, State College, Pennsylvania.

Pres. Henry E. Alvord, Maryland Agricultural College, College Park, Md.

Pres. O. Clute, Agricultural College, Michigan.

Pres. Charles W. Dabney, Jr., University of Tennessee.

Dr. Charles W. Eliot, President Harvard University, Cambridge, Mass.

Prof. George T. Fairchild, Manhattan, Kas.

Pres. M. C. Fernald, Maine State College, Orono, Me.

Gov. Joseph W. Fifer, Springfield, Ill.

Dr. D. C. Gilman, Baltimore, Md., President John Hopkins University.

Dr. Merrill E. Gate, LL.D., Amherst, Mass., President Amherst College.

His Eminence, Cardinal James Gibbons, Baltimore, Md.

Prof. G. Brown Goode, Assistant Secretary Smithsonian Institution, Washington.

Pres. H. H. Goodell, Massachusetts Agricultural College, Amherst, Mass.

Hon. W. T. Harris, United States Commissioner of Education, Washington.

Col. Thomas W. Higginson, Cambridge, Mass.

The Rev. Edward Everett Hale, Boston.

Prof. F. G. Hammond, Dean, Law School, St. Louis, Mo.

His Grace, Archbishop John Ireland, St. Paul, Minn.

Prof. Edmund J. James, University of Pennsylvania, Philadelphia, Pa.

Prof. G. E. Morrow, University of Illinois, Champaign, Ill.

A. M. McAllister, President, etc., Philadelphia, Pa.

James McCosh, D. D., LL.D., ex-President, etc., Princeton, N. J.

Dr. S. H. Peabody, President University of Illinois, Champaign.

Dr. William Pepper, Philadelphia, Pa.

Bishop J. L. Spalding, Peoria, Ill.

John G. Whittier, Haverhill, Mass.

Prof. D. W. Whitney, LL.D., Yale College, New Haven, Conn.

Francis A Walker, President Boston Institute of Technology, Boston.

The Hon. Carroll D. Wright, Bureau of Labor, Washington.

Dr. George W. Atherton, Pennsylvania State College, State College, Pa.

Prof. Richard T. Ely, John Hopkins University, Baltimore.

Dr. Washington Gladden, Columbus, O.

Dr. A. L. Gihon, Washington.

The Hon. J. M. Rusk, Washington.

Dr. C. K. Adams, President Cornell University.

Dr. E. B. Andrews, President Brown University

Rev. Dr. George Dana Boardman, Christian Arb. and Peace Society, Philadelphia.

George·W. Cable, Northampton, Mass.

Dr. I. C. Chamberlain, President University of Wisconsin.
Pres. George S. Coe, ex-President American Bankers' Association.
Rev. Dr. Robert Collyer, New York.
Prof. James A. Dana, New Haven, Conn.
Hon. William L. Gross, Secretary State Bar Association.
Hon. George Hunt, Attorney-General of Illinois.
Dr. Abraham Jacobi, New York.
Hon. Seth Low, President Columbia College.
Prof. Edwin D. Mead, Boston, Mass.
Hon. J. W. Noble, Secretary of the Interior.
Rt. Rev. J. H. Vincent, Buffalo, N. Y.
Dr. Francis A. Walker, President of Boston Institute of Technology.
Pres. W. F. Warren, Boston, University Ho.
Hon. Andrew D. White, ex-President Cornell University.
Col. F. D. Grant, U. S. Minister to Austria.
Hon. William Walter Phelps, U. S. Minister to Germany.
Hon. George S. Batchelder, U. S. Minister to Portugal.
Lord Chief Justice Coleridge, London, Eng.
Mr. Walter Besant, Author, London, Eng.
Prof. F. Max Muller, Oxford University, Eng.
Prof. Emile de Laveleye, University of Liege, Belgium.
Prof. George Ebers, Egyptologist, Munich, Germany.
Rt. Hon. James Bryce, British Parliament, London.
Lord Tennyson, Poet Laureate of England.

The immediate work of these committees is to open communications with persons and societies interested; to receive and answer inquiries and suggestions; and to form, mature, and report plans of action. The Special Committees will report to General Committees, which will report to the Auxiliary. Conferences between the Committees of Women and the Committees of Men, on subjects of mutual interest, will be held whenever desirable.

According to the titles of the various committees appointed the congresses will cover the widest range of subjects. There are committees on educational matters, from the kindergarten to the university and technical instruction, on scientific and philosophic congresses, on temperance, moral and social science, labor, literature, law reform, religion, medicine and surgery, commerce and finance, agriculture, arbitration and peace societies, music, art, politics. There is a special woman's branch of the auxiliary with committees on congresses on household

16

economics, social reforms, temperance, charities, churches, missions, physicians, authors, painters, sculptors, and other artists.

LANDSCAPE AND ARCHITECTURAL PLAN.

In more ways than one the World's Columbian Exposition marks a departure in the arrangement of enterprises of this character. This implies in reality more than merely the matter of arrangement. It carries with it the realization of a new principle. The first world's expositions were intended merely to afford room for the exposition of goods. There was no idea of making the exposition in itself an object of interest by giving it features of beauty and introducing attractions entirely apart from the mere exhibition of the products of industry or the arts.

This idea was first successfully carried out at the Paris Exposition in 1889. Here, also, the division of the exposition into departments, each of which had practically a separate exposition in its own building, was first made a prominent feature. Here attempts were made to make the exposition attractive as a whole by paying attention to the general architectural and landscape features.

None of these ideas were, however, carried out so completely and successfully as they are at the World's Columbian Exposition. The Parisians claim a sense of art and the beautiful superior to that of the Americans, but if their claim is true then they were hampered at their exposition in 1889 by the insufficiency of the available space. It may be safely asserted that the landscape and architectural features of the World's Columbian Exposition will be, among its greatest attractions. A description of each of the buildings is given elsewhere, but attention should be directed to the architectural grouping of these buildings. It was not so difficult for each architect to produce a superbly beautiful building. The principal difficulty consisted in grouping these huge buildings in such a manner that the picture they would present to the eye from any point of the grounds or outside might be one of perfect artistic beauty. There was the severe Doric style and the graceful Ionic, the light French and Italian renaissance, the Spanish and Moorish,

HORTICULTURAL BUILDING.

and the ponderous modern style as exemplified in the Transportation Building; there were tall domes and long flat structures, solid masses of iron and stone and broken lines of airy fabric. To arrange all these various elements under a system that would combine beauty and usefulness was a task that had never confronted an architect before on such a stupendous scale.

It is true, the architect was materially assisted by the unrivaled natural opportunities offered by the site. The proximity of Lake Michigan and the vast space set aside for exposition purposes enabled the landscape artists and architects to produce a picture that lacks but little of perfection.

The entire Exposition falls easily into three groups according to its architectural and landscape features. At 59th street a canal connects the little park lakes with Lake Michigan. This canal or lagoon runs to the westward and sweeps around to the southward, embracing between two arms an oblong wooded island, then after the juncture of the two arms continues to the south end of the principal Exposition section. Near its south end a wide basin branches off to the eastward and empties into Lake Michigan. This basin forms the center of the south or main group of buildings. Upon its north bank close upon the shore of Lake Michigan stands the huge Manufactures Building. West of this comes the Electricity, then the Mines and Mining Building. Facing them and standing on the south side of the basin are the Agricultural and Machinery Buildings connected by a colonnade that encloses the south end of the lagoon. South of all these buildings is the live stock exhibit, a series of long low buildings and stables. All the buildings in this group work up gradually towards the magnificent dome of the Administration Building which stands at the west end between the Machinery and Mining Buildings. It rises to a lofty height, forming a fitting climax to the group.

In this group must also be included the harbor improvements, the long pier reaching out into the lake, and the Casino at the extreme end of it. From the superb proportions of the Administration Building there is a gradual tapering down toward the light and graceful structures making up this thoroughly Venetian group in the lake. Viewed from the lake the impression made by this group is one of grandeur and splendor, while from the other end the eye roams along the pleasing façades of the long buildings along the basin and rests in the background upon the delightful resort that is surrounded on all sides by the waves of Old Michigan.

If the first group relies mainly on the architectural features of the magnificent buildings for its effect the eye is gratefully relieved when the visitor comes to the second group adjoining it to the northward. Here it is nature and landscape gardening that form the main features. The wooded island in the midst of the lagoons and ponds form a central point of the very opposite character to that of the south group with the Administration Building. On the east the U. S. Government Building rises to a moderate height, and to the west the low Horticultural Building with its glass roofs and domes remains in perfect harmony with the surroundings. The Transportation Building is too far removed to destroy this sylvan character. To the northward lies the Fisheries Building, probably the most graceful of all the structures of the Exposition. Situated on a peninsula, its Moorish columns and slender walks seem to rival the trees on the island in gracefulness and faithfulness to nature, while its fanciful ornamentation serves only to intensify the effect.

The third group occupies the north end of the grounds. It has for its center the Palace of Fine Arts, a moderately tall, modest building surrounded by wide lawns. The massive building of the State of Illinois concludes this group to the south, while the buildings of the various States of the Union and foreign governments enclose it to the northward. A long street of buildings with minarets and domes of a quaint character stretches to the westward along the Midway Plaisance, the site for attractions not included in the regular Exposition programme.

The general effect of the landscape and the grouping of the buildings is emphasized by a most skillful use of color. The buildings at the north end of the park are kept in a subdued tone of color, but suddenly there rises the roof of the Fisheries Building in a deep, rich blue, made still more prominent by the immediate proximity of the bright red roof of the U. S. Government Building. A quiet blue tint lies over the Manufactures Building, giving its character to the entire southern group, but the tall dome of the Administration Building is gilded and sparkles in the bright sunshine. Opposite to it the variegated colors of the Casino lend life to this group, relieving the sombreness of the great Manufactures Building with their brightness, which is reflected a thousandfold by the waves around it, and still further assisted by the gay colors of the boats of all descriptions that keep moving to and fro along the shore and in the vicinity of the pier.

LIGHTING OF THE GROUNDS AND BUILDINGS.

The grounds and all of the Exposition Buildings except the Woman's and Administration will be illuminated by arc electric lights. The exceptive buildings as well as the State and foreign government buildings will be lighted with incandescent lights. Special attention will be given to artistic effects in illumination, and the architect of each building is now making a special study of his building, with a view to artistic illumination.

In all of the buildings, with the exceptions noted, a street system of lighting will be followed. The floors will be laid out in aisles, and aisles treated as streets lighted by ornamental lamp-posts of the ordinary height bearing an arc light. These lights will be shielded and present an opalescent glow rather than a fierce sputtering spark. This system will constitute the illumination of the building proper; the exhibits in each building will be illuminated by incandescent lights, according to the demands of the exhibitors who will make their arrangements for light and pay a stated price per lamp to the Exposition company. Structural lighting will be effected in the area space under the roof by artistic groups of arc lights. Clusters of incandescent lights will illuminate and decorate all the entrances and domes. The grounds will be illuminated by arc lights on ornamental posts and no tower lighting will be attempted.

Electric power for exhibition purposes will be used in the following buildings: Agriculture, Transportation, Forestry, Dairy, Manufactures, Fisheries, Mines and Electricity. These buildings will require a total of 3250 horse-power. Electric power will operate the elevated railroad which will encircle the grounds; 18,000 horse-power of electricity will be required for all purposes. This will be generated by 24,000 horse-power steam plant in Machinery Hall and conducted over the grounds partly by the elevated railway structure and partly by underground sub-ways. The two sub-ways or tunnels are 6 by 6 feet square and carry 150 wires each. They extend from Machinery Hall north to the Fisheries Building, a distance of half a mile. One tunnel supplies the Administration, Electricity and Mines Buildings and adjacent grounds. The Mines and Electricity Buildings will require more electric power than any other—800 horse-power each. The second tunnel supplies power for the Electric Fountain, Manufactures, Government and Fisheries Buildings and adjacent grounds.

The many pleasure boats on the grounds will be driven by electric power. So far, 60 of these pleasure boats have been designed. To supply the storage batteries to these boats a charging station will be located on the Lake Shore.

Structural decoration with incandescent lights will be elaborately carried out in the buildings facing the main court. The Administration Building marks the head from the west of this court with the water basin in the center and the emblematic columns on the peristyle at the mouth of the basin, on the Lake Shore, marking the foot of the court.

On the north side of the court are the Manufactures, Electricity and Mines Buildings. On the south, Agriculture Building with its annex and Machinery Hall. On the east, the peristyle, Casino and Music Hall. At night, this Central court or Main court and its surrounding buildings will blaze and twinkle with electric fire, and the effect will be magnificent. The architectural lines of the buildings will be delineated against the black sky in myriads of electric stars. The shore lines of the basin and its intersecting canal and the architectural lines of the bridges will be outlined in fire, and the spectacular Administration Building with its dome of gold will blaze like a diamond crown. The great Electric Fountain in the center of the court will spout an irridescent deluge and the search lights will bathe the marble like unto palaces in ever-changing floods of color.

RAILWAY EXHIBIT.

There will be shown in the Transportation Department a historical exhibit of the passenger railway train. The exhibit will be given by the Baltimore & Ohio Railroad and on 500 feet of railroad track. The evolution of the passenger train will be shown, from the time of the little four-wheel car drawn by a gray horse, a distance of 32 miles, up to the Baltimore & Ohio's "Royal Blue," which now runs between Washington and New York, With the evolution of the passenger train will be shown in the same exhibit the evolution of the railroad rail and track bed With the first car and the gray horse will be shown the flat rail laid on a stone sill. Following the gray-horse car will come the old original Thomas sail car that was propelled along the track like any other sailboat. It is in railroad history that this car made several trips until an eccentric gust of wind blew it off the bridge one day and ended its usefulness. The " Peter Cooper " engine will follow the sail car, and the original " crab " engine will be shown. This engine drew the first train of cars over the Allegheny Mountains, from Baltimore to Parkersburg, W. Va., and carried among its passengers the President of the United States.

In connection with this railroad exhibit the development of the modern railroad ticket will also be shown. Originally the railroad passenger was billed as a keg of nails is at the present time. All forms of railroad passenger tickets will be shown, from this old bill of lading down to the coupon ticket. Lewis M. Cole, who died two years ago, and who was in the employ of the Baltimore & Ohio Railroad for fifty years, and for a long time its general ticket agent, was the inventor of the present coupon ticket.

In this same connection there will be shown in the Electricity Building a reproduction of the first Morse telegraph line. It is a curious fact that the first telegraph wire was laid in the ground rather than suspended in the air. Morse laid his first line along the Baltimore & Ohio Railroad, from Baltimore to the Relay Station, a distance of nine miles. The wire was what is still known in trade as bonnet wire. This wire was inclosed in a lead pipe, and laid in a ditch. The ditch was made by a plow, drawn by sixteen oxen. In view of the world-wide use of the telegraph, the thousands of miles of wire, and the wonderful improvements over the first crude methods, it is a remarkable fact that the men who made the plow and laid this first telegraph wire are still alive.

MINERAL AND METAL EXHIBIT.

In no other department of the World's Columbian Exposition, perhaps, will be seen a greater diversity of exhibits than in that of Mines and Mining. Not only will there be a dazzling array of diamonds, opals, emeralds and other gems, and of the precious metals, but a most extensive collection of iron, copper, lead and other ores, and of their product ; of coal, granite marble, sandstone and other building stone ; of soils, salt, petroleum, and, indeed, of almost everything, useful or beautiful, belonging to the mineral kingdom. How extensive the mineral exhibit from other countries will be, it is yet too early to know, but the indications are that it will surpass any that has heretofore been made. However that may be, there is no doubt that the mineral resources and products, not only of this country as a whole, but of each State and section, will be of the most complete and representative description. Chief Skiff, of the Department of Mines and Mining, is confident that this will be the result of the plans which he is pursuing.

Owing to the fact that what has been published thus far, relating to the exhibit in this department, has been almost exclusively concerning gold, silver and the various precious stones and rare collections of minerals, many may have inferred, perhaps, that the baser metals and minerals are to receive scant attention. This is far from being the case. In fact, so important does Chief Skiff consider it, that the representation of the latter shall be fully commensurate with their surpassing industrial importance that he has determined to organize soon a subdepartment to take special charge of the coal and iron exhibit, and later of that of copper and lead.

The coal industry in the United States is of gigantic proportions, involving the investment of many millions of capital and the subsistence of many hundreds of thousands of people.

According to recent census bulletins the output of coal in 1889 alone aggregated 104,576,299 tons, the value of which at the mines was $131,421,172. Fully two-thirds of the States and Territories are coal producing. But great as is the annual production of coal in this country it is insignificant in comparison with the possibilities. Our coal resources are simply enormous. Vast areas of coal measures, thousands of miles in extent, lie distributed between the Atlantic and Pacific and the northern and southern boundaries. Throughout the West and South coal mining is rapidly increasing in importance.

The exhibit of coal at the Exposition, of course, will be qualitative rather than quantitative. Not only will the different varieties of coal, which the different localities produce, be shown, but chemical analyses of each and the results of tests determining economic value and adaptability to various uses. The coal resources of the different States and sections will be shown by geological maps and drawings showing configuration, stratification, etc., which will render apparent the extent and accessibility of the coal beds and veins. For example, it will be shown that coal measures of varying thickness underlie a great portion of the State of Texas—some forty or fifty counties—and that, although the coal production of Texas has thus far been comparatively small, the supply is practically inexhaustible, and that much of the coal is of excellent quality. Chief Skiff is enlisting the co-operation of large coal exchanges and corporations and expects to have a very extensive and complete exhibit.

So, too, as regards iron. The most strenuous efforts will be made to have an exhibit worthy of that great branch of industry. This country is now the first nation in the world in iron production, having recently forged ahead of Great Britain, its only real competitor. Our production of pig-iron now exceeds 10,000,000 tons, annually, or nearly four times what it was ten years ago, and the production of steel now aggregates about 5,000,000 tons a year, a growth of nearly 300 per cent. in the decade. The development of the iron resources of the Southern States has been especially great and rapid. The display at the Exposition will be prepared and collected under the fullest appreciation of the magnitude and importance of the iron industry. There will be shown all the many varieties of ores, with full data as to the location and extent of their beds, the analysis of each ore, and, so far as possible, the different processes of treatment in the manufacture of iron and steel.

Another exhibit which will be very extensive and varied will be that of building stone. Granite, limestone, marble, sandstone and bluestone, in scores of varieties and scores of colors, will be shown by the finest specimens procurable. Nearly every State has quarries of native material of excellent quality. From one to half a dozen of the twenty or more recognized varieties of granite, for example, are quarried in twenty-eight States—Massachusetts, Maine, California and Connecticut being the largest producers. The value of the granite output in 1889 was $14,464,095, an increase of more than $9,000,000 over that of 1880. Limestone is quarried in almost every State, Pennsylvania and Illinois taking the lead. The value of the output in 1889 was $19,095,179. This is exclusive of the output of marble, which, as is well known, is a species of limestone, the quarrying of which in a number of the States is an important and extensive industry. Sandstone, including bluestone, was quarried in 1889, to the value of $11,758,081, nearly every State being a producer. The exhibit of building stone, Chief Skiff intends, will be given the importance it justly demands. Thousands of specimens, many of them highly polished and very beautiful, will be shown, and accompanying each will be the results of tests made to determine strength, durability and other merits as construction material. The exhibit, which will be made in the Mines and Mining Department, will, it is believed, mean very much in the matter of rapid development of newly discovered mines and quarries, and the attraction of capital to many which, through lack of it, have been but little worked.

THE MUSICAL ISLAND.

In the vicinity of the main lagoon entrance, just south of the Manufactures Building, and about one thousand feet from the shore, will be a peristyle 60 feet wide and 500 feet long, extending north and south and spanning the lagoon entrance by a grand arch. Ranged along this peristyle will be emblematic columns representing all of the States and Territories. At the north end of the peristyle will be placed the Music Hall, which for a time it was thought would have to be put on the wooded island. It will measure 140 by 200 feet, and will have an auditorium large enough to seat two thousand people with an orchestra of seventy-five pieces and a chorus of three hundred persons. It will also have a rehearsal hall 50 by 80 feet, capable of seating six hundred people. This Music Hall is designed to be used by musical talent and connoisseurs of the art rather than by the mass of people who will visit Jackson Park. It is intended that here shall gather the fine singers and instrumentalists who may wish to be heard and criticised by the best representatives of their art or profession.

The grand choruses and band concerts—the popular musical entertainments—will be held in an amphitheater accommodating fifteen thousand people or more. This will be in the extreme southern part of the park, and, after the close of the projected musical program, will be transformed into a live-stock show ring.

At the south end of the peristyle there will be a restaurant and cafe, of the same size and style as Music Hall. The plans for these improvements were made by Designer-in-chief Atwood, of the Construction Bureau. The estimated cost is $206,000, or $1,000 less than would be necessary to carry out the plans which were abandoned.

The pier, extending 1,000 feet into the lake, is already completed. At its extremity will be erected a tower 250 feet high. This will be of iron, covered with staff, and will resemble a light-house in appearance. From its summit electrical displays of exceeding brilliancy will be made, and by means of electric "search-lights" the grounds, or any particular portion of them, can be flooded with light on fête nights.

A MODEL HOSPITAL.

One of the curious as well as useful and instructive features of the Exposition will be a model hospital in the Woman's Building. This is, of course, separate and distinct from the official hospital of the Exposition, of which Dr. Owen is director, being rather in the nature of an exhibit. It will, however, be fully equipped with physicians and trained nurses, a veritable model hospital, prepared to handle the gravest cases of accident or illness, and here women will find another magnificent opportunity to show their skill in the divine art of healing—in that field where delicate touch and tender sympathy have fullest scope.

Adjoining the model hospital, and in connection with it, will be the Department of Public Comfort, which promises to become a novel and important feature of the World's Fair. In this room will be couches and hospital beds for such cases of indisposition or accident as do not require serious or regular medical attention. Here old persons, invalids, sufferers from sudden faintness, swoons or hysterics, children who are temporarily indisposed, weak people of all ages needing rest and a spot in which to lie down, will find what they want in this room. A moment's reflection will reveal the excellence of the arrangement. It is scarcely possible to overestimate its value, in view of the innumerable exigencies arising from the flurry, confusion, consequent exhaustion, and unavoidable accidents attendant upon such crowds as will come to the World's Fair. The weary pilgrims to the Centennial and to the Paris Exposition who fell by the wayside can fully appreciate the plan.

It is further contemplated to extend the Department of Public Comfort throughout the entire Exposition by establishing branch rooms in all the main buildings. The Director-General has favorably considered a proposition to this effect, and although no official action has as yet been taken in the matter, it is reasonably certain that these branch rooms will be established. They will be duplicates of the main room in the Woman's Building and used for similar purposes, thus greatly relieving the pressure upon the Exposition Hospital. All these rooms will be under the management of the Board of Lady Managers.

RESTAURANTS.

Arrangements have so far been made to feed eight thousand people at one time on the Exposition grounds. In the corridors and loggias of the various buildings there will be twenty-seven

ELECTRICAL BUILDING,

cafés, one hundred and fifteen dining rooms, and three distinctly characteristic lunch counters. The supplies will issue from seventeen complete hotel kitchens manned by more than one thousand waiters, cooks and scullions. The dining-rooms so far designed cover about five acres of space.

There will be sixteen restaurants on the main floor of the Manufactures Building, located under the galleries, on the east and west sides of the building. Entrance to the restaurants will be made both from the inside and outside, and in fair weather guests will be served in the loggias and corridors. These restaurant rooms are of a uniform size of 22 by 100 feet, and will comfortably seat one thousand seven hundred and fifty guests at one time. They are supplied by eight kitchens, also on the main floor, with store rooms and dining-rooms for servants in the basement. Each kitchen will have a complete hotel outfit. In the galleries are seventy-six dining-rooms, connected with the kitchens and restaurants by dumb-waiters. These private dining-rooms are twenty-five feet square, and will.have a seating capacity of two thousand three hundred people, but they are designed with a view of being used by parties of from four people upward in number.

In the gallery of the Mines Building there will be a restaurant which will accommodate three hundred and twenty-five people. There will also be in connection with it, five private dining-rooms.

The restaurants in the Electricity Building will be most attractively located, and they will probably become the most popular place of refreshment on the grounds. They will fill the two round bays in the gallery at the north end of the building. These bays overlook the lagoon and the island, and the view from this point should be sufficiently charming and spirited to induce digestion to wait on appetite. The entire area of each bay is 96 by 68 feet, and the café in this space will be surrounded by a semicircle of nine private dining-rooms, each 16 by 18 feet in size. There will be a kitchen to supply each restaurant and its series of dining-rooms. In each bay, outside of the semicircle of dining-rooms, is a balcony 24 feet wide and 115 in length. In fair weather guests will be served with refreshments on this balcony.

Machinery Hall will have four cafés on the ground floor, each 128 by 88 feet in size, and sixteen private dining-rooms in the galleries. There will be two large cafés in the Horticultural Building, one in each of the end pavilions. These rooms are 100 feet square, and will seat one thousand persons. The café in the Fisheries Building will be exclusively an oyster and fish house.

The Agricultural Building will have no café, but will be equipped with an immense lunch counter, where sandwiches, hard boiled eggs and such like delicacies will be served in innumerable courses. In the Transportation Building will be instituted a typical American railroad counter. Besides feeding the hungry the counter will serve as an exhibit of an exclusive American institution. The guests, however, will probably not be limited to three minutes' time in which to swallow their food, but the food itself and the conduct of the business and the counter will constitute an exhibit.

The Dairy Building will have a lunch counter, wherein the cow will play the principal part as a source of supply.

The ladies will refresh themselves in the summer gardens on top of the Woman's Building, surrounded by flowers and tropical plants, and shielded from the sun by oriental canopies. The ladies can here sip their tea and discuss the merits of Miss Ridout's groups of statuary which will adorn the eight plinths in the beautiful columns which inclose the garden.

In addition to the cafés in the buildings there will be six restaurant buildings on the lake shore, in front of the Manufactures Building. These buildings will stand on the esplanade at equal distances apart. They will be but 25 by 40 feet in size, but will be of elaborate architecture, in keeping with the classic designs of the other buildings, and will serve the purposes of usefulness and ornamentation, while at the same time giving a comparative idea of the monster building sheltering them.

FLOWERS AT THE FAIR.

There have been flower shows and flower shows, but the flower show of the world will be seen at the Exposition. During the six months of the Exposition every flower and every blooming shrub known to floriculture will be shown. When the gates are opened on the first day there will be spread before the visitor, in front of Horticultural Hall, a great carpet of tulips— three million of them, in one vast bank. These will all come from Holland, and will be contributed by the celebrated growers of that home of the tulip. This is the most spectacular of flowers, and the sight of this great bed in all the shades and hues of crimson, pink, maroon and gold, is beyond description. Opening the Exposition, the indoor display will be inaugurated with ten thousand orchids in bloom, and representing in value more than half a million dollars. These wonderful air plants, which bear the same relation to other flowers that champagne does to other liquors, will be seen through a tropical forest of ferns and palms, and will give a view of fairyland. The flower display will be panoramic, both indoor and out. Following the tulips, in the outdoor display will come the daffodil and the pansy. Immense quantities of them will be contributed from the florists of the world. In June will come the rhododendrons and a greater display of these beautiful flowers will be made than has ever before been attempted. Varieties infinite in number will be shown in all colors, from pure white through all the tints of pink and crimson to deep purple. With the rhododendrons will be shown azalias, with all the shades of pink, bronze and yellow. Through the warm summer months the wooded island will be a great rose garden, and not less than one million of these royal flowers will be in bloom at one time. Later will come the gladioli and dahlia, the iris and other hardy plants. Everywhere about the island and in front of the Horticultural Building will be great banks of phlox, asters, verbenas, nasturtiums, and zenias—all spectacular flowers. The outdoor display will close with a great show of chrysanthemums. A special feature of the outdoor display will be the work done with foliage plants by all the park superintendents of the country, who have promised to produce something unique in the way of designs. The Fair grounds will abound in floral surprises, in figures of animals, carpets, scrolls, etc. Each superintendent will be given a space sufficient in which to work, and each will select his own design. In the indoor display the Indian

azalia will follow the orchid, and one view of the indoor panorama will show ten thousand lilies in bloom.   There will be a collection of over two thousand varieties of fern.   There will be
special displays of geraniums, gloxanias and calladiums.   There
will also be an educational display of economic plants—the
cocoa-nut, the palm, the arrow-root plant, the croton-oil plant,
the various plants that produce rope and cordage, and the visitor
can see here, in its.first stage, coffee, tea, sugar, cinnamon,
pepper and all the other spices.

The American Society of Florists is enthusiastic as a body
over the proposed flower show at the Fair, and its individual
members seem to consider it their personal duty to see that
this display is the greatest ever made.

Under the big dome of the Horticultural Building will be
shown the most rare and wonderful plants in the world, which
will be contributed to the show by wealthy amateurs all over the
country.   Jay Gould, who is not generally known as one of the
most enthusiastic of floriculturists, will give some valuable plants
to the Exposition.   He has promised palms from 40 to 45 feet
high.   From Fairmount Park, Philadelphia, will come bamboos
that have reached a height of 50 feet.   There are but six of
these plants in the United States.   From the same park will
come some India-rubber plants, 30 feet high, and a large tree-fern
imported from Australia.   There will be shown a number of
cyanophyllums, from Assam.   These plants are very rare.   They
have leaves like great spreads of green velvet, two feet wide and
five feet long.   Mr. George W. Childs, who is a philanthropist in
various directions, contributes to the display his largest Chinese
fern-palm, a magnificent specimen, 24 feet high, and 20 feet in
diameter.   He will also send two sago palms, whose stems are a
foot in diameter and six feet high.   From him, too, will come
the araucaria, the Australian monkey-puzzle.   The plant is a
monkey-puzzle sure enough, for Nature has so constructed it that
a monkey cannot climb it to get its fruit.   But for this wonderful provision of Nature there would be no araucaria, for the mon-
keys would have destroyed the plant long ago.   There will be
shown two sabals from Florida, with their peculiar wing-shaped
leaves, and two large date palms.   Mr. H. H. Hunnewell, of

Boston, has contributed to the Exposition the largest plant in the United States. It is known to the learned in floriculture as the pandanus reflexus. It is 20 feet high and 24 feet in diameter. Mr. Hunnewell has also contributed two cocoa-nut palms, 30 feet high, and some tree-ferns that have been in his conservatory more than thirty years. There will be a number of variegated holly, similar to pyramid bay trees, their leaves being covered with gold and silver decorations. One of the most curious plants to be seen resembles a baptismal font or basin. Its leaves so grow that they will hold three or four gallons of water. This plant is contributed by Mr. T. H. Spaulding, of New Jersey. Mr. Charles A. Dana will contribute some of his Japanese trees. The Japanese are experts in dwarfing trees, and have succeeded in reducing some of their largest trees to mere shrubs.

JAPAN'S BIG EXHIBIT.

Japan has appropriated $630,765 for the World's Fair. On December 8, the house of peers of the imperial parliament voted the appropriation by a large majority. This appropriation is the largest that has been made by any foreign power for the World's Fair. It is larger than any appropriation made to date, except those by the State of Illinois and the Congress of the United States. The bill, as it passed the house of peers, provides that there shall be expended $51,495 during the year 1891, $313,098 during 1892, $241,536 during 1893 and $24,635 during 1894. The expenditures of 1891 are for preliminary organization, that of 1892 is for the preparation of exhibits, and that of 1893 will be devoted largely to transportation. What is left will be spent in settling up the affairs of the Japanese commission.

The government of Japan is making elaborate plans for its exhibit at the Fair. Architects are now designing a building for headquarters of the Japanese commission that is expected to surpass any other office building on the grounds. This building will probably be made of durable material and after the Exposition presented to the city of Chicago. It will be surrounded by gardens containing the rarest flowers of Japan in great profusion. These also will be given to the city of Chicago. The

17

Japanese government is aware of the decision of the South Park board that all buildings must be removed, but it intends to make this building and the surrounding grounds so attractive that the park commissioners will allow them to remain. Commissioner Goward writes that the passage of the appropriation bill meets with great favor, in spite of the fact that the country is in great distress on account of the recent earthquakes. The Japanese press is enthusiastic and the industrial and art societies are well pleased. The Japanese government is well aware of the great advantages to be derived from taking part in the Exposition, and justifies the large outlay by saying that Japan could ill afford to make anything but a creditable exhibit. There is an exceedingly close relation existing between Japan and the States. Large exports of merchandise come to us from that country, and the leading Japanese statesmen claim that there is no other nation with equal claims to their generous consideration. The government has already set about preparing exhibits, and articles manufactured for the purpose, specimens and designs are named by the hundreds. The results of the measure will be to improve the country's relations and increase its prestige abroad, and to promote its institutions and content its industries at home.

AN UNDERGROUND THEATER.

The plans are ready for the construction in Chicago of the most novel playhouse ever conceived since theaters were first invented. A company with plenty of money at its command has been formed, with the intention of having an underground theater complete and in operation in time for the World's Fair.

There will be, a few feet above the street level, a handsome building which is to be the entrance to the caverns underneath, and also a café fitted with tables and fountains for soda and mineral waters. An elevator fitted with tiers of opera chairs, arranged as in a theater, and giving accommodations to one hundred persons, will connect the upper and lower regions. There will be a solid concrete or granite shaft about the elevator extending downward.

The visitors to the underground theater are to be given

checks for seats in the huge elevator-car, and at stated intervals
the door of the car will be closed and the elevator set in motion.
It will shoot down past the gray rocks until it has reached a
depth of 200 feet, where a stop will be made before the mouth of
a huge cavern, and there before the eyes of the audience will be
shown a coal-mine extending hundreds of feet away with dozens
of miners working with pick and shovel by the light of miners'
lamps worn on the hats. During the time the car is stopped a
mine will be exploded and tons of coal thrown out by the
force of the dynamite.

After full time has been given for seeing the practical workings
of the coal-mine the elevator will again go on its downward trip.
Another 200 feet and a second cavern will be shown, and as the
car stops before the mouth there will be seen a view of snow-fields
and icebergs, with fur-clothed Esquimaux in ice-sledges and
others spearing walruses and seals. The bright glow of the
aurora borealis will sweep up the northern heavens and the
spectators will have a view of that wonder of the polar regions.
Then 200 feet more descent, while the shaft above the car grows
smaller and smaller until there is but a patch of light to mark
where Chicago and its smoke are, and another cave will stretch
out into the earth.

The third cave is to be a direct concession to Dr. Patton and
his orthodoxy. It will be a scene from Dante's Inferno, and the
gates of adamant and solid brass will be thrown wide open on
invitation. There before the pools of burning sulphur, waiting
for the sinners who died unrepentant, will be Mephistopheles
and the smaller satans, attended by imps of darkness in fantastic
red. It will be orthodox enough to suit the most orthodox.

The fourth stop, 200 feet below the last-named and 800 feet
beneath the granite pavements of Chicago streets, there will be a
cavern representing a submarine view. A sunken ship will be
shown stranded on a coral bed and about it will be divers working in complete divers' suits. Fishes of all sorts will swim about
before the entrance to the cave.

Just one more drop of 200 feet and the elevator will stop
before a cavern 1,000 underground. It will be a cavern of dazzling brilliancy, with stalactites and stalagmites reflecting the

light of hundreds of electric lights in globes of various colors. This will be the last stop, and here the passengers will alight and the elevator will start on its upward trip. At the tables, with which the cave is to be liberally provided, ice cream and cakes and various other refreshments will be served. The idea is to have the waiters and other attendants in costumes fitting the surroundings and indicating the great depth to which the visitor has been carried.

After those who have made the long descent have seen sufficient of the glories of the cavern and are ready to get up to earth again, they will be shown into a dimly lighted passage, two big folding-doors will suddenly fly open, and through the blinding flood of light that flows in will be seen passing teams and street-cars, and if all is quiet in the neighborhood a policeman may be seen standing on the street corner.

Instead of descending hundreds of feet into the earth the car containing the audience of one hundred persons has in reality gone down a distance of only ten feet and the lowest cavern is say five feet below the level of the street.

The descent in the elevator, the narrowing of the shaft of light, the four intermediate caverns, and the bottommost cave, all are to be illusions. It will be done so skillfully, so true to nature, that. the visitor will fully believe that he has been going down and down from one cavern to the next unless it is fully explained to him before he enters the car.

The effect of the descent is to be obtained by having the four walls of the elevator shaft painted on canvas, which will run on rollers both above and beneath. When the passenger-audience is seated and the door of the car is shut the elevator will go down the distance of ten feet below the level of the entrance floor. Then the car will stop, and the sensation of further descent is caused by the four walls passing by at the same rate of speed that would be made by the elevator if it were descending. When 200 feet of canvas has been unrolled there is an opening through which the coal-mining scene is viewed. When the canvas starts again it continues to roll by until the same opening comes around once more, and, presto! the scene has changed. The Inferno, or the submarine view, or the ice-fields are shown.

When the curtain rolls around the last time the scenes have disappeared and the cave is there, where ice cream and soda water may be purchased singly or in the way of commutation tickets. To heighten the effect of the descent the elevator-car will be given a realistic motion.

The plan of the inventor for the changing of the scenes is no less novel than his plan of sliding elevator walls. There will be a large, movable round table at one end of the cave, and this will be divided into five sections, each divided from the others by canvas partitions. One of these will be turned toward the elevator opening and scenes let down along the sides to correspond. The miners don their suits and lamps before the first opening in the canvas gets even with the elevator-car. Before the next one gets by they will have costumed as imps, and the round table has been given a turn while another set of curtains has been lowered. Another turn of the table, some more scenes let down, and the satans in diving-suits will make a respectable-looking submarine view. So on to the last one, the cave scene, when the miner, imp, diver, et al., will serve ice cream in a swallow-tail coat. A judicious use of mirrors will heighten the effect. In short it will be a living panorama on a large scale.

The plans for the café on the entrance floor are also unique. The idea is to have it a model of the Mammoth Cave with long stalactites in which electric lights will be placed and mineral waters flow from springs the counterpart in miniature of the famous springs from which the water came—Carlsbad, Kissingen, and Manitou, for example. Every novelty in the way of soda fountains, ice-cream stands, and other necessaries of such a café will be there.

ELECTRICAL DISPLAY.

It is the intention of the management to make the World's Fair site and the buildings one grand exemplification of the progress that has been made in electricity.

The electrical exhibits will not be confined to a few of the buildings, but on every hand there will be a display of electricity. The ground, including the water-ways, the wooded island, the streets and avenues and boulevards approaching the World's

Fair site, will all be lighted by electricity, and in harmony with the general effect which it is desired to produce. According to Chairman Jeffery, of the Committee on Grounds and Buildings, the great structures of the Exposition will be turned into a panoramic view at night by the aid of powerful electric search-lights. On the gilded dome of the Administration Building, on the center pavilion of the Casino, and at other suitable points, these search-lights will be placed. During the evenings on which the Exposition is open the lights will be turned on the several main buildings and water-ways, so as to flood them with a sudden burst of electric splendor. Glimpses of the outlines of woods, water and buildings will suddenly flash before the eye. And this panoramic view will be had from different points of observation.

Special attention will be paid to artistic effect in the arrangement of the lights, and the architects are making a special study of all the buildings, and the plans when completed will be submitted to Electrical Engineer Sargent, of the Department of Construction.

In all the buildings, except the Administration and Woman's, the "street system" of lighting will be followed. The floors will be laid out in aisles and the aisles treated as streets—lighted by ornamental lamp-posts, of the ordinary height, bearing arc lights. These lights will be shielded, and will present an opalescent glow, rather than a fierce, sputtering spark. This system will constitute the illumination of the building proper. The exhibits will be illuminated by incandescent lights, according to the demands of the exhibitors, who will shape their own arrangements of light and pay a stated price per lamp to the Exposition company.

In each building structural lighting will be effected in the area of space under the roof by artistic groups of arc lights. Clusters of incandescent lights will illuminate and decorate all the entrances and domes.

Electric power for exhibition purposes will be used in the following buildings: Agriculture and annex, transportation and annex, forestry, dairy, manufactures, fisheries, mines and electricity. These buildings will require a total of 3,250 horse-power.

Electric power will operate the elevated railroad which will encircle the grounds. For all purposes 18,000 horse-power of

FISH AND FISHERIES BUILDING

electricity will be required.   This will be generated by the 24,000 horse-power steam plant in Machinery Hall, and conducted over the grounds, partly by the elevated railroad structure and partly by underground subways, or tunnels, 6 x 6 feet square, and carrying 150 wires each.   They extend from Machinery Hall north to the Fisheries Building, a distance of about half a mile.   One tunnel supplies the Administration, Electricity and Mines buildings and adjacent grounds.

The Mines and Electricity buildings will use more electric power than any other—800 horse-power each.   The second tunnel supplies power for the electric fountain, the Manufactures, Government, and Fisheries buildings, and adjacent grounds.

It is probable that the pleasure-boats at the interior waterways will be driven by electric power.   There will be sixty of these pleasure-boats, and to supply their storage batteries a charging-station will be established on the Lake Shore.

Structural decoration with incandescent lights will be elaborately carried out on those buildings facing on the main court. The Administration Building marks the head or west end of this court, with the water basin in the center and the emblematic columns on the peristyle at the mouth of the basin, on the Lake Shore, marking the foot of the court.   On the north side of the court are the Manufactures, Electricity and Mines buildings, and on the south the Agriculture Building and its annex, the Machinery Hall, the Peristyles, the Casino, and the Music Hall.

HOTEL ACCOMMODATIONS.

While the number of people who will come to the World's Fair will be greater than that of any gathering ever before known, preparations are going forward for their ample accommodations. It is estimated that there are at present in Chicago one thousand four hundred and sixty-three hotels with a total capacity of one hundred and thirty-five thousand guests.   This does not include the Great Northern at Jackson and Dearborn streets, with a probable entertaining capacity of two thousand people, nor does it include any of the hundreds of apartment houses being erected on the South Side for the accommodation of World's Fair visitors.

In addition to hotels it is estimated that there are eighteen thousand boarding-houses with room for more than fifty thousand guests, and there are spare rooms by the thousand in private residences that will be utilized as sources of income during the Exposition. These are some of the permanent reasons Chicago has to offer for its assertion that everybody in the country can come to the big show and feel easy on the question of temporary homes.

Then there are projects for entertaining visitors by the thousand. One syndicate has already bought and laid out a tract of land south of the Exposition site where two thousand five hundred cottages will be built and rented to families for such a term as may be arranged. The ground is laid off in state sections so that families from California will have neighbors from their own State. Each cottage will be arranged for the comfortable housing of from five to eight persons, and restaurants in plenty will be available for the cottagers. Besides such plans as this all the lake steamer lines are to have their fleets in port, plying to and fro on excursions, and a careful judge of such things estimates that at least fifteen thousand people will be able to find shelter and food on these steamers every day.

Taking the most careful figures on all these places for visitors, including hotels, boarding and apartment houses, lake steamers and cottage camping establishments, and the city can tuck away two hundred and fifty thousand strangers within its borders without annexing any more suburbs. When it comes to a big emergency, hotels, and Chicago hotels especially, have the dilating powers of the anaconda, and are able to tuck in anybody and everybody who can get to the office desk. Four such big hotels as the Auditorium, Grand Pacific, Palmer House and Leland can furnish sleeping-quarters for nearly eight thousand guests without hanging anybody on the hat rack. If occasion should arise, the landlords and landladies of Chicago could probably entertain all the people of New York and Boston at once— but they are not inviting that kind of trouble.

Taking a conservative estimate and calculating on two hundred and fifty thousand people as the utmost limit of accommodation, a comparison with the Paris exposition crowds is very comfort ing to the World's Fair management. The average daily attendance at the Paris exposition was one hundred and thirty thousand. The largest number admitted in one day was four hundred thousand. Concluding half of these to be strangers, and Paris had two hundred thousand visitors to care for in one day, it is estimated that the actual number of foreign visitors during the entire period of the Paris exposition was one million five hundred thousand and the average number of strangers who resided in Paris during the exposition was sixty thousand.

The Centennial offers the only American basis of estimates, though the attendance at Chicago will naturally be very much larger than at Philadelphia. The largest number in attendance on any one day at the Centennial was two hundred and seventy-four thousand nine hundred and nineteen; the smallest, twelve thousand seven hundred and twenty. The average was sixty-two thousand three hunded and thirty-three.

The World's Fair managers expect as large an attendance or larger than at Paris, and are making their plans accordingly. Special bureaus of information for strangers are in contemplation, the most complete facilities for handling passengers and baggage are being studied, and everything is being arranged that can conduce to the comfort of the wayfarer within the city's gates during the World's Fair.

WATER TRANSPORTATION.

In addition to the present railroad and street-car lines running between Chicago and the World's Fair grounds, several additional lines, both service and elevated, are projected and will no doubt be completed before the opening of the Exposition. The broad breast of Lake Michigan, however, offers too tempting a means of transportation to be neglected, and several projects, looking to the building of docks along the lake-shore front, from which pleasure crafts may ply between the heart of the city and the Exposition proper, have already been presented to Commissioner of Public Works Aldrich. The latest and most elaborate of these is that suggested by F. S. Ingoldsby. His plan comprehends not only pleasure-boat docks, a World's Fair depot 1,200 feet long by 100 feet wide, and a suburban depot 600 feet long by 50 feet wide, but a grand elevated promenade of thirty-two acres, over which citizens and visitors can pass to the lake craft or trains with perfect safety. The viaduct, 200 feet wide, is to be so constructed that people can pass over or through it as they may elect, the arrangement of the delivery to or from the trains being such that no crush is possible, and in wet weather passengers will be under cover, and thoroughly protected. In the covered viaduct will be waiting-rooms, smoking-room, ticket offices, etc.

The docks, 50 feet wide by 300 feet long, will radiate from the base of the statue building "Freedom Raising the World," which has been examined by the best engineering and architectural experts and pronounced practical and possible. This building, located so far out into the lake—1,000 feet east of Michigan avenue—will be no more obstruction to view than a fence 50 feet long and 25 feet high built on the present park, and its ample interior accommodations would supply the city's need for a permanent exposition building and memorial of the World's Columbian Exposition. This arrangement is difficult to fully describe, but with the broad stairway leading to the viaduct, the promenade, the ornamental docks, and the colossal statue of "Freedom Raising the World" in triumph 450 feet above it all, it would present a sight worthy of contemplation.

The cost of this improvement will be $2,500,000, and if the plan meets with proper indorsement by the city, the World's Fair and the Illinois Central railroad, private Chicago capital will construct it.

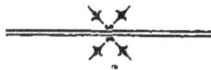

Work of the Congress Auxiliary.

The World's Congress Auxiliary is an organization authorized and supported by the Exposition corporation for the purpose of bringing to Chicago a series of World's Conventions of leaders in the various departments of human progress during the Exposition of 1893. The Auxiliary has also been recognized

by the Government of the United States as the appropriate
agency through which to conduct this important work, and its
announcement has been sent to foreign governments by the
Department of State. An appropriation on account of its expenses has been made by act of Congress.

The Auxiliary consists of an active membership of persons
residing in Chicago, or sufficiently near to attend committee
meetings without inconvenience, and a non-resident membership,
divided into advisory councils of the different departments of
progress, and honorary and corresponding members. Each
committee has its own advisory council, composed of the eminent leaders of the world in the department to which it relates.
Honorary and corresponding members are persons not assigned
to a particular department, but whose prominence and influence
make their aid and co-operation desirable. The officers of the
Auxiliary are as follows :

President, Hon. Charles C. Bonney; vice-president, Hon.
Thomas B. Bryan ; treasurer, Hon. Lyman J. Gage ; secretary,
Hon. Benjamin Butterworth. There is also a president of the
Woman's Branch of the Auxiliary, Mrs. Potter Palmer, and a
vice-president, Mrs. Charles Henrotin.

These general officers are aided by a long list of general
committees for the various departments, with appropriate
special committees for the chapters and sections into which the
departments are divided. Many of the committees are dual in
form, a committee of men and a committee of women on the
same general subject, authorized to meet separately or jointly,
as may be most convenient, under regulations intended to secure
uniformity of action in the arrangements of the plans for each of
the contemplated congresses.

This arrangement will preserve the identity of woman and her
work, and will at the same time secure all the advantages of co-
operation of men and women in the various congresses appropriate to both.

The general committees so far as created, are as follows:

Executive committee, committee of arrangements, committee on places of meeting ; education, science and philosophy,
literature, public press, music, artists, government and law

reform, religion, moral and social reform, temperance, labor, health and medicine, commerce and finance, engineering, agriculture, and a committee on a Youth's World's Congress.

These general departments have been divided into appropriate divisions, and committees appointed for each. To illustrate—the Department of Commerce and Finance, under the chairmanship of Hon. Lyman J. Gage, includes transportation, exchange and distribution, with divisions of banking, stock exchange, boards of trade, water commerce, railway commerce, and insurance. Each subject has a special committee and each committee has its advisory council.

The work of these general and special committees, now ninety-five in all, is very distinct and well defined. Each committee first issues its preliminary address, which states the objects of the Auxiliary with especial reference to its own department. This address is sent to appropriate persons and societies throughout the world, and the advisory councilors are requested to make any suggestions they may deem necessary, and to furnish appropriate themes for discussion in the particular congress in which they are interested.

The permanent Memorial Art Palace, to be erected on the shore of Lake Michigan in the heart of Chicago, will be devoted during the entire six months' exposition season, to the exclusive use of the congresses. This building will have two large audience rooms with a seating capacity of about thirty-five hundred each, and twenty smaller rooms which will be used for the meetings of the various divisions into which a congress is divided. The great Auditorium theater will also be at the disposal of the Auxiliary, and as many as twenty great meetings in this building are now contemplated.

The proposed congresses in each department will be of a twofold character: First, Special Congresses of existing organizations, under the general direction of the Auxiliary, which will consider such living questions as they may deem appropriate, conducted by their own proper officers. Second, Popular Congresses, arranged by the Auxiliary for the purpose of presenting to the people of the world, as represented by those who will be in attendance at the Columbian Exposition, the results of human progress in all the leading departments of civilized life, voiced by the ablest living representatives whose attendance can be secured on that occasion. This method of Special Congresses on the one hand, and Popular Union Congresses on the other, will secure the greatest relative freedom and independence of existing organizations in the conduct of their own proper work, and also afford the largest practicable opportunities for the people to see and hear the living leaders of mankind. It is also proposed that the speakers and writers, both in the Special Congresses and the Popular Congresses, shall be selected a year in advance of the date when the congress in which they will participate will be convened, in order that the maturest thought of the world may be presented on that occasion. The discourses and papers so to be presented will, it is expected, be permanently preserved in an encyclopedic publication, which will naturally find its way into all the leading languages of the world, and will constitute the most imposing and enduring monument of the World's Columbian Exposition.

The Auxiliary has at present an active membership of above 2,000. Of these, 750 are residents of Chicago. Acceptances to participate in the congress are being received from all parts of the world. Although the formal invitations have been but recently issued, more than 500 acceptances have been received. Nothing could be more comprehensive than the work planned for this great congress of thinkers, and its results for good on the thought of the world is not to be estimated. Every question of importance in human life and human labor will be discussed, and, judging from the names of those who will participate, these questions will be handled by the ablest minds of the world.

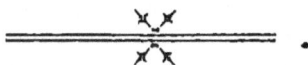

· Grand Dedicatory Ceremonies.

While the World's Columbian Exhibition will not be formally opened until August, 1893, the buildings and grounds will be dedicated in October, 1892, the anniversary of the discovery of Amer-

ica by Columbus.   The ceremonious demonstrations at this time
promise to eclipse anything of the kind ever before attempted.
If rare Ben Jonson could only come back to view the processions,
parades, and glory of those four days, how it would gladden his
heart, that so delighted in such scenes of mimic splendor.   Two
hundred and fifty thousand dollars has been appropriated by the
World's Fair directors for the dedicatory ceremonies.

The plans outlined by the Committee on Ceremonies embrace
a civic and industrial display, a military parade, dedication services
on Wednesday, October 12, a grand dedication ball, and one day
wholly devoted to military manœuvers, in which all or most of the
service will be represented.

The industrial display promises to be the greatest event of its
kind ever held in any country.   The general design is to illustrate
the growth and development of America during the last 400 years.
The first three centuries will be devoted to historical events, which
will be correctly reproduced on floats.   Careful attention will be
given to costumes and the accurate representation of the historical characters.   The last hundred years will illustrate every great
industry and invention, showing the primitive methods, the gradual improvement and what is now regarded as the perfection of
machinery.

From a short account of " the joyful and magnificent pageant
of 1788, in honor of the adoption of the constitution of the United
States," which was pronounced by Francis Hopkinson, who himself participated in the procession, " an exhibition which for novelty, splendor and decorum justly merited universal admiration
and applause," we select the following curious displays, to give an
idea of what was regarded at that time as marvelous :

" The manufacturing society, with spinning and carding
machines, looms, etc.   The carding-machine, worked by two men,
carding cotton at the rate of fifty pounds weight per day, was
placed on a carriage 30 feet long, 18 feet wide and 13 feet high,
drawn by ten horses ; also several other machines in full operation.   The carriage was followed by a large number of weavers.

" Farmers, headed by Messrs. Richard Peters, Richard Willing,
Samuel Meredith, Isaac Warner, George Gray, Charles Willing.
and others.   One of the plows in this department was drawn by

four oxen and directed by Richard Willing, in the character and dress of a farmer."

Who can tell but that an anniversary celebration 100 years hence will show as much improvement over the great display the committee is arranging for next year as will that over the celebration described by Francis Hopkinson.

One of the most interesting features of the World's Columbian Exposition will be the military display. The aggregate organized strength of the militia of the United States, from figures compiled by Lieutenant R. H. Wilson, of the Eighth United States Infantry, is 106,506 men. From the zeal already displayed in the matter of inquiry by military commanders, it appears that 25,000 of these State troops will answer reveille in Washington Park at sunrise October 13, 1892. The Government of the United States can, without detriment to the service, order something óver 3,000 men to rendezvous for four days at Chicago. A proper balancing would divide the regulars as follows : Five regiments of infantry, 2,000 men; two regiments of cavalry, 1,000 men ; and four batteries of light artillery, 250 men.

With the regular contingent to hold the right of line there would be in the marching column 28,250 troops, a number still 1,750 men less than that which made up the Philadelphia parade in 1887. In platoon formation averaging 40 privates to a company and 20 to a platoon, the number of men given would suffice to form over 1,400 platoons and to make a procession about eight miles in length. The simplicity of the regulation uniform of the United States army does not yet mark the clothing of the troops of all the States, and blue is not by any means the only color to be seen among the militia. There are nodding plumes on dozens of regiments of civilian soldiers, and bearskin chapeaux are not unknown. Take these, with the white and blue of the infantry, the yellow of the cavalry, the red of the artillery, the somber black of the engineers, and the almost numberless tints of the militiamen's apparel, and that array as it swings from line into column will present a sight that will be an ample excuse for the sounding by Chicago of an assembly that has caused troops from the North and South, the East and the West, to fall into line.

General Nelson A. Miles has been appointed by the War Department to have charge of the military features of the World's Fair.

So far as the dedicatory ceremonies are concerned, Gen. Miles thinks there should be 15,000 troops, 10,000 of the National Guard and 5,000 of the United States regulars, and he has also suggested that in the parade there be 2,000 Indians.

The military ceremonies will probably conclude with an attack and the defense of a fortified position. There would be ample room for the proper distribution of the offensive and defensive troops at Washington Park. Young Americans would have the opportunity of witnessing a spectacle now only to be witnessed on rare occasions in European countries.

The following States have agreed to send military delegations: Colorado, California, North Dakota, Kansas, Indiana, Ohio, and Pennsylvania. From these States and others will come the pick of their militia, and Chicago will see the Ancient and Honorable Artillery of Boston, with its 253 years of existence, in the column with the last company of Nebraska militia organized to protect Rushville from the Sioux. Illinois will be represented, of course, in full force.

The possibilities for drill and dress ceremonies at Jackson and Washington Parks are unlimited. There is room for everything, from the "setting up" drill to the evolutions of the brigade, and it is the intention to take advantage of the troops' mobilization to drill in mass.

Gen. Miles also wants the big show in 1893 to have 90,000 troops present. His idea is to establish a military camp somewhere in the suburbs of Chicago, and hold the troops here at least thirty days. This, he thinks, would give foreign visitors an idea of the military resources of this country.

Some Things Projected for the World's Fair.

HANGING GARDENS.

"The Hanging Gardens of Babylonia," is the name given by Bernard Jacoby to a novel structure which he would like to erect in the World's Fair grounds. The plans are for two steel and glass buildings, 150 feet long, 50 feet wide and 50 feet high, to be arranged on cables between steel columns, one to be suspended in air while the other is on the ground, the weight of one to balance the other. The sixteen steel columns for the proposed hanging gardens are to be 400 feet high, according to the plans, so that the building suspended will be 350 feet above ground. There will be a restaurant in each one, with music and with roof-gardens containing flowers and light trees. Two thousand people could be accommodated on each trip, which would occur once every hour. The gardens are to be brilliantly lighted by electricity, and handsome marble steps will lead up to the platforms on which the buildings are to rest. The originator of the plan estimates the cost at $500,000.

QUAINT STREETS OF CAIRO.

There are many novel and interesting things projected for the World's Fair which will astonish and delight the hundreds of thousands of spectators in 1893. One of the most unique and attractive of these will be a complete reproduction of a street in Cairo, Egypt.

The privilege for representing the street has been granted to George Pangalo by the Ways and Means Committee. Mr. Pangalo is a manager of a bank in Egypt and a citizen of Cairo. He came to this country expressly to make the exhibit, and has been working to secure this privilege for months. It will embrace 50,000 square feet of ground, and the site will be on Midway Plaisance.

The exhibit will embrace a single street, furnishing a

18

composite picture of the buildings characteristic of Cairo. The
street will be 421 feet long and its width will vary from 20
to 35 feet. The features will be a mosque, with its drinking
fountain and the richly ornamented minaret. It will be ninety-
five feet high, and the striking feature of the architecture. Its
style will be that of the Cherkess dynasty, and it will be an
accurate reproduction of a Mohammedan place of worship.

Another feature will be a large amusement hall, where, if
objections be not raised, there will be dancing-girls to amuse the
visitors. There will be a barber-shop, Arab coffee-shops, and
representations of the residences of prominent Egyptians. Exclusive of the monuments and buildings, there will be sixty shops
of various kinds. It is intended to bring a number of donkeys,
donkey-boys, camels, snake-charmers and fortune-tellers, to
represent the coffee-shops, refreshment rooms, and various street
scenes seen in the market, wedding processions, etc., together
with the quaint furniture and dress and decorations of this
ancient people.

PLAN TO INTEREST THE CHILDREN.

An elaborate and interesting scheme by which some fifteen
million children or more, both in the United States and foreign
lands, will become directly interested in booming the World's
Fair, has been prepared by Bishop Fallows, the Rev. F. F. Bliss,
and others.

The plan involves nothing less than the formation of an
International Youths' World's Fair Association, which will enlist
the sympathies of children up to the age of sixteen years all
over the world. They will be primarily reached through the
public schools, Sunday schools and churches, and the promoters
feel confident that in this association there will be formed a
working auxiliary of inestimable value in inciting general interest among older folks in the World's Fair and its doings.

The American Society of Patriotic Knowledge, through
Bishop Fallows, its first vice-president, stands sponsor for the
enterprise ; C. C. Bonney, of the World's Fair auxiliary, Frances
Willard, Anna Gordon, Dr. Frances Dickinson, Supt. A. G. Lane,
Judge Waite, A. R. Abbott, M. J. Sands, Mrs. A. G. Lane, C. S.

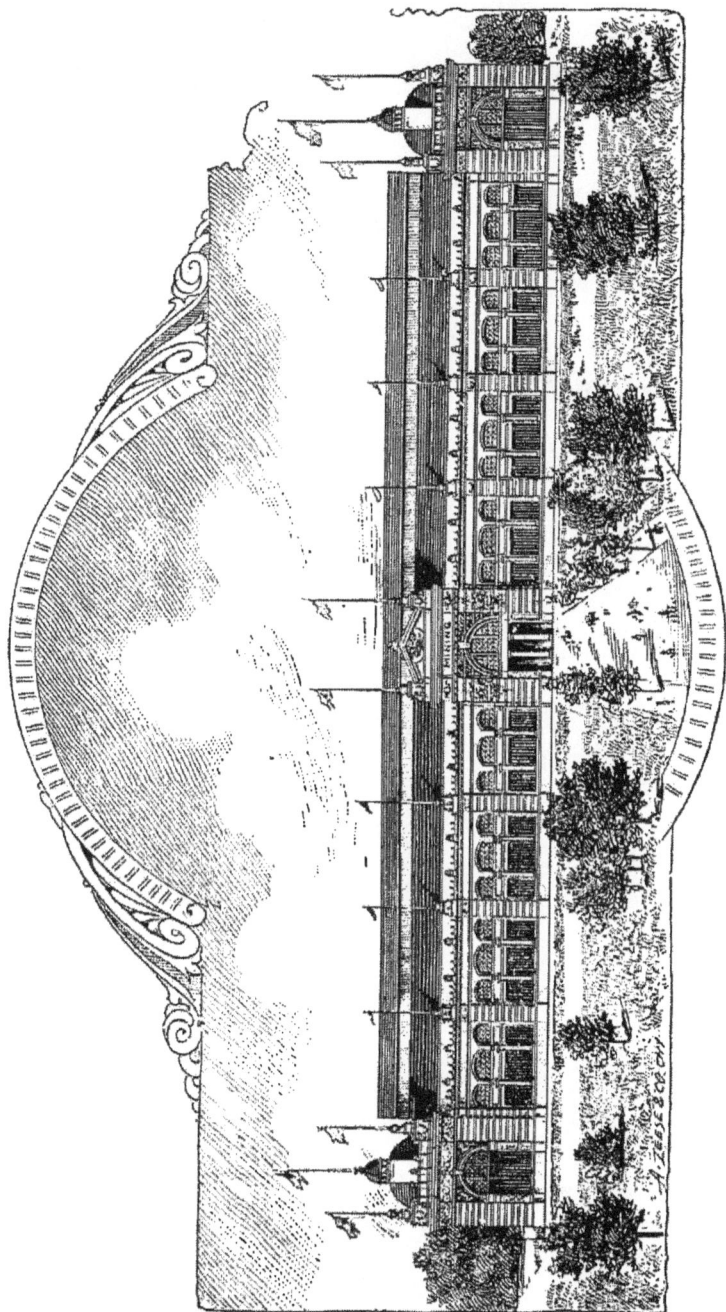

MINES AND MINING BUILDING.

Brown, J. M. Bullens, Prof. Marks, Ford and Claflin, and many other prominent Chicago people, are interested in and supporting the movement; while Mrs. Isabella Beecher Hooker, Connecticut; Mesdames ex-Gov. Bagley and E. P. Howes, Michigan; Mrs. Gov. Eagle, Arkansas; Mrs. D. F. Verdenal, New York; Mrs. Mary E. Lockwood, Washington, D. C.; Mrs. Alexander Thompson, Maryland; Mrs. M. R. Kindler, Delaware; Mesdames M. S. Briggs and C. S. Langworthy, Nebraska; Mrs. Elizabeth Fry, Texas; Prof. W. W. Parsons, Indiana; Prof. F. Buck, Iowa; Miss Emma Winosatt, Washington, D. C.; Mrs. Miller, Iowa, and Mrs. E. N. Hailman, of Indiana, the well known head of the kindergarten movement, are supporting the project on the outside.

WAUKESHA WATER AT A CENT A CUP.

Water is to be piped from the springs of Waukesha, Wis., to the Exposition grounds. The Hygeia Spring Water Company was given the privilege of supplying water during the Fair. The company has already laid pipes part of the way. William B. Keep represents the company. About 300 drinking-booths will be built on the grounds and Waukesha water furnished to thirsty visitors for one cent a cup.

AMERICAN SPORTSMAN'S EXHIBIT.

The American Sportsman's Exhibit at the Columbian Exposition will be a complete exhibition of every weapon and utensil used in hunting, fishing and trapping since the discovery of the country down to the present day. "We have," says Theodore Roosevelt, who has interested himself in this display, "the greatest hunting country on earth; the Boone and Crockett Club, of which I am a member, is enthusiastic over it, and we want nothing but what is American. For instance, I know where the rifles used by Davy Crockett may be secured." Nothing could be more interesting than such a collection. It would embrace not only the thing suggested but the heads of all kinds of American game of the larger sort and specimens of the smaller game, animals, birds, and fishes; the old wigwam, hunting-shacks of pioneer days, all kinds of Indian weapons and all the conveniences which go to make up a modern hunting-camp. Such a display would have a peculiar fascination for the sportsmen of all countries.

A DUTCH EXHIBIT.

Van Houten & Zoon, the manufacturers of cocoa at Weesp, Holland, have set apart $100,000 with which to make a splendid exhibit at the Exposition in Chicago in 1893. They intend to erect a large building in the style of old Holland architecture of the fifteenth century, and to put in it, besides an exhibit in their own line of business, paintings, views, bric-a-brac, etc., illustrative of the Netherlands and the life and characteristics of the Dutch people. They will have there a "cocoa school," where Dutch maidens, clad in picturesque native attire, will make delicious cocoa beverages according to the most approved methods, and will serve it to visitors.

The Patent Office will exhibit a comprehensive array of models to illustrate the wonderful progress of mechanical civilization. One group of models will show the progress of the printers' art from Gutenberg's crude invention to the latest rotary perfecting and folding printing-press, capable of turning out newspapers at the rate of many thousands per hour. Other groups will show the development of the steam-engine, sewing-machine, agricultural machinery, application of electricity, etc.

BRITISH COLUMBIA WOODS

British Columbia has decided to build a structure, which will be a novelty in architecture, composed of every variety of wood known to the British Columbia forests. The building will be built first in sections of contrasting woods neatly mortised together. The roof will be of native slate and a variety of cedar shingles, making in all a pleasing effect. It is intended to ship the building in sections, ready to be erected on its arrival. The display will be unique in every way, the government and cities of the province subscribing to the fund.

THE CONVENT OF LA RIBADA.

Tl e Exposition Directors have appropriated $50,000 for the expense of reproducing at the Exposition the Convent of La Ribada, Palos, Spain, where Çolumbus lived while perfecting his plans for his voyage of discovery. The building will be used for housing an extensive collection of Columbus relics, and its ancient appearance, it is believed, will afford a pleasing contrast to that of the magnificent palaces by which it will be surrounded.

RELIGIOUS RECORDS OF EARLY VOYAGERS.

At the request of the Latin-American Bureau of the World's Columbian Exposition, Cardinal Gibbons has requested the proper officers of the several religious orders of the Roman Catholic church, both in Europe and America, to cause their archives to be searched for historical records bearing upon the discovery and settlement of the New World. It is known that every ship that left Spain, beginning with the first voyage of Columbus, carried among its crew a priest or a friar, and that these missionaries made voluminous reports to the heads of their different orders, few of which were ever published. It is believed that the archives of the church are filled with valuable historical material.

PARAGUAY FINE ART WORKERS.

Dr. Bertolette, Commissioner to the La Platte Republics, has informed the Latin-American Department that he is endeavoring to secure for the Exposition a colony of lace makers and gold and silver workers from Paraguay. These people are ingenious, their product being equal to that of the Brussels working-women, and the fact that they use vegetable fiber exclusively makes their work of even greater value and interest. It has been planned by the Latin-American Department to have a group of these lace makers on the Exposition grounds; also a group of workers in gold and silver filigree.

Word has been received that the Corcovado Railway Company, of Rio de Janeiro proposes, making an exhibit in miniature of its railway. It is the purpose to have large photographs illustrating the mountain route through which the railway passes, the bridges, the stations, the hotel at the summit, and interesting scenery adjacent. They will have molded, in papier maché, the mountain of Corcovado in miniature, with the railway laid down as in actual operation. The total length of the road is two miles. The rise from the station at the upper end of the road to the summit is 2,300 feet.

<h3 style="text-align:center">INDIAN RELICS.</h3>

The Department of Ethnology is making researches among the Indian tribes of the United States and Canada with a view to making a big display in that division of the work. Chief Putnam, in his July report to Director-General Davis, said his assistants were taking measurements and noting facts which will furnish the material for the tablets, charts and molds which will constitute the exhibit. One of these assistants, who is making a study of the Bannock and Shoshone Indians, has made a collection of war bonnets, dress and accoutrements worn during burial ceremonies, at their ghost dances, and at their religious ceremonies. He has secured complete costumes with which to dress the Indian models, and will make an exhibit of the training and treatment of children, burial ceremonies, religious myths and traditions of the race.

Miss Alice C. Fletcher, who holds the Thaw fellowship in connection with this department of Harvard University, and who has spent several years in actual life among the Indians, will direct the reproduction of types of Indian habitations that have passed out of use. Mrs. Zelia Nuttall, an assistant of the Peabody Museum, is transcribing and translating Mexican photographs and making drawings of Indian houses. She has discovered, in a library in Florence, some precious old manuscripts of the time of Cortez, which contain pictures of Mexican houses. Edward H. Thompson, United States consul to Merida, Yucatan, intends to bring to the Exposition a native Maya house with complete furnishings, a Maya family and a native potter, who will make his vessels during the Fair.

A model is to be made of the famous Turner group of earth-workers in Ohio. Ernest Volk is working in the Delaware Valley, exploring the ancient argellite workshop discovered there and is getting material concerning the existence of man on the American continent in remote ages. United States Consul Thompson is now at Uxmal, Yucatan, making molds of portions of façades and cornices used in adornment of these majestic ruins.

Of the structure known as the "House of the Governor of Uxmal," he says, "each square yard is a mosaic gem. A section of this structure would, if of a size sufficient to show the symmetry of the design, be a revelation to many who believe the mines of Yucatan to be mud piles and stone heaps."

George A. Dorsey is working at Anco, Peru, and has already opened fifty-three graves at the famous burial-place at Anco, and taken out several perfect mummies. He found one in a remarkable state of preservation—the body and trappings appearing as if they had been buried but a few days. In the grave with the body was a pot of fish, a pot of corn, a calabash of beans and two jugs which had probably contained some sort of beverage. Over the shoulders of the body was a beautiful poncho.

As the World's Fair is to be an exhibition of the purest and highest culture of the American people, much depends upon the three elements of art, ethnology and the liberal arts. The directors understand this, and while great attention is being paid to the more stirring accomplishments of agricultural and mechanical arts and sciences, these finer arts are in no wise neglected.

Progress of the Columbian Exposition.

A brief resumé of the work already done on the ground and the Exposition buildings cannot fail to be of interest to the reader. The opening of the year 1892 finds the World's Columbian Exposition fairly in possession of the great field which it is soon to occupy fully. Nine months before the day fixed for the dedication of the great buildings at Jackson Park, and eighteen months before the Exposition itself is to be thrown open to the public, it can be said without reserve that every grand division was thoroughly organized. The grounds are in an advanced condition of preparation. The buildings are well under way. The finances are in a most prosperous and promising condition ; and from every quarter of the world there is assurance of exhibits which in extent, interest and variety will surpass those on view at any previous national exposition. The States and the people of the American Union are substantially unanimous in support of the enterprise. Every nation in the civilized world has bidden God-speed to the celebration of the birthday of the great Venetian discoverer.

Never since Nomads were transformed into city builders and capitols of empires became sights of international exhibitions has there been such universal interest displayed in any project conceived by man. The greatest of expositions which has passed into history will compare but feebly with the grandeur of this stupendous undertaking. No spot in all the world could have been selected susceptible to so many advantages as is the site of the Columbian Exposition on the shores of the beautiful lake Michigan.

Its ground area, comprising more than eleven hundred acres of undulating lawn, is more than double that hitherto covered by the greatest international exposition.

Its glorious structures, outnumbering many times those of the last universal exposition of Paris, and exceeding individually, each in its department, all predecessors, have reached a stage of construction which foreshadow the beauties and grandeur of the whole as conceived and designed by the corps of architects whose genius has been expended in their conception.

Interest concentrates, of course, upon the series of big elevations that show the main buildings which will occupy the Exposition grounds in 1893. Taken singly they prove great ability on the part of their designers. Taken together they show that the Exposition authorities were wise in selecting a number of different architects to do their work, and that these architects were wise in consulting together before they began. Each of the structures will have individuality, yet all will harmonize in a general effect that promises to be dignified, imposing and beautiful enough to do infinite credit to American art and appropriate enough to be as creditable to American good sense, if, indeed, art and good sense can be even nominally dissevered when works of architecture are in question. Of course, however, one must regret, even more than in former years, that the space at the league's command is so small that plans and sections as well as exterior views could not be shown.

A simple type of renaissance art has been chosen for all the buildings, but, as was not undesirable, some are much more richly treated than others. The richest of all is the Agricultural Hall, with its far-spreading Corinthianesque colonnades. The plainest is the Horticultural Hall, which, however, is so good in the massing of its varied parts that no lack of elaboration is felt when it is compared with any of the others. In the Gallery of Fine Arts colonnades appear again, but of an Ionic type. The largest of all, yet the simplest in structure, is the Exhibition of Manufactures and Liberal Arts, but its immense size seems impressive and monumental enough to sustain the monotony of its lines. The Transportation Building is excellent, and Machinery Hall, which from its name might suggest the most prosaic outlines, is treated with architectural grandeur. The combination of the great semicircular glazed ends of the divisions of the hall with the colonnaded porticoes which run beneath them is striking and the two large porches, each projecting from a wall crowned by a pair of elaborate towers, are distinctly ecclesiastical in air. These central fronts recall the churches of Venice or of Spanish America, instead of suggesting a Chicago home for the spirit of steam. When one studies all these buildings together, and fancies them enlivened by color and sculpture, based on broad green lawns and standing near the borders of the great lake and the newly constructed canals, a picture is called up which arouses deep satisfaction in the patriotic heart. However great or small may be the success of the Exposition in other ways, there need be no doubt that as far as architectural art is concerned we shall not blush in the presence of the " intelligent foreigner." It is nothing short of an artistic triumph thus to have struck, in these vast and difficult structures, a happy medium between inorganic diversity and monotonous uniformity, and between a utilitarian poverty of effect and an undue degree of monumental elaboration.   How excellent they are is proved by the fact that we cannot even try to criticise them from any point of view except the one from which they were designed.   We judge them simply as exposition buildings, and are not for a moment tempted to compare or contrast them with buildings of any other kind.   It is interesting to reflect upon the style that was selected for them by the many distinguished architects concerned.   Doubtless no other style suggested itself as possible.   Probably no one even thought that it might be best to choose some form of Gothic, though Gothic lends itself so well to picturesqueness of general effect and to variety in the treatment of special features ; or to choose that type of Romanesque which Americans have so generally practiced in recent years, and have so commonly believed to be adaptable to all modern needs. When it came to the designing of structures which had to be at once very monumental and very practical, and in which economy had to be considered, renaissance art must have been recognized at once as the only adequate resource.   And, as has been well remarked, the fact has a wider significance than as a mere justification of these architects' choice in this special case.

When one reads the exact state of the finances of the Exposition, the part the city corporate has done, the part the citizens have contributed, and the sum the national government has given for the support of the enterprise, with the additional sums required to complete the great undertaking, a somewhat vague conception may be had of the magnitude of the great World's Fair, which, a little more than a year hence, will bring together the nations of the earth.

That the Exposition will be opened at the time set need not be doubted.   The date for the opening of the Paris exposition was set forth five years in advance of the event.   A little more than a year has gone by since the World's Columbian Exposition was inaugurated, and yet it is more nearly ready for dedication in October of this year and an installation for the formal opening in May next year, than the buildings of the Paris exposition were nine months before the exposition began.

Everything has been done that could be done to enlist the co-operation of foreign countries. Congress has passed a law removing the duty from all articles duly entered from foreign ports before authorized officials for exhibition at Chicago in 1893.

The Bureau of Publicity and Promotion have disseminated throughout all the world volumes of literature explaining in detail every step in the progress of the Exposition, and all nations are keenly alive to the benefits to be derived from a complete display of their manufactures and products at the Fair.

The National Commission, the Board of Lady Managers and the Chicago Directory —all of them agents authorized under the act of Congress for the creation of an exposition to celebrate the discovery of America, have diligently, unitedly and heartily carried on their work. Comprehending much more than has heretofore been attempted, grander in its ideal, its beauty and its lesson than any undertaking which a power of less importance than one of the great nations of the earth could undertake, each of the great agencies authorized by the nation for its construction has become more and more consolidated in united action and the great departments of administration, finance, exploitation and construction have overcome seemingly insurmountable obstacles, and, pushing their work with intelligence and vigor, have secured unparalleled results.

The progress of the World's Fair enterprise during the year 1891 has been veritably marvelous. A short twelve months ago the World's Columbian Exposition lived chiefly in the favor and enthusiasm of the people. Comparatively little had been done besides planning and projecting. Congress had awarded the prize of location to Chicago; Chicago citizens had subscribed $5,000,000; the city council had voted to issue $5,000,000 of bonds in aid of it, and the President of the United States had invited foreign nations to participate.

That was about all that had been accomplished. Ground had not been broken; not a building had been planned; not a contract let. The National Commission and the Exposition Directory were at variance as to their respective powers and duties.

The perplexing site question had not been settled, and it was not until the year was well advanced that the Lake Front was

finally abandoned. At the beginning of the year it was understood that the Art Palace, the Decorative Art Palace, the Water
Palace, the Electrical Building, the Temple of Music and probably the Woman's Building, would be on the Lake Front, and as
late as January 28, ground was broken on the Lake Front for
the erection of what was then termed the first World's Fair
building. ·

Nearly a month later the Lake Front was abandoned and
work was begun at Jackson Park. Just before 1890 closed the
Lady Managers had elected Mrs. Potter Palmer president, but
their ideas as to what they were to accomplish were very indefi-
nite and they can hardly be said to have formed any plan. The
World's Congress Auxiliary lived at that time in the minds of its
projectors only.

With the advent of 1891 the practicable work of making the
World's Fair commenced. The officers were transferred from
cramped quarters in the Pullman and Adams Express Buildings
to the present commodious accommodations in the Rand-McNally
Building.

The Board of Architects was appointed, and to each member
was assigned the task of submitting plans and designs for one
of the projected Exposition buildings. These have all been
submitted and approved. Contracts for the construction of all
of the buildings have been let and their erection is now progressing day and night. Several of the buildings are completely
under roof.

At the beginning of the year but two of the department
chiefs had been appointed by the Director-General. These were
M. P. Handy, Bureau of Publicity and Promotion, and W. I.
Buchanan, Agriculture. They did not get fairly to work, however,
until January; since then chiefs of thirteen departments have
been selected and the work of each has long since been at an
advanced stage.'

MAKING A WORLD'S FAIR.

The offices and rooms where the work of the World's Columbian Exposition is being done are on the fourth and a portion of
the fifth floors of the Rand-McNally Building on Adams and

Quincy streets. About 50 rooms are occupied. Besides these the twelth floor of the Rookery Building and a portion of the rooms of Mr. Burnham, supervising architect, in the same building, are being used by a small army of draughtsmen engaged upon unfinished plans and designs. There are 687 officers and employes on the pay-roll, and the amount of money paid out for their services each month is $36,000. This number and amount include the force at the Rand-McNally Building and that at the Rookery. The work is divided into departments with a chief at the head of each. These departments are lettered in alphabetical order—to wit:

Department A.—Agriculture, Food and Food Products, Farming Machinery and Appliances.   W. I. BUCHANAN, Chief.

Department B.—Horticulture.   J. M. SAMUELS, Chief.

  Sub. Department—Floriculture.   JOHN THORP.

Department C.—Live Stock—Domestic and Wild Animals.   EBER W. COTTRELL, Chief.

Department D.—Fish, Fisheries, Fish Products and Apparatus of Fishing.   J. W. COLLINS, Chief.

Department E.—Mines, Mining and Metallurgy.   FREDERICK J. V. SKIFF, Chief.

Department F.—Machinery.   L. W. ROBINSON, Chief.

Department G.—Transportation Exhibits, Railways, Vessels and Vehicles.   WILLARD A. SMITH, Chief.

Department II.—Manufactures.   JAMES ALLISON, Chief.

Department J.—Electricity and Electrical Appliances.   J. P. BARRETT, Chief.

Department K.—Fine Arts, Pictorial, Plastic and Decorative.   HALSEY C. IVES, Chief.

Department L.—Liberal Arts, Education, Engineering, Public Works, Architecture, Music and the Drama.   S. H. PEABODY, Chief.

Department M.—Ethnology, Archæology, Progress of Labor and Invention —Isolated and Collective Exhibits.   F. W. PUTNAM, Chief.

Department N.—Forestry and Forest Products.   THOS. B. KEOGH, Chief.

Department O.—Publicity and Promotion.   MOSES P. HANDY, Chief.

Department P.—Foreign Affairs.   WALKER FEARN, Chief.

Secretary of Installation,
JOS. HIRST.

This list does not include the Board of Lady Managers, of which Mrs. Potter Palmer is the head, nor does it include a number of other adjuncts and divisions, which will be noted further on.

The duties of the National Commission, of which T. W. Palmer is the head, require that he shall be here once a month, or oftener as occasion demands. President Palmer and his assistants meet in conference with the local directors. He is also a member, as is his staff, of the Board of Control. Associated with Mr. Palmer is J. A. McKenzie, Vice-Chairman. He is always in his office during business hours. He is a typical Kentuckian.

When President Palmer is not in the city Mr. McKenzie takes his place. John P. Dickinson, secretary of the National Commission, is another of the assistants to the president. All correspondence growing out of the work of the commission goes through his hands. All expenses incurred by the commission in its national capacity are audited by the secretary. The president, vice-president and secretary each draws a salary of $5,000 a year.

While the National Commission is essential to such an enterprise as this, and while its work is not by any means to be despised, its labor is trifling compared with the local directory.

The president of the local directory is W. T. Baker, president of the Chicago Board of Trade. By virtue of his office he is ex-officio a member of all the committees and must confer daily with such committees as have held sessions or are holding them. He also entertains foreign visitors.

Next to President Baker comes Vice-President T. B. Bryan, the gentleman who did so much to secure the Fair for Chicago. Foreign delegations are very much at home in the presence of this distinguished orator and linguist and skilled diplomat. It must not be understood from this that Mr. Bryan is in his present position for no other purpose than that of being an agreeable gentleman of leisure. He is a worker. He is conferred with daily by the heads of the various departments. He gives general advice. He is also the general checking agent of the directory, signing all vouchers before they reach the auditor. In addition to all these duties he, being a skillful lawyer, gives much legal advice on Fair matters requiring consideration of that character.

In the room adjoining that of Vice-President Baker is the secretary of the local directory, and Solicitor-General Benjamin Butterworth. All ordinances relating to the World's Fair, as between the commission and the directory and the city are drawn by Mr. Butterworth. All legal questions are referred to him.

The auditor of the directory is Mr. W. K. Ackerman, who has a large corps of aides. His position is strictly one of business. Every bill that is incurred on account of the World's Fair has to come to Mr. Ackerman. His is the halfway place between the business end of the Fair and the treasurer, who hands out the cash. It follows as a common-sense result, that Mr. Ackerman is frequently consulted by the chiefs of various departments and by the heads of the local directory.

Mr. A. F. Seeberger is treasurer of the World's Columbian Exposition. He is one of the successful business men of the city, who has shown his faith in the work before him by devoting a considerable portion of his time to the duties of the office herein named. This department is one of the most important of the World's Fair. Every pound of nails, every bit of ornamentation, every item in the great expense account of this enterprise must be paid from this department. The collection of every dollar on shares subscribed is paid here. From this department all collectors are employed. When the work of gathering subscriptions was undertaken, the men employed for that were instructed from this department. In order to facilitate the work it was necessary to obtain from every factory and storehouse in the city a list of the names of the employes. After the subscriptions were obtained and the collection of the first assessment was begun, it was found that very many who had subscribed had changed their residences and business, so that it was difficult to find them. All this devolved upon Mr. Seeberger and his assistants. Sometimes a man was found who, for one reason or another, declined to pay his assessment. Then missionary work had to be done to bring the delinquent over. It fell to Mr. Seeberger's lot to devise means to accomplish this. In doing so he had a two-fold duty to perform, for if one delinquent were permitted to escape it opened the door for others.

All that has passed, and the thanks of the interested are due to Mr. Seeberger's patience and ingenuity. This department has nothing of the ornamental about it. It is as free from anything like dress parade as a bank. Its employes are selected on account of their quick knowledge and business qualifications only.

When every department shall have finished its work, and the announcement is made that all is ready for the opening of the World's Columbian Exposition, Director-General Davis will give the word. He will touch the button, not literally, for that will be left to the next President of the United States, but that will not be before Director-General Davis says the word. Besides being director-general, he is in consultation with all committees and sub-committees. He makes the nominations of all heads of departments. His nominations, however, like those which the President of the United States sends to the Senate, are not final. They must be passed upon by the National Commission and the local directory. There are forty-four local directors—one for each star on the flag, and his nominations must be satisfactory to both directors and commission. Every scheme and plan must in some manner come to the director-general. All department-chiefs' work goes through Col. Davis, and if there is any friction it is his ingenuity which must cool it off. All applications must be approved by him. The clerical force of the director-general is necessarily large. The business of this department is wide in its ramifications. It frequently calls the head away from home. The commission appointed to go abroad in the interest of the Fair was a suggestion by Col. Davis. The people appointed to go on that mission were named by him.

One of the most important departments in connection with the great event of 1893 is put down as the Department of Publicity and Promotion. This is the editorial department to which come all matters pertaining to the Exposition, and from which is issued all information concerning the Fair. It is under the supervision of Major Moses P. Handy, who laid aside the more active duties of general newspaper work to give the directory the benefit of his knowledge in the promotion of this work. His department is composed of well-trained writers. For the most part they are

TRANSPORTATION BUILDING.

young men who had their journalistic schooling in the newspaper offices of Chicago, which is equivalent to saying that they understand their business. In this department fourteen languages are spoken and written, or can be when the occasion calls for it. The work of this department is of great importance to the success of the World's Fair. Accurate articles on every branch of thought or industry to be represented at the Fair are written in this department. If there is to be an exhibit of the boot and shoe interest, an article is prepared in English, in which every possible fact in connection therewith is given, from a description of the building or the department where such an industry will be exhibited to the manner of shipment of such goods, and all other information which an exhibitor would want. This article is translated into French, German, Spanish, Danish, Swedish, Portuguese and Italian. Copies are made of these translations and sent to every newspaper printed in the languages named which is devoted to the interest discussed. They are also sent to every leading manufacturer in the world whose name the department has in its possession. What is true of this industry is true of every one which will be exhibited here in 1893. Nothing will be seen at the Exposition which has not or will not have been discussed by the writers of this department.

Nor is this more than a beginning of the duties required of the workers in this department. A newspaper in Germany wants a special and an illustrated article on the Exposition. A newspaper in Mexico wants a special article prepared on mining. A newspaper in Denmark wants a general article on the Fair, a description of the grounds, of the buildings, of the means of transporting articles, and so on. These applications are made to the Department of Publicity and Promotion, which at once complies with the requests. A journal in India recently asked for and obtained an illustrated article on Jackson Park and the buildings which are in the course of erection.

There is also an exchange list of every daily newspaper in this country, most of the weeklies, and the principal ones in Europe. When these papers arrive here they are carefully examined by a corps of clippers, distinct from the writers, who cut out every item of news bearing on the Exposition, credit it, and place it in

19

a scrapbook, which is labeled, so that if it is desired to know what the paper in Kamchatka has said about the affair the article will be found in the scrap-book with the name of that country printed upon it. There are at present one hundred of these scrap-books, most of which are well filled with matter pertaining to the coming Exposition. After the Exposition shall have become a thing of the past, these books are to be put away in a place of safety where they will be accessible to the curious.

There have been spread upon the records of this department the names of forty thousand prominent people throughout the world. They are members of legislatures, congressmen, all possible exhibitors in the world; consuls, officers of the Farmers' Alliance, people connected with arts and manufactures, commercial and educational organizations—each one of these gets from time to time all the information gathered by this department, and whatever, queries they make, and they are many, are answered in the fullest and most courteous way.

In the large room above the editorial department are men and women engaged in mailing the pamphlets printed in every language that has been named. Not only pamphlets, but every article bearing on the great event. There are one hundred and fifty thousand various documents on every conceivable topic touching the great exhibit in this department. The postage of this section of Major Handy's department amounts to over $200 a week, and a good deal of the matter goes at second-class rates.

There is a room set aside in connection with the publicity and promotion bureau for reporters and outside newspaper men who come to it for information. Every facility is afforded the press of the city and country for the accumulation of news concerning the Exposition. For the papers in Milwaukee and adjacent cities, special reports of the day's doings in all the departments are prepared and sent out. In addition to this, plate matter is prepared and sent out to that class of papers which use plate matter. In these plates are all the new cuts that have been made of grounds and buildings.

The statement having been made that few of the foreign countries have taken any interest in the coming Exposition, Mr. Dorr, assistant to Major Handy, has had prepared a sheet of clippings from the foreign press, which embraces a list of papers printed in London, Liverpool, Manchester, Dublin, Plymouth, Dundee, Melbourne, Gibraltar, Frankfort-on-the-Main, Berlin, Hamburg, Munich, Bremen, Vienna, Berne, St. Petersburg, Luxemburg, Stockholm, City of Mexico, Milan, Constantinople, Havana, Guatemala, Panama, Paris, Evora in Portugal, and other cities, each of which shows the most intense interest in the World's Fair to be held in Chicago. This sheet of clippings, printed in all the languages mentioned in this article, has been scattered broadcast.

All employes whose salaries are over $2,000 are paid monthly; those who receive $2,000 and less are paid semi-monthly. The head of each department makes out his or her pay-roll. It is sent to Col. Davis, who certifies to it and sends it to President Baker or Vice-President Bryan, who passes upon it and then sends it to the auditor, from whose department it goes to the treasurer.

The business of the local directory is to raise money and erect buildings. Then there is what is called the Board of Control, which is commissioned by the National Commission. This committee passes upon all plans of buildings and all the details of the Fair. It is composed of President Palmer, J. M. McKenzie, E. B. Martindale, G. V. Massur, M. H. DeYoung, J. W. St. Clair, T. M. Waller and W. Lindsay. These gentlemen meet once a month and listen to the reports of Col. Davis, which embrace all the suggestions which that official has to communicate and all the reports which the heads of the various departments have made to him.

It is not too late to state that in the local directory there are thirteen standing committees. They locate buildings on the grounds and fix the price of admission to the same. In addition to these thirteen committees there is the executive committee. It is composed of the chairmen of the thirteen committees. To this executive committee is delegated a great deal of the business of the thirteen committees. The local directory meets once a month. The executive committee meets once a week.

An important committee is that on grounds and buildings. It meets every day except Wednesday and Saturday. It is to the department of Supervising Architect Burnham what the Committee of Control is to Col. Davis. It passes on the appointments of Mr. Burnham, on the letting of all contracts, and on the business of expending any large sum of money, from $8,000,000 to $10,000,000. Mr. E. T. Jeffery is chairman of this committee. None of the chairmen of committees or committeemen get any pay as such. The president of the National Commission and his staff of officers draw salaries. So do the officers of the local board, the treasurer, auditor, director-general and chairman of the Publicity and Promotion Bureau.

The committee of which Mr. H. N. Higinbotham is chairman is the Ways and Means. It meets twice a week. It is the committee which will have charge of the Bazaar of All Nations, in which each nation will erect a booth or house representing its business customs. To this committee must also come whosoever wishes to erect or get the privilege for any sort of stand on the grounds, from a peanut vender to the Parsee merchant. All the unique features of the Fair will be under the wing of Mr. Higinbotham's committee.

The committee, or, as it is known in the technique of the Fair people, the Bureau of Subscriptions, is under the management of Mr. Harmon E. Spruance. All delinquent subscribers are looked up by the employes of this committee. And to the same workers . will be intrusted the labor of securing new subscriptions. It is calculated that not less than $15,000,000 will have been expended in connection with the Fair by the time the gates are opened. Ten millions have been subscribed and collected. The general government has been asked to loan an additional $5,000,000 and take the gate receipts for that amount, and there is every reason to believe the request will be granted. To this Committee on Subscriptions will fall the work of getting the other $5,000,000.

The Bureau of Construction is under the care and supervision of Mr. D. H. Burnham, the architect. The quarters of this bureau are in the Rookery Building, occupying a portion of Mr. Burnham's rooms and all of the twelfth floor. Connected with the bureau are A. Gottlieb, chief engineer, and F. L. Olmstead & Co., landscape architects. It is the business of this department to lay out all grounds at Jackson Park; to build and construct the island, which will remain forever afterward one of the attractive spots of Chicago. On the twelfth floor referred to all plans are being made for whatever buildings that are yet to be agreed upon. Under the direction of this bureau at the park are men whose duty it is to go over the grounds almost daily for the purpose of making whatever changes in the plans may have been agreed upon by Mr. Burnham's department. To the building temporarily erected at the park all engineers and others interested in that line go to consult Mr. Gottlieb, who has charge of the plans and specifications there.

Mr. Joseph Hirst is Secretary of Installation. All applications for space are made to him. He makes a memorandum of the same and they are then referred to the heads of the department to which they belong. Mr. Hirst is in close and frequent communication, of course, with the director-general. His department is one of the busy and important ones of the general offices.

The work being done by the Board of Lady Managers is of a character which will tell and be appreciated by the public later on. It does not show upon its face. This department is under the attention of Mrs. Potter Palmer and occupies three rooms on the Adams street front of the building. The board consists of 115 members. There are two managers from each State and Territory. At this Exposition every woman of this country and Europe will be given an opportunity to place her work conspicuously before the world. They will be represented by States and Nations. Whatever, for instance, the women of the State of Alabama have to offer will be reported to the managers from that State, who will communicate the same to Mrs. Palmer, who will make arrangements for the exhibit from that State. These lady managers in the various States and Territories are also interested in urging upon their respective localities all which can be of any possible benefit to the Fair as a whole. Some of the lady managers, for instance, did excellent work in their State legislatures when the time came for such legislatures to make appropriations for exhibits. This department is fully equipped for its work, and has a corps of women who are fully aware of the importance of

the coming event. Many of the adjuncts to the various departments come from this one of Mrs. Palmer's. All articles on
fashion, women's work elsewhere touching the Fair, which appear
in women's publications, are clipped by a lady who has had experience in newspaper work, arranged and sent over to Maj.
Handy. Translations from all literature across the water, where
the same relates to the Fair, are made in this department.

There is a Board of Reference and Control composed of eight
men from the national commission and eight from the local directory. Before this combination of conservatism all disputes
and questions connected with or arising out of the work of the
Fair are submitted and the action of the board is final.

The last committee to be appointed was the Committee on
Ceremonies, composed of members of the national and local
boards. Its duties, so far as the Fair proper is concerned, have
not yet been explicitly defined, but it will be called upon to do
a great work before the Fair.

On the 12th day of October, 1892, next year, there will be an
informal opening of all the buildings. There will be grand military
and industrial parades, military and civic balls and many august
ceremonies bearing on the voyage of Columbus and his discovery
of America. All this will occur under the direction of the Committee on Ceremonies. The celebration will occupy three days.
And then it will be some time before the World's Columbian
Exposition proper will open. By that time Chicago will have
become familiar with the ground and buildings.

The various departments occupied by the people who are
making the World's Fair are furnished in business-like manner.
The rooms of the chiefs are handsomely carpeted. Every em-
ployé in any clerical position has a cylinder desk and a revolving
chair. The rooms give evidence of work being done in a business-like manner.

It cost Chicago $90,674.97 to secure the World's Columbian
Exposition. This preliminary fund was produced by an organization of which Mr. James W. Scott was chief and W. J.
Onahan treasurer. They made a levy on the subscribers of the
first $5,000,000 worth of stock of 2 per cent., which proved to be
ample funds to carry on the campaign and permitted the treas-

urer of the preliminary organization to turn a respectable amount of cash to the treasurer of the permanent organization.

On March 10, France—the first foreign nation to accept—decided to participate in the Exposition. Since that date forty nations and twenty-four colonies have voted their acceptance, and are energetically preparing to participate. Previous to January 1, but one or two States had made any World's Fair appropriation. Now twenty-eight States and Territories have voted appropriations, and nearly if not quite all of the remaining ones are planning either to secure appropriations or to raise by private subscription the sums deemed necessary for a creditable exhibit of their respective resources and products.

The construction department has accomplished wonders. After plans for the various Exposition buildings had been submitted and approved, the working plans and drawings had to be made. This required the work of several hundred men for weeks. Contracts involving in the aggregate millions of dollars were advertised and let. Meantime work was pushed at the park to prepare it for the great structures. At an expense of nearly half a million dollars the park, the greater portion of which was a swamp, was drained and graded. Lagoons and waterways, ranging from 100 to 300 feet wide, were dredged out. Raised sites for the buildings were made. About 1,200,000 cubic yards of earth had to be moved. The park was inclosed by a high tight board fence. Huge boarding-houses or cheap hotels for the workmen were built in the park, and numerous shops and other buildings for construction purposes were put up. Many miles of pipe were laid in carrying out the extensive water and sewerage systems which had been adopted; pumping-works were built; fire-department stations, fully equipped with men and apparatus, were established; police protection was provided; a hospital was built and manned. More than fifteen miles of railroad track were laid in the park for transporting lumber and other construction material to the sites of the various Exposition buildings.

The actual erection of the Exposition buildings cannot be said to have begun until last June, though of course the plans for most of them had been well advanced before that time and contracts for several of them had been let. The contract for the last of the great buildings was not let until October. Contracts for some of the minor structures are yet to be let. When it is considered that all of the buildings which the visitor beholds at Jackson Park to-day have been erected within the last six months, it must be admitted that the results which have been accomplished are remarkable.

The tables given below show concisely the dimensions, area and cost of the principal Exposition buildings.

BUILDINGS.	DIMENSIONS IN FEET.	AREA IN ACRES.	COST.
Manufactures and Liberal Arts..........	787x1687	30.5	$1,500,000
Mines	350x700	5.6	265,000
Electricity	345x690	5.5	401,000
Administration.....................	262x262	1.6	435,000
Transportation	256x960	5.6 }	370,000
" Annex.................	425x900	8.8 }	
Woman's	199x3881	1.8	138,000
Art Galleries.........................	320x500	3.7 }	670,000
" Annexes (2).......................	120x200	1.1 }	
Fisheries.............................	165x365	1.4 }	224,000
" Annexes (2)	135 diameter	.8 }	
Horticulture	250x998	5.7	300,000
Machinery	492x846	9.6 }	1,200,000
" Annex......................	490x550	6.2 }	
" Power house	100x461 ⎫		
" Pumping works	77x84 ⎬	2.1	85,000
" Machine shop	146x250 ⎭		
Agriculture	500x800	9.2 }	618,000
" Annex	300x550	3.8 }	
" Assembly Hall.............	125x450	1.3	100,000
Forestry	208x528	2.5	100,000
Saw Mill............................	125x300	.9	35,000
Dairy...............................	100x200	.5	30,000
Live Stock (3).........................	65x200	.9 ⎫	
" Pavilion	280x440	2.8 ⎬	335,000
" Sheds......................		40. ⎭	
Casino	120x250	.7 }	*210,000
Music Hall...........................	120x250	.7 }	
		153.3	$7,016,000
U. S. Government	345x415	3.3	400,000
" Battleship.......	69.25x348	.3	400,000
Illinois State ....:	160x450	1.7 }	250,000
" " Annexes (2)		.3 }	

*With connecting peristyle.........................,.....158.9 $7,766,000

The last three buildings are being erected, the first two by the United States Government and the third by the State of Illinois. The visitor, however, will naturally class them among the great Exposition structures. All of the annexes will be scarcely less imposing and architecturally beautiful than the main buildings themselves. The live-stock sheds, which will cover an immense area, as indicated, are to be constructed as inexpensively as possible without marring the general architectural effect. There will be several Exposition buildings in addition to those named above, but plans for these are not yet perfected. Among them will be a press building and a reproduction of a Spanish convent La Rabida, within which are to be exhibited Columbus relics. The total cost of the Exposition buildings proper is estimated at $8,000,000 approximately. This estimate does not include the government structures or those of the State and foreign countries. These, it is now thought, will be fully 75 in number. They will show a great diversity of architecture and represent the expenditure of more than a million dollars, it is estimated.

The work of construction of the buildings at Jackson Park is at an advanced stage, and is proceeding day and night upon a number of them. All of the buildings named in the list are in process of erection except the live-stock structures and several of the annexes.

Work is proceeding energetically on the power-houses, machine-shops, pumping-works, and the water and sewerage systems are being brought rapidly into operating condition. Nearly 5,000 men are now employed in the work of construction. Insurance is placed and increased on the buildings as their construction proceeds. The amount now carried is about $1,000,000. It has been stated that it is the intention to carry an aggregate of $300,000,000 on the buildings and exhibits during the summer of 1893.

The Exposition Company has very large expenditures to meet in addition to the cost of the buildings. In fact, the latter does not constitute one-half of the total amount necessary to carry through the enterprise. In a report made by the grounds and

buildings committee some time ago, the following estimates
of such expenses were given :

Grading, filling, etc	$ 450,400
Landscape gardening	323,490
Viaducts and bridges	125,000
Piers.	70,000
Waterway improvements	225,000
Railways	500,000
Steam plant.	800,000
Electricity	1,500,000
Statuary on buildings	100,000
Vases, lamps and posts.	50,000
Seating	8,000
Water supply, sewerage, etc..	600,000
Improvement of Lake Front	200,000
World's Congress Auxiliary.	200,000
Construction department expenses, fuel, etc	520,000
Organization and administration	3,308,563
Operating expenses	1,550,000
	$10,530,453

Adding to this the amount estimated to be necessary for buildings ($8,000,000), the grand total sum to be expended by the
Exposition Company alone foots up $18,530,453.

The following shows the resources of the Exposition Company :

Stock subscriptions	$ 5,710,140
City of Chicago bonds.	5,000,000
Prospective gate receipts	10,000,000
Concessions and privileges	1,500,000
Salvage .	2,000,000
Interest on deposits	35,000
	$24,245,140

To the resources will be added future interest on bank
deposits and future subscriptions to stock. Subscriptions are
coming in daily, and the amount which will thus be realized is
certain to be large, though how much it will be cannot, of course,
be estimated now even approximately. Of the subscriptions
already received 60 per cent. has been called for, and $3,350,000
has been paid in. The number of subscribers is over 30,000.
Death, impoverishment, etc., have caused thus far a delinquency

in collections of between 7 and 8 per cent. of the whole amount due. This is much less than was anticipated. Quite a number of subscribers have anticipated the calls and have paid up in full. The $5,000,000 from city bonds is certain to be realized in full, as Chicago's credit is excellent. The gate receipts, concessions and privileges and salvage are necessarily prospective, and the amounts given are of course estimates. It is believed they are moderate. As a large share of the resources, as given above, cannot be realized until the Exposition opens, it is naturally the desire to anticipate a portion of them in some way in order to meet the heavy expense attending the erection of buildings and preparation of the grounds. Accordingly it is contemplated asking Congress to appropriate $5,000,000 to insure the carrying out of the Exposition enterprise on the magnificent lines on which it has been projected, and which have been pursued thus far. Up to date $3,000,000, approximately, has been expended. A large proportion of this has been paid on construction contracts and the rest for organization and administration purposes.

The various Exposition departments are fully organized and are doing an immense amount of work in arranging for the exhibits to be under their respective supervision ; conducting a very large correspondence extending to all parts of the world; enlightening intending exhibitors as to the rules and regulations governing them and the placing and care of their exhibits ; and answering innumerable inquiries upon Exposition affairs. All of this work is done systematically, and reports concerning it are made regularly to the director-general by the respective chiefs. It would be impossible within the compass of this article to specify in detail what these departments have accomplished. It can only be stated in general that their work is being efficiently done and that it is fully abreast of that being done at Jackson Park by the construction department.

The Department of Publicity and Promotion, which was organized to advertise the Fair—to bring it to the favorable attention of the world, and to counteract hostility and correct misapprehensions concerning it—has done excellent work in that direction. No previous exposition has had this promotion work so systematically and extensively done. The department has a large force of writers, translators, typewriters, and mailing-clerks. Special articles and notes upon Exposition affairs, setting forth the scope, progress of construction of buildings, arrangements for exhibits, preparations being made for participation by the States, territories, and by foreign nations and colonies, exhibits that are expected, attractions that visitors will enjoy, and in short, information of every sort relating to the Exposition, is sent each week in five or six languages to thousands of interested persons in all parts of the world. Matter descriptive of the Exposition and relating to its interests, which is prepared by the department, is sent to a mail list comprising thirty-five thousand five hundred addresses, divided as follows: American, twenty-five thousand; German, four thousand five hundred; French, two thousand five hundred; Spanish, two thousand five hundred; others, one thousand. The number of different pieces of mail matter sent out each week ranges all the way from fifty thousand to two hundred thousand. In the week ending December 12 the number of pieces reached two hundred and forty-nine thousand five hundred and twenty-two. The weekly average runs about eighty thousand, but has been greatly increased of late owing to the fact that a large number of lithographs and other extra matter are being sent out.

The result of the work of the Department of Publicity and Promotion is that the World's Fair is known and talked about from one end of the earth to the other. Newspapers are received from South Africa, Constantinople, India, Japan, Central America, Sandwich Islands and Australia, as well as from France, England, Germany, and other countries in frequent and direct communication with the United States, containing columns of matter relating to the Exposition. A large proportion of this was furnished by the Department of Publicity and Promotion. Indifference and hostility to the Fair have been transformed into interest and enthusiasm by the work of this department.

Throughout Europe interest in the Exposition received an immense impetus through the tour made last July and August by the special Exposition Commission composed of Secretary and Solicitor-General Butterworth, Promoter-General Handy, Commissioners Lindsay and Bullock and Director Peck. These envoys did very effective work in promoting foreign participation in the Fair, a work for which the field had been prepared by Major Handy's Department of Publicity and Promotion. A second commission, compòsed of Vice-President Bryan, and Director Higginbotham is now engaged in a like work in the countries of southern Europe and northern Africa. The Exposition is being widely and effectively advertised, and it is assured that the results will be abundantly apparent in the thoroughly international character of the Fair and the thoroughly representative nature of the exhibits.

HOME AND FOREIGN EXHIBITORS.

The foreign nations and colonies which have formally determined to participate in the Exposition, and the amounts of their appropriations made or officially proposed, as far as information concerning them has been received at headquarters, will be found on pages 277-278 of thiˉ volume.

While Egypt and the Netherlands are not expected to participate as nations, they have given assurances that they will render aid and encouragement to such of their citizens as desire to be exhibitors. Italy now stands in the same category, but it is thought not improbable that it will reconsider its former determination and decide to participate officially.

The United States Government has appropriated $1,500,000, of which $400,000 is available for its buildings alone. Congress will be asked at the present session to appropriate, besides the $5,000,000 already referred to, some $700,000 for the awards and expenses attending the judging of exhibits, $50,000 for representation by the District of Columbia, and also a large sum for the expenses of the national commission and Bcard of Lady Managers.

In Colorado an additional $42,000 has been raised by the counties, and in Indiana $8,000 or more has been raised by school pupils and teachers. In several States, notably New York and Virginia, the legislatures now in session are expected to make liberal appropriations. It is confidently reported from several of the States, notably Iowa and Minnesota, that they will double or even treble the appropriations they have

already made. In nine States which made no Fair appropriations, either because of constitutional restriction or by reason of political bickerings, State conventions have been held,
and plans, generally of the stock subscription sort, have been
inaugurated and are in operation to raise amounts deemed necessary for proper representation at the Exposition. These States
and the sums they are endeavoring to raise are:

Alabama ..	$ 50,000	Oregon . .	$100,000
Arkansas. 100,000		South Dakota	80,000
Florida 100,000		Tennessee.	100,000
Georgia 100,000		Texas	300,000
Kansas 100,000		Total	$1,030,000

The expenditure by the States and territories, it is reasonable
to believe, will aggregate more than $4,000,000.

The Board of Lady Managers has proved to be one of the most
energetic branches of the Exposition enterprise. The women,
not only of America, but of many foreign countries, are manifest-
ing very deep interest in the project of showing as completely as
possible at the Fair the achievements of their sex in every branch
of human endeavor to which it has devoted its ability and skill.
To this purpose the lady managers have labored effectively, and
as a result women are organized both here and in European
nations and are bending their energies toward making the
women's exhibit complete in every respect, believing that it will
be a revelation to the world, that it will tend mightily toward
destroying existing prejudices and discriminations, and that it
will prove a powerful incentive to women to enter broader fields
of usefulness.

The World's Congress Auxiliary has arranged to bring to
Chicago in 1893 many of the world's greatest specialists and
thinkers to participate in congresses, where an interchange of
ideas and discussions of the important questions in their respective fields will occur.

Arrangements, almost complete, have been made for the
formal dedication of the Exposition buildings on October 12,
1892. The ceremonies will begin on October 11 and conclude on October 13. The ceremonies will be very elaborate,

ILLINOIS STATE BUILDING.

and will include as prominent features music, oratory, mobiliza-tion of ten thousand troops, a procession of twenty or more sym-bolical floats in the Exposition lagoon, and magnificent displays of fireworks.

The World's Columbian Exposition is an enterprise stupen-dous beyond the present conception of the people. Even those active in its organization and management declare that it has ex-panded and developed so rapidly since its inauguration that they themselves can scarcely comprehend its magnitude. The present indications are so strong as to amount almost to positive proof that the Exposition will, in every respect, far surpass all previous World's Fairs. Notwithstanding all that could be said and writ-ten concerning the preparations that have been made, the enor-mous work already done, and the enormous work still to be done, it is doubtless a fact that only when the gates are thrown open on May 1, 1893, will the people be able to comprehend its mag-nitude and magnificence. But when the citizens of the world shall congregate to celebrate the four hundredth anniversary of the landing of Columbus in America, Jackson Park will have been transformed into a city as large as Vienna and as beautiful as Venice.

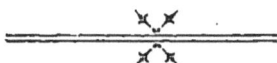

Former World's Fairs.

"Men are but children of an older growth." They must have their holidays and half-holidays their Fourth of Julys and their Christmases. Especially is this true of the Western World wherein a year is but a whirling drum of dusty activity. The whirring spindle must rest or be consumed by the heat of its own friction. In the Orient, where life is indolent and voluptuous, people do not feel so urgently the need of these play-spells that have come to be a part of the life of the more rugged and ad-venturous people of the earth. At first these short "play-spells" in the round of industry were given up entirely to pleasure, carnivals in which license often led to debauchery. A growing intelligence; however, recognized the fact that rest did not mean idleness, but change of thought and occupation. Booths exhibiting the industrial features of the country were added to the amusement displays of these pleasure gatherings, and fairs, at which the mechanical, industrial and fine arts were the principal features, became popular. Out of these have grown the World's Fairs, of which the Columbian Exposition to be held in Chicago in 1893 will be by far the grandest and most important.

The first one of national importance was held in Paris in 1778, under the auspices of the Marquis d'Aveze. A second and larger one was held in Paris in 1802, and another in 1805, and others in the same city at intervals of three years and designated Triennial Expositions, the series continuing for a period of a half-century. The exhibits were, however, of French origin, care being early taken that specimens from other countries should be excluded.   `

The public interest in these fairs extended to large cities in other countries, and between the years 1820 and 1860 extensive industrial displays were made in Berlin, Vienna, Brussels, Moscow, St. Petersburg, Lisbon, Madrid, Stockholm, Dublin, Birmingham, Liverpool, New York, Philadelphia, and other large places.

FIRST INTERNATIONAL EXPOSITION, LONDON, A. D. 1851.

In the spring of 1849, Prince Albert, Royal Prince Consort of Great Britain, President of the Society of Arts, suggested the project of an International Exhibition on a plan much more extended than any preceding one, with hearty invitations to other countries to participate in the same, the exposition to be held in 1851. In July, 1849, a Royal Commission, at the head of which was Prince Albert, was appointed to organize and manage the exposition. The work was energetically pushed forward,. exciting wide-spread interest, to completion, and on May 1, 1851, the exposition was opened in Hyde Park, London, by Queen Victoria. It was held in a vast iron and glass structure, named the Crystal Palace (now located at Sydenham) and planned by Sir Joseph Paxton. The building was 1851 feet long by 408 feet wide, with an additional width of 48 feet for half that length. The highest portion was a center transept 108 feet high. The area covered was 19 acres. The exhibitors numbered nearly fifteen thousand, about one-half from Great Britain and the other half from foreign countries. The cost of the structure was $850,000 ; other expenses to the close of the exposition $613,975; total cost $1,463,975. The number of visitors was 6,039,195, averaging 41,938 per day. The total receipts from admission and other sources aggregated $2,525,535 ; net cash profit, $1,062,540. The number of exhibitors exceeded 17,000, of whom 2,918 received prize medals, and 170 received council medals. The greatest number of visitors at any one day was 109,760 (Oct. 8, 1851), and the greatest present at one time was at 2 o'clock P. M. on that day, when over 93,000 were found to be present. These persons were not present in an open area, like an ancient amphitheater, but within a single roofed, windowed and floored build-ing — presenting a single assemblage larger than any other recorded, up to that time, in the annals of ancient or modern history.

The exposition closed October 11, 1851, after continuing for 144 days—May 1 to October 11. The prices for admission were one pound sterling, half a crown, and one shilling per day.

The ground floor and galleries contained 1,000,000 square feet of flooring ; there were altogether in the structure 4,000 tons of iron and 17 acres of glass in the roof, besides about 1,500 glazed sashes. The first subscription ($5,000) was made by the Queen, March 21, 1850; the edifice was commenced September 26, 1850, and on February 12, 1851, the contractors delivered it to the royal commissioners, who on the same day opened it for the reception of goods and for the sale of season tickets.

The exhibition building of 1851 having been surrendered to Messrs. Fox and Henderson on December 1, 1851, the materials were sold for 350,000*l.* to a company, who soon after commenced re-erecting the Crystal Palace on its present site, near Sydenham, in Kent, under the direction of Sir Joseph Paxton, Owen Jones, Digby Wyatt and others. The proposed capital of 2,500,000*l.*
20

(in 100,000 shares of $25 each) was increased in January, 1853, to $5,000,000.

The following is a condensed chronological record of the principal uses to which the structure has been devoted:

First column raised by S. Laing, M.P.............. .　.... Aug. 5, 1852
During the progress of the works as many as 6,400 men were engaged at one time.　By the fall of scaffolding, 12 men were killed... . Aug. 15, 1853
Dinner given to Professor Owen and others in the interior of the model of the iguanodon, constructed by Mr. Waterhouse Hawkins . .Dec. 31, 1853
The palace opened by the queen ... ...　.............. . June 10, 1854
Grand musical *fete* on behalf of the Patriotic Fund .. . . Oct. 28, 1854
The palace visited by the Emperor and Empress of the French, etc.,
　　　　　　　　　　　　　　　　　　　　　　　April 20, 1855
First grand display of the great fountains, before the queen and 20,000 spectators .... June 18, 1856
The receipts were 115,627*l.*; the expenditure 87,872*l.*, not including payments for preference shares, etc., in year ending　..　... April 30, 1857
On the fast-day (for the Indian mutiny) Rev. C. Spurgeon preached here to 23,000 persons; 476*l.* were collected, to which the C. P. company added 200*l.*.. ... 　......-........ .... Oct. 7, 1857
The preliminary Handel festivals ..... .June 15, 17, 19, 1857, and July 2, 1858
Centenary of the birth of Robert Burns celebrated; the directors awarded 50*l.* to a prize poem on the subject, which was obtained by Miss Isa Craig .... Jan. 25, 1859
The Handel festival　.. .... .June 20, 22, 24, 1859
Festival kept in honor of Schiller, Nov. 10, 1859; of Mendelssohn, May 4, 1860
London charity children sing here ... .June 6, 1860
3,000 Orpheonistes (French musical amateurs) perform choral music, June 25; the Imperial band of Guides perform June 26; both dine in the palace .　...... ....June 30, 1860
115 brass bands perform ....July 10, 1860
Annual rose show began 1860
North wing injured by a gale of wind ....Feb. 20, 21, 1861
Haydn's "Creation" performed (Costa, conductor)...............May 1, 1861
Successful Handel festival; a new arched roof constructed for the orchestra ; about 4,000 vocal and instrumental performers,
　　　　　　　　　　　　　　　　　　　June 23, 25, 27, 1862
Successful Handel festival.................... ....June 26, 28, 30, 1865
North wing containing tropical department, the Alhambra, and other courts, destroyed by fire (about 150,000*l.*).....................Dec. 30, 1866
Prince of Wales present at a grand concert to raise funds to restore the palace.. ....June 26, 1867
Visit of the Viceroy of Egypt (gives 500*l.*), July; of the sultan (gives 1,000*l.*).. ....July 16, 1867
Conservative working-men's demonstration ....Nov. 11, 1867

Meeting of shareholders decide by ballot that free tickets shall not be
issued to admit non-shareholders on Sundays..... ....Dec. 31, 1867
North wing restored and re-opened to the public .. ..Feb. 15, 1868
An aeronautical exhibition opened.. . ...June 25, 1868
Protestant meeting to defend the Irish church....... ....Aug. 17, 1868
Reception of the Vicomte de Lesseps ...   .July, 1870
Death of Mr. Robert K. Bowley, fourteen years manager of the com-
pany   .   . . . Aug. 25, 1870
Successful Handel festival .. . .June 19, 21, 23, 1871
The Grand Duke Wladimir of Russia entertained here by the Prince of
Wales   .   ... .June 26, 1871
Dividend on stock, 1½ per cent ....Dec., 1871
Inauguration of the great aquarium by Prof. Owen .. ..Jan. 12, 1872
Lecture by Prof. Flower...... .. .. Jan. 12, 1872
Thanksgiving festival for the recovery of the Prince of Wales. May 1, 1872
Meeting of National Union of Conservative and Constitutional Associa-
tions ....June 24, 1872
National music meetings; competition and concerts..... June 27, July 6, 1872
Scottish southern gathering, highland sports.... ....July 25, 1872
Grand commemoration of the opening of the palace; the Paxton memo-   '
rial unveiled   . ..   .June 10, 1873
Visit of the Shah of Persia.............................June 30, July 3, 1873
National music meetings . ...July 3, 5, 8, 10, 12, 1873
Resignation of Mr. George Grove, many years secretary, announced Sept.;
succeeded by Capt. Flood Page. ....Dec., 1873
Visit of the Czar...May 16, 1874
Handel festival; successful.............................June 22, 24, 26, 1874
Visit of the Sultan of Zanzibar ....June 19, 1876
National music meeting ....July 1, 10, 1875
Visit of the King and Queen of Greece and Prince and Princess of
Wales ....July 19, 1876
Great clock completed...Nov., 1876
Handel festival ....June 25, 27, 29, 1877
Handel festival; successful ....June 21, 23, 25, 1880
Great damage done by bursting of a water-tank; no lives lost .. Sept. 30, 1880
International woolen exhibition opened by the Duke of Connaught,
June 2, 1881
Several notable musical performances patronized by many royal person-
ages who participated in the queen's jubilee coronation festivities..... 1887

DUBLIN, 1853.

The next international exhibition of importance was that of
Dublin, Ireland, opening May 12, 1853. It owed its existence
to the great liberality and enterprise of Mr. Dargan, of that city,

who contributed $400,000 for the purpose. It was erected by Sir John Benson, in the Dublin Society's grounds near Merrion Square, and consisted of one large and two smaller halls, lighted from above. It was opened by the Lord Lieutenant, and was visited by Queen Victoria and Prince Consort. Its visitors numbered 1,140,000, but its receipts amounted to only about $250,000, leaving a deficiency of about $150,000.

CRYSTAL PALACE, NEW YORK, 1853.

This was held under the auspices of a joint-stock company and opened by President Pierce on July 12, 1853. The structure and expenses aggregated $640,000, but its receipts were only about $340,000. The main buildings and galleries covered an area of 173,000 square feet. At the close of the exhibition the palace was used by the American Institute for its fairs, and for meetings of various kinds. The fine edifice was designed by Messrs. Carstensen and Gildemeister, of New York, and located on Reservoir square. October 5, 1858, the edifice, with a great number of articles on exhibition, was destroyed by fire; estimated loss, $2,000,000. The building was regarded as a beautiful piece of architecture.

SECOND LONDON EXPOSITION, 1862.

The second great London exposition was held in a great building, covering an area of about 24 acres, in South Kensington. The main building was of massive brickwork. The annexes and two immense cupolas were chiefly of glass and iron. The total covered space was nearly 1,300,000 feet, including corridors, staircases, etc. About 700,000 square feet were ground-floor space, the remainder galleries. So wisely were the arrangements carried out that the exhibitors had 1,032,352 square feet of horizontal flooring and 284,670 square feet of vertical wall-space. About one-half was allotted to the United Kingdom and its colonies, the other half to foreign countries. The total number of exhibitors was 28,653, of whom 26,348 were in one or other of thirty-six industrial classes; the remainder in one or other of four fine-art classes. There were 3,370 paintings in oil and water colors, 1,275 etchings and engravings, 983 architectural drawings, etc., and 901 pieces of sculpture. The exhibition was open 171 days, nearly a month longer than that of 1851. The visitors numbered in all 6,211,103 persons, but though the number was greater than in 1851, the average per day was less. The receipts from all sources (admission at the doors, season tickets, refreshment contracting, etc.) amounted to the grand total of $2,243,-160, but the cost of the building was so great ($1,600,000, virtually for six months' use only) that the receipts did not cover the outlay, and a deficit of about $50,000 was the result.

The second London international exhibition was followed by several of less magnitude in different cities; some of them, however, were of the international type. The chief among them were the following: Constantinople, 1863; Bayonne, 1864; Dublin, 1865 (opened by the Prince of Wales, Feb. 24, and closed Nov. 19—held under the auspices of a joint-stock company, and resulting in a financial failure); Cologne, 1865; Oporto, 1865; Melbourne, Austria, 1866; Stockholm, 1866, and Agra, 1867.

SECOND PARIS INTERNATIONAL EXHIBITION.

This exposition exceeded in magnitude of conception and in general arrangement and outlay any of its predecessors. It was a really great undertaking. The building was a vast oval, 1,550 feet by 1,250, with a series of twelve concentric galleries running around it, and a small garden in the center. In each gallery a separate branch of science and art was illustrated, and the entire oval was divided into sections, one of which was devoted to each country. The oval covered 11 acres, and the complete exhibition, counting the various annexes and outside grounds, close upon 100. The number of exhibitors was 50,226, and the total expense $3,200,000, half of which was defrayed by the public attendance, half by the imperial government and the Paris municipality. The number of visitors was 10,200,000. Great Britain, it may be, did not figure very favorably in this exhibition, whereas Germany, France and Belgium showed a marked advance in the excellence of their exhibits.

The location of the exhibition was on the Champs de Mars (with a new park of more than 100 acres). The oblong edifice was designed by Leplay and enclosed about 35 acres. The exterior corridor was a belt of iron 85 feet high and 115 feet wide. It was opened by the French Emperor and Empress April, 1 1867. Among other dignitaries it was visited by the Prince of Wales, the Kings of Greece, Belgium, Prussia, and Sweden, the Czar of Russia, the Viceroy of Egypt, the Sultan of Turkey and the Emperor of Austria. The distribution of prizes to exhibitors was made by the Emperor in the presence of the Prince of Wales, the Sultan and other royal personages July 1. The exhibition finally closed November 3, 1867.

Following the above were several other notable exhibitions, viz.: Havre, 1868; Amsterdam, 1869; Sydney, 1870; Milan, Naples and Peru, 1871; Copenhagen, Moscow, and Lyons, 1872.

VIENNA INTERNATIONAL EXHIBITION, 1873.

The exhibits of this exposition occupied an enormous building, with annexes, the whole designed by Mr. Scott Russell, ably assisted by Austrian architects and engineers. The grand central rotunda was 312 feet in diameter, with a lofty dome, greatly exceeding that of St. Peter's at Rome. The exhibition was opened by the Austrian Emperor May 1, 1873, in the presence of the Prince of Wales and numerous other royal dignitaries. The Czar visited it June 1 to 7; the Shah of Persia, July 30, and Victor Emmanuel, King of Italy, September 17 to 22. The exhibition closed November 2. During its progress there arose a great financial panic, greatly affecting Vienna and other chief monetary centers in Europe and America. The entire cost of the exhibition was about $12,000,000. The Austrians contributed $3,000,000 toward the enterprise, but, owing to unwise management, the prevalence of the extraordinary financial stringency and other detrimental causes, the really great exhibition proved to be a huge financial failure. There were many Austrian writers, however, who claimed that the nation received ample compensation from the monetary losses by the advantages which resulted from the introduction into the country of American inventions and products.

A series of annual international exhibitions began in London in 1871, but they failed to prove popular, and were relinquished in 1874.

CENTENNIAL EXPOSITION, PHILADELPHIA, 1876.

Many of the features of this exposition are yet fresh in the minds of those who traveled thousands of miles over land and sea to witness the displays of art and science and join in the festivities of this memorable occasion. It was an international exhibition, in celebration of the hundredth year of the Independence of the United States of America. The congressional bill, providing for the exhibition, was signed by the President, March 3, 1871. The Centennial commission was formed March 24, 1872; Centennial board of finances, created by act of Congress June 1, 1872. The exhibition was opened by President Grant May 19, 1876. Exhibition stock was issued by the Centennial commission. Subscription lists were opened in all of the principal cities of the country. By act of Congress the government contributed $1,500,000, and so from all these sources the sum of money estimated to be necessary ($8,500,000) was raised, though not without much opposition. As the work progressed, however, all obstacles—even those inseparable from so great an undertaking—were overcome. To erect buildings suitable in character and capacity—buildings illustrative of the taste, equal to the enterprise, and worthy of the genius of the American people—was the next great duty devolved upon the Centennial commission. Here success was necessary. To succeed was to elicit the admiration of every people; to fail was to fail ingloriously.

After much deliberation, the Centennial commission determined upon the erection of five principal buildings, the name and character of each to be determined by the nature of the materials therein to be displayed.

The first of these principal buildings was called the Main Building. It was designed for the exhibition of the products of mines, workmanship in the metals, manufactures in general, and for educational and scientific displays. It was in the form of a parallelogram, having a length from east to west of 1,880 feet, and a breadth from north to south of 464 feet. The building throughout its greatest extent was only one story high, the main cornice being 45 feet from the foundation.   The general hall within was 70 feet, rising to 90 feet under the principal arcades. From each of the four corners rose a rectangular tower 48 feet square and 75 feet high.   The water and drainage pipes laid underneath the floor were more than four miles in length.

The third principal building was named Machinery Hall, and was designed for the display of machines of every pattern and purpose known to man—motors, generators of power, pneumatic and hydraulic apparatuses, railway enginery, and contrivances for aërial and water transportation.   In its general plan and outline Machinery Hall was similar to the Main Exposition Building, and only second thereto in dimensions.   The ground plan was a rectangular parallelogram 1,402 feet in length, and 360 in width.   On the south side the central transept of the main hall projected into an annex, 208 feet in depth by 210 feet in breadth.   This hall could hardly be called a thing of beauty ; it was too long and low for that ; but was admirably adapted to the purpose of its construction.

The fourth edifice projected by the commissioners was called Agricultural Hall, and was planned for the exhibition of all tree and forest products, fruits of every grade and description, agricultural products proper, land and marine animals, including the apparatus used in the care and culture of the same; animal and vegetable products, textile materials, implements and processes peculiar to agriculture, farm engineering, tillage and general management of field, forest and homestead.   The ground plan presented a central nave 820 feet in length, and 125 feet in width.   As to its style, Agricultural Hall had a touch of the Gothic, suggested by the Howe truss-arches of the nave and transepts, in its construction.   Over the bisection of the central avenue and main transept rose an elegant cupola surrounded by a weather-vane.   The entrances were ornamental, and at each side were handsome turrets.   This building, being devoted to the general purposes of an agricultural display, had the necessary concomitant of yards for an exhibition of all domestic fowls and animals.

The fifth and last great building was named Horticultural

Hall. It was designed for the proper display of ornamental trees, shrubs and flowers—hot-houses and conservatories—graperies, tools, accessories, designs, construction and management of gardens.

Such was the general plan in which the chief edifices were planned and erected. Other buildings, illustrative of other interests and enterprises, were also rapidly planned and constructed. A Women's Pavilion was projected and completed by an organization called the Women's Centennial Executive Committee. It was designed in October, 1875, and completed in the following January. The building was designed for the special exhibition of whatever woman's skill, patience and genius have produced and are producing, in the way of handicraft, invention, decorations, letters and art. Next came the several States and Territories, selecting grounds and constructing a series of State buildings commemorative of the spirit and illustrating the resources of the respective commonwealths of the Union. Nearly all the foreign nations participating in the exposition made haste to erect, for their own convenience and for the honor of their native land, elegant government buildings—French, Spanish or British —which became a kind of headquarters and rendezvous for the several nationalities. Then came model dwellings and bazars, school-houses and restaurants, judges' halls and model factories, newspaper buildings and ticket-offices—until the Centennial grounds (capacious as they were) were filled with—shall it be called a city?—the most imposing, spacious and ornate ever seen in the world.

The main building covered 21 acres, and the five principal buildings, with their "annexes," covered 75 acres. Including the foreign and State buildings, the total number of structures was 199. The number of visitors admitted was 9,910,966. The number present on the opening day was ———. The largest number present on any one day was 274,919. The number of exhibitors was about 40,000. Of the total space covered by the exhibits of various countries the United States used about 1,000,-000 square feet; Great Britain and her colonies, 200,000 square feet; France and French dependencies, 100,000 square feet; Germany over 60,000 square feet. The receipts for admission aggregated $3,761,598, and the total receipts were about $4,300,-000. The exhibition after being open to the public for 158 days was closed November 10, 1876.

THIRD PARIS INTERNATIONAL EXHIBITION, 1878.

The site of this exhibition was divided by the Seine into two unequal parts. The main building in the Champ de Mars covered 263,593 square yards (765 by 360 yards); the Trocadéro palace is a stone structure, with a rotunda, supported by columns, crowned by a dome, flanked by two lofty towers, the exterior gallery ornamented with statues. The exhibition was opened by the President, Marshal MacMahon ("in the name of the Republic"), in presence of the Prince of Wales, the Duc d'Aosta, and other distinguished persons, May 1, 1878; 111,955 persons visited exhibition (a fête day) August 15. Grand distribution of medals by Marshal MacMahon, with speech, October 21. The exhibition closed Sunday, November 10. Total admissions, 16,032,725; daily average, 82,000; gross receipts, 12,653,746 francs, equivalent to $2,530,000. International Exhibition of Applied Science opened July 24.

During the decade following the Paris exhibition of 1878 the chief industrial displays were the following: Sydney and Berlin in 1879; Melbourne, 1880; Berlin, Moscow and Buenos Ayres, 1882; Louisville, Ky.; Caracas, and Amsterdam, 1883; Calcutta, and New Orleans, 1884; Antwerp, 1885; Edinburg and Liverpool, 1886; Manchester, England, 1887; Melbourne Centennial, Glasgow, and Brussels, 1888.

There have been held, also, numerous special exhibits engaging considerable attention on the part of the public. The following were held in London: An Electrical Exhibition (1882), an International Fisheries Exhibition (1883), a Health Exhibition (1884), an Inventions Exhibition (1885), a Colonial Exhibition (1886), an American Exhibition (1887), the Italian, Irish and Anglo-Danish Exhibitions (1888), and a Spanish Exhibition (1889). In Paris there were held in 1881, an Electrical Exhibition and Congress; in 1884-5, an "Exhibition of Manufactures and Processes."

FOURTH PARIS INTERNATIONAL EXHIBITION, 1889.

On May 9, 1889, the "Paris Universal Exhibition" was opened in the Champs de Mars. It occupied an area of 173 acres and in magnitude and comprehensiveness excelled all its predecessors. On the opening day there were present, exclusive of official sightseers and invited guests, 112,294 persons. During the first week the paying visitors numbered 350,000.

During the year 1889 there were also held, industrial and largely attended exhibitions as follows: "Exhibition of Arts and Industries" at Hamburg; the "Accident Prevention Exhibition" at Berlin; and the "Goldsmiths' Exhibition" at Vienna.

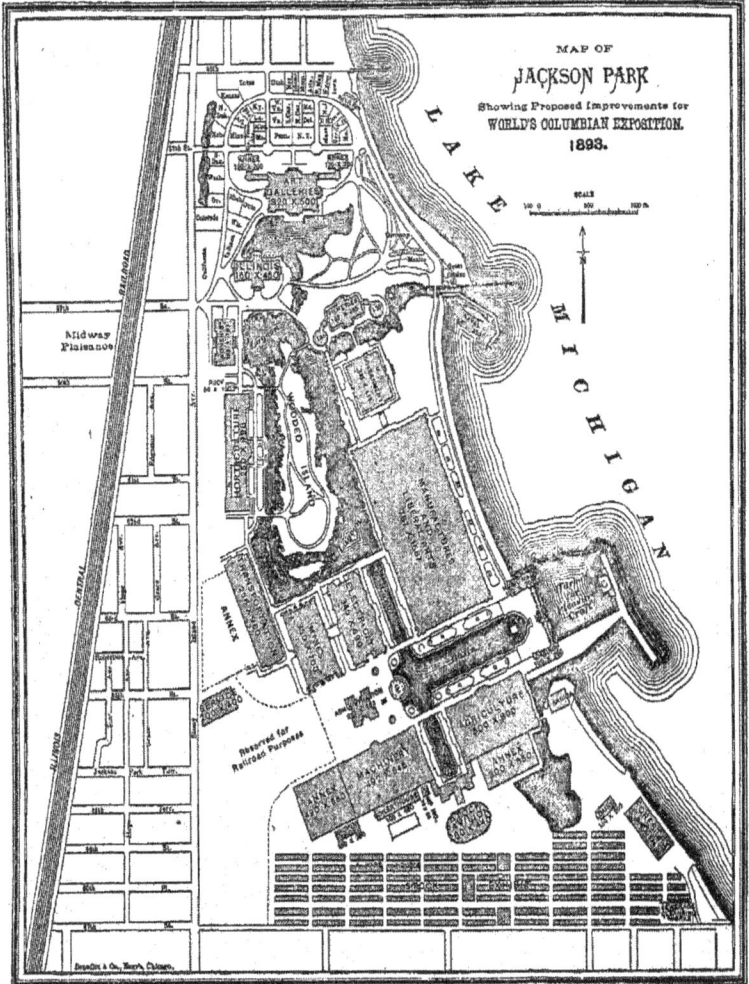

MAP OF
JACKSON PARK
Showing Proposed Improvements for
WORLD'S COLUMBIAN EXPOSITION.
1893.

Classification of Exhibits.

DEPARTMENTS.

A—AGRICULTURE, FOOD AND ITS ACCESSORIES, FORESTRY AND FOREST PRODUCTS, MACHINERY AND APPLIANCES.

B—HORTICULTURE.

C—LIVE STOCK: DOMESTIC AND WILD ANIMALS.

D—FISH, FISHERIES, FISH PRODUCTS, AND APPARATUS OF FISHING.

E—MINES, MINING, AND METALLURGY.

F—MACHINERY.

G—TRANSPORTATION: RAILWAYS, VESSELS, VEHICLES.

H—MANUFACTURES.

J—ELECTRICITY AND ELECTRICAL APPLIANCES.

K—FINE ARTS: PAINTING, SCULPTURE, ARCHITECTURE, DECORATION.

L—LIBERAL ARTS: EDUCATION, ENGINEERING, PUBLIC WORKS, CONSTRUCTIVE ARCHITECTURE, MUSIC AND THE DRAMA.

M—ETHNOLOGY, ARCHÆOLOGY: PROGRESS OF LABOR AND INVENTION. ISOLATED AND COLLECTIVE EXHIBITS.

DEPARTMENT A.

AGRICULTURE, FOOD AND ITS ACCESSORIES, FORESTRY AND FOREST PRODUCTS. MACHINERY AND APPLIANCES.

GROUP 1.
CEREALS, GRASSES AND FORAGE PLANTS.

Class 1. Wheat and its culture.
Varieties of wheat grown in America and abroad.
Statistics of products and of prices.
Class 2. Indian corn—all varieties
Illustrations of methods of planting, tilling and harvesting. Statistics of products and of prices.
Class 3. Oats.
Class 4. Barley.
Class 5. Rye.
Class 6. Rice and its culture.
Class 7. Buckwheat and other grains.
Class 8. Grasses, various species ; hay and hay-making.
Class 9. Forage plants—clover, alfalfa, cow-pea, cornstalks.
Class 10. Ensilage—silos, etc.
Class 11. Flours, meals, decorticated grains, grits, etc.

GROUP 2.
BREAD, BISCUITS, PASTES, STARCH, GLUTEN, ETC.

Class 12. Bread and its manufacture ; baking powder, yeast and its preparations.
Class 13. Cakes and pastry.
Class 14. Biscuit industry, crackers of all kinds.
Class 15. Italian paste, semolino, vermicelli, macaroni, etc.
Class 16. Starch and its manufacture from all sources; from cereals, tubers, arrow-root, plantain, cassava, zamia, manioc, tapioca, sago, pearl flour, etc.

GROUP 3.
SUGAR, SYRUPS, CONFECTIONERY, ETC.

Class 17. Sugar cane, its cultivation and treatment; manufacture of sugar.
Class 18. Cane sugar, syrup, molasses, etc.
Class 19. Grape and fruit sugars.
Class 20. Beet root sugar.
Class 21. Maple sugar, syrups, etc.
Class 22. Palm sugar.
Class 23. Milk sugar.
Class 24. Sorghum, its culture and uses, and preparation of syrup and sugar.
Class 25. Glucoses, etc., prepared.
Class 26. Honey-bees and honey ; hives and appliances.
Class 27. Confectionery, confections, etc. (For jams, jellies, etc., see Group 21.)

GROUP 4.
POTATOES, TUBERS, AND OTHER ROOT CROPS

Class 28. Potatoes, sweet potatoes, yams, etc.
Class 29. Sugar beets, mangel wurzel.
Class 30. Carrots, turnips, beets, artichokes, etc.
Class 31. Peanuts ; methods of cultivation, statistics, etc.

378

GROUP 5.
PRODUCTS OF THE FARM NOT OTHERWISE CLASSED.
Class 32. Broom corn, pumpkins, squashes, peas, beans, as crops. (For garden vegetables, etc., see Group 23.

GROUP 6.
PRESERVED MEATS AND FOOD PREPARATIONS.
(For fish product as food, see also Group 40.)
Class 33. Dried meats, jerked beef.
Class 34. Smoked beef, hams and bacon.
Class 35. Salted meats.
Class 36. Canned meats, including fish, flesh and fowl, pâtés, sardines, lobsters, oysters, etc.
Class 37. Meat extracts, soups and food preparations.
Class 38. Extracts of beef.
Class 39. Milk, dried or in cans, evaporated or condensed.
Class 40. Milk and coffee and similar preparations, in tin or glass.

GROUP 7.
THE DAIRY AND DAIRY PRODUCTS.
Class 41. Milk and cream, with apparatus and method of treatment.
Apparatus and methods of transporting and delivering milk and cream.
Concentrated or partly evaporated milk. (For condensed milk, see Class 39.)
Class 42. Butter.
Class 43. Cheese and its manufacture.
Class 44. Dairy fittings and appliances—churns for hand and power, butter workers, cans and pails, cheese presses, vats and apparatus.

GROUP 8.
TEA, COFFEE, SPICES, HOPS, AND AROMATIC AND VEGETABLE SUBSTANCES.
Class 45. Tea, coffee, cocoa, chocolate and substitutes.
Class 46. Hops; culture, statistics, etc.
Class 47. Peppers, cloves, cinnamon and other spices.
Class 48. Tobacco in the leaf, and tobacco not manufactured.
Class 49. Machines and appliances for the curing of tobacco and for the manufacture of tobacco, cigars, cigarettes and snuff.
Class 50. Insecticides. Methods and appliances for the destruction of the tobacco worm and other parasites.
Class 51. Commercial forms of chewing and smoking tobacco.
Class 52. Cigars, cigarettes and snuff.

GROUP 9.
ANIMAL AND VEGETABLE FIBRES.
Class 53. Cotton on the stalk—its several varieties; long and short staples, shown by living examples, by engravings, photographs, etc.
Class 54. Methods of planting and culture.
Class 55. Machines and appliances for planting, cultivating, picking, ginning and baling.
Class 56. Cotton seed and its uses.
Class 57. Remedies and appliances for destroying insects.
Class 58. Literature, history and statistics.
Class 59. Hemp, flax, jute, ramie and other vegetable fibres not enumerated, in primitive forms and in all stages for spinning.
Class 60. Wool in the fleece, in sacks and in bales.

Class 61. Silk worms, silk in the cocoon; apparatus and appliances used in silk culture.
Class 62. Hair as a textile material.

GROUP 10.
PURE AND MINERAL WATERS, NATURAL AND ARTIFICIAL.
Class 63. Distilled water, for use in the arts and for drinking.
Class 64. Spring water, mineral water, natural and artificial.
(See also Group 48.)
Class 65. Aerated waters.

GROUP 11.
WHISKIES, CIDER, LIQUEURS AND ALCOHOL.
Class 66. High wines—whisky and its manufacture.
Class 67. Rum and other distilled spirits, as saki, samshoo, etc.
Class 68. Alcohol—pure spirits.
Class 69. Cordials and liqueurs.
Class 70. Bitters and mixed alcoholic beverages.
Class 71. Cider and vinegar.

GROUP 12
MALT LIQUORS.
Class 72. Preparation of the grain. Malt and extracts of
Class 73. Beers, ales, porter, stout, etc.

GROUP 13.
MACHINERY, PROCESSES AND APPLIANCES OF FERMENTING, DISTILLING, BOTTLING AND STORING BEVERAGES.
Class 74. Apparatus of fermenting—vats, cellars, etc.
Class 75. Distilling. Ordinary and vacuum stills, etc.
Class 76. Rectifying apparatus and methods.
Class 77. Machinery and appliances for bottling beer.

GROUP 14.
FARMS AND FARM BUILDINGS.
Class 78. Farms and farm administration and management, shown by farms, or by maps, models, records, statistics and other illustrations.
Class 79. Irrigation, drainage methods, machinery and appliances. Models of fences, construction of roads; literature and statistics.
Class 80. Systems of planting, cultivating harvesting and fertilizing.
Class 81. Systems of breeding and stock feeding.
Class 82. Farm buildings, houses, barns, stables, etc., shown by reference to special examples, or by models, drawings or other illustrations. Stable fittings.

GROUP 15.
LITERATURE AND STATISTICS OF AGRICULTURE.
Class 83. Statistics of farms; reports of agricultural societies, etc.

GROUP 16.
FARMING TOOLS, IMPLEMENTS AND MACHINERY.
Class 84. Tillage—manual implements—spades, hoes, rakes, etc. Animal power machinery—plows, cultivators, horse hoes, clod crushers, rollers, harrows, etc. Steam-power machinery—plows, breakers, harrows, cultivators, etc.
Class 85. Planting—manual implements—planters and hand-drills, hand-seeders, etc. Animal power machinery—grain and fertilizer drills, seeders, planters. etc. Steam-power machinery—grain and fertilizer drills, seeders, planters, etc.

Class 86. Harvesting—manual implements—scythes, rakes, forks, grain cradles, sickles, reaping hooks, etc. Animal power machinery—reapers, binders, and headers, mowers, tedders, rakes, hay elevators, hay loaders and stackers, potato diggers, corn harvesters, combined harvesters, binding twine, etc.

Class 87. Preparatory to marketing—threshers, clover hullers, corn shellers, winnowers, and apparatus for bailing hay, straw and other products, etc.

Class 88. Applicable to farm economy—portable engines, wind mills, chaffers, hay and feed cutters, vegetable and root cutters, feed grinders, corn-mills, farm-boilers and steamers, stump extractors, etc.

Class 89. Traction engines and apparatus for road making and excavating, with illustrations.

GROUP 17.

MISCELLANEOUS ANIMAL PRODUCTS—FERTILIZERS AND FERTILIZING COMPOUNDS.

Class 90. Miscellaneous animal products—hides, horns, ivory, bones, scales, tortoise shell, shells, glue, gelatine, etc. Animal perfumes—musk, castorium, civet, ambergis, etc., in their crude state, not manufactured.

Class 91. Hair—for masons' use; for upholsterers, heavy felting, bristles, feathers, down, etc.

Class 92. Fertilizers of living animals; guanos, raw and mixed.

Class 93. Fertilizers of fossil origin. Commercial fertilizers—phosphatic, ammoniacal, calcareous, potash, salts, etc.

GROUP 18.

FATS, OILS, SOAPS, CANDLES, ETC.

Class 94. Animal oils and fats—lard, tallow, butterine, oleomargarine, lard oil, whale oil. (For fish oils see also Department D.)

Class 95. Vegetable oils, cotton-seed oil, olive oil, rape-seed oil, linseed oil, palm-oil, etc., with the seeds and residues.

Class 96. Soaps and detergent preparations. (For perfumery and toilet soaps, see also Group 87.)

Class 97. Stearine, glycerine, paraffine, etc. Spermaceti, ozocerite, wax, candles, etc.

Class 98. Lubricating oils, axle grease, etc.

GROUP 19.

FORESTRY, FOREST PRODUCTS.

Class 99. Logs and sections of trees; samples of wood and timber of all kinds generally used in construction or manufactures, either in the rough or hewed, sawed or split, including square timber, joists, scantling, plank and boards of all sizes and kinds commonly sold for building purposes. Also ship timber, as used in ship-building, or for masts and spars; spiles, timber for fencing, for posts, for paving or for timbering mines. Miscellaneous collections of wood.

Class 100. Worked timber or lumber, in form of clapboards, shingles, sheathing or flooring, casings, moldings, stair rails, or parts of furniture.

Class 101. Ornamental wood used in decorating and for furniture; veneers of hard and fancy woods; mahogany logs, crotches and veneers; rosewood; satin-wood, ebony, birdseye maple, madrona, black walnut veneers and other fancy woods suitable for and used for ornamental purposes.

21

Class 102. Timber prepared in various ways to resist decay.
Class 103. Dyeing, tanning and coloring—dye-woods, barks, and various vegetable substances in their raw state, ısed for dyeing and coloring,
such as log-wood, Brazil wood. peach wood, fustic, sumac.
Barks of various kinds, Brazilian acacias, oak, hemlock, murici,
bicida, gordonia. Galls, excrescences and abnormal woody products. Mosses used for dyeing and coloring.
Class 104. Cellular substances—corks, and substitutes for cork of vegetable
growth; porous woods for special uses, pitch, rice-paper, etc.
Class 105. Lichens, mosses, pulu, ferns and vegetable substances used for bedding, for upholstering, or for mechanical purposes, as teazels, Dutch
rushes, scouring grass, etc., "Excelsior."
Class 106. Gums, resins, vegetable wax or tallow wax, including caoutchouc,
gum senegal, tragacanth, Arabic, mesquite gum, myrrh, copal, etc.
Class 107. Seeds and fruits, for ornamental purposes; vegetable ivory, coquilla
nuts, cocoa-nut shells, ganitrus beads, bottle gourds, etc.
Class 108. Medicinal: roots, herbs, barks, mosses, berries, etc.
Miscellaneous products.
Class 109. Wood pulp for making paper and other objects.
Class 110. Paper and wooden ware generally, as pails, tubs, platters, brooms,
coopers' stock.
Class 111. Basket industry—willow-ware, etc.
Class 112. Rattan, bamboo and cane work in part. (For rattan furniture, see
also Group 90.)
Class 113. Forest botany—distribution of forests, of genera, of species (maps).
Wood sections and herbarium specimens of the economically im-
portant timber trees.
Seed collections, not herbarium—etc.
Illustrations of forest growth, typical trees, botanical features.
Anatomy and structure of woods. (Veneer sections and photo-
micographs.)
Peculiarities of forest growth—cypress-knees, burls.
Diseases of forest trees and timber. Injurious insects.
Class 114. Timber culture.—Plant material.—Conifers, seedlings, and trans-
plants.
Broad-leaved trees. Seedlings, transplants of various sizes, cuttings.
Seed collections and means for storing seed.
Means employed in gathering and preparing seed and other plant
material for the market, and seed testing.
Class 115. Timber culture and cultivation.—Implements for the cultivation of
the soil. Special adaptations.
Sewing machines and tools.
Implements and machines used for planting.
Implements used in after-culture. Means of protection against
insects, animals, climate.
Seed-beds and other graphic illustrations of nursery practice.
Class 116. Forest management.—Maps, plans, illustrations, calculations illus-
trating forest management.
Instruments for measuring standing timber.
Growth of different ages and soils. Graphic or other illustrations
showing rate of growth. Graphic or other illustrations showing
influence of various managements on tree-growth.
Statistics of lumber trade and of forestry.
Exhibits showing relation of forests to climate.
Literature and educational means.

Class 117. Lumbering and harvesting of forest products. The lumbering industry. Logging and transportation. Implements, machines, plans,
drawings, and statistical material. Loggers' tools, stump-pulling
devices, marking devices, measuring tools. Loading devices,
slides, rope tram-ways, railroads, methods of water transportation,
rafts, booms, etc.
The tan-bark industry. Other barks.
The turpentine industry.
The charcoal industry.

Class 118. Preparation and manipulation of lumber. Dressing, shaping and
preparation of wood. Hewing of logs, spars, etc. Shaping of
knees. Sawing and milling.
Drying and seasoning of wood, kiln-drying, steambending, etc.

DEPARTMENT B.

HORTICULTURE, VITICULTURE, POMOLOGY, FLORICULTURE, ETC.

GROUP 20.

VITICULTURE, MANUFACTURED PRODUCTS. METHODS AND APPLIANCES.

Class 118. Preparation and manipulation of lumber. Dressing, shaping and
preparation of wood. Hewing of logs, spars, etc. Shaping of
knees. Sawing and milling.
Drying and seasoning of wood, kiln-drying, steam-bending, etc.

Class 119. The vine and its varieties—shown by living examples, by cuttings,
by engravings, photographs, etc.

Class 120. Methods of planting, staking, and training the vine.

Class 121. Vineyards and their management.

Class 122. Grapes for the table.

Class 123. Grapes for wine-making.

Class 124. Grapes for drying—raisin grape culture.

Class 125. Methods of and appliances for cultivating, harvesting, curing, packing, and shipping grapes.

Class 126. White wines.

Class 127. Red wines, Clarets, Zinfandel, Burgundies.

Class 128. Sherries, Madeira, Port.

Class 129. Sparkling wines.

Class 130. Methods of expressing the juice of the grape ; of fermenting, storing,
racking, bottling, and packing. Wine cooperage.

Class 131. Brandy of all kinds ; methods and apparatus for the production of
brandy.

Class 132. Literature, history, and statistics of viticulture.

·GROUP 21.

POMOLOGY, MANUFACTURED PRODUCTS. METHODS AND APPLIANCES.

Class 133. Pomaceous and stone fruits—pears, apples, plums, peaches, necta-
rines, apricots, cherries, etc.

Class 134. Citrus fruits—oranges, lemons, limes, shaddocks, etc.

Class 135. Tropical and subtropical fruits—bananas, pineapples, guavas, man-
goes, sapodillas, tamarinds, figs, olives, etc.

Class 136. Small fruits—strawberries, raspberries, blackberries, gooseberries,
currants, etc.

Class 137. Nuts—almonds, pecans, chestnuts. filberts, walnuts, etc.
Class 138. Casts and models of fruits; imitations in wax, etc.
Class 139. Dried and evaporated apples, peaches, pears and other fruits. Prunes, figs, dates, etc., in glass or boxes.
Class 140. Fruits in glass or cans, preserved in syrup or alcohol.
Class 141. Jellies, jams, marmalades.
Class 142. Fruits glaced.
Class 143. Cider, perry, vinegar and expressed juices of berries.
Class 144. Methods for crushing and expressing the juices of fruits and berries. Apparatus and methods of desiccating; apparatus for making vinegar, etc. Cider mills and presses.
Class 145. Methods for preserving all fruits by cold storage or chemical appliances; their keeping, packing and shipping.
Class 146. Literature, history and statistics.

GROUP 22.
FLORICULTURE.

Class 147. Roses.
Class 148. Carnations.
Class 149. Orchids.
Class 150. Rhododendrons, azaleas, etc.
Class 151. Chrysanthemums.
Class 152. Dahlias, gladiolus, etc.
Class 153. Ornamental bulbous flowering plants. Hyacinths, narcissus, etc.
Class 154. Pelargoniums, zonal and show.
Class 155. Bedding plants and flowering annual plants.
Class 156. Climbing plants.
Class 157. Perennials and flowering shrubs not otherwise specified.
Class 158. Miscellaneous annuals, phlox, asters, etc.
Class 159. Palms.
Class 160. Ferns.
Class 161. Ornamental leaf plants.
Class 162. Cactacae.
Class 163. Aquatic plants.
Class 164. Native wild plants and flowers.
Class 165. Ornamental grasses and reeds.
Class 166. Rare exotic plants.
Class 167. Cut flowers. Floral designs, pressed flowers, leaves, sea-weeds and bouquets.
Class 168. Plants grown for commercial purposes.
Class 169. Receptacles for plants, flower pots, plant boxes, fern cases, tubs, jardinieres, plant and flower-stands, ornate designs in flower-stands.
Class 170. Literature, history and statistics.
Class 171. Miscellaneous.

GROUP 23.
CULINARY VEGETABLES.

Class 172. Leguminous; cereal and fruit-like vegetables. Beans, peas, okra, peppers, tomatoes, cucumbers, squashes, pumpkins, melons, etc.
Class 173. Radicaceous and tuberous vegetables. Beets, turnips, carrots, potatoes, radishes, etc.
Class 174. Vegetables cultivated for their leaves and sprouts. Cabbage, lettuce, rhubarb, spinach, endive, asparagus, etc.
Class 175. Miscellaneous culinary vegetables not included in the above.
Class 176. Vegetables dried or in cans or glass.
Class 177. Pickles, champignons, truffles, chutney, mustard, etc.
Class 178. Methods for preserving vegetables by cold storage or chemical appliances, their keeping, packing and shipping.

GROUP 24.

SEEDS, SEED RAISING, TESTING, AND DISTRIBUTION.

Class 179. Display of vegetable and flower seeds, grown in different latitudes.
Class 180. General display of flower and vegetable seeds by seed-houses or growers.
Class 181. Methods of growing, harvesting, and preparing flower, vegetable, tree, and shrub seeds.
Class 182. Seed warehouse, methods of burnishing and packing for the retail trade. Work of packing, etc., in operation.
Class 183. Methods of testing vitality of seeds, as practiced by different seed houses.
Class 184. Tree and shrub seeds, and seeds used for condiments and medicines.

GROUP 25.

ARBORICULTURE.

Class 185. Ornamental trees and shrubs. Methods of growing, transplanting, etc.
Class 186. Fruit trees and methods of raising, grafting, transplanting, pruning, etc. Means of combatting insects and other enemies.
Class 187. Nurseries and the nursery trade.

GROUP 26.

APPLIANCES, METHODS, ETC.

Class 188. Hot-houses, conservatories, methods of construction, management and operation.
Class 189. Heating apparatus for hot-houses and conservatories.
Class 190. Seats, chairs and adjuncts for the garden and conservatory.
Class 191. Ornamental wire-work, trellises, fences, borders, labels for plants and trees, etc.
Class 192. Garden and nursery administration and management. Floriculture and Arboriculture, as arts of design and decoration. Laying out gardens, designs for the laying out of gardens, and the improvement of private residences. Designs for commercial gardens, nurseries, graperies; designs for the parterre; treatment of water for ornamental purposes; cascades, fountains, reservoirs, lakes; formation and after treatment of lawns. Garden construction, building, etc. Rock-work grottoes: rustic construction and adornment for private gardens, and public grounds. Planting, fertilizing, cultivating, and appliances.

DEPARTMENT C.

LIVE STOCK—DOMESTIC AND WILD ANIMALS.

GROUP 27.

HORSES, ASSES, MULES.

Class 193. Draft horses—all breeds.
Class 194. Coach horses.
Class 195. Trotting horses.
Class 196. Thoroughbred horses.
Class 197. Saddle horses.
Class 198. Hunters.

Class 199. Educated and trick horses.
Class 200. Ponies.
Class 201. Jacks and jennets.
Class 202. Mules.
Class 203. Literature and statistics; copies of the constitution and by-laws of national horse-breeding associations.

GROUP 28.
CATTLE.

Class 204. Beef.
Class 205. Dairy.
Class 206. For general purposes.
Class 207. Oxen.
Class 208. Crosses of cattle with buffalo, etc.
Class 209. Collections of brands and registers of brands and marks, with implements of herding, tying, etc.

GROUP 29.
SHEEP.

Class 210. Fine wooled sheep.
Class 211. Combing wooled sheep.
Class 212. Middle wooled sheep.
Class 213. Sheep for mutton.

GROUP 30.
GOATS, LLAMA, CAMELS AND OTHER DOMESTICATED ANIMALS.

Class 214. Goats, camels, elephants, llama, vicugna, alpaca, guanaco, yaks, etc.

GROUP 31.
SWINE.

Class 215. Swine of all varieties.
Class 216. Methods of raising, feeding, fattening, breeding, killing and packing. Statistics, literature and history of the industry.

GROUP 32.
DOGS.

Class 217. Hunting, watch, coach, pet and all other varieties, of dogs.
Class 218. Dog collars, chains, muzzles, etc.
Class 219. Breeding kennels, bench shows, registers, standards and literature.

GROUP 33.
CATS, FERRETS, RABBITS, ETC.

Class 220. Breeds of the domestic cat; illustrations of uses and value.
Class 221. Ferrets and their uses.
Class 222. Rabbits, and methods of raising and hunting, and of their destruction as pests.

GROUP 34.
POULTRY AND BIRDS.

Class 223. The breeds of poultry and pigeons, and all domesticated birds. Poultry Shows. Standards of perfection, literature.
Class 224. Fowls and capons.
Class 225. Ducks and geese. Swans.
Class 226. Turkeys.
Class 227. Pigeons and pigeon lofts. Homing pigeons.
Class 228. Guinea fowls, pea-fowls, ostriches, etc.
Class 229. Pheasants and other ornamental birds. Pet birds in general. Cages.

Class 230. Birds of all countries, alive and as stuffed specimens. Taxidermy. Methods and appliances.

Class 231. Poultry and bird houses, and their fittings. Incubators and brooders.

Class 232. Poultry and eggs for market. Feathers, down, quills, and all products. Methods of and appliances for packing and transportation. Prices, Statistics, etc.

GROUP 35.

INSECTS AND INSECT PRODUCTS.

Class 233. Leeches, leech culture; methods and statistics.

Class 234. Care of the cochineal bugs. Gathering and primary preparation of cochineal.

Class 235. Other insects, useful or injurious. Apparatus for the destruction of injurious insects; insecticides and methods of application.

GROUP 36.

WILD ANIMALS.

Class 236. Animals of all countries, alive and as stuffed specimens.

Class 237. Methods of collecting, housing, caging, etc. Protection of wild animals and game.

Class 238. Game preserves, copies of game laws and regulations.

DEPARTMENT D.

FISH, FISHERIES, FISH PRODUCTS, AND APPARATUS OF FISHING.

GROUP 37.

FISH AND OTHER FORMS OF AQUATIC LIFE.

Class 239. Aquatic life. Scientific collections and literature.
Works on aquatic zoology and botany. Maps illustrating geographical distribution, migration, etc., of fishes and other aquatic animals.
Specimens and representations illustrative of the relations between extinct and existing forms of life.
Specimens (marine and fresh water), fresh, stuffed or preserved, in alcohol or otherwise, casts, drawings and representations of objects named in the following classes:

Class 240. Algæ, genera and species, with localities.

Class 241. Sponges, corals, polyps, jelly-fish.

Class 242. Entozoa and epizoa.

Class 243. Oysters, clams, and mollusca of all kinds; shells.

Class 244. Star-fishes, sea-urchins, holothurians.

Class 245. Worms used for bait, or noxious; leeches, etc.

Class 246. Crustacea of all kinds.

Class 247. Fishes, living or preserved, or represented by casts, drawings or otherwise.

Class 248. Reptiles, such as tortoises, turtles, terrapins, lizards, serpents, frogs, newts.

Class 249. Aquatic birds.

Class 250. Aquatic mammalia, otters, seals, whales, etc.

Class 251. Characteristic plant and animal life at great depths.

Class 252. Fishing grounds.

GROUP 38.

SEA FISHING AND ANGLING.

Class 253. History of fishing, fishery laws, and fish commerce.
Ancient fishing implements or their reproductions.
Models, pictures, books, emblems.
    Charters and seals of ancient fishermen's guilds.
    Fishery laws of different countries.
    Copies of treatises, conventions, etc., dealing with international fishery relations.
    Reports, statistics, and literature of fish, fishing and fisheries. Reports of acclimatization of fish and of attempts in that direction.

Class 254. Gear of every description and of all nations, used in trawl, herring, long line, hand line and every other mode or system of fishing, fishing lines and rigged gear.

Class 255. Fish hooks, jigs and drills.

Class 256. Fishing rod and reels for lines and nets.

Class 257. Nets and seines, rakes and dredges, and materials used in their manufacture.

Class 258. Fish traps, weirs, and pounds.

Class 259. Fishing stations and their outfit.

Class 260. Knives, gaffs, and other apparatus.

Class 261. Illustration of special fisheries. The whale and seal, cod, mackerel, halibut, herring, haddock, pollock, menhaden, sword-fish, bluefish, oyster, sponge and other sea fisheries.

Class 262. Fishing boats and vessels.

GROUP 39.

FRESH WATER FISH AND ANGLING.

Class 263. History and literature of angling. Waltonian literature. Folk-lore. Angler's trophies.

Class 264. Salmon nets and fixed appliances for catching salmonidæ in all their varieties.

Class 265. Salmon rods, reels, lines, artificial flies and baits, gaffs, spears, creels, etc.

Class 266. Bass, pike, perch rods, reels and tackle, artificial spinning baits, etc.

Class 267. Traps, nets, bucks, wheels, and all kind of apparatus for catching eels, lampreys, etc.

Class 268. Angler's apparel of every description.

Class 269. The angler's camp and its outfit.

Class 270. Illustrations of special fresh water fishery. Shad and alewife, sturgeon, eel, salmon, whitefish, the Great-Lake fisheries, etc.

GROUP 40.

PRODUCTS OF THE FISHERIES AND THEIR MANIPULATION.

(See also, in part, Groups 6 and 17.)

Class 271. Models of fish-curing and canning establishments. Methods of, and models, and other representations of any appliances for drying, curing, salting, smoking, tinning, cooking, etc.

Class 272. Fish, dried, smoked, cured, salted, tinned or otherwise prepared for food.

Class 273. All products prepared from fish, such as oils, roses, isinglass, etc.

Class 274. Antiseptics suitable for preserving fish for food.

Class 275. Oils, manures and other products prepared from fish.

Class 276. Methods of, and models, and other representations of appliances for preparing oils and manures from fish.

Class 277. Sea and fresh water pearl shells, mother-of-pearl, manufactured ; pearl, sorted.

Class 278. Preparation and application of sponges, corale, pearls, shells and all parts of products of aquatic animals, etc., to purposes useful and ornamental, with specimens.

Class 279. Appliances for carrying fish and for preserving fish during transport or otherwise, and models of the same. Models of fish markets and appliances connected with the same

GROUP 41.

FISH CULTURE.

Class 280. The history of fish culture.

Class 281. Hatching, breeding and rearing establishments, including oyster and other shell-fish grounds.

Class 282. Apparatus and implements connected with fish culture and for transporting fish and fish ova. Food for fry.

Class 283. Representations illustrative of the development and progressive growth of fish.

Class 284. Models and drawings of fish-ways and fish ladders.

Class 285. Diseases of fish, with special reference to their origin and cure. Models and drawings.

Class 286. Processes for rendering streams polluted by sewerage and chemical or other works innocuous to fish life. (Illustrated by models and drawings.)

Class 287. Physico-chemical investigation into those qualities of salt and fresh water which affect aquatic animals ; investigation of the bottom of the sea and of lakes, shown by samples; aquatic plants in relation to fishing, etc.; researches into the aquatic fauna (animals of the several classes preserved in alcohol, or prepared, etc.) ; apparatus and implements used in such researches.

Class 288. Acclimatization of fish. Marking of introduced fish for purposes of identification.

Class 289. Statistics of the results of fish culture. Specimens of fish artificially propagated or introduced.

DEPARTMENT E.

MINES, MINING, AND METALLURGY.

GROUP 42.

MINERALS, ORES, NATIVE METALS, GEMS AND CRYSTALS. GEOLOGICAL SPECIMENS.

Class 290. Collections of minerals systematically arranged.

Class 291. Collections of ores and the associated minerals. Diamonds and gems, rough, uncut and unmounted.
Specimens illustrating the formations of the earth, systematically arranged. Crystallography.

GROUP 43.

MINERAL COMBUSTIBLES—COAL, COKE, PETROLEUM, NATURAL GAS, ETC.

Class 292. Coal—Anthracite, semi-bituminous and bituminous; coal waste, "slack," coke and pressed coal.

Class 293. Asphaltite and asphaltic compounds—Uintaite, wortzilite, grahamite, albertite, bitumen, mineral tar, amber.
Class 294. Petroleum—Illuminating and lubricating oil.
Class 295. Natural gas—Methods of conveying and using.

GROUP 44.

BUILDING STONES, MARBLES, ORNAMENTAL STONES AND QUARRY PRODUCTS.

Class 296. Building stones, granites, slates, etc., rough hewn, sawed or polished —For buildings, bridges, walls, or other constructions, or for interior decoration, or for furniture.
Marble, white, black, or colored.—Stalagmitic marbles, onyx, brecciated marbles, silicified wood, agates, jaspers, porphyries, etc., used in building, decoration, statuary, monuments, vases, or furniture.

GROUP 45.

GRINDING, ABRADING AND POLISHING SUBSTANCES.

Class 297. Grindstones, hones, whetstones, grinding and polishing materials, sand, quartz, garnet, crude topaz, diamond, corundum, emery in the rock and pulverized, and in assorted sizes and grades.

GROUP 46.

GRAPHITE AND ITS PRODUCTS; CLAYS AND OTHER FICTILE MATERIALS AND THEIR DIRECT PRODUCTS; ASBESTOS, ETC.

Class 298. Crude graphite, in blocks and in powder.
Class 299. Graphite and compounds for coating iron.
Class 300. Graphite lubricants.
Class 301. Electrotypers' graphite.
Class 302. For pencils, crayons, etc.
Class 303. Graphite crucibles and melting pots.
Class 304. Clays, kaolin, silex, and other materials for the manufacture of porcelain faience, and of glass, bricks, terra cotta, tiles, and firebrick ; various examples.
Class 505. Refractory stones for lining furnaces, sandstone, steatite, etc., and refractory furnace materials. Muscotive ; kidney, sheet or ground.
Class 306. Bauxite clay for the manufacture of aluminum.
Class 307. Asbestos, crude and manufactured.
Class 308. Meerschaum.

GROUP 47.

LIMESTONE, CEMENT, AND ARTIFICIAL STONE.

Class 309. Lime, cement and hydraulic cement, raw and burned, accompanied by specimens of the crude rock or material used; also artificial stone, concrete, beton.
Specimens of lime, mortar and mixtures, with illustrations of the process of mixing, etc. Hydraulic and other cements.
Class 310. Beton mixtures and results, with illustrations of the processes.
Class 311. Artificial stone for building purposes, building blocks, cornices, etc. Artificial stone mixtures for pavements, walls, or ceilings.
Class 312. Asphaltic mastics and mixtures, asphaltic sand, asphaltic limestone.
Class 313. Gypsum, crude and boiled, calcareous; plaster mastics, etc.

GROUP 48.

SALT, SULPHUR, FERTILIZERS, PIGMENTS, MINERAL WATERS, AND MISCELLANEOUS USEFUL MINERALS AND COMPOUNDS.

Class 314. Salt from beds or from brines.
Class 315. Nitre and other nitrates.
Class 316. Sulphates, alums, and other salts.
Class 317. Sulphur and pyrites for the manufacture of sulphuric acid.

Class 318. Boracic acid and its salts; borax.
Class 319. Pigments, iron oxides, ochres, vermilion, etc.
Class 320. Mineral fertilizing substances, gypsum, phosphate of lime, marls, shells, coprolites, etc., not manufactured. (For commercial fertilizers and compounds, see Group 17).
Class 321. Mineral waters, artesian well water (for commercial forms, as bottled and as beverages, see Group 10); natural brines, saline and alkaline efflorescences and solutions.

GROUP 49.

METALLURGY OF IRON AND STEEL, WITH THE PRODUCTS.

Class 322. Ore mixtures, fluxes and fuels.
Class 323. Blast furnaces—stacks, stoves, blowing apparatus and arrangement.
Class 324. Pig-iron, cast-iron, and mixtures.
Class 325. Cupola furnaces.
Class 326. Direct processes—Sponge and blooming plant and apparatus.
Class 327. Puddling—Furnaces and appliances.
Class 328. Besemer machinery—Details and arrangements.
Class 329. Basic process and apparatus.
Class 330. Open-hearth steel—Plant and apparatus.
Class 331. Crucible steel—Plant and apparatus.
Class 332. Nickle steel.
Class 333. Manganese iron and steel, chrome steel, aluminum steel, tungsten steel,'other forms of steel.
Class 334. Iron and steel. Bars, rods, sheets, wire.

GROUP 50.

ALUMINUM AND ITS ALLOYS.

Class 335. Aluminum, pure and commercial; ingots, castings, bars, rods, wire sheets, and partly manufactured.
Class 336. Aluminum alloys.
Class 337. Aluminum alloy wire and wire-cloth.
Class 338. Process for the extraction of aluminum; electric reduction and results.

GROUP 51.

COPPER AND ITS ALLOYS. METALLURGY.

Class 339. Native copper, and the methods of extracting, melting and refining it.
Class 340. Copper ores and their treatment by fire. Copper smelting. Pneumatic process. Converter system.
Class 341. Copper extraction in the "wet" way.
Class 342. Copper in ingots, bars, and rolled, with specimens illustrating its various stages of production. Copper and zinc. Brass industry, and products regarded as materials of manufacture.
Class 343. Copper and aluminum, aluminum bronze.

GROUP 52.

METALLURGY OF TIN, TIN-PLATE, ETC.

Class 344. Tin ores and their treatment.
Class 345. Block tin and its extraction from tin ore.
Class 346. Tin-plate and methods of cleaning and coating iron and steel plates.

GROUP 53.

METALLURGY OF ZINC, NICKEL AND COBALT.

Class 347. Production of spelter.
Class 348. Sheet and bar zinc.
Class 349. Production of zinc oxide.
Class 350. Nickel in ingots, bars, rods, sheets and wire.

Class 351. Nickel-covered steel and iron by rolling.
Class 352. Nickel "plating."
Class 353. Nickel salts.
Class 354. Special nickel alloy, as German silver, etc.
Class 355. Nickel steel. (See Class 332.)

GROUP 54.
METALLURGY OF ANTIMONY AND OTHER METALS NOT SPECIFICALLY CLASSED.
Class 356. Crude and star antimony.
Class 357. Antimony compounds and principal alloys.
Class 358. Arsenic, white arsenic, orpiment, and realgar.
Class 359. Bismuth and alloys. Quicksilver and amalgams.

· GROUP 55 -
EXTRACTION OF GOLD AND SILVER BY MILLING.
Class 360. Gold mills and accessories.
Class 361. Silver mills and accessories.
Class 362. Apparatus and accessories of amalgamation; handling quicksilver.
Class 363. Retorting, melting, stamping, shipping bullion.

GROUP 56.
EXTRACTION OF GOLD AND SILVER BY LIXIVIATION.
Class 364. Roasting and chloridizing furnaces.
Class 365. Chlorination process and adjuncts.
Class 366. Other processes.

GROUP 57.
EXTRACTION OF GOLD, SILVER, AND LEAD BY FIRE.
Class 367. Furnace plant and appliances.
Class 368. Lead bullion molds and bars.
Class 369. Refining operations.

GROUP 58.
QUARRYING AND WORKING STONE.
Class 370. Quarrying, channeling, and cutting engines.
Class 371. Derricks and fittings.
Class 372. Slate-cutting, sawing, and planing machines.
Class 373. Machines and apparatus for cutting, turning and polishing marble granite, and other stone. (See Group 78.)

GROUP 59.
PLACER, HYDRAULIC, AND "DRIFT" MINING.
Class 374. Apparatus and machines for washing gravel; sluices, cradles, toms, rockers, rifles, etc.
Class 375. Construction of ditches, flumes, penstocks, etc.
Class 376. Pipes for conveying water.
Class 377. "Giants," nozzles, and appurtenances.

GROUP 60.
TOOLS AND APPLIANCES OF UNDERGROUND MINING, TIMBERING AND SUPPORTING.
Class 378. Timber cutting and framing machines.
Class 379. Methods of timbering shown by examples.
Class 380. Underground chutes, gates, and appliances for delivering ores. Methods and appliances for ventilating, lighting and signaling.

GROUP 61.

BORING AND DRILLING TOOLS AND MACHINERY, AND APPARATUS FOR
BREAKING OUT ORE AND COAL.

Class 381. Picks, gads, and hammers.
Class 382. Hand drills, hammers, and blasting implements.
Class 383. Drilling by steam or compressed air,—"power drills."
Class 384. Diamond drills for prospecting or for sinking and driving.
Class 385. Well and shaft boring (various systems).
Class 386. Boring for water, oil, or gas—tools and methods.
Class 387. Machines, apparatus and implements for cutting coal.

GROUP 62.

PUMPS, ENGINES AND APPARATUS USED IN MINING FOR PUMPING,
DRAINING AND HOISTING.

GROUP 63.

MOVING, STORING AND DELIVERING ORES, COALS, ETC.

Class 388. Tramways, turn-tables, automatic hoisting and conveying on the
surface, contrivances for loading and unloading ores and coal.
Class 389. Cars of all kinds.
Class 390. Automatic dumping.
Class 391. Ore bins and appliances.

GROUP 64.

APPARATUS FOR CRUSHING AND PULVERIZING.

Class 392. Rock breakers.
Class 393. Rolls.
Class 394. Large stamps.
Class 395. Stamps and mortars.
Class 396. Revolving grinding mills.
Class 397. Coal breakers.

GROUP 65.

SIZING APPLIANCES.

Class 398. Grizzlys and bar screens and sieves.
Class 399. Perforated plates.
Class 400. Wire-mesh sieves and trammels.
Class 401. Sizing by currents of water or air. Overflows.
Class 402. Sizing by belts.

GROUP 66.

ASSAYING APPARATUS AND FIXTURES.

Class 403. Plans of assay offices.
Class 404. Furnaces, muffles and appliances.
Class 405. Scorification and cupelling.
Class 406. Volumetric methods and apparatus.
Class 407. Fluxes and their receptacles.
Class 408. Assay balances, etc. (See Group 112.)
Class 409. Assay tables, assay schemes and methods.

GROUP 67.

HISTORY AND LITERATURE OF MINING AND METALLURGY.

Class 410. Maps, relief-models and pictures to illustrate the geology and distribution of minerals and mines and the methods of working mines.
Class 411. History and statistics of mines and mining districts.
Charts, diagrams and tabular representations. Statistics of mineral
production.

Class 412.　Mine engineering—surface and underground surveying and plotting, projection of underground work, location of shafts, tunnels, etc.; surveys for aqueducts and for drainage.

Boring and drilling rocks, shafts and tunnels, etc.; surveys for aqueducts and for ascertaining the nature and extent of mineral deposits.

Construction—Sinking and lining shafts by various methods, driving and timbering tunnels and the general operations of opening, stoping and breaking down ore; timbering, lagging and masonry.

Hoisting and delivering at the surface, rock, ore or miners; pumping and draining by engines, buckets or by adits.

Ventilating and lighting.

GROUP 68.

ORIGINALS OR REPRODUCTIONS OF EARLY AND NOTABLE IMPLEMENTS AND APPARATUS USED IN MINING AND METALLURGY.

DEPARTMENT F.

MACHINERY.

GROUP 69.

MOTORS AND APPARATUS FOR THE GENERATION AND TRANSMISSION OF POWER—HYDRAULIC AND PNEUMATIC APPARATUS.

Class 413.　Boilers and all steam or gas generating apparatus for motive purposes.

Class 414.　Water wheels, water engines, hydraulic rams.

Class 415.　Steam, air and gas engines.

Class 416.　Apparatus for the transmission of power—shafting, hangers, belting, pulleys, couplings, clutches, cables, gearing. Transmission of power by compressed air, etc.

Class 417.　Pumps and apparatus for lifting and moving liquids, water filters. (See also Department E.)

Class 418.　Pumps and apparatus for moving and compressing air or gas.

Class 419.　Pumps and blowing engines, blowers and ventilating apparatus.

Class 420.　Hydraulic presses, freight elevators and lifts. Traveling cranes and derricks.

Class 421.　Beer engines, soda water machines, bottling apparatus, corking machines. (See also Department A.)

Class 422.　Iron and other metallic pipes, tubes and fittings, stop valves, cocks, etc.

Class 423.　Diving apparatus and machinery.

Class 424.　Ice machines. Refrigerating apparatus.

GROUP 70.

FIRE ENGINES—APPARATUS AND APPLIANCES FOR EXTINGUISHING FIRE.

Class 425.　Engines.

Class 426.　Hose-carts and hose.

Class 427.　Ladders and escapes.

Class 428.　Standpipes, etc.

Class 429.　Chemical fire-extinguishing apparatus.

GROUP 71.

MACHINE TOOLS AND MACHINES FOR WORKING METALS.

Class 430. Small tools for machinists' use, drills, taps and dies, gauges, etc.
Class 431. Squares, rules and measuring tools.
Class 432. Steam hammers, trip-hammers, drop forging and swaging machines, hydraulic forging, etc.
Class 433. Planing, drilling, slotting, turning, shaping, milling, punching and cutting machines. Wheel-cutting and dividing machines.

GROUP 72.

MACHINERY FOR THE MANUFACTURE OF TEXTILE FABRICS AND CLOTHING.

Class 434. Machines for the manufacture of silk goods.
Class 435. Machines for the manufacture of cotton goods.
Class 436. Machines for the manufacture of woolen goods.
Class 437. Worsted working machinery and appliances.
Class 438. Machines for the manufacture of linen goods.
Class 439. Machines for the manufacture of rope and for twine-making and for miscellaneous fibrous materials.
Class 440. Machines for paper-making and felting.
Class 441. Machines for the manufacture of India-rubber goods.
Class 442. Machines for the manufacture of mixed fabrics.
Class 443. Machines used in the manufacture of tapestry, including carpets, lace, floor-cloth, fancy embroidery, etc.
Class 444. Sewing machines for heavy materials.
Class 445. Machines for preparing and working leather.
Class 446. Machines for making boots and shoes.

GROUP 73.

MACHINES FOR WORKING WOOD.

(See also Departments A and E.)

Class 447. Direct-acting steam sawing machines, with gang saws, band saws, circular saws.
Class 448. Sawmills and sawmill tools.
Wood-working machinery for sawmills.
Wood-working tools and minor appliances for sawmills.
Class 449. Planing, sawing, veneering, grooving, mortising, tonguing, cutting, molding, stamping, carving and cask-making machines, etc.; cork-cutting machines. Lathes for wood-work and machinery for the manufacture of matches, toothpicks, etc.

GROUP 74.

MACHINES AND APPARATUS FOR TYPE-SETTING, PRINTING, STAMPING, EMBOSSING, AND FOR MAKING BOOKS AND PAPER WORKING.

Class 450. Steam power presses.
Class 451. Hand-printing presses.
Class 452. Job presses.
Class 453. Hydraulic presses.
Class 454. Ticket printing and numbering machines.
Class 455. Type casting and setting machines. Linotypes.
Class 456. Hand-casting molds.
Class 457. Machines and printing blocks.
Class 458. Typographic electrotyping.
Class 459. Stereotyping.
Class 460. Book-binding machinery.
Class 461. Envelope machines.
Class 462. Paper-cutters, card-cutters.
Class 463. Printers' cabinets and printers' furniture generally.

Class 464. Composing sticks, cases.
Class 465. Brass and type-metal labor-saving appliances.
Class 466. Specimens of plain and ornamental types, cuts, music, borders and electrotype plates.
Class 467. Type-founders' specimen books of type and typographical ornaments.
Class 468. Miscellaneous machinery used by printers and newspapers not otherwise specified. Folding machines, addressing, stamping, embossing, etc.

GROUP 75.
LITHOGRAPHY, ZINOGRAPHY AND COLOR PRINTING.

Class 469. Lithography—Tools, materials and appliances. The various methods of lithography, crayon, pen and ink; engraving, brush work, color printing, etc. Transferring, printing. Zinography.
Class 470. Color printing—Historical illustrations from the 16th Century to the present time. (Relief engraving. The old chiaro-oscuros. Modern wood-engravings. The Baxter process. Intaglio engraving, printed at one impression; *i. e.*, from the plate rubbed in different colors, printed from several plates. Stenochromy. Chromolithography. Wax process, etc. The modern photo-mechanical processes applied to color printing).

GROUP 76.
PHOTO-MECHANICAL AND OTHER MECHANICAL PROCESSES OF ILLUSTRATING, ETC.

Class 471. Relief processes—Photo-mechanical processes producing relief blocks for printing in the type-press (etching, swell-gelatine and washout processes). Line processes (photo-typographic etchings, typogravures, etc.)
Class 472. Half-toned processes—Gelatine grain processes. (Paul Pretsch's and later). Screen processes. (Meisenbach, etc.) The Ives process.
Class 473. Photo-lithography, etc.—Photo-mechanical processes involving the production of printable designs on stone or zinc ;. *i. e.*, photo-lithography and zincography. Half-toned processes (the Bitumen process, Poitevin's process, Asser's process, etc.) Recent grain processes. Screen process. Line processes. (Osborne's process.)
Class 474. Collographic processes—Photo-mechanical processes, involving the production of gelatine or other glutinous films, to be used as printing surfaces in the lithographic press; *i. e.*, collographic or photo-gelatine processes (albertype, heliotype, artotype, etc.)
Class 475. Photo-mechanical processes—Producing intaglio plates for printing in the copperplate press ; *i. e.*, photo-gravure. Etching processes, deposit processes, heliotypes, heliogravures, etc. The Woodbury . type-molds and impressions.
Class 476. Mechanical processes—Partly chemical, partly mechanical, devised as substitutes for the other hand processes, but not involving photography. Chalcotype, Comte process, Gillot process, etching in relief, typographic etching, properly so-called (chemitype, the graphotype, kaolitype), the wax process and allied processes (glyphography, kerography, stylography, typographic etching, improperly so-called, etc.) Machine relief engraving, machine intaglio engraving (medal ruling), galvanography, stenochromy, mineralogy, nature printing, the anastatic process, etc. Appendix Etching on glass (improperly so called, which involves photography, but not the use of the press)
Class 477. Drawings for process work.

Class 478. Aids to drawing for process work (used by lithographers and draughtsmen). Grained and embossed papers. Pasting tints. The air brush. Day's shading mediums, etc. Methods of reducing and enlarging. Photo-mechanical processes.
Class 479. Applications of the photo-mechanical processes in the industrial arts—prints on metal work, cloth, etc.

GROUP 77.
MISCELLANEOUS HAND-TOOLS, MACHINES AND APPARATUS USED IN VARIOUS ARTS.

Class 480. Machines for making clocks, watches and watch cases.
Class 481. Machines for making jewelry.
Class 482. Machines for making buttons, pins, needles, etc.
Class 483. Wire-working machinery.
Class 484. Machines for ironing, drying, scouring and laundry work generally.
Class 485. Machines for making capsules and other pharmaceutical products.
Class 486. Machines used in various manufacturing industries not specifically mentioned.
Class 487. Emery and corundum wheels.
Class 488. Street rollers, sweepers and sprinklers.
Class 489. Steam guages, oil cocks and all kinds of appliances used in connection with machinery.
Class 490. For testing the strength of materials. Dynamometers.

GROUP 78.
MACHINES FOR WORKING STONE, CLAY AND OTHER MINERALS.
(See also Department E.)

Class 491. Stone-sawing and planing machines, dressing, shaping and polishing, sand blasts, Tilghman's machines, glass-grinding machines, etc.
Class 492. Brick, pottery and tile machines. Machines for making artificial stone.
Class 493. Rolling-mills and forges—roll trains, hammers, squeezers, engines, boilers and other driving power; heating furnaces (coal and gas), special machines for shaping metal, such as spike, nail, and horse-. shoe machines; tire mills, etc.

GROUP 79.
MACHINERY USED IN THE PREPARATION OF FOODS, ETC.

Class 494. Mills for the preparation of cereals.
Class 495. Sugar-refining machines. Confectioners' machinery.
Class 496. Oil-making machinery; presses and stills.
Class 497. Mills and machinery for spices, coffee, etc.
Class 498. Evaporating machinery for condensing milk, etc.

22

DEPARTMENT G.

TRANSPORTATION—RAILWAYS, VESSELS, VEHICLES.

GROUP 80.
RAILWAYS, RAILWAY PLANT AND EQUIPMENT.

Class 499. Railway Construction and Maintenance.—Maps, profiles, etc. Grading, track-laying and ballasting machinery. Samples of Standard Permanent Way. Systems of drainage. Ballast, culverts, ties, methods of preserving ties. Rails, rail fastenings, frogs, crossings, switches, etc. Cattle guards. Railway bridges, trestles, viaducts, with models and drawings. Tunneling, with machinery, models, maps. Methods of constructing, lighting and ventilating tunnels. Turn-tables and transfer tables. Water supply and machinery and fixtures used by railroads in connection therewith. Track tools. Systems of maintenance. Snow sheds and other protection against snow. General plans, elevations and models of stations and other railroad structures.

Class 500. Railway Equipment.—Locomotives for passenger and freight service. Locomotive appliances—head lights, bells, whistles, brake valves and apparatus, etc. Plans, drawings and photographs of locomotives and locomotive shops.
  Passenger cars.—Mail, baggage and express coaches, drawing-room, parlor, dining, officers' and private cars, etc. Passenger car furnishings and appliances.
  Freight cars.—Box, caboose, stock, horse, milk, refrigerator, and other varieties. Working cars—sweeping, ditching, wrecking, etc.; snow plows; hand, inspection, push and velocipede cars, baggage barrows and trucks. Freight car appliances of all descriptions. Plans, drawings and photographs of cars and car works.

Class 501. Railway Operation.—Purchasing department. Methods of purchasing, storing and distributing material and disposition of condemned material. Railway stationery.
  Mechanical Department.—Organization. Records, plans and management of shops. Devices for coaling locomotives, etc. Testing laboratories. Machines, apparatus and methods of testing.
  General train management.—Dispatching, signaling, etc. Speed indicators and recorders. Interlocking switches and signals. Block systems, etc. Crossing protection by gates, signals, etc. Wrecking tools and appliances. Plans of yards and methods of storing, cleaning and keeping cars. Car interchange and inspection. Systems of accounting, records, tracers.
  Railway employes.—Methods of testing for color-blindness, etc. Uniforms, organizations, etc. Railway sanitation and surgery and appliances used therein.

Class 502. Railway management.—Legal department, treasury and accounting departments, passenger department. Advertising. Tickets, ticket cases, punches, baggage checks, etc. Freight department, methods of rate-making, soliciting. handling, billing, etc.; plans, arrangements and appliances for handling and housing of freight. Freight-handling machinery, track scales, apparatus for transferring grain from car to car. Traffic Associations, their objects, methods, etc.

Class 503. History and statistics, exemplified by exhibits of old locomotives, cars, track material and other relics. Railway law and legislation. Railway technical engineering and mechanical associations. Railway literature.

GROUP 81.

STREET CAR AND OTHER SHORT LINE SYSTEMS.

Class 504. Cable roads and cars. Construction, equipment, methods of operation. Grips and other appliances.

Class 505. Electric railway cars. Systems of track construction, equipment and supplies for electric roads, methods of operation, appliances and furnishings.

Class 506. Cars for street railways or tramways operated by horse-power or other means of propulsion not specified. Construction. Equipment and supplies. Methods of operation.

Class 507. Elevated and underground railways. Plans, models, and maps, showing systems of construction. Systems of operation and maintenance.

GROUP 82.

MISCELLANEOUS AND SPECIAL RAILWAYS.

Class 508. Mountain railways, spirals, switchbacks, rack rails and all systems for climbing inclines, ship railways, multiple speed railways (moving platforms and sidewalks), gravity roads, sliding railways, plans, profiles, drawings, photographs and models.

GROUP 83.

VEHICLES AND METHODS OF TRANSPORTATION ON COMMON ROADS.

Class 509. Hand-barrows, wheel-barrows, trunk and barrel-trucks.

Class 510. Carts, trucks, drays, farm wagons, garden truck wagons.

Class 511. Freight wagons and other heavy wagons for special purposes, beer wagons, express wagons, wagons for moving heavy objects, as timbers, stone, iron, etc. Sprinkling carts (for fire engines and ladder trucks see Group 70.)

Class 512. Large wagons for pleasure parties, picnic parties and excursions, "breaks," "barges," "wagonettes," etc.

Class 513. Omnibuses, herdics, cabs, hansoms, etc.

Class 514. Drags, Concord leather spring coaches; mud wagons for mail, express and passenger service.

Class 515. Pleasure carriages, coaches, Victorias, Broughams, dog carts, etc.

Class 516. Light pleasure carriages, buggies, phaetons, etc.; trotting wagons and sulkies.

Class 517. Sleighs, sleds, cutters, toboggans, snow shoes, etc.

Class 518. Steam and electric carriages, and all vehicles for carrying passengers on common roads, operated by other than horse-power.

Class 519. Ambulances for special purposes—for the sick and injured. Hearses.

Class 520. Bicycles, tricycles and the appurtenances.

Class 521. Rolling chairs for invalids and others, baby carriages, etc.

Class 522. Wagon and carriage woodwork, hardware and fittings.

Class 523. Harness, saddlery, robes, whips and accessories of the stable.

GROUP 84.

ÆRIAL, PNEUMATIC AND OTHER FORMS OF TRANSPORTATION.

Class 524. Transportation of letters and parcels in pneumatic tubes.

Class 525. Shop-fittings for the transportation of parcels and money.

Class 526. Balloon transportation and captive balloons for observation and experiment.

Class 527. Passenger elevators and lifts.

GROUP 85.

VESSELS, BOATS—MARINE, LAKE AND RIVER TRANSPORTATION.

Class 528. Sailing vessels and boats. Sailing vessels used in commerce, pilot boats, fishing vessels, sailing yachts, ice boats, ship's boats, pleasure boats, canoes and small boats of all kinds propelled by sails, oars or paddles. Models, designs, drawings, descriptions, specifications, photographs, paintings, etc.

Class 529. Steamships and all vessels propelled by steam, electricity or motive power other than sails, oars or paddles. Ocean steamships, coasting, lake and river steamers. Tank steamers, cable steamers, steam pilot vessels, steam fishing vessels, steam fire, police and patrol boats, steam schooners, tow-boats, steam yachts, steam launches, naphtha launches, vessels designed for jet propulsion or be propelled by any unusual device. Models, designs, etc.

Class 530. Vessels, boats and floating structures for special purposes. Docks and other receptacles for vessels and structures used for docking or hauling out vessels or boats. Transports for carrying railway trains or cars, barges, canal boats; coal rafts and coal boxes; water boats, dredges, floating derricks, elevators, etc. Dry docks and marine railways. Models, designs, drawings, etc.

Class 531. Marine mechanical appliances. (For nautical instruments, see Group 151. For marine engines, boilers, pumps, condensers and appurtenances, see Group 69) Devices for propulsion, devices for obtaining forced draft, steam capstans, windlasses, deck winches, appliances to facilitate loading and discharging cargoes, steering apparatus; marine electric motors, electric indicators, engine room and bridge signal systems and apparatus; boat-lowering and detaching apparatus, speed indicators and speed registers, appliances for laying, picking up and repairing ocean telegraph cables, etc.

Class 532. Construction, outfit, equipment and repair of vessels.—Methods, articles, fittings or appurtenances. Methods and materials used; special designs for hull or fittings; plates, cellulose, woodite, etc.; water-tight compartments, rudders, masts and spars, rigging; anchors, chains and cables; hawsers, ropes, cordage, wire rope, etc.; sales, blocks and tackles, gear, etc.

Class 533. Methods of lighting, heating, ventilation and refrigeration of ships.

Class 534. Protection of life and property and communication at sea. Harbors; light-houses; buoys and similar aids to navigation and all pertaining thereto; life-saving service, boats, rafts, belts, etc.; precaution against fire aboard ship and devices for extinguishing it; storm and coast signals; marine signals. Models, plans, samples, etc.

Class 535. Wrecking apparatus. Sub-marine armor and divers' appliances, pontoons for raising vessels, equipment for wrecking-steamers, etc.

Class 536. Miscellaneous. Trophies of yacht and boat clubs, relics of merchant marine and river transportation, relics of arctic and other exploration, seamen's associations, uniforms and designations of rank, flags and ensigns of merchant marine, yacht clubs, etc., designs, maps, charts, boats.

GROUP 86.

NAVAL WARFARE AND COAST DEFENCE.

Class 537. Armored vessels. Battle-ships, rams, cruisers, coast defense ships. Models, designs, drawings, descriptions, specifications, photographs, paintings, etc.

Class 538. Unarmered vessels. Frigates, sloops and gun vessels, cruisers, dispatch vessels and tenders, torpedo vessels and torpedo boats, sub-marine boats, public vessels for special service, revenue vessels, surveying vessels, etc. Man-of-war boats, etc. Models, designs, etc.

Class 539. Ships and boats of war of barbarous and semi-civilized nations. Models, drawings, photographs, etc.

Class 540. Models and relics of famous ships of war, relics of naval battles, etc.

Clrss 541. Training ships; naval schools; naval institutes, naval reserve, etc.

Class 542. Guns and armor, and adjuncts and appliances of naval warfare (see also Group 113). Guns, armor, torpedoes, small arms for naval use, projectiles and ammunition, fuses, sub-marine mines, methods, devises, fittings or appliances designed for use in naval warfare and coast defense.

DEPARTMENT H.

MANUFACTURES.

GROUP 87.

CHEMICAL AND PHARMACEUTICAL PRODUCTS—DRUGGISTS' SUPPLIES.

Class 543. Organic and mineral acids.

Class 544. The alkalies and alkaline earths.—Potash, soda, ammonia, caustic soda, carbonate of soda, lime, magnesia, barytes, etc., with their salts and compounds. Bleaching powders, etc.

Class 545. Metallic oxides and salts of the metals, and other commercial chemical compounds.

Class 546. Pure chemicals for chemists' use.

Class 547. Drugs and pharmaceutical preparations and compounds.

Class 548. Chemists' and druggists' wares and supplies.

Class 549. Flavoring extracts, essences, essential oils, toilet soap, perfumery, pomades, cosmetics, etc.

Class 550. Explosive and fulminating compounds.—Powder, giant powder, etc., shown only by empty cases and packages, "dummy packages," and cartridges, to illustrate the commercial forms.

Class 551. Pyrotechnics. (In harmless forms, not charged.) Pyrotechnic displays.

GROUP 88.

PAINTS, COLORS, DYES AND VARNISHES.

(See also Group 48.)

Class 552. Colors and pigments—natural and artifical, dry and ground in oil. Printing inks, writing inks, blacking, cochineal, etc.

Class 553. White lead and white zinc industry.

Class 554. Painters' and glaziers' supplies.

Class 555. Artists' colors and artists' materials.

GROUP 89.

TYPEWRITERS, PAPER, BLANK BOOKS, STATIONERY.

Class 556. Paper, pulp, and paper stock.

Class 557. Cardboard, cards, pasteboard, binders-board, building-boards, and felts for walls and roofing; for floors, ceilings, and for decorations; embossed-boards, etc. Papier mache; useful articles made from paper.

Class 558. Wrapping papers, manilla paper, paper bags, tissue papers.
Class 559. Printing paper for books and for newspapers.
Class 560. Writing papers, bond paper, drawing papers, tracing papers and tracing linen; envelopes; blotting paper.
Class 561. Blank books; sets of account books, specimens of ruling and binding, including blanks, bill-heads, etc.; book-binding.
Class 562. Ornamental and decorated paper; marbleized papers, etc.
Class 563. Wall papers, oil papers.
Class 564. Typewriters, stationery, and stationers' goods, ink-stands, weights, rulers, pens, pencils, filing-cases, letter presses, etc.

GROUP 90.

FURNITURE OF INTERIORS, UPHOLSTERY, AND ARTISTIC DECORATION.

Class 565. Chairs of all grades, rockers, lounges, settles, etc.
Class 566. Tables for various purposes—billiard, card, dining, etc.
Class 567. Suites of furniture for the hall, parlor, drawing-room, library, dining-room, and for the bed-chamber.
Class 568. Upholstery for windows, doors; curtains, portières, etc.
Class 569. Mirrors and their mountings.
Class 570. Treatment of porches, doorways, halls, and stair-cases, mantels, etc.
Class 571. Floors, ceilings, walls, doors, and windows.
Class 572. Artistic furnishing, illustrated by completely furnished apartments, with selections of furniture and various objects of adornment from other groups.
Class 573. Sewing and embroidering. (See also Group 72.)

GROUP 91.

CERAMICS AND MOSAICS.

(For clays and other materials see Group 46.)

Class 574. Bricks and terra cotta for building purposes, plain and enameled. Terra cotta ware for decorative purposes. Reproductions of ancient Roman and Grecian red ware.
Class 575. Stoneware and pottery, lead-glazed and salt-glazed ware, Doulton ware.
Class 576. Earthenware, stone, china, and semi-porcelain ware, faience, etc., with soft glazes, and with high-fire, feld-spathic glazes and enamels.
Class 577. Porcelain with white or colored body, painted, incised or pâté-sur-pâté decoration.
Class 578. Tiles.—Plain, encaustic and decorated tiles, bosses, tessaræ, etc., for pavements, mural and mantel decoration, etc.
Class 579. Mural decoration; reredos and panels; borders for fire-places and mantels.
Class 580. Designs for and examples of pavements in tiles and mosaics.

GROUP 92.

MARBLE, STONE AND METAL MONUMENTS, MAUSOLEUMS, MANTELS, ETC.— CASKETS, COFFINS AND UNDERTAKERS' FURNISHING GOODS.

Class 581. Marble, stone and metal monuments, and mausoleums and fittings.
Class 582. Marble and stone fountains, balustrades and miscellaneous ornaments.
Class 583. Marble, stone and metal mantels and ornaments.
Class 584. Coffins, caskets and undertakers' furnishing goods.

GROUP 93.

ART METAL WORK—ENAMELS, ETC.

Class 585. Art metal work; selected examples of iron forgings, bronzes, bas-reliefs, repoussé and chiseled work.

Class 586. Cloisonné enamels.
Class 587. Champ lévé enamels.
Class 588. Niello work.

GROUP 94.

GLASS AND GLASSWARE.

Class 589. Plate glass in the rough, as cast and rolled, and as ground and polished.
Class 590. Blown glass, ordinary window glass, bottles, tubes, pipes, etc.
Class 591. Pressed glass and glassware generally for the table and various purposes ; skylights, insulators, etc.
Class 592. Cut-glassware for the table and various purposes. Engraved and etched glass.
Class 593. Fancy glassware—plain, irridescent, opalescent, colored, enameled, painted, beaded, gilded, etc. Millefiori and aventurine glass.
Class 594. Crackled glass in layers, onyx glass, sculptured glass ; reproductions of ancient glassware.
Class 595. Glass mosaics, beads, spun glass, and glass fabrics.

GROUP 95.

STAINED GLASS IN DECORATION.

Class 596. Civic and domestic stained glass work, panels, windows, etc.
Class 597. Ecclesiastical stained glass work.

GROUP 96.

CARVINGS IN VARIOUS MATERIALS.

Class 598. Wood carving.
Class 599. Ivory carving.
Class 600. Bamboo incised work.
Class 601. Metal carving and chiseling.
Class 602. Sculptured and engraved glass.
Class 603. Sculpturing, carving, and modeling in porcelain. Pâté-sur-pâ

GROUP 97.

GOLD AND SILVER WARE, PLATE, ETC.

Class 604. Gold ware and silver, gilt ware for the table and for decoration.
Class 605. Silver table ware generally.—Plates, salvers, tureens, bowls, dishes, baskets, candelabra, épergnes, etc.
Class 606. Knives, forks and spoons.
Class 607. Fancy bonbon and other spoons; miscellaneous fancy articles in silver.—Snuff-boxes, match-boxes, cane-heads, handles, chatelaines, etc.
Class 608. Ware of mixed metals.—Monkumé ware, inlaid and incrusted ware, enameled and niello work.
Class 609. Plated ware on hard or nickel silver foundation.
Class 610. Nickel ware ; nickel-silver ware, aluminum ware and aluminum-silver ware.
Class 611. Plated ware on soft metal alloys.

GROUP 98.

JEWELRY AND ORNAMENTS.

Class 612. Gold ornaments for the person, plain, chased, or otherwise wrought or enameled, rings, bracelets, necklaces, chains, etc.
Class 613. Diamonds and various colored gems, as rubies, sapphires, emeralds, chrysoberyls, tourmalines, topazes, etc., mounted in various ornaments.
(For gems in the rough and unmounted in parts, see Department E.)
Class 614. Agates, onyx, jasper, ornaments for the person.

Class 615. Pastes and imitations of precious stones, mounted or unmounted.
Class 616. Gold-covered and gilt jewelry and ornaments.

GROUP 99.

HOROLOGY—WATCHES, CLOCKS, ETC.
(See also Group 151.)

Class 617. Watches of all kinds.
Class 618. Watch movements and parts of watches.
Class 619. Watch-cases.
Class 620. Watch-makers' tools and machinery in part. (For machines requiring power, see Department F.)
Class 621. Clocks of all kinds.
Class 622. Clock movements.
Class 623. Clock-making machinery.
Class 624. Watchmen's time register.

GROUP 100.

SILK AND SILK FABRICS.

Class 625. Raw silk as reeled from the cocoon, thrown or twisted silks in the gum; organzine, tram, spun-silk yarn.
Class 626. Thrown or twisted silks, boiled off or dyed, in hanks, skeins or on spools; machine twist and sewing silk.
Class 627. Spun-silk yarns and fabrics and the materials from which they are made.
Class 628. Plain woven silks, lute-strings, sarsnets, satins, serges, foulards, tissues for hat and millinery purposes, etc.
Class 629. Figured-silk piece goods, woven or printed. Upholstery silks, etc.
Class 630. Crapes, velvets, gauzes, cravats, handkerchiefs, hosiery, knit goods, laces, scarfs, ties, veils; all descriptions of cut and made-up silks.
Class 631. Ribbons—plain, fancy and velvet.
Class 632. Bindings, braids, cords, galoons, ladies' dress trimmings, upholsterers', tailors', military and miscellaneous trimmings.

GROUP 101.

FABRICS OF JUTE, RAMIE AND OTHER VEGETABLE AND MINERAL FIBRES.

Class 633. Jute cloth and fabrics, plain and decorated.
Class 634. Ramie and other fabrics.
Class 635. Mats and coarse fabrics of grass, rattan, cocoanut and bark; mattings, Chinese, Japanese, palm-leaf, grass and rushes; floor cloths of rattan and cocoa-nut fibre, aloe fibre, etc.
Class 636. Floor oil-cloths, and other painted and enameled tissues, and imitations of leather with a woven base.
Class 637. Woven fabrics of mineral origin. Fine wire-cloths, sieve-cloth, wire screen, bolting cloth. (See also Group 117.) Asbestos fibre, spun and woven, with the clothing manufactured from it. Glass thread, floss and fabrics. (See also Class 595.)

GROUP 102.

YARNS AND WOVEN GOODS OF COTTON, LINEN AND OTHER VEGETABLE FIBRES.

Class 638. Cotton fabrics.—Yarns, twines, sewing-cotton, tapes, webbings, battings, waddings, plain cloths for printing and converting, print cloths, brown and bleached sheetings or shirtings, drills, twills, sateens, ginghams, cotton flannels, fine and fancy woven fabrics, duck, ticks, denims, stripes, bags and bagging. Upholstery goods, Tapestries, curtains and chenilles.

Class 639. Linen fabrics.—Linen thread, clothes and drills, plain and mixed; napkins, tablecloths, sheetings, shirtings, etc.; cambrics, handkerchiefs, and other manufactures of linen.

GROUP 103.

WOVEN AND FELTED GOODS OF WOOL AND MIXTURES OF WOOL.

Class 640. Woolen and worsted fabrics—Woolen yarns, union or merino worsted tops, noils and yarns, shoddy and mungo.

Class 641. Woolen goods.—All woolen cloths, doeskins, casimeres, indigo flannels and broadcloth, overcoatings, cloakings and kerseys, flannels, dress goods, etc., for both men and women.

Class 642. Blankets, robes, traveling rugs, horse blankets, shawls, bunting, etc.

Class 643. Worsted goods.—Coatings, serges, suitings, cashmeres, etc.

Class 644. Cotton and woolen-mixed woven goods.—Unions, tweeds, cheviots, flannels, linseys, blankets, etc.

Class 645. Woven on cotton warps.

Class 646. Upholstery goods.

Class 647. Sundries and small wares, webbings and gorings, bindings, beltings, braids, galloons, fringes and gimps, cords and tassels, and all elastic fabrics, dress trimmings, embroideries, etc.

Class 648. Felt goods, felt cloths, trimming and lining felt, felt skirts and skirting, table and piano covers, felts for ladies' hats, saddle felts, druggets, endless belts for printing machines, rubber shoe-linings and other foot wear, hair feltings.

Class 649. Carpets and rugs, ingrains (two-ply and three-ply) and art carpets, tapestry and body Brussels, tapestry velvet, Wilton or Wilton velvet, Axminster, tapestry Wilton, Moquette, ingrain and Smyrna rugs, other woolen rugs, rag carpets.

Class 650. Wool hats of every description.

Class 651. Fabrics of hair, alpaca, goat's hair, camel's hair, etc., not otherwise enumerated.

GROUP 104.

CLOTHING AND COSTUMES.

Class 652. Ready-made clothing—Men's and boys'.

Class 653. Dresses, gowns, habits, costumes.

Class 654. Hats and caps.

Class 655. Bonnets and millinery.

Class 656. Boots and shoes.

Class 657. Knit goods and hosiery, woven gloves, gloves of leather and skins.

Class 658. Shirts, collars, cuffs, cravats, suspenders, braces, and appliances.

Class 659. Sewing machines for domestic purposes.

GROUP 105.

FURS AND FUR CLOTHING.

Class 660. Furs and skins, dressed and tanned. Of the cat tribe, of the wolf tribe, of the weasel tribe, of the bear tribe, of the seal tribe. Fur seals—Alaska, Oregon, South Georgia, Shetland and Siberia, undressed, plucked and dyed. Hair seals—Greenland and Labrador seals, spotted seals, silver seal, harp seal, saddle-back. Furs of rodent animals—squirrels, chinchilla, beaver, hares, rabbits, and other fur-bearing animals. Birds' skins treated as furs. Swans and swan's-down. Skins. Goose and goose-down used as swan's-down. Grebe, eider-down, and penguin.

Class 661. Fur mats and carriage or sleigh robes.

Class 662. Fur clothing.

Class 663. Fur trimmings.

GROUP 106.

LACES, EMBROIDERIES, TRIMMINGS, ARTIFICIAL FLOWERS, FANS, ETC.

Class 664. Laces of linen and cotton, of silk, wool, or mohair, made with the needle or the loom ; silver and gold lace.
Class 665. Embroideries, crochet-work. etc., needle-work.
Class 666. Artificial flowers for trimming and for decoration of apartments.
Class 667. Fans.
Class 668. Trimmings in variety, not otherwise classed.—Buttons, hooks and eyes, pins and needles.
Class 669. Art embroidery and needle-work.
Class 670. Tapestries, hand-made.
Class 671. Tapestries, machine-work.

GROUP 107.

HAIR WORK, COIFFURES, AND ACCESSORIES OF THE TOILET.

Class 672. Hair-work, as souvenirs and ornaments.
Class 673. Coiffures, wigs, switches, etc.
Class 674. Barbers' and hair-dressers' tools and appliances.
Class 675. Combs, brushes. (See also Class 549).

GROUP 108.

TRAVELING EQUIPMENTS—VALISES, TRUNKS, TOILET-CASES, FANCY LEATHER-WORK, CANES, UMBRELLAS, PARASOLS, ETC.

Class 676. Tents, shelters and apparatus for camping, camp stools, etc., hampers, baskets, etc.
Class 677. Shawl and rug straps and pouches, gun cases.
Class 678. Valises of various materials; dress-suit cases, satchels, hand-bags, etc.; toilet articles.
Class 679. Trunks of leather, paper, canvas and of wood and metal.
Class 680. Fancy-bags, pouches, purses, card cases, portfolios, pocket-books, cigar cases, smoking pipes, cigar holders, etc.
Class 681. Canes.
Class 682. Umbrellas and parasols.

GROUP 109.

RUBBER GOODS, CAOUTCHOUC, GUTTA PERCHA, CELLULOID, AND ZYLONITE.

Class 683. Clothing ; Mackintoshes, capes, coats, boots, shoes, hats, etc.
Class 684. Piano and table covers, horse covers, carriage cloth.
Class 685. Stationers' articles.
Class 686. Druggists' articles, toilet articles.
Class 687. Medical and surgical instruments. (See also Group 147.)
Class 688. House furnishing articles, mats, cushions.
Class 689. Hose, tubes, belting and packing.
Class 690. Insulating compounds.
Class 691. Toys of rubber.
Class 692. Gutta-percha fabrics.

GROUP 110.

TOYS AND FANCY ARTICLES.

Class 693. Automatic and other toys and games for the amusement and instruction of children.
Class 694. Bon-bons, fancy boxes and packages for confectionery.
Class 695. Miscellaneous fancy articles not especially classed.

GROUP 111.

LEATHER AND MANUFACTURES OF LEATHER.

Class 696. Hides and skins.
Class 697. Tanned leathers.—Belting, grain, and harness leather. Sole-leather —Calf, kip and goat skins, sheep skins.
Class 698. Curried leathers.
Class 699. Patent and enameled leathers ; morocco.
Class 700. Alligator, porpoise, walrus, and kangaroo leather.
Class 701. Russian leathers.
Class 702. Oil leathers, wash leather, and all other varieties of leather not before named.
Class 703. Parchment for commissions, patents, deeds, diplomas, etc. Vellum for similar purposes, and for books and book-binding; for drums and tambourines ; for gold-beaters' use, etc.
Class 704. Leather belting.
Class 705. Embossed leather for furniture, wall decoration, etc.
   (For trunks, see Class 679. For harness, saddlery, etc., see Class 523.)

GROUP 112.

SCALES, WEIGHTS AND MEASURES.
(See also Group 151.)

Class 706. Scales for commercial use in weighing groceries, produce and merchandise. Counter scales, etc., portable platform scales.
Class 707. Scales for weighing heavy and bulky objects, as hay, ice, ores, coal, railway cars, etc.
Class 708. Druggists' and prescription scales.
Class 709. Bullion scales. Assayers' and chemists' scales. (See also Class 408.)
Class 710. Postal balances.
Class 711. Gas and water meters.
Class 712. Commercial weights and sets of weights.—Avoirdupois, troy, and apothecaries', with the weights of the metric system.
Class 713. Commercial examples of the measures of capacity, for solids and fluids—measuring glasses for the kitchen and for the laboratory.

GROUP 113.

MATERIAL OF WAR ; ORDNANCE AND AMMUNITION. WEAPONS AND APPARATUS OF HUNTING, TRAPPING, ETC.; MILITARY AND SPORTING SMALL-ARMS.

Class 714. Military small-arms, rifles, pistols, and magazine-guns, with their ammunition.
Class 715. Light artillery, compound guns, machine guns, mitrailleuses, etc.
Class 716. Heavy ordnance and its accessories.
Class 717. Knives, swords, spears and dirks.
Class 718. Fire-arms used for sporting and hunting ; also other implements for same purpose. (See also Group 161.)

GROUP 114.

LIGHTING APPARATUS AND APPLIANCES.

Class 719. Lamps for burning petroleum, burners, chimneys, shades, table lamps, hanging lamps.
Class 720. Lanterns, coach lamps, street and special lights and lanterns.
Class 721. Illuminating gas ; fixtures, burners and chandeliers.
Class 722. Electroliers and electric lamps.
Class 723. The "Lucigen" and similar lighting apparatus.

GROUP 115.

HEATING AND COOKING APPARATUS AND APPLIANCES.

Class 724. Fire-places, grates, and appurtenances for burning wood, coal or gas.
Class 725. Hot-air heating furnaces.
Class 726. Steam heaters, hot-water heaters, radiators, etc.
Class 727. Stoves for heating, cooking stoves, kitchen ranges, grills, roasting jacks, ovens, etc. Stove polish.
Class 728. Gas burners for heating gas logs, gas stove
Class 729. Petroleum stoves.
Class 730. Kitchen utensils and other miscellaneous articles for household purposes.

GROUP 116.

REFRIGERATORS, HOLLOW METAL WARE, TINWARE, ENAMELED WARE.

Class 731. Refrigerators. Soda and aerated water fountains and appliances
Class 732. Cast hollow-ware—kettles, pots, etc.
Class 733. Hollow-ware of copper, nickel, tin-plate and iron bells.
Class 734. Enameled ware, granite ware and porcelain-lined ware. Enameled letters and signs.

GROUP 117.

WIRE GOODS AND SCREENS, PERFORATED SHEETS, LATTICE WORK, FENCING, ETC.

Class 375. Wire cloth of brass or of annealed iron and steel.
Class 736. Wire cloth of special alloys, as aluminum bronze wire, etc.
Class 737. Sieves of various grades and materials.
Class 738. Screens for special purposes.
Class 739. Perforated metal plates.
Class 740. Artistic lattice work.
Class 741. Wire netting.
Class 742. Wire fencing. (For trellis work for gardens and flowers, see also Group 26.)

GROUP 118.

WROUGHT-IRON AND THIN METAL EXHIBITS.

Class 743. Wought-iron gates, railings, crestings, and artistic forgings, not otherwise specifically classed. (See also Department K.)
Class 744. Repoussé, hammered and stamped metal ornaments used for buildings, bridges, and other structures.
Class 745. Beams, girders, columns, angle-irons, etc.
Class 746. Horse-shoes and crude forgings.

GROUP 119.

VAULTS, SAFES, HARDWARE, EDGE TOOLS, CUTLERY.

Class 747. Builders' hardware—Locks, latches, spikes, nails, screws, tacks, bolts, hinges, pulleys; furniture fittings; ships' hardware and fittings.
Class 748. Axes, hatchets, adzes, etc.
Class 749. Edge tools of various descriptions.
Class 750. Saws, files.
Class 751. Cutlery,—knives, scissors, shears, razors, etc.; table cutlery.
Class 752. Vaults, safes and appliances; machinists' and metal workers' tools.

GROUP 120.

PLUMBING AND SANITARY MATERIALS.

Class 753. Bath tubs, bathing appliances and attachments.
Class 754 Water closets, syphons, flushing tanks ; apparatus and receptacles for ventilation and sewerage.

Class 755. Porcelain laundry tubs, basins, cocks, drains, and other appliances.
Class 756. Plumbers' and gas-fitters' hardware and miscellaneous appliances.

GROUP 121.

MISCELLANEOUS ARTICLES OF MANUFACTURE NOT HERETOFORE CLASSED.

DEPARTMENT J.

ELECTRICITY AND ELECTRICAL APPLIANCES.

GROUP 122.

APPARATUS ILLUSTRATING THE PHENOMENA AND LAWS OF ELECTRICITY
AND MAGNETISM.

Class 757. Statical electricity.
Class 758. Thermo electricity; thermo-electric batteries.
Class 759. Magnets, temporary and permanent.
Class 760. Induction coils, converters, etc.

GROUP 123.

APPARATUS FOR ELECTRICAL MEASUREMENTS.

Class 761. Standard resistance coils.
Class 762. Standard condensers.
Class 763. Standard batteries.
Class 764. Instruments of precision; voltmeters, ammeters, wattmeters, etc.

GROUP 124.

ELECTRIC BATTERIES, PRIMARY AND SECONDARY.

GROUP 125.

MACHINES AND APPLIANCES FOR PRODUCING ELECTRICAL CURRENTS BY
MECHANICAL POWER—DYNAMICAL ELECTRICITY.

Class 765. Dynamos of direct current, constant electro motive force; varying
quantity.
Class 766. Dynamos of direct current, constant quantity and varying E. M. F.
Class 767. Dynamos of alternating current, constant E. M. F., and varying
quality.
Class 768. Dynamos of alternating current, constant quantity, and varying
E. M. F.

GROUP 126.

TRANSMISSION AND REGULATION OF THE ELECTRICAL CURRENT.

Class 769. Cables, wires, and insulation ; rheostats, switches, indicators, regis-
tering meters ; ammeters, volt-meters.
Class 770. Safety and protective appliances ; lightning rods, lightning arresters,
insulators, fusible cut-outs, safety switches, etc.
Class 771. Conduits, interior and underground.

GROUP 127.

ELECTRIC MOTORS.

Class 772. Direct constant current.
Class 773. Direct constant E. M. F
Class 774. Alternating current.

GROUP 128.

APPLICATION OF ELECTRIC MOTORS.

Class 775. Street, underground, mining and other railways.
Class 776. Elevators, pumps, printing presses, and general machinery
Class 777. Toys, novelties, and domestic appliances.

GROUP 129.

LIGHTING BY ELECTRICITY.

Class 778. The arc systems, their lamps, fixtures, and appliances.
Class 779. The incandescent systems, their lamps, fixtures and appliances.

GROUP 130.

HEATING BY ELECTRICITY.

Class 780. For warming and heating apartments
Class 781. For heating flat irons, soldering irons, and other objects used in industrial operations.
Class 782. Maintenance of constant high temperature in ovens.
Class 783 Electric heating furnaces.

GROUP 131.

ELECTRO-METALLURGY AND ELECTRO-CHEMISTRY.

Class 784. Electrotyping.
Class 785. Electro-plating, gilding and nickeling.
Class 786. Electro-deposition of iron and other metals.
Class 787. Electrolytic separation of metals from their ores or alloys.

GROUP 132.

ELECTRIC FORGING, WELDING, STAMPING, TEMPERING, BRAZING, ETC.

Class 788. Apparatus for, and methods of forging, welding or joining iron, steel and other metals.
Class 789. Brazing, stamping, tempering, etc.

GROUP 133.

ELECTRIC TELEGRAPH AND ELECTRIC SIGNALS.

Class 790. Various systems of transmitting and receiving.
Class 791. Chronographs.
Class 792. Annunciators.
Class 793. Thermostats.
Class 794. Fire alarm apparatus.
Class 795. Police telegraph and burglar alarm apparatus.
Class 796. Railroad signal apparatus.

GROUP 134.

THE TELEPHONE AND ITS APPLIANCES. PHONOGRAPHS.

Class 797. Cables; construction and underground work.
Class 798. Special protective devices.
Class 799. Switch boards.
Class 800. Transmitting apparatus.
Class 801. Receiving apparatus.
Class 802. Signalling apparatus.
Class 803. Long distance systems.
Class 804. Various systems of operation.
Class 805. Subscriber's apparatus: Numbers, code, registers, etc.
Class 806. Phonographs.—Receiving and recording apparatus.
Class 807. Apparatus for the reproduction of recorded sounds and articulate speech.

GROUP 135.

ELECTRICITY IN SURGERY, DENTISTRY AND THERAPEUTICS.

Class 808. Cautery apparatus.

Class 809. Apparatus for the application of the electrical current as a remedial agent—surgical and dental.

Class 810. Apparatus for diagnosis.

Class 811. Apparatus for the destruction of life.

GROUP 136.

APPLICATION OF ELECTRICITY IN VARIOUS WAYS NOT HEREINBEFORE SPECIFIED.

Class 812. Ignition of explosives; gas lighting, etc.

Class 813. Control of heating apparatus by electricity, as applied to steam and hot air pipes and registers.

Class 814. Electric pens.

Class 815. Application in photography.

GROUP 137.

HISTORY AND STATISTICS OF ELECTRICAL INVENTION.

Class 816. Objects illustrating the development of the knowledge of electricity and of the application of electricity in the arts.

Class 817. Collections of books and publications upon electricity and its applications.

GROUP 138.

PROGRESS AND DEVELOPMENT IN ELECTRICAL SCIENCE AND CONSTRUCTION, AS ILLUSTRATED BY MODELS AND DRAWINGS OF VARIOUS COUNTRIES.

Class 818. United States Patent Office and other exhibits of electrical models and drawings.

Class 819. Foreign exhibits of electrical models and drawings.

DEPARTMENT K.

FINE ARTS; PAINTING, SCULPTURE, ARCHITECTURE AND DECORATION.

GROUP 139.

SCULPTURE.

Class 820. Figures and groups in marble; casts from original works by modern artists; models and monumental decorations.

Class 821. Bas-reliefs in marble or bronze.

Class 822. Figures and groups in bronze.

Class 823. Bronze from *cire-perdue.*

GROUP 140.
PAINTINGS IN OIL.

GROUP 141.
PAINTINGS IN WATER COLORS.

GROUP 142.
PAINTINGS ON IVORY, ON ENAMEL, ON METAL, ON PORCELAIN OR OTHER
WARES; FRESCO PAINTING ON WALLS.

GROUP 143.
ENGRAVINGS AND ETCHINGS; PRINTS.

GROUP 144.
CHALK, CHARCOAL, PASTEL, AND OTHER DRAWINGS.

GROUP 145.
ANTIQUE AND MODERN CARVINGS; ENGRAVINGS IN MEDALLIONS OR IN GEMS;
CAMEOS, INTAGLIOS.

GROUP 146.
EXHIBITS OF PRIVATE COLLECTIONS.

DEPARTMENT L.

LIBERAL ARTS—EDUCATION, LITERATURE, ENGINEERING, PUBLIC WORKS; MUSIC AND THE DRAMA.

GROUP 147.
PHYSICAL DEVELOPMENT, TRAINING AND CONDITION—HYGIENE.

Class 824. The nursery and its accessories.

Class 825. Athletic training and exercise gymnasiums; apparatus for physical development and of gymnastic exercises and amusement; skating, walking, climbing, ball-playing, wrestling, acrobatic exercises; rowing, hunting, etc. Special apparatus for training in schools, gymnasia; apparatus for exercise, drill, etc.

Class 826. Alimentation.—Food supply and its distribution; adulteration of food, markets, preparation of food, cooking and serving, school kitchens and arrangements for school canteens, methods of warming childrens' meals, etc. Dinner-pails, or receptacles for carrying meals for school children, working men, and others. Restaurants, dining halls, refectories, etc.

Class 827. Dwellings and buildings characterized by the conditions best adapted to health and comfort, including dwellings for working men and factory operatives, houses and villages for operatives in connection with large manufacturing establishments, tenement houses, "flats," suites of apartments, city and country residences, club-houses, school houses; designs and models of improved buildings for elementary schools, infant schools and crèches, court-rooms, theatres, churches, etc.

Class 828. Hotels, lodging-houses.

Class 829. Public baths, lavatories; public and domestic hygiene. Sanitation.
—Sanitary appliances and methods for dwelling-houses, buildings
and cities. Direct renewal of air. Heating, ventilating, lighting,
in their relation to health. Conduits of water and sewage.
Drains and sewers. Sinks, night-soil apparatus, sanitary plumb-
ing, walls, bricks, roofs, flooring, etc. Sanitary house decoration.—
Non-poisonous paints and wall papers, floor coverings, washables,
decorations, etc.
Apparatus for carrying off, receiving and treating sewage.
Slaughter-house refuse, city garbage.
Apparatus and methods for filtering water and cleansing water-
courses.
Apparatus intended for the prevention of infectious diseases.
Methods, materials and instruments for purifying and destroying
germs; disinfectors.
Apparatus and fittings for warming, ventilating, and lighting schools;
school latrines, closets, etc.
Special school fittings for storing and drying clothing.
Precaution in schools for preventing the spread of infectious dis-
eases; school sanitaria, infirmaries, etc.

Class 830. Hygiene of the workshop and factory.—(Classification modified
from that of the London health exhibition).
Designs and models for improvement in the arrangement and construction of workshops, especially those in which dangerous or
unwholesome processes are conducted.
Apparatus and fittings for preventing or minimizing the danger to
health or life from carrying on certain trades. Guards, screens,
air-jets, preservative solutions, washes, etc.
Objects of personal use—mouth-pieces, spectacles, dresses, hoods,
etc., for use in certain unhealthy and poisonous trades.
Illustrations of disease and deformities caused by unwholesome trades
and professions; methods of combating these diseases; preservative measures, etc.
Sanitary construction and inspection of workshops, factories, and
mines; new inventions and improvements for ameliorating the
condition of life of those engaged in unhealthy occupations; means
for economizing human labor in various industrial operations.

Class 831. Asylums and homes.—Asylums for infants and children; foundling and orphan asylums; children's aid societies. Homes for
aged men and women; for the maimed and deformed; for soldiers and for sailors.
Treatment of paupers; alms-houses.
Treatment of aborigines; Indian reservations and homes.

Class 832. Hospitals, dispensaries, etc.; plans, models, statistics. Shed hospitals for infectious fevers and epidemic diseases; tent hospitals,
hospital ships; furniture and fittings for sick rooms.

Class 833. Protective supervision; sanitary supervision; vaccination and its
enforcement; isolation of contagious diseases; quarantine; prevention and elimination of animal epidemics.
Food inspection.—Treatment of adulterated foods; inspection and
analysis; treatment of stale food substances; regulation of abat-
toirs, mills, etc.; regulation of sale of horses; protective devices.
Building inspection, etc.—Building regulations and inspection;
building drainage and plumbing; fire regulations, fire escapes, etc.
Personal inspection.—Color tests, etc.; professional examination
for licenses.
Immigration.—Reception, care and protection of immigrants.

GROUP 148.

INSTRUMENTS AND APPARATUS OF MEDICINE, SURGERY AND PROSTHESIS.

Class 834. Pharmacology, drugs, pharmacy, etc.—Medicines, officinal (in any authoritative pharmacopœia) articles of the materia medica, preparations unofficinal. (See Group 87.)

Class 835. Dietetic preparations intended especially for the sick. (For beef extracts, see Class 38.)

Class 836. Instruments for physical diagnosis, clinical thermometers, stethoscopes, ophalmoscopes, etc.

Class 837. Surgical instruments, appliances and apparatus, with dressings, anæsthetics, antiseptics; obstetrical instruments, etc.

Class 838. Prosthesis.—Apparatus for correcting deformities; artificial limbs.

Class 839. Instruments and apparatus of dental surgery and prosthesis.

Class 840. Vehicles and appliances for the transportation and relief of the sick and wounded, during peace or war, on shore or at sea. (See also Department G.)

GROUP 149.

PRIMARY, SECONDARY AND SUPERIOR EDUCATION.

Class 841. Elementary instruction.—Infant schools and kindergartens. Descriptions of the methods of instruction, with statistics.

Class 842. Primary schools, city and country.—School houses and furniture. Apparatus and fittings. Models and appliances for teaching, text-books, diagrams, examples. Specimens of work in elementary schools.

Class 843. Domestic and industrial training for girls.—Models and apparatus for the teaching of cookery, housework, washing and ironing, needle-work and embroidery, dress-making, artificial flower-making, painting on silk, crockery, etc. Specimens of school work.

Class 844. Handicraft teaching in schools for boys.—Apparatus and fittings for elementary trade teaching in schools. Specimens of school work.

Class 845. Science teaching.—Apparatus and models for elementary science instruction in schools. Apparatus for chemistry, physics, mechanics, etc.; diagrams, copies, text-books, etc.; specimens of the school work in these subjects.

Class 846. Art teaching.—Apparatus, models and fittings for elementary art instruction in schools ; diagrams, copies text-books, etc., specimens of art work, modeling, etc., in schools.

Class 847. Technical and apprenticeship schools.—Apparatus and examples used in primary and secondary schools for teaching handicraft ; models, plans and designs for the fitting up of work-shop and industrial schools ; results of industrial work done in such schools.

Class 848. Special schools for the elementary instruction of Indians.

Class 849. Education of defective classes.—Schools for the deaf, dumb, blind, and feeble-minded ; adult schools for the illiterate.

Class 850. Public schools.—Descriptions, illustrations, statistics, methods of instruction, etc.

Class 851. Higher education.—Academies and high schools. Description and statistics.

Colleges and universities.—Descriptions, illustrations of the buildings, libraries, museums, collections, courses of study, catalogues, statistics, etc.

Class 852. Professional schools.—Theology, law, medicine and surgery, dentistry, pharmacy ; mining, engineering, agriculture, mechanic arts ; art and design ; military, naval, normal, commercial ; music.

Class 853. Government aid to education.—National Bureau of Education.— Reports and statistics,

GROUP 150.

LITERATURE, BOOKS, LIBRARIES, JOURNALISM.

Class 854. Books and literature, with special examples of typography, paper and binding. General works.—Philosophy, religion, sociology, philology, natural sciences, useful arts, fine arts, literature, history, and geography; cyclopedias, magazines, and newspapers; bindings, specimens of typography.

Class 855. School books.

Class 856. Technical industrial journals.

Class 857. Illustrated papers.

Class 858. Newspapers and statistics of their multiplication, growth, and circulation.

Class 859. Journalism, statistics of; with illustrations of methods, organization and results.

Class 860. Trade catalogues and price-lists.

Class 861. Library apparatus; systems of cataloguing and appliances of placing and delivering books.

Class 862. Directories of cities and towns.

Class 863. Publications by governments.

Class 864. Topographical maps. Marine and coast charts; geological maps and sections; botanical, agronomical, and other maps, showing the extent and distribution of men, animals and terrestrial products; physical maps; meteorological maps and bulletins; telegraphic routes and stations; railway and route maps; terrestrial and celestial globes, relief maps and models of portions of the earth's surface, profiles of ocean beds and routes of submarine cables.

GROUP 151.

INSTRUMENTS OF PRECISION, EXPERIMENT, RESEARCH, AND PHOTOGRAPHY. PHOTOGRAPHS.

Class 865. Weights, measures; weighing and metrological apparatus.—Balances of precision, instruments for mechanical calculation, adding machines, pedometers, cash registers, water and gas meters, etc.; measures of length, graduated scales, etc.
(For ordinary commercial forms, see also Group 112.)
(For testing machines see Class 490.)

Class 866. Astronomical instruments and accessories.—Transits, transit circles, mural circles, zenith sectors, altazimeters, equatorials, collimators, comet-seekers.

Class 867. Geodetic and surveying instruments.—Transits, theodolites, artificial horizons; surveyor's compasses, goniometers; instruments for surveying underground in mines, tunnels, and excavations; pocket sextants, plane tables, and instruments used with them; ship's compasses, sextants, quadrants, repeating circles, dip-sectors, etc.

Class 868. Leveling instruments and apparatus—hand-levels, water-levels, engineers' levels, of all patterns and varieties; cathetometers, leveling staves, targets, and accessory apparatus.

Class 869. Hydrographic surveying; deep sea sounding.

Class 870. Photometic apparatus and methods.

Class 871. Photographic apparatus and accessories. Photographs.

Class 872. Meteorological instruments and apparatus, with methods of recording, reducing and reporting observations. Thermometers—mercurial, spirit, air; ordinary or self-registering, maximum and minimum Barometers—mercurial, aneroid; anemometers, rain gauges, etc.

Class 873. Chronometric apparatus.—Chronometers, watches of precision, astronomical clocks, church and metropolitan clocks, clepsydras, hour-glasses, sun-dials, chronographs, electric clocks, metronomes. (For commercial clocks and watches, see also Group 99.)

Class 874. Optical and thermometric instruments and apparatus.

Class 875. Electric and magnetic apparatus. (See also Department J.)

Class 876. Acoustic apparatus.

GROUP 152.

CIVIL ENGINEERING, PUBLIC WORKS, CONSTRUCTIVE ARCHITECTURE.

Class 877. Land surveying, topographical surveying.—Surveys and locations of towns and cities, with systems of water supply and drainage.

Class 878. Surveys of coasts, rivers, and harbors.

Class 879. Construction and maintenance of roads, streets, pavements, etc.

Class 880. Bridge engineering (illustrated by drawings and models.)
Bridge designing.—Drawings and charts, showing methods of calculating stresses.
Foundations, piers, abutments and approaches of stone, wood, etc.
Arch bridges of stone, wood or iron.
Suspension bridges of fiber, iron chain, and cable.
Truss bridges of wood, iron and steel.—Pony, bow-string and plate girders, lattice girders, Fink, Bollman, Howe, Pratt, Warren, Post, Long, Whipple and other trusses of special design.
Cantilever bridges, draw-bridges, rolling and swinging machinery.
Tubular bridges.
Railway, aqueduct, and other bridges of special design not elsewhere classed.
(A chart showing date of completion, span, rise, weight, and cost of the great bridges of the world, would be of interest).

Class 881. Subaqueous constructions.—Foundations, piers, harbors, breakwaters, building of dams, water-works and canals.

Class 882. Irrigation.—Irrigating canals and systems.

Class 883. Railway engineering.—Surveying, locating and constructing railways.

Class 884. Dynamic and industrial engineering.—The construction and working of machines ; examples of planning and construction of manufacturing and metallurgical establishments.

Class 885. Mine engineering.—Surveying underground, construction of tunnels, subaqueous tunnels, etc. ; locating and sinking shafts, inclines, and winzes ; driving levels, draining, ventilating, and lighting. (See also Department E).

Class 886. Military engineering.—Construction of earth-works, breast-works and temporary fortifications.

Class 887. Permanent works.—Fortifications, magazines, arsenals, mines.

Class 888. Roads, bridges, pontoons, etc.; movement of troops and supplies.

Class 889. Constructive architecture.—Plans of public buildings for special purposes ; large and small dwelling-houses.
Drawings and specifications for foundations, walls, partitions, floors, roofs, and stairways.
Estimates of amount and cost of material.
Designs of models and special contrivances for safety, comfort, convenience in the manipulation of elevators, doors, windows, etc.
Working plans for the mason, carpenter and painter ; designs and models of bonds, arches, coping, vaulting, etc.; plastering and construction of partitions ; painting and glazing.
Plans of appliances for hoisting, handling and delivering building materials to artisans.—Scaffolding and ladders, special scaffolding for handling great weights ; portable cranes and power elevators.
Illustrations of the strength of materials.

Class 889. Plans and sections of special architectural forms. Metallic floor beams and girders ; hollow bricks and other architectural pottery for heating and ventilation ; metallic cornice and conduits, shingles and sheathing, glass roofs, floors and accessories, architectural hardware.
Methods of combining materials.
Protection of foundations, areas and walls against water.
Working plans for paving and draining.

GROUP 153.
GOVERNMENT AND LAW.

Class 890. Various systems of government illustrated.—Government departments, legislative, executive, and judicial.
Class 891. International law and relations.—Fac-similes of treaties, etc.
Class 892. Protection of property in inventions. Patent offices and their functions, statistics of inventions and patents.
Class 893. Postal systems and the appliances of the postal service. Letter-boxes, pouches, mail-bags, postage stamps, etc.
Class 894. Punishment of crime.—Prisons and reformatories, prison management and discipline, transportation of criminals, penal colonies, houses of correction, reform schools, naval or marine discipline, punishment at sea, police stations, night lock-ups, etc.; dress and equipment of prisoners, example of convict workmanship.

GROUP 154.
COMMERCE, TRADE, AND BANKING.

Class 895. History and statistics of trade and commerce.
Class 896. Railway and transportation companies.
Class 897. Methods and media of exchange.—Money, coins, paper money, etc.
Class 898. Counting houses, stores, and shops.—Arrangement, furniture, fittings; methods of management, book-keeping, devices for distributing change and goods to customers.
Class 899. Warehouse and storage systems.—Grain elevators.
Class 900. Boards of trade and their functions illustrated.
Class 901. Exchanges for produce, metals, stocks, etc.
Class 902. Insurance companies.
Class 903. Banks and banking.—Illustrations of buildings, interiors, methods, and statistical information ; clearing-houses, etc.; savings and trust institutions.
Class 904. Safes and vaults for storage of treasure and valuables; safe deposit companies.
Class 905. Book-keeping.—Books and systems of book-keeping and accounting, commercial blank forms, etc.
Class 906. Express companies, freighting, etc.

GROUP 155.
INSTITUTIONS AND ORGANIZATIONS FOR THE INCREASE AND DIFFUSION OF KNOWLEDGE.

Class 907. Institutions founded for the increase and diffusion of knowledge, such as the Smithsonian Institution, the Royal Institution, the Institute of France, British Association for the Advancement of Science, and the American Association, etc.; their organization, history and results.
Class 908. Academies of science and letters.—Learned and scientific associations, geological and mineralogical societies, etc.; engineering, technical, and professional associations; artistic, biological, zoological, medical, astronomical societies and organizations.

Class 909. Museums, collections, art galleries, exhibitions of works of art and industry; agricultural fairs, state and county exhibitions, national exhibitions, international exhibitions, international congresses.
Class 910. Publication societies.
Class 911. Libraries—Public and private; statistics of operations.

GROUP 156.

SOCIAL, INDUSTRIAL, AND CO-OPERATIVE ASSOCIATIONS.

Class 912. Social organizations.—Clubs—political, military, university, travelers', press clubs, science clubs, and others.
Class 913. Political societies and organizations.
Class 914. Workingmen's unions and associations.—Their · organization, statistics, and results.
Class 915. Industrial organizations.
Class 916. Co-operative trading associations.
Class 917. Secret societies. ·
Class 918. Miscellaneous organizations for promoting the material and moral well-being of the industrial classes.

GROUP 157.

RELIGIOUS ORGANIZATIONS AND SYSTEMS—STATISTICS AND PUBLICATIONS.

Class 919. Religious organizations and systems.—Origin, nature, growth, and extent of various religious systems and faiths. Statistical, historical and other illustrations ; pictures of buildings; plans and views of interiors.
Class 920. Religious music, choirs, hymnology.
Class 921. Missionary societies, missions, and missionary work ; maps, reports, statistics.
Class 922. Spreading the knowledge of religious systems by publications; Bible societies, tract societies, and their publications.·
Class 923. Systems and methods of religious instruction and training for the young; Sunday-schools, furniture, apparatus and books.
Class 924. Associations for religious or moral improvement.
Class 925. Charities and charitable associations connected with ecclesiastical societies.

GROUP 158.

MUSIC AND MUSICAL INSTRUMENTS—THE THEATRE.

Class 926. History and theory of music.—Music of primitive people. Crude and curious instruments. Combinations of instruments, bands and orchestras. Music books and scores. Musical notation.
History and literature of music. Portraits of great musicians.
Class 927. Self-vibrating instruments. — Drums and tambourines; cymbals, triangles, gongs, castanets, "bones."
Bells, chimes and peals.
Bell-ringers' instruments. Musical glasses.
Glockenspiels, zylophones, marimbas.
Music boxes.
Class 928. Stringed instruments played with the fingers or plectrum.
Lutes, guitars, banjos and mandolins.
Harps and lyres. .
Zithers and dulcimers.
Class 629. Stringed instruments played with the bow.
The violin.
The viol, viola, viola da gamba, viola di amore.
The violoncello and the bass viol.
Mechanical instruments:—Hurdy-gurdy and violin piano.

Class 930. Stringed instrumsnts with key-board.—The piano-forte—square, upright and grand.
Actions and parts of a piano.
The predecessors of the piano.—Clavicytherium clavicymbal, clavichord, manichord, virginal, spinet, harpsichord, and hammer harpsichord.
Instruments and methods of manufacture.
Street pianos.

Class 931. Wind instruments, with simple aperture or plug mouthpiece. The flute, flute-a-bec Syrinx. Organ-pipes. Flageolet.

Class 392. Wind instruments, with mouthpiece regulated by the lips. The clarionet, oboe and saxophone.

Class 933. Wind instruments with bell mouthpiece, without keys. The trumpet (simple) and the bugle. Oliphant. Alpenhorn. The trombone (with slide and with finger holes). The serpent, bassoon and bagpipe.

Class 934. Wind instruments with bell mouthpiece, with keys. Key bugles, cornets, French horns. Cornopeans, orphicleides.

Class 935. Wind instruments with complicated systems.
The pipe organ.
Reed organs, melodeons and harmonicas.
Accordions, concertinas and mouth organs.
Hand organs and organettes. Automatic organs, orchestrions, etc.

Class 936. Accessories of musical instruments—strings, reeds, bridges.
Conductor's batons, drum-majors' staves. Mechanical devices for the orchestra.
Tuning forks, pitch-pipes, metronomes, music stands, etc.

Class 937. Music in relation to human life.—Musical composers. Great performers. Great singers. Portraits. Biographies.
Concerts and the concert stage.
The opera. The oratorio. Masses.
Church music and sacred music of all periods. Hymnology, ballads.
Folk-song, and folk-music of all lands. National airs.

Class 938. The theatre and the drama. The stage. Plans and models of stages and theatres.
History of the drama, so far as can be shown by literary record.
Portraits of actors. Relics of actors.
Playbills, etc. Costumes, masks, armor. Scenery. Appliances of illusion, etc. Plays of all ages and people.

DEPARTMENT M.

ETHNOLOGY, ARCHÆOLOGY, PROGRESS OF LABOR AND INVENTION.

GROUP 159.

VIEWS, PLANS OR MODELS OF PREHISTORIC ARCHITECTURAL MONUMENTS AND HABITATION.

Class 939. Caves—natural, artificial ; dwellings, natural and artificial.

Class 940. Lacustine dwellings—dolmens, tumuli, menhirs, cromlechs, alignments, cup-stones, graves, cists, crematories.

Class 941. Cliff and other dwellings—models of dwellings, shelters, skin lodges, yourts, huts (of bark, grass, etc.), wooden houses.

Class 942. Appurtenances.—Sweat-houses (models), totem-posts (originals and models), gable ornaments, locks.

GROUP 160.

FURNITURE AND CLOTHING OF ABORIGINAL, UNCIVILIZED AND BUT PARTLY CIVILIZED RACES.

Class 943. Household utensils and furniture.
Class 944. Articles serving in the use of narcotics—pipes, etc.
Class 945. Articles used in transportation.
Class 946. Clothing and adornment.

GROUP 161.

IMPLEMENTS OF WAR AND THE CHASE.
(See also Groups 86 and 113.)

GROUP 162.

TOOLS AND IMPLEMENTS OF INDUSTRIAL OPERATIONS.

Class 947. Gathering and storing food other than game.—Water vessels.
Class 948. Articles used in cooking and eating.
Class 949. Apparatus of making clothing and ornaments and of weaving.

GROUP 163.

ATHLETIC EXERCISES—GAMES.

GROUP 164.

OBJECTS OF SPIRITUAL SIGNIFICANCE AND VENERATION—REPRESENTATIONS OF DEITIES—APPLIANCES OF WORSHIP.

GROUP 165.

HISTORIC ARCHÆOLOGY—OBJECTS ILLUSTRATING THE PROGRESS OF NATIONS.

GROUP 166.

MODELS AND REPRESENTATIONS OF ANCIENT VESSELS, PARTICULARLY OF THE PERIOD OF THE DISCOVERY OF AMERICA.

GROUP 167.

REPRODUCTIONS OF ANCIENT MAPS, CHARTS, AND APPARATUS OF NAVIGATION.

Class 950. Charts and maps of the world anterior to the voyage of Columbus.
Class 951. Charts and maps following the discovery.
Class 952. Charts and maps of the period of the early colonization of America.
Class 953. Charts and maps of America and the world at the period of the Revolution and since.

GROUP 168.

MODELS AND REPRESENTATIONS OF ANCIENT BUILDINGS, CITIES, OR MONUMENTS OF THE HISTORIC PERIOD ANTERIOR TO THE DISCOVERY OF AMERICA.

GROUP 169.

MODELS AND REPRESENTATIONS OF HABITATIONS AND DWELLINGS BUILT SINCE THE DISCOVERY OF AMERICA.

GROUP 170.

ORIGINALS, COPIES, OR MODELS, OR GRAPHIC REPRESENTATIONS OF NOTABLE INVENTIONS,

WORLD'S COLUMBIAN EXPOSITION. 421

GROUP 171.

OBJECTS ILLUSTRATING GENERALLY THE PROGRESS OF THE AMELIORATION OF THE CONDITIONS OF LIFE AND LABOR.

Class 954. The evolution of the dwelling and its furniture.
Class 955. The evolution of the plow and other implements of the farm and garden.
Class 956 Evolution of tools.—The ax, saw, and other implements of handicraft.
Class 957. Labor-saving machines and their effects.

GROUP 172.
WOMAN'S WORK.

GROUP 173.
STATE, NATIONAL, AND FOREIGN GOVERNMENT EXHIBITS.

GROUP 174.
THE NORTH AMERICAN INDIAN.

Class 958. Special monographic exhibit of the tribes of America.
Class 959. Villages or families of various tribes engaged in their native occupations.
Class 960. Specimens of their special work and industries. Collections of Indian "trinkets" or curiosities.
Class 961. Books or papers, written or printed, in his native tongue.
Class 962. Means and methods of communication between tribes by "sign" language and "picture letters," etc. Status of females under tribal regulations.
Class 963. Treaties and acquisition of territory from the various tribes, and how obtained.
Class 964. Progress of Indian civilization through the efforts of the Government, missionaries, or by his own efforts and choice. His industrial pursuits and capabilities, as exemplified in the shop, on the farm, and in the school-room. Inventions, etc.
Class 965. Music. The "Columbian Indian Band," consisting of sixty or more instruments.
Class 966. The allotment of lands to families, and individuals, and its effects.
The Indian as an American citizen.
The hope of the Indian.
Class 967. Other attainments and industries not specially mentioned. (For treatment of Indians, reservations, etc., see Class 831, also special Indian schools, see Class 848.)

GROUP 175.
PORTRAITS, BUSTS, AND STATUES OF GREAT INVENTORS AND OTHERS, WHO HAVE CONTRIBUTED LARGELY TO THE PROGRESS OF CIVILIZATION, AND THE WELL-BEING OF MAN.

GROUP 176.
ISOLATED AND COLLECTIVE EXHIBITS.

Class 968. The Latin-American Bureau.

www.ingramcontent.com/pod-product-compliance
Lightning Source LLC
Chambersburg PA
CBHW032309280326
41932CB00009B/750